THE HEROIC LEGEND OF
ARSLAN

STORY BY
YOSHIKI TANAKA

MANGA BY
HIROMU ARAKAWA

2

The Heroic Legend of
ARSLAN

TABLE OF CONTENTS

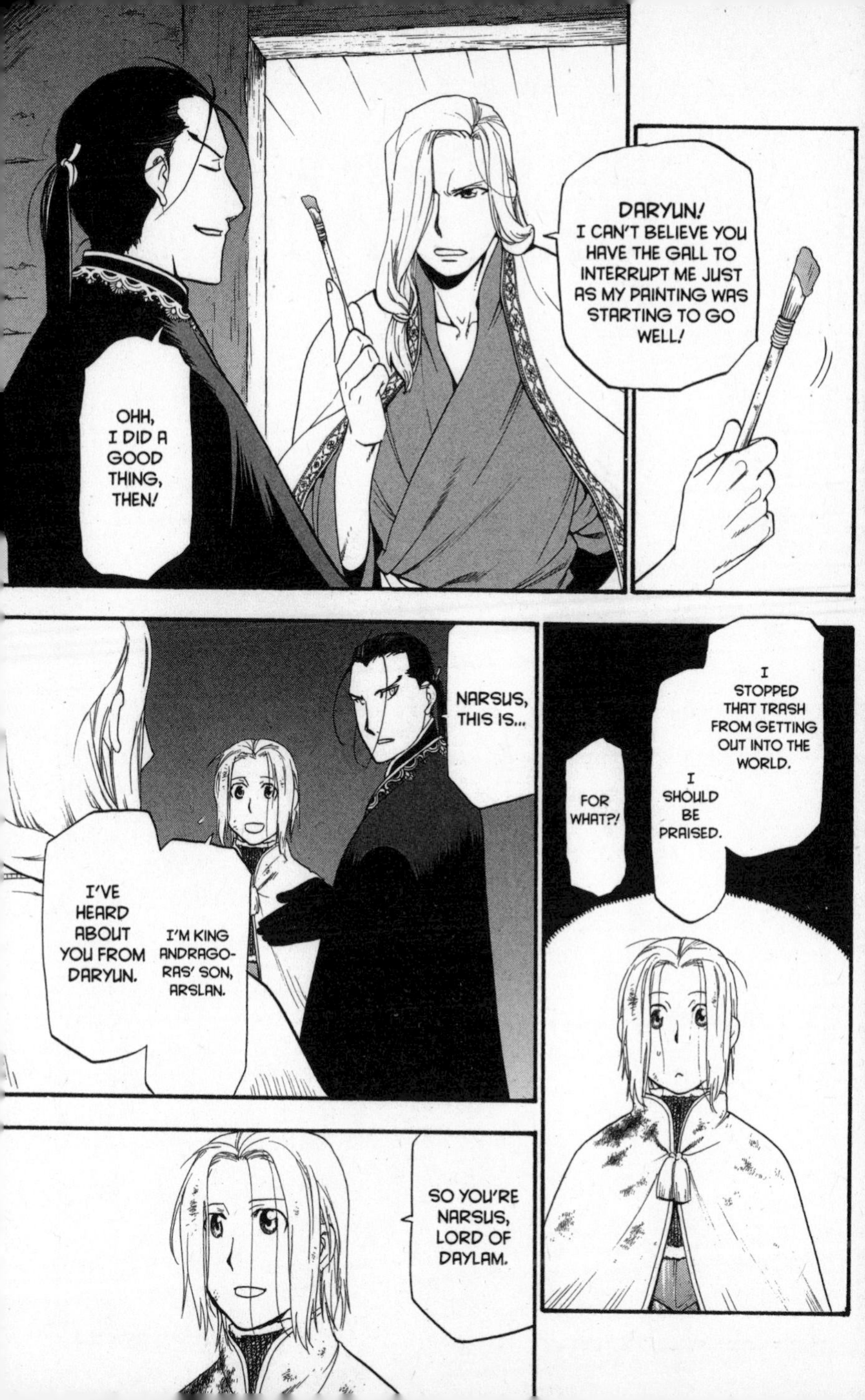
DARYUN! I CAN'T BELIEVE YOU HAVE THE GALL TO INTERRUPT ME JUST AS MY PAINTING WAS STARTING TO GO WELL!
OHH, I DID A GOOD THING, THEN!
I STOPPED THAT TRASH FROM GETTING OUT INTO THE WORLD.
I SHOULD BE PRAISED.
FOR WHAT?!
NARSUS, THIS IS...
I'M KING ANDRAGO-RAS' SON, ARSLAN.
I'VE HEARD ABOUT YOU FROM DARYUN.
SO YOU'RE NARSUS, LORD OF DAYLAM.

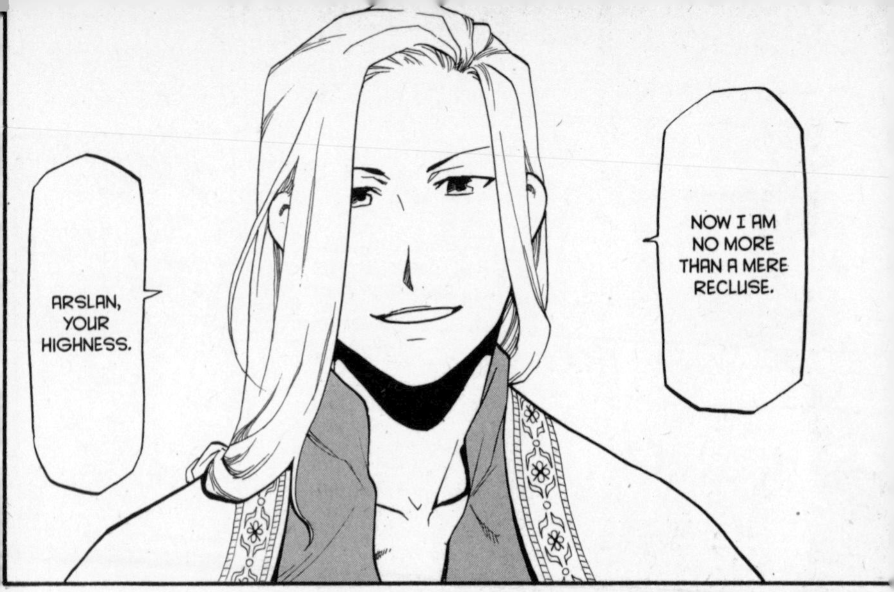
NOW I AM NO MORE THAN A MERE RECLUSE.
ARSLAN, YOUR HIGHNESS.

CHAPTER 5: A Monarch's Generosity

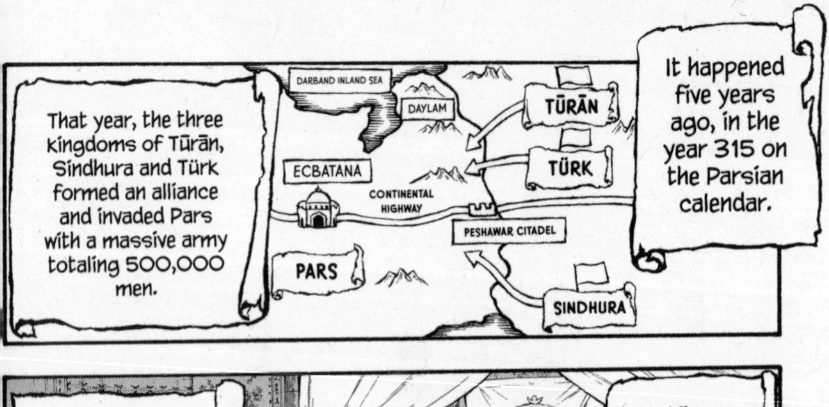
It happened five years ago, in the year 315 on the Parsian calendar.
TŪRĀN
TÜRK
SINDHURA
PESHAWAR CITADEL
CONTINENTAL HIGHWAY
DAYLAM
DARBAND INLAND SEA
ECBATANA
PARS
That year, the three kingdoms of Tūrān, Sindhura and Türk formed an alliance and invaded Pars with a massive army totaling 500,000 men.

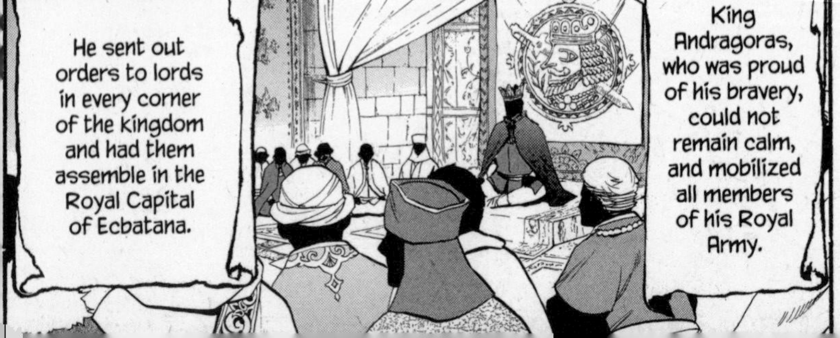
King Andragoras, who was proud of his bravery, could not remain calm, and mobilized all members of his Royal Army.
He sent out orders to lords in every corner of the kingdom and had them assemble in the Royal Capital of Ecbatana.

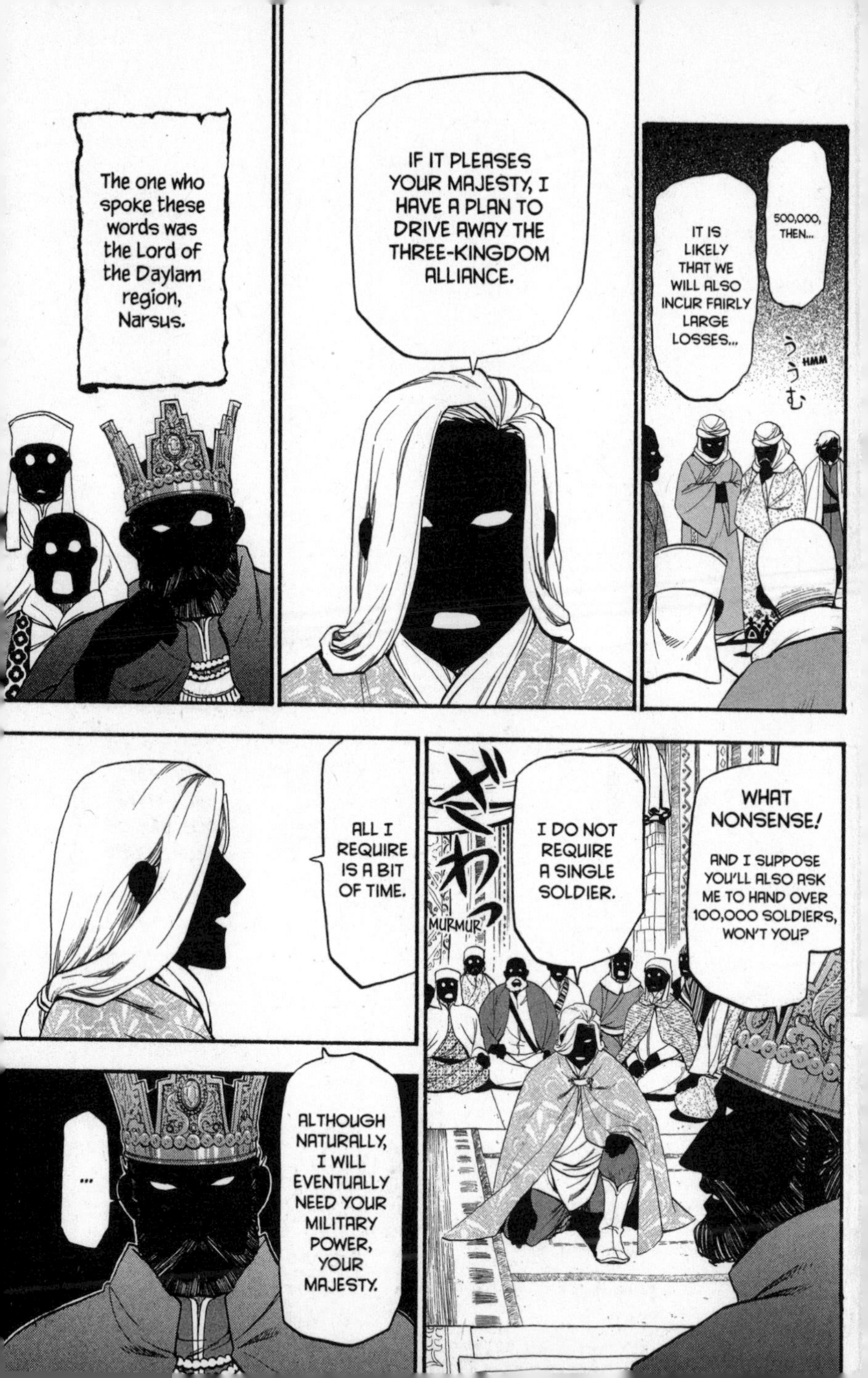

500,000, THEN...
IT IS LIKELY THAT WE WILL ALSO INCUR FAIRLY LARGE LOSSES...
うむ
HMM
IF IT PLEASES YOUR MAJESTY, I HAVE A PLAN TO DRIVE AWAY THE THREE-KINGDOM ALLIANCE.
The one who spoke these words was the Lord of the Daylam region, Narsus.
WHAT NONSENSE!
AND I SUPPOSE YOU'LL ALSO ASK ME TO HAND OVER 100,000 SOLDIERS, WON'T YOU?
I DO NOT REQUIRE A SINGLE SOLDIER.
ざわっ
MURMUR
ALL I REQUIRE IS A BIT OF TIME.
ALTHOUGH NATURALLY, I WILL EVENTUALLY NEED YOUR MILITARY POWER, YOUR MAJESTY.
...

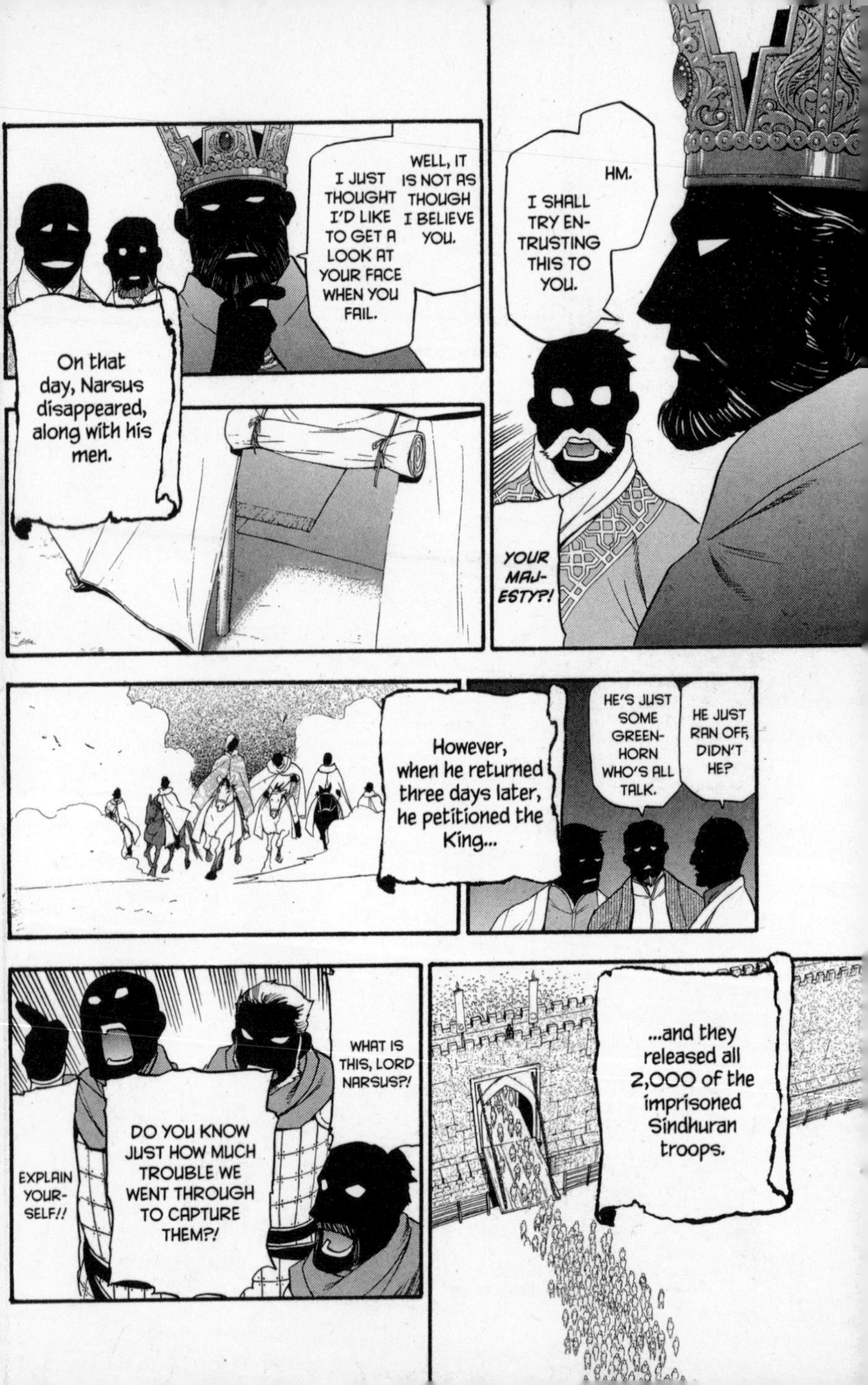
HM.
I SHALL TRY ENTRUSTING THIS TO YOU.
YOUR MAJESTY?!
WELL, IT IS NOT AS THOUGH I BELIEVE YOU.
I JUST THOUGHT I'D LIKE TO GET A LOOK AT YOUR FACE WHEN YOU FAIL.
On that day, Narsus disappeared, along with his men.
HE JUST RAN OFF, DIDN'T HE?
HE'S JUST SOME GREENHORN WHO'S ALL TALK.
However, when he returned three days later, he petitioned the King...
...and they released all 2,000 of the imprisoned Sindhuran troops.
WHAT IS THIS, LORD NARSUS?!
DO YOU KNOW JUST HOW MUCH TROUBLE WE WENT THROUGH TO CAPTURE THEM?!
EXPLAIN YOURSELF!!

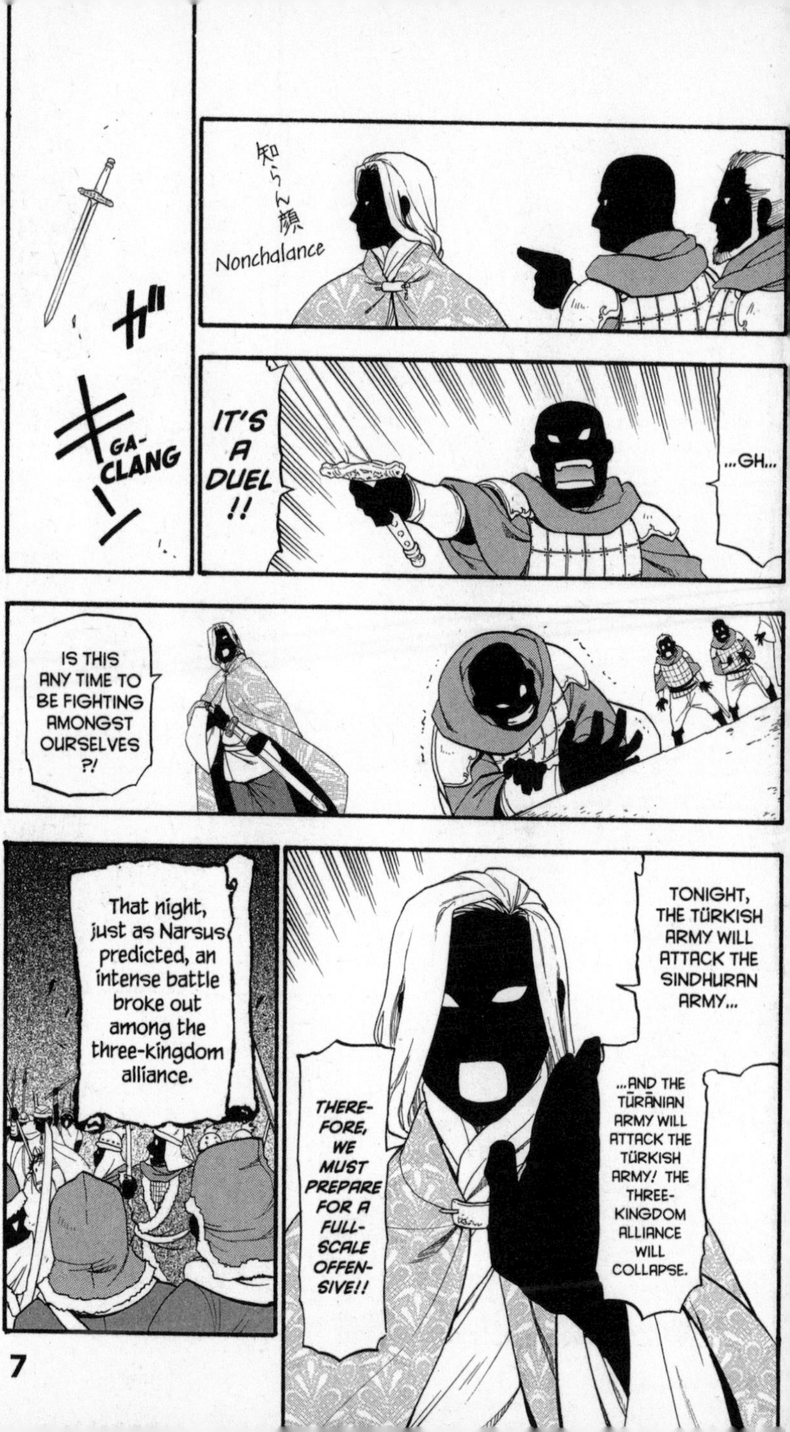
知らん顔
Nonchalance
...GH...
IT'S A DUEL!!
ガ キーン
GA-CLANG
IS THIS ANY TIME TO BE FIGHTING AMONGST OURSELVES?!
TONIGHT, THE TÜRKISH ARMY WILL ATTACK THE SINDHURAN ARMY...
...AND THE TŪRĀNIAN ARMY WILL ATTACK THE TÜRKISH ARMY! THE THREE-KINGDOM ALLIANCE WILL COLLAPSE.
THEREFORE, WE MUST PREPARE FOR A FULL-SCALE OFFENSIVE!!
That night, just as Narsus predicted, an intense battle broke out among the three-kingdom alliance.

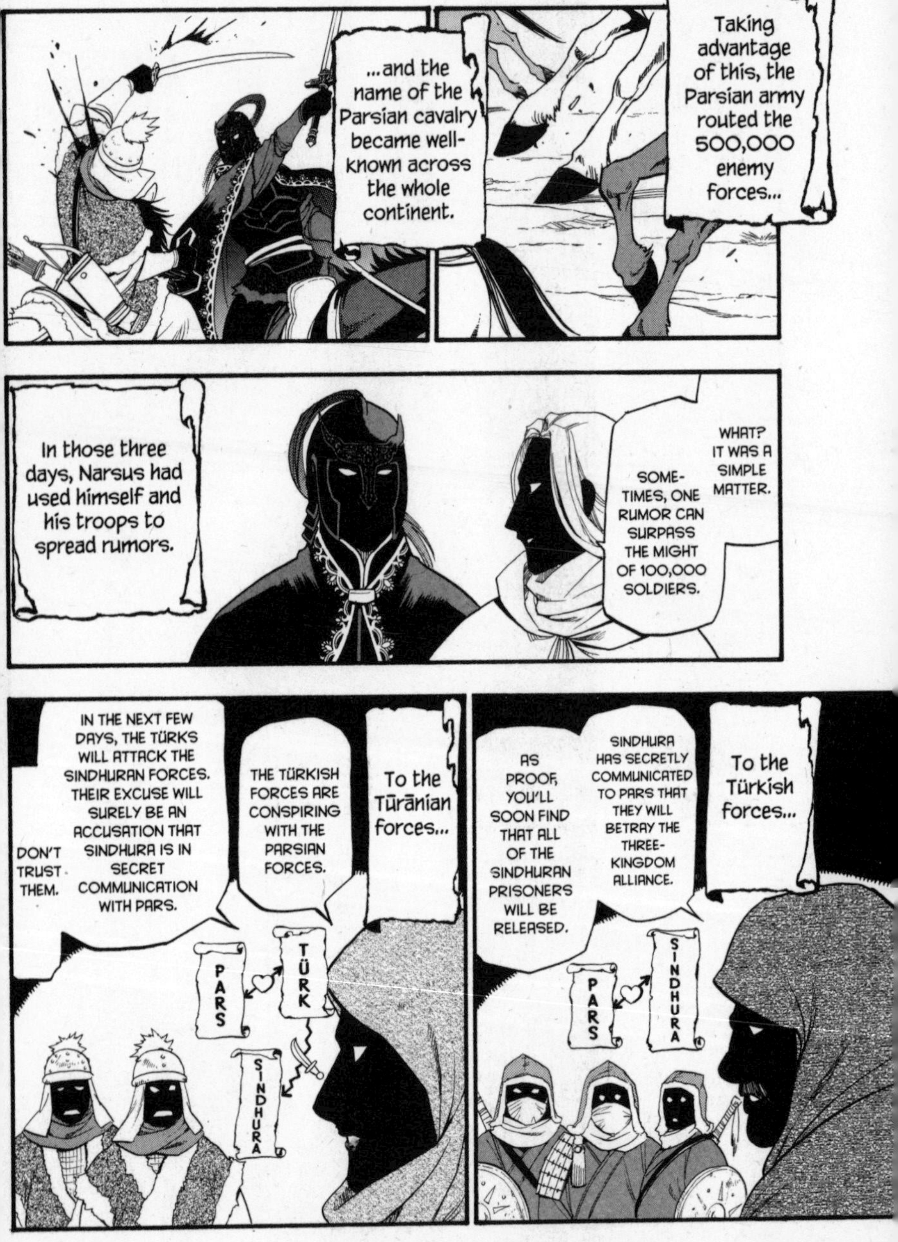
Taking advantage of this, the Parsian army routed the 500,000 enemy forces...
...and the name of the Parsian cavalry became well-known across the whole continent.
WHAT? IT WAS A SIMPLE MATTER.
SOME-TIMES, ONE RUMOR CAN SURPASS THE MIGHT OF 100,000 SOLDIERS.
In those three days, Narsus had used himself and his troops to spread rumors.
To the Türkish forces...
SINDHURA HAS SECRETLY COMMUNICATED TO PARS THAT THEY WILL BETRAY THE THREE-KINGDOM ALLIANCE.
AS PROOF, YOU'LL SOON FIND THAT ALL OF THE SINDHURAN PRISONERS WILL BE RELEASED.
SINDHURA
PARS
To the Tūrānian forces...
THE TÜRKISH FORCES ARE CONSPIRING WITH THE PARSIAN FORCES.
IN THE NEXT FEW DAYS, THE TÜRKS WILL ATTACK THE SINDHURAN FORCES. THEIR EXCUSE WILL SURELY BE AN ACCUSATION THAT SINDHURA IS IN SECRET COMMUNICATION WITH PARS.
DON'T TRUST THEM.
TÜRK
PARS
SINDHURA

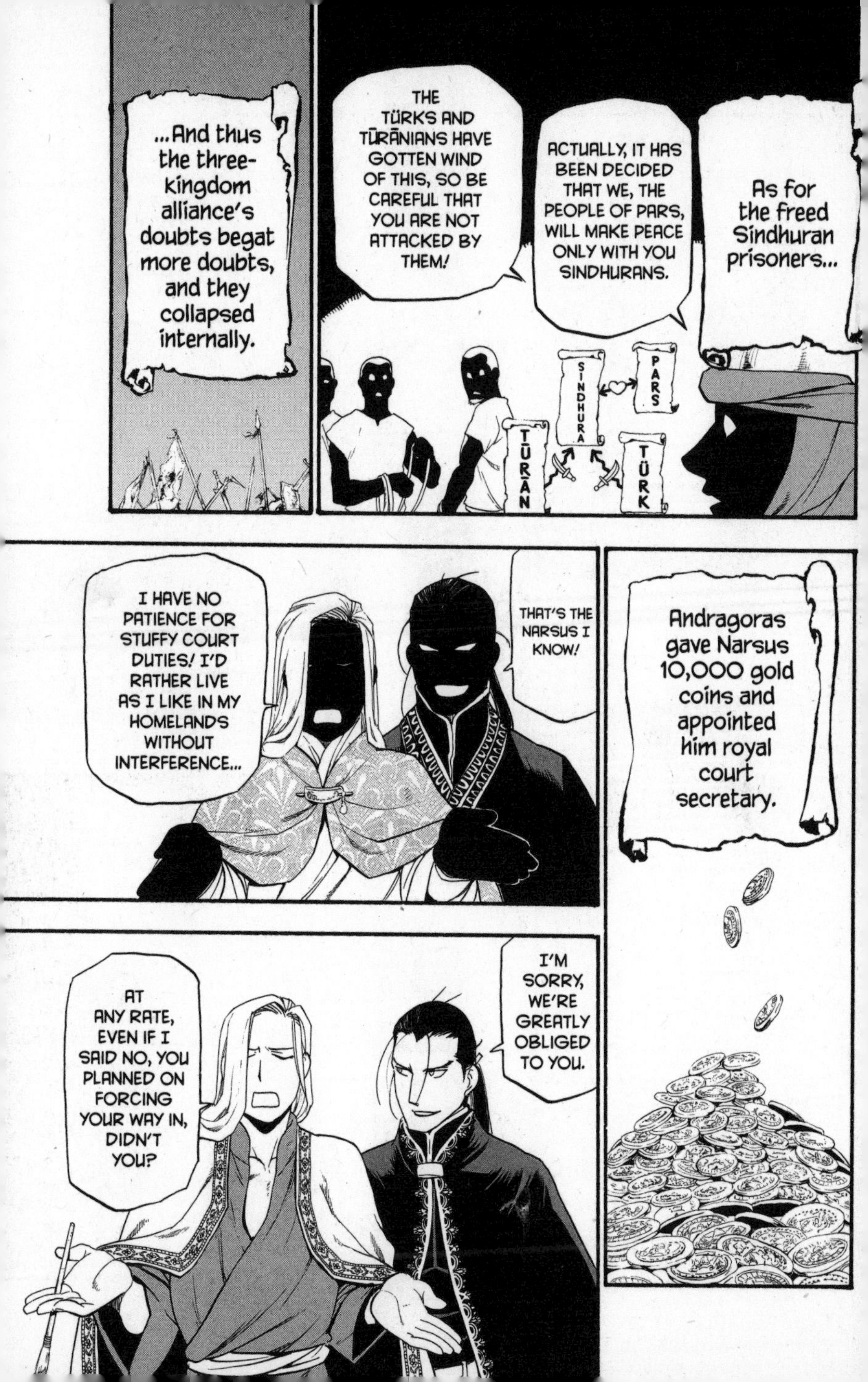
As for the freed Sindhuran prisoners...
ACTUALLY, IT HAS BEEN DECIDED THAT WE, THE PEOPLE OF PARS, WILL MAKE PEACE ONLY WITH YOU SINDHURANS.
THE TÜRKS AND TŪRĀNIANS HAVE GOTTEN WIND OF THIS, SO BE CAREFUL THAT YOU ARE NOT ATTACKED BY THEM!
PARS
SINDHURA
TŪRĀN
TÜRK
...And thus the three-kingdom alliance's doubts begat more doubts, and they collapsed internally.
Andragoras gave Narsus 10,000 gold coins and appointed him royal court secretary.
THAT'S THE NARSUS I KNOW!
I HAVE NO PATIENCE FOR STUFFY COURT DUTIES! I'D RATHER LIVE AS I LIKE IN MY HOMELANDS WITHOUT INTERFERENCE...
I'M SORRY, WE'RE GREATLY OBLIGED TO YOU.
AT ANY RATE, EVEN IF I SAID NO, YOU PLANNED ON FORCING YOUR WAY IN, DIDN'T YOU?

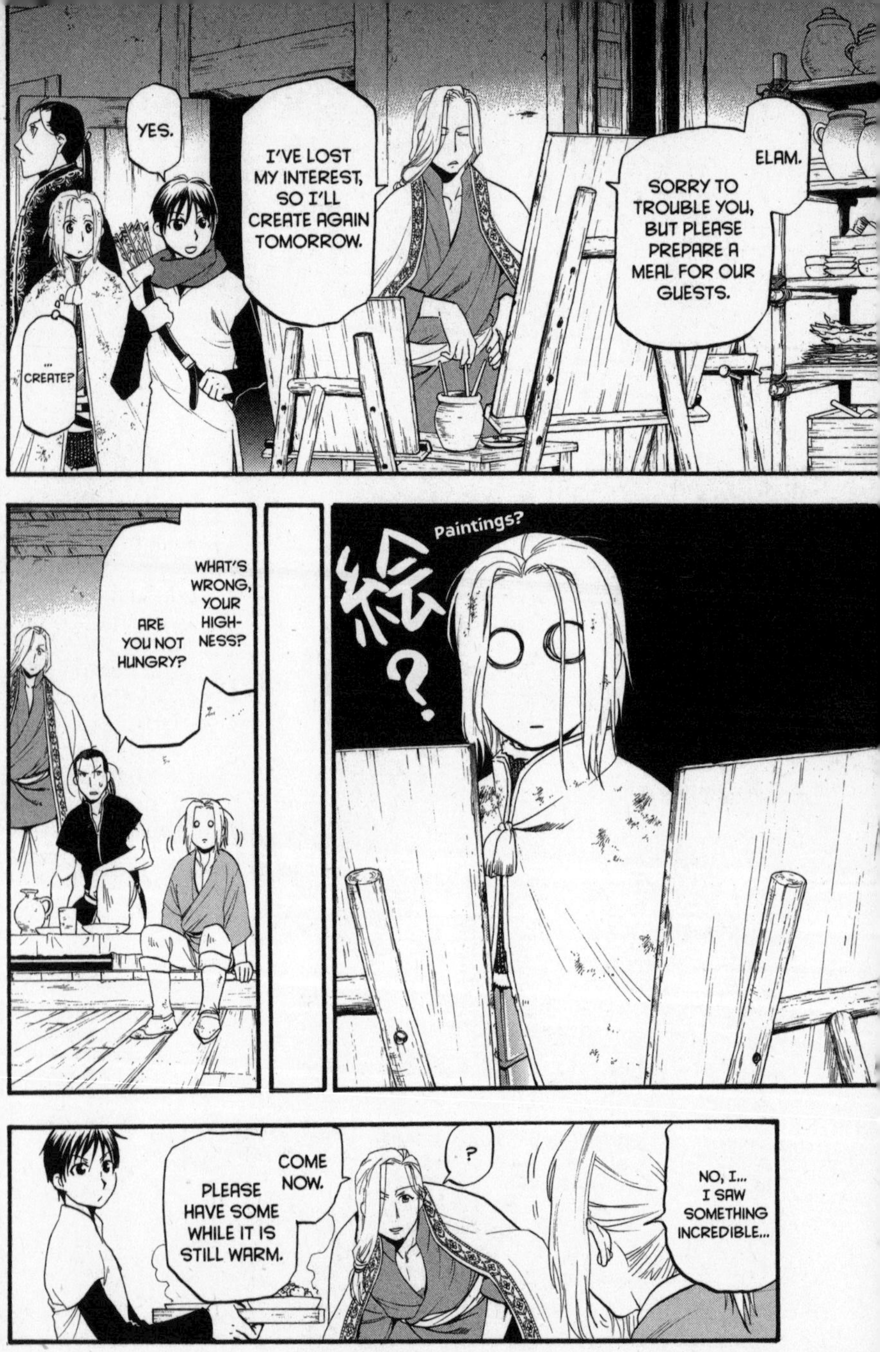
ELAM.
SORRY TO TROUBLE YOU, BUT PLEASE PREPARE A MEAL FOR OUR GUESTS.
I'VE LOST MY INTEREST, SO I'LL CREATE AGAIN TOMORROW.
YES.
... CREATE?
Paintings?
絵?
WHAT'S WRONG, YOUR HIGHNESS?
ARE YOU NOT HUNGRY?
NO, I... I SAW SOMETHING INCREDIBLE...
?
COME NOW.
PLEASE HAVE SOME WHILE IT IS STILL WARM.

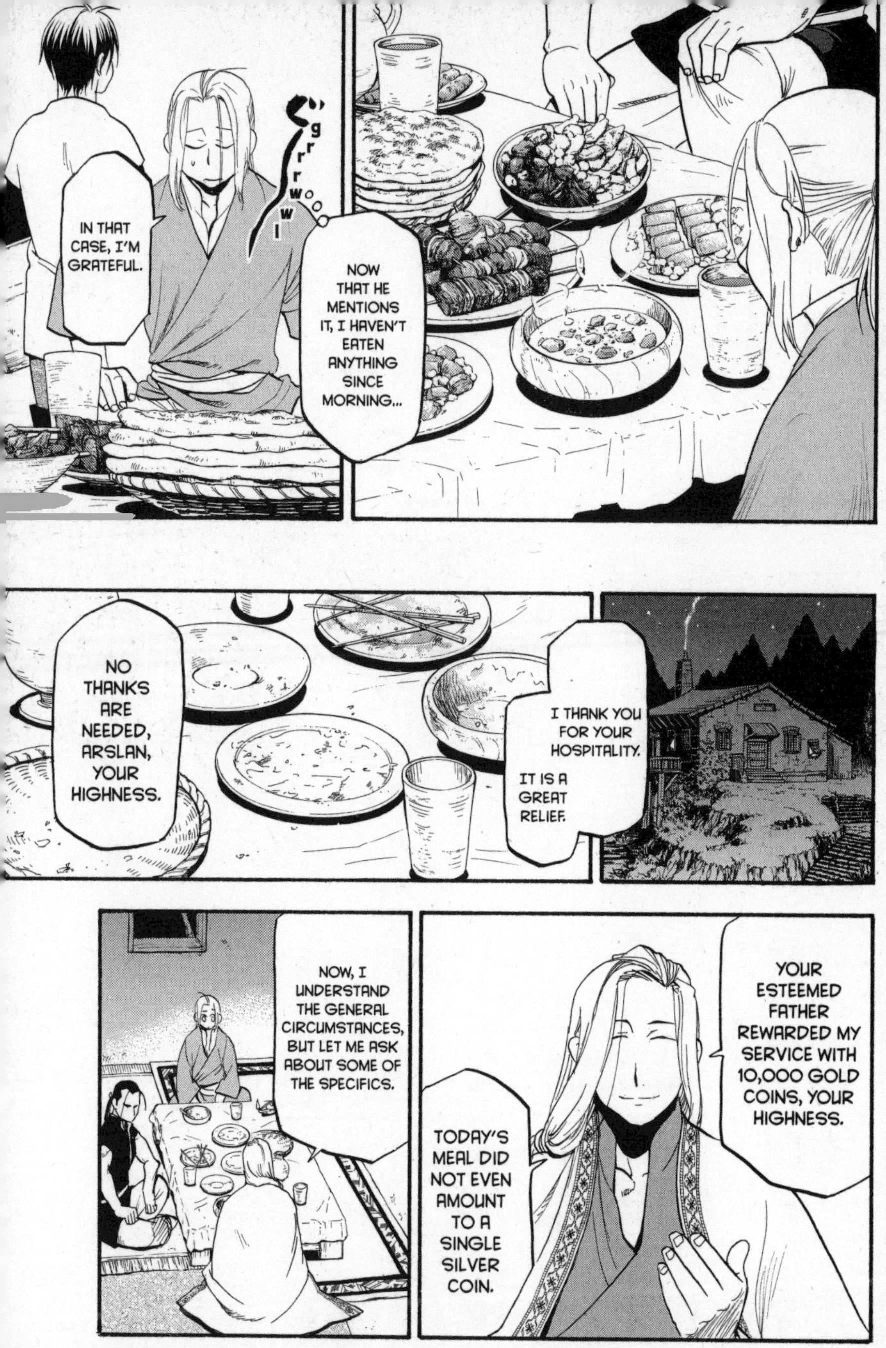
IN THAT CASE, I'M GRATEFUL.
ぐ grrrwoowl
NOW THAT HE MENTIONS IT, I HAVEN'T EATEN ANYTHING SINCE MORNING...
I THANK YOU FOR YOUR HOSPITALITY.
IT IS A GREAT RELIEF.
NO THANKS ARE NEEDED, ARSLAN, YOUR HIGHNESS.
YOUR ESTEEMED FATHER REWARDED MY SERVICE WITH 10,000 GOLD COINS, YOUR HIGHNESS.
TODAY'S MEAL DID NOT EVEN AMOUNT TO A SINGLE SILVER COIN.
NOW, I UNDERSTAND THE GENERAL CIRCUMSTANCES, BUT LET ME ASK ABOUT SOME OF THE SPECIFICS.

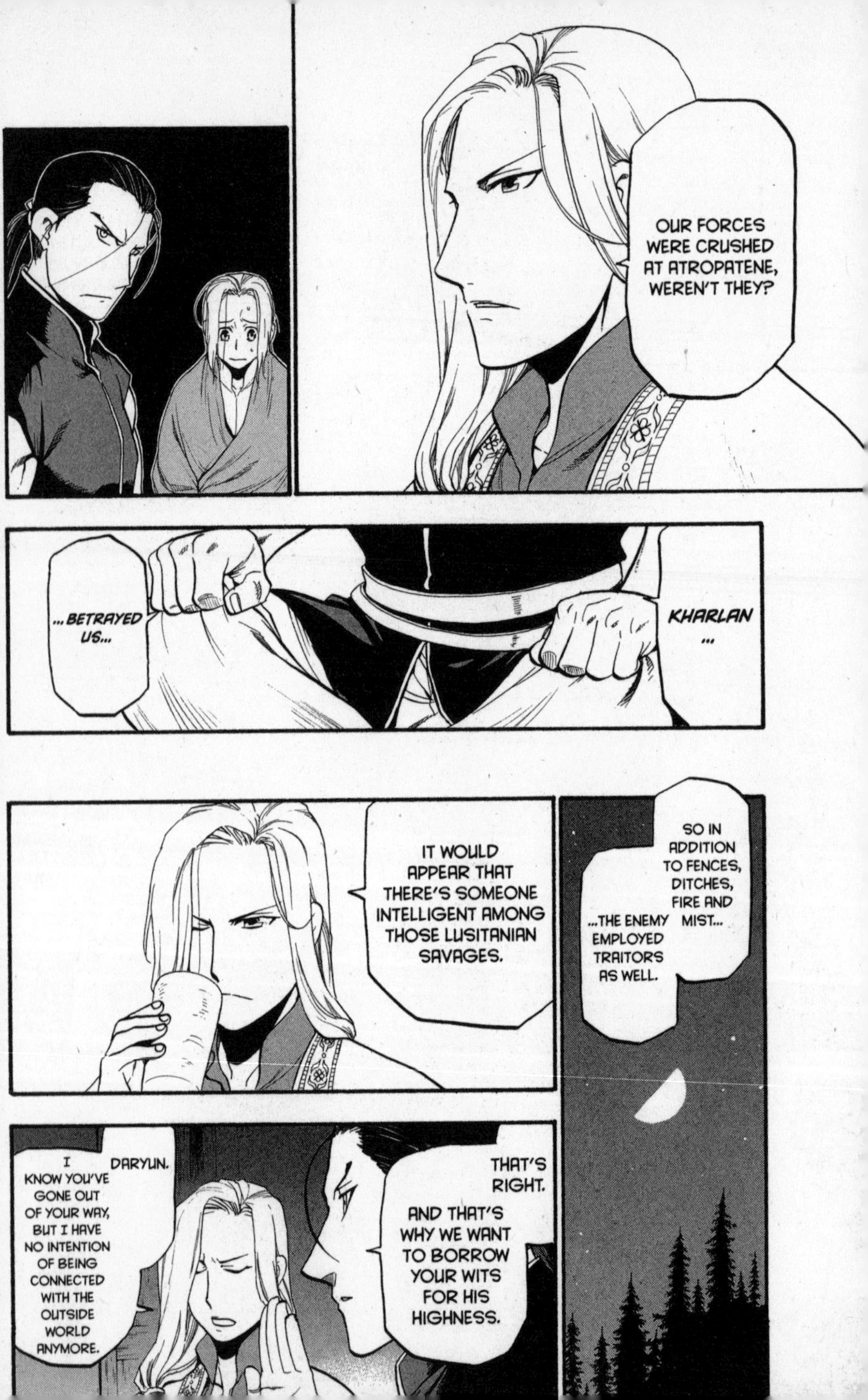
OUR FORCES WERE CRUSHED AT ATROPATENE, WEREN'T THEY?
KHARLAN ...
...BETRAYED US...
SO IN ADDITION TO FENCES, DITCHES, FIRE AND MIST...
...THE ENEMY EMPLOYED TRAITORS AS WELL.
IT WOULD APPEAR THAT THERE'S SOMEONE INTELLIGENT AMONG THOSE LUSITANIAN SAVAGES.
THAT'S RIGHT.
AND THAT'S WHY WE WANT TO BORROW YOUR WITS FOR HIS HIGHNESS.
DARYUN.
I KNOW YOU'VE GONE OUT OF YOUR WAY, BUT I HAVE NO INTENTION OF BEING CONNECTED WITH THE OUTSIDE WORLD ANYMORE.

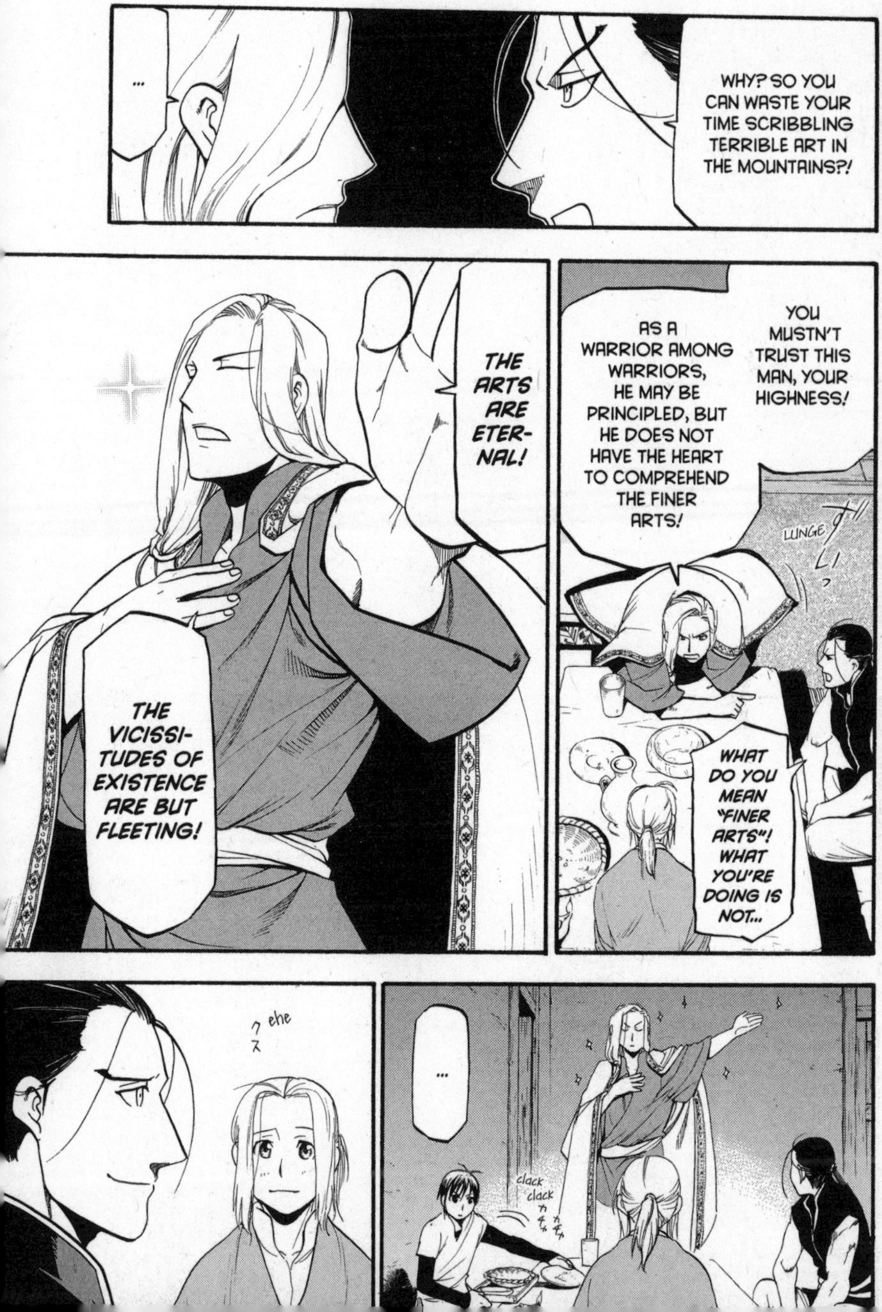
WHY? SO YOU CAN WASTE YOUR TIME SCRIBBLING TERRIBLE ART IN THE MOUNTAINS?!
...
YOU MUSTN'T TRUST THIS MAN, YOUR HIGHNESS!
AS A WARRIOR AMONG WARRIORS, HE MAY BE PRINCIPLED, BUT HE DOES NOT HAVE THE HEART TO COMPREHEND THE FINER ARTS!
LUNGE
WHAT DO YOU MEAN "FINER ARTS"! WHAT YOU'RE DOING IS NOT...
THE ARTS ARE ETER-NAL!
THE VICISSI-TUDES OF EXISTENCE ARE BUT FLEETING!
...
clack clack
ehe

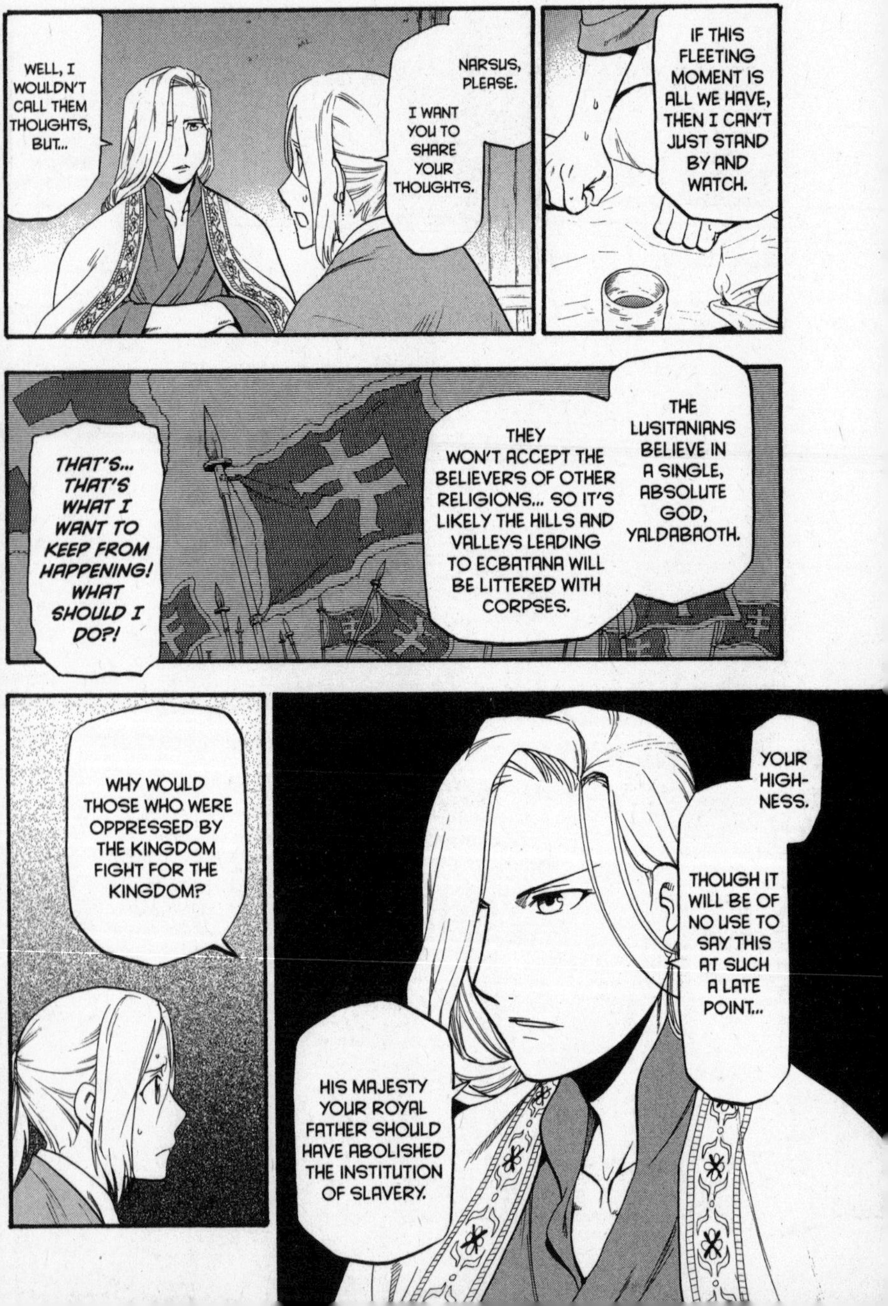
IF THIS FLEETING MOMENT IS ALL WE HAVE, THEN I CAN'T JUST STAND BY AND WATCH.
NARSUS, PLEASE.
I WANT YOU TO SHARE YOUR THOUGHTS.
WELL, I WOULDN'T CALL THEM THOUGHTS, BUT...
THE LUSITANIANS BELIEVE IN A SINGLE, ABSOLUTE GOD, YALDABAOTH.
THEY WON'T ACCEPT THE BELIEVERS OF OTHER RELIGIONS... SO IT'S LIKELY THE HILLS AND VALLEYS LEADING TO ECBATANA WILL BE LITTERED WITH CORPSES.
THAT'S... THAT'S WHAT I WANT TO KEEP FROM HAPPENING! WHAT SHOULD I DO?!
YOUR HIGHNESS.
THOUGH IT WILL BE OF NO USE TO SAY THIS AT SUCH A LATE POINT...
HIS MAJESTY YOUR ROYAL FATHER SHOULD HAVE ABOLISHED THE INSTITUTION OF SLAVERY.
WHY WOULD THOSE WHO WERE OPPRESSED BY THE KINGDOM FIGHT FOR THE KINGDOM?

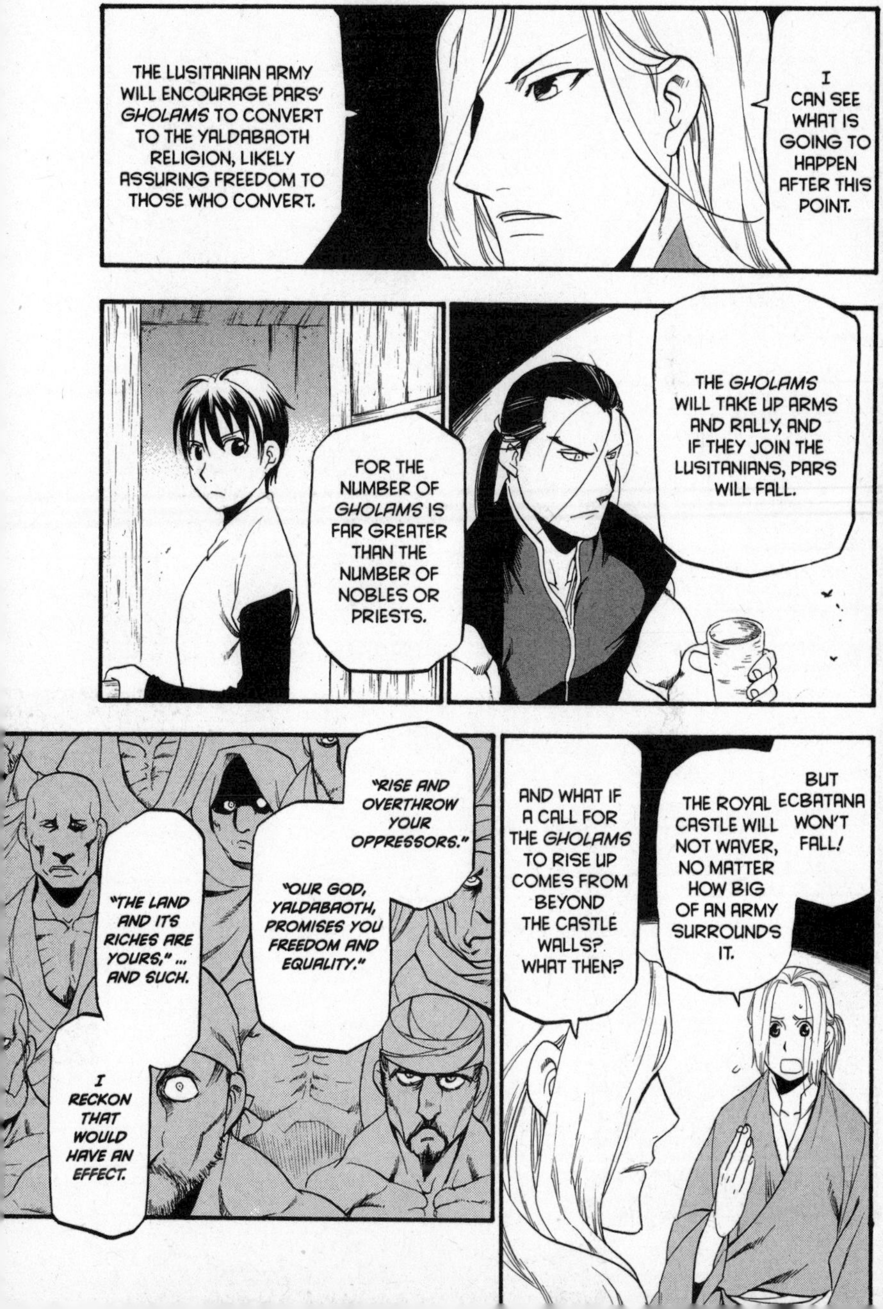
I CAN SEE WHAT IS GOING TO HAPPEN AFTER THIS POINT.
THE LUSITANIAN ARMY WILL ENCOURAGE PARS' *GHOLAMS* TO CONVERT TO THE YALDABAOTH RELIGION, LIKELY ASSURING FREEDOM TO THOSE WHO CONVERT.
THE *GHOLAMS* WILL TAKE UP ARMS AND RALLY, AND IF THEY JOIN THE LUSITANIANS, PARS WILL FALL.
FOR THE NUMBER OF *GHOLAMS* IS FAR GREATER THAN THE NUMBER OF NOBLES OR PRIESTS.
BUT ECBATANA WON'T FALL!
THE ROYAL CASTLE WILL NOT WAVER, NO MATTER HOW BIG OF AN ARMY SURROUNDS IT.
AND WHAT IF A CALL FOR THE *GHOLAMS* TO RISE UP COMES FROM BEYOND THE CASTLE WALLS? WHAT THEN?
"RISE AND OVERTHROW YOUR OPPRESSORS."
"OUR GOD, YALDABAOTH, PROMISES YOU FREEDOM AND EQUALITY."
"THE LAND AND ITS RICHES ARE YOURS," ... AND SUCH.
I RECKON THAT WOULD HAVE AN EFFECT.

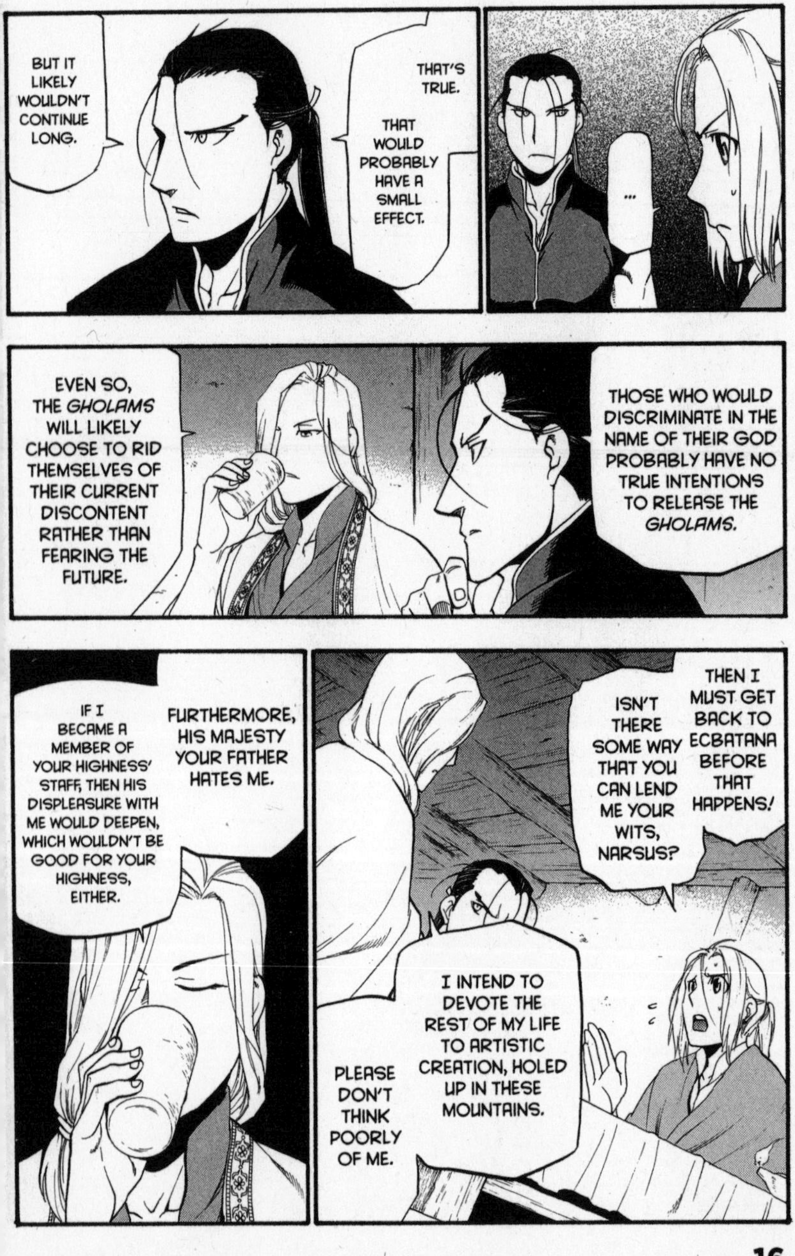
...
THAT'S TRUE.
THAT WOULD PROBABLY HAVE A SMALL EFFECT.
BUT IT LIKELY WOULDN'T CONTINUE LONG.
THOSE WHO WOULD DISCRIMINATE IN THE NAME OF THEIR GOD PROBABLY HAVE NO TRUE INTENTIONS TO RELEASE THE *GHOLAMS.*
EVEN SO, THE *GHOLAMS* WILL LIKELY CHOOSE TO RID THEMSELVES OF THEIR CURRENT DISCONTENT RATHER THAN FEARING THE FUTURE.
THEN I MUST GET BACK TO ECBATANA BEFORE THAT HAPPENS!
ISN'T THERE SOME WAY THAT YOU CAN LEND ME YOUR WITS, NARSUS?
I INTEND TO DEVOTE THE REST OF MY LIFE TO ARTISTIC CREATION, HOLED UP IN THESE MOUNTAINS.
PLEASE DON'T THINK POORLY OF ME.
FURTHERMORE, HIS MAJESTY YOUR FATHER HATES ME.
IF I BECAME A MEMBER OF YOUR HIGHNESS' STAFF, THEN HIS DISPLEASURE WITH ME WOULD DEEPEN, WHICH WOULDN'T BE GOOD FOR YOUR HIGHNESS, EITHER.

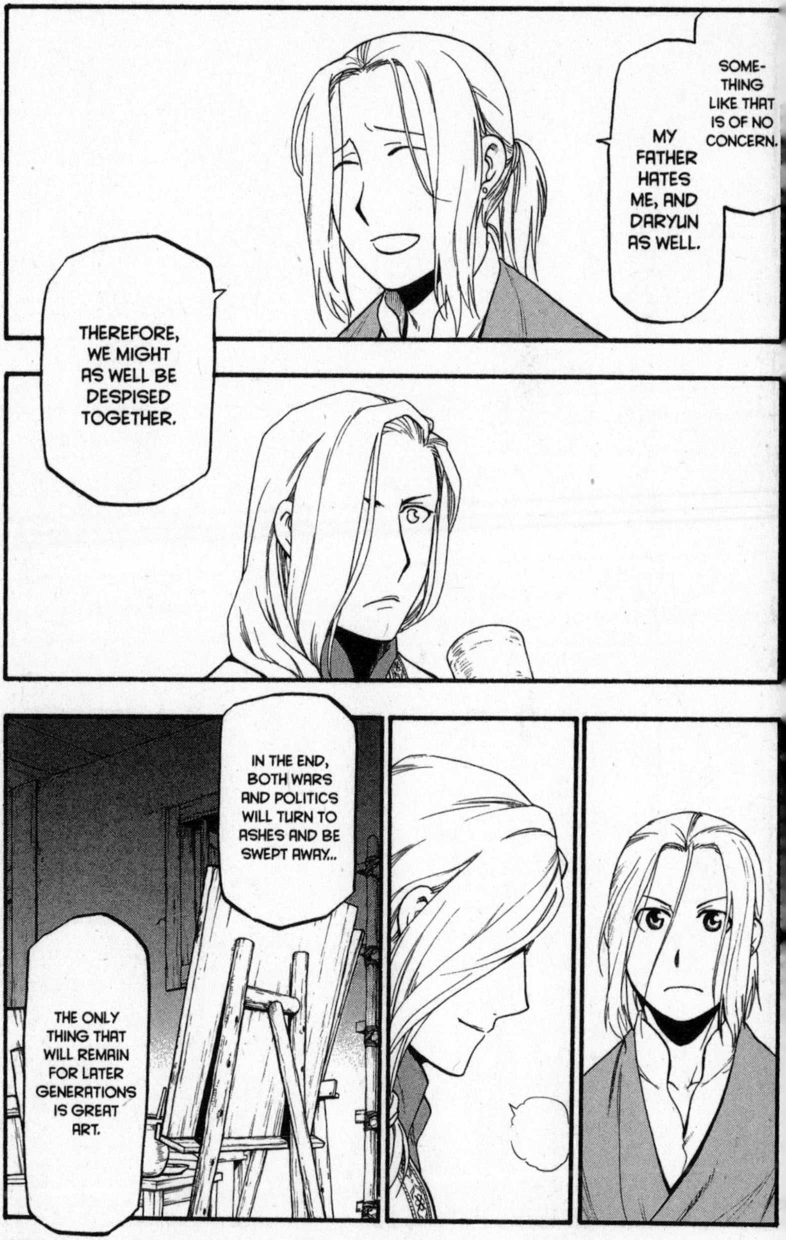
SOME-THING LIKE THAT IS OF NO CONCERN.
MY FATHER HATES ME, AND DARYUN AS WELL.
THEREFORE, WE MIGHT AS WELL BE DESPISED TOGETHER.
IN THE END, BOTH WARS AND POLITICS WILL TURN TO ASHES AND BE SWEPT AWAY...
THE ONLY THING THAT WILL REMAIN FOR LATER GENERATIONS IS GREAT ART.

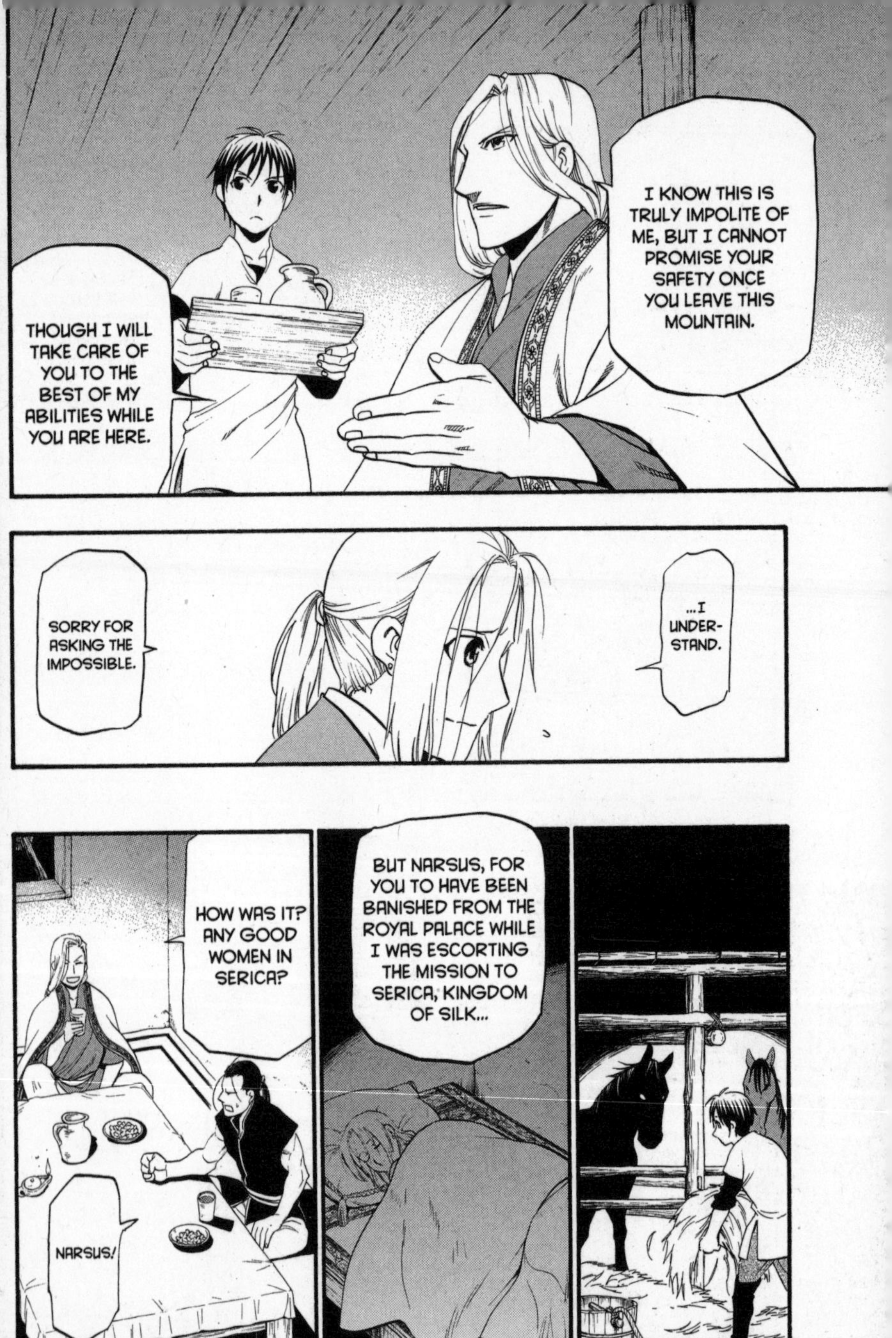
I KNOW THIS IS TRULY IMPOLITE OF ME, BUT I CANNOT PROMISE YOUR SAFETY ONCE YOU LEAVE THIS MOUNTAIN.
THOUGH I WILL TAKE CARE OF YOU TO THE BEST OF MY ABILITIES WHILE YOU ARE HERE.
...I UNDER-STAND.
SORRY FOR ASKING THE IMPOSSIBLE.
BUT NARSUS, FOR YOU TO HAVE BEEN BANISHED FROM THE ROYAL PALACE WHILE I WAS ESCORTING THE MISSION TO SERICA, KINGDOM OF SILK...
HOW WAS IT? ANY GOOD WOMEN IN SERICA?
NARSUS!

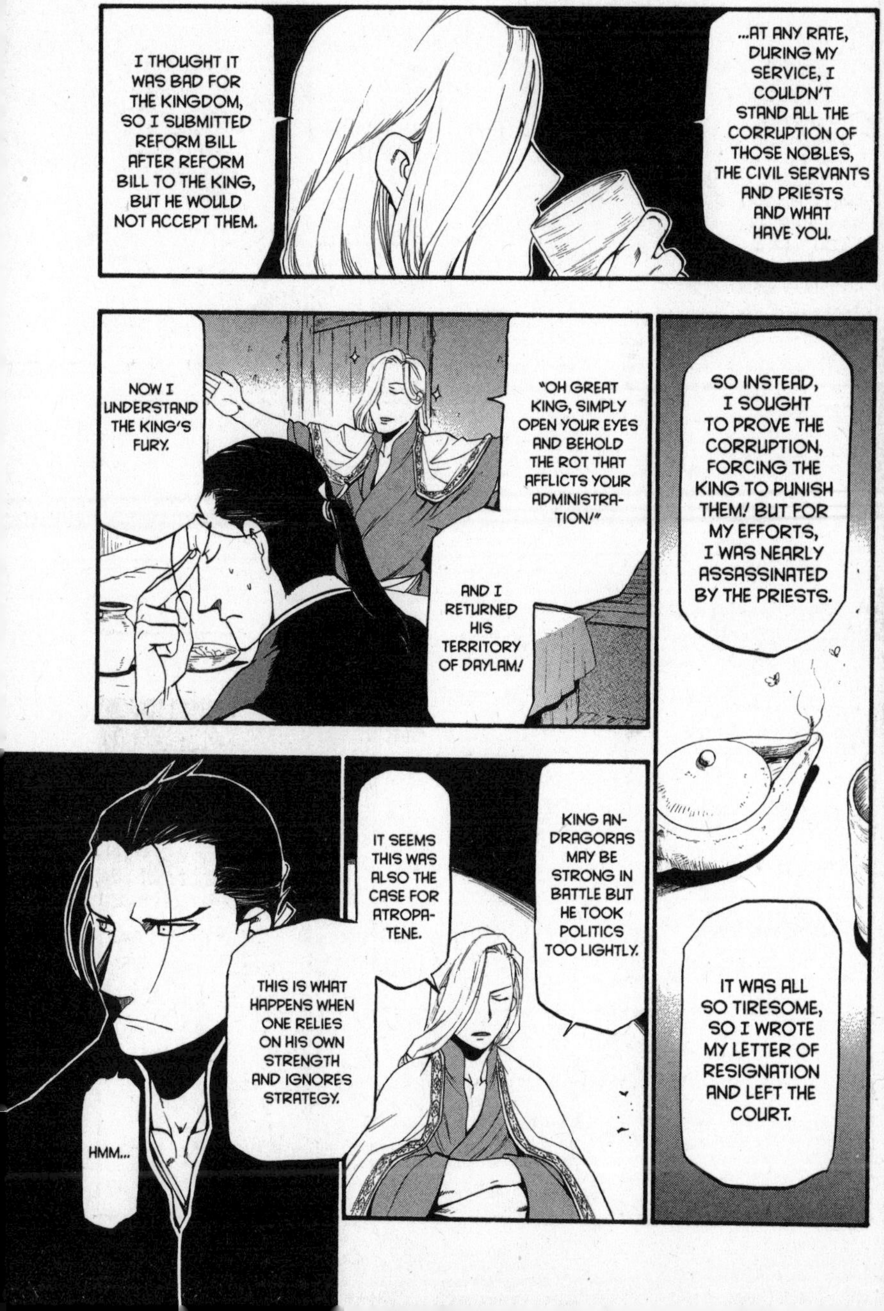
...AT ANY RATE, DURING MY SERVICE, I COULDN'T STAND ALL THE CORRUPTION OF THOSE NOBLES, THE CIVIL SERVANTS AND PRIESTS AND WHAT HAVE YOU.
I THOUGHT IT WAS BAD FOR THE KINGDOM, SO I SUBMITTED REFORM BILL AFTER REFORM BILL TO THE KING, BUT HE WOULD NOT ACCEPT THEM.
SO INSTEAD, I SOUGHT TO PROVE THE CORRUPTION, FORCING THE KING TO PUNISH THEM! BUT FOR MY EFFORTS, I WAS NEARLY ASSASSINATED BY THE PRIESTS.
IT WAS ALL SO TIRESOME, SO I WROTE MY LETTER OF RESIGNATION AND LEFT THE COURT.
"OH GREAT KING, SIMPLY OPEN YOUR EYES AND BEHOLD THE ROT THAT AFFLICTS YOUR ADMINISTRATION!"
AND I RETURNED HIS TERRITORY OF DAYLAM!
NOW I UNDERSTAND THE KING'S FURY.
KING ANDRAGORAS MAY BE STRONG IN BATTLE BUT HE TOOK POLITICS TOO LIGHTLY.
IT SEEMS THIS WAS ALSO THE CASE FOR ATROPATENE.
THIS IS WHAT HAPPENS WHEN ONE RELIES ON HIS OWN STRENGTH AND IGNORES STRATEGY.
HMM...

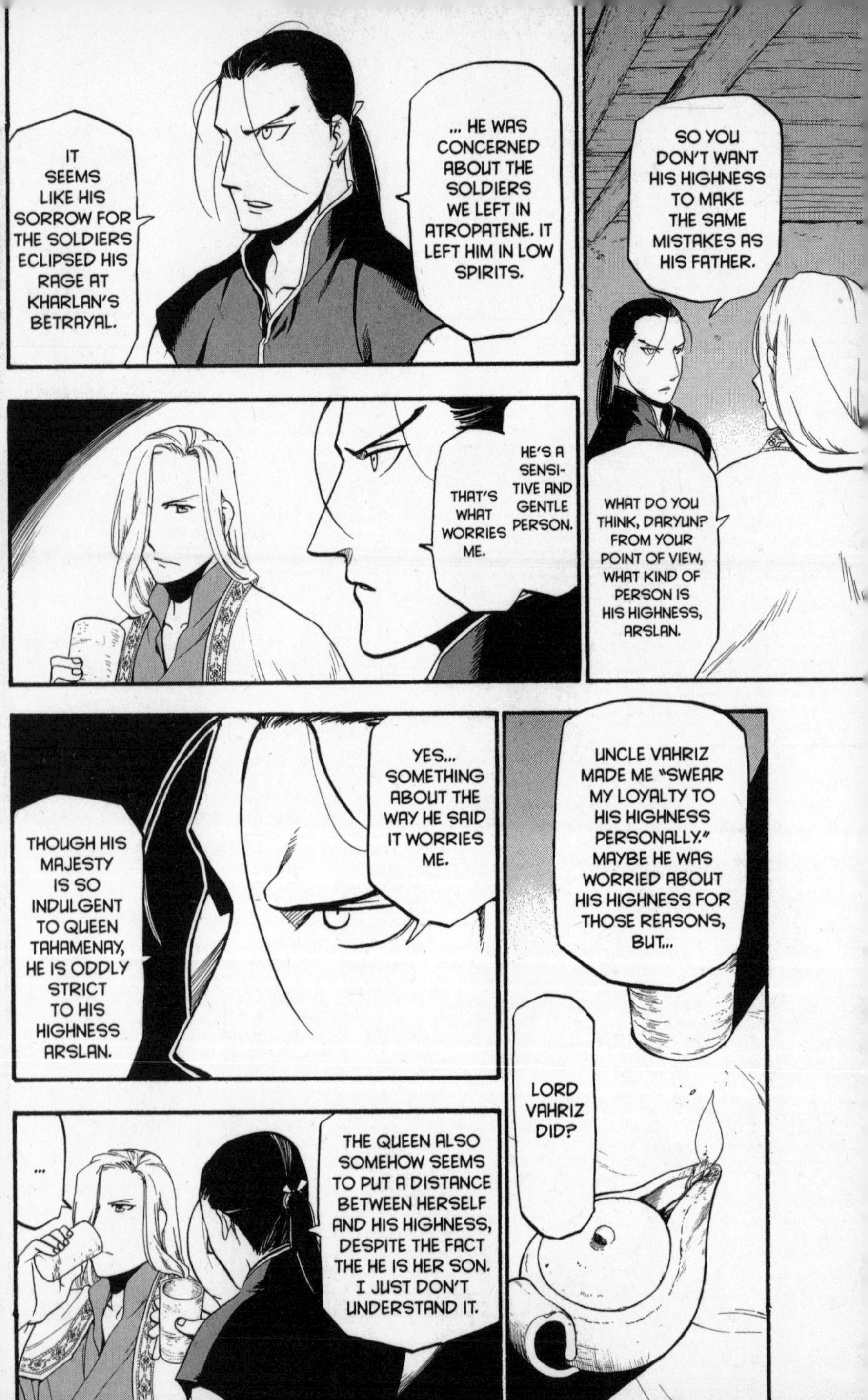
SO YOU DON'T WANT HIS HIGHNESS TO MAKE THE SAME MISTAKES AS HIS FATHER.
WHAT DO YOU THINK, DARYUN? FROM YOUR POINT OF VIEW, WHAT KIND OF PERSON IS HIS HIGHNESS, ARSLAN.
... HE WAS CONCERNED ABOUT THE SOLDIERS WE LEFT IN ATROPATENE. IT LEFT HIM IN LOW SPIRITS.
IT SEEMS LIKE HIS SORROW FOR THE SOLDIERS ECLIPSED HIS RAGE AT KHARLAN'S BETRAYAL.
HE'S A SENSITIVE AND GENTLE PERSON.
THAT'S WHAT WORRIES ME.
UNCLE VAHRIZ MADE ME "SWEAR MY LOYALTY TO HIS HIGHNESS PERSONALLY." MAYBE HE WAS WORRIED ABOUT HIS HIGHNESS FOR THOSE REASONS, BUT...
LORD VAHRIZ DID?
YES... SOMETHING ABOUT THE WAY HE SAID IT WORRIES ME.
THOUGH HIS MAJESTY IS SO INDULGENT TO QUEEN TAHAMENAY, HE IS ODDLY STRICT TO HIS HIGHNESS ARSLAN.
THE QUEEN ALSO SOMEHOW SEEMS TO PUT A DISTANCE BETWEEN HERSELF AND HIS HIGHNESS, DESPITE THE FACT THE HE IS HER SON. I JUST DON'T UNDERSTAND IT.
...

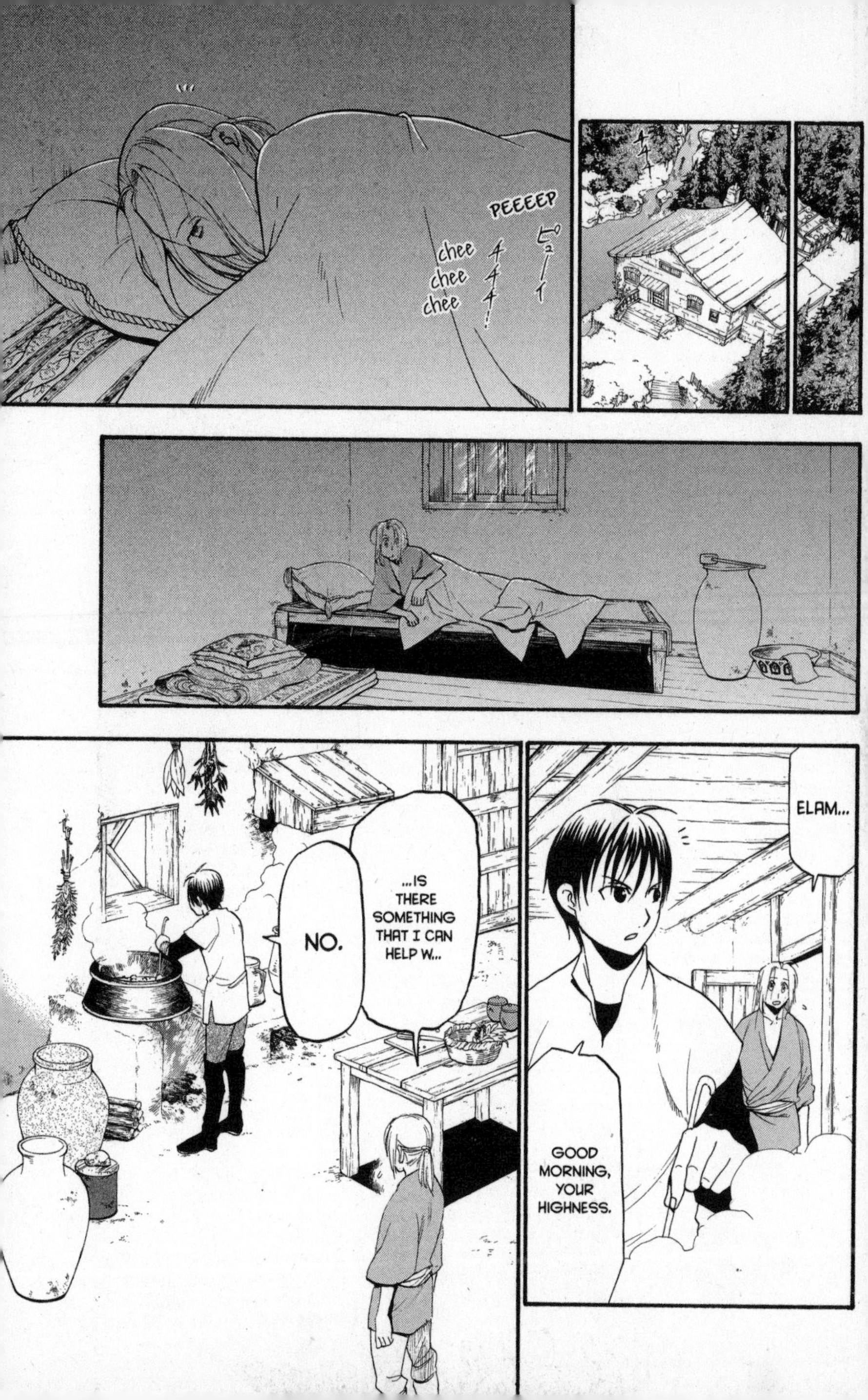
PEEEEP
ピューイ
chee chee chee
チチチ！
ELAM...
GOOD MORNING, YOUR HIGHNESS.
...IS THERE SOMETHING THAT I CAN HELP W...
NO.

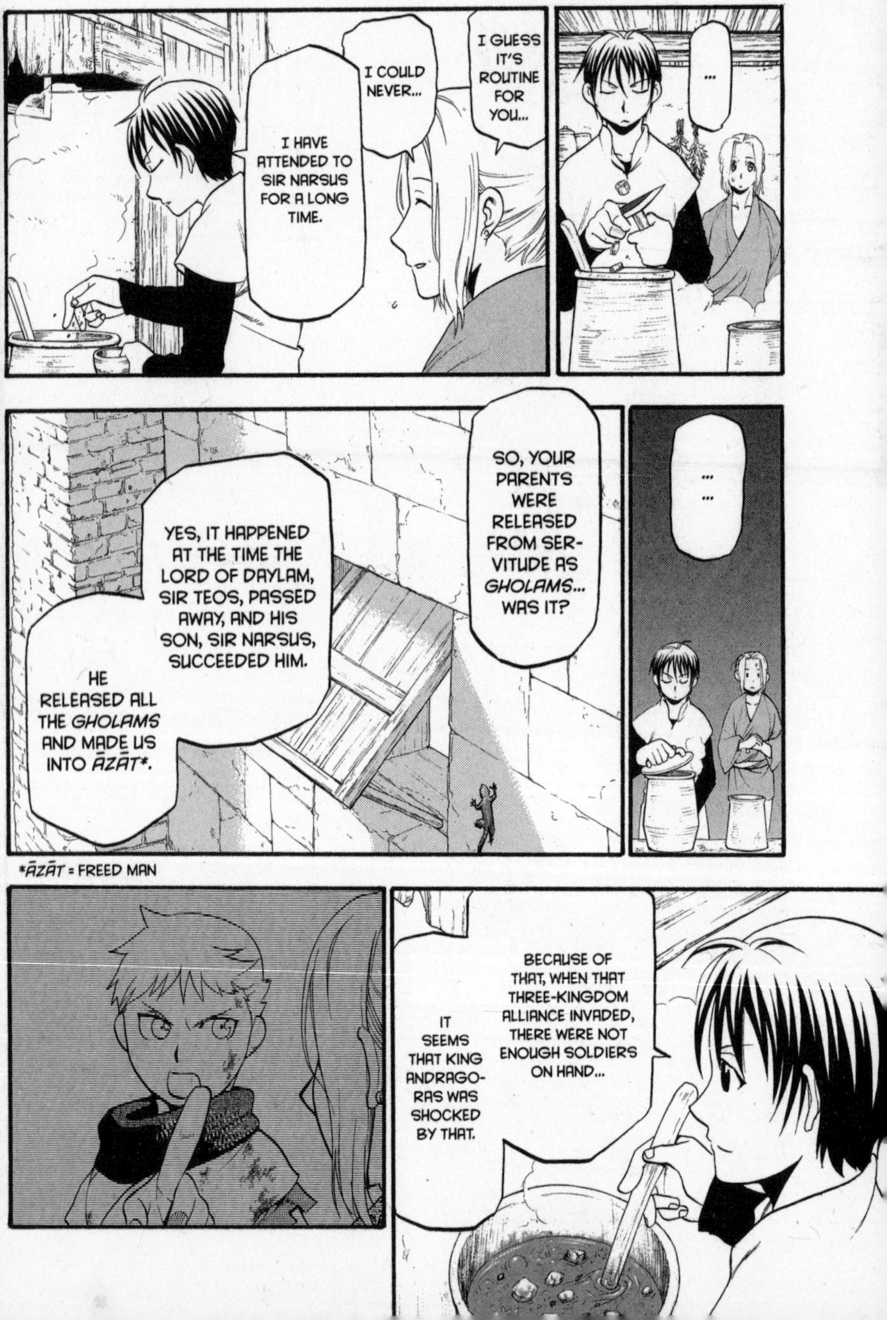
...
I GUESS IT'S ROUTINE FOR YOU...
I COULD NEVER...
I HAVE ATTENDED TO SIR NARSUS FOR A LONG TIME.
...
...
SO, YOUR PARENTS WERE RELEASED FROM SER-VITUDE AS *GHOLAMS*... WAS IT?
YES, IT HAPPENED AT THE TIME THE LORD OF DAYLAM, SIR TEOS, PASSED AWAY, AND HIS SON, SIR NARSUS, SUCCEEDED HIM.
HE RELEASED ALL THE *GHOLAMS* AND MADE US INTO *ĀZĀT**.
BECAUSE OF THAT, WHEN THAT THREE-KINGDOM ALLIANCE INVADED, THERE WERE NOT ENOUGH SOLDIERS ON HAND...
IT SEEMS THAT KING ANDRAGO-RAS WAS SHOCKED BY THAT.

**ĀZĀT* = FREED MAN

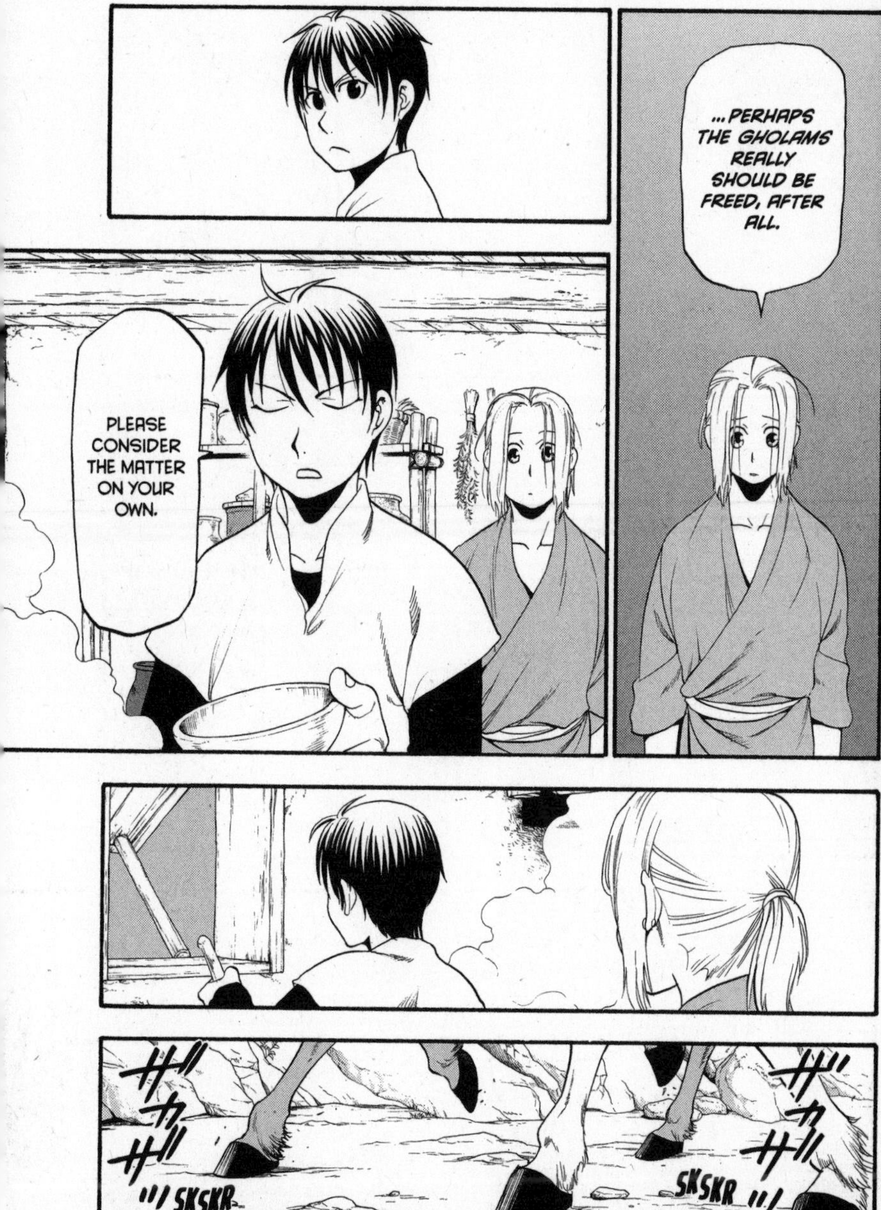
...PERHAPS THE GHOLAMS REALLY SHOULD BE FREED, AFTER ALL.
PLEASE CONSIDER THE MATTER ON YOUR OWN.
SKSKR
SKSKR

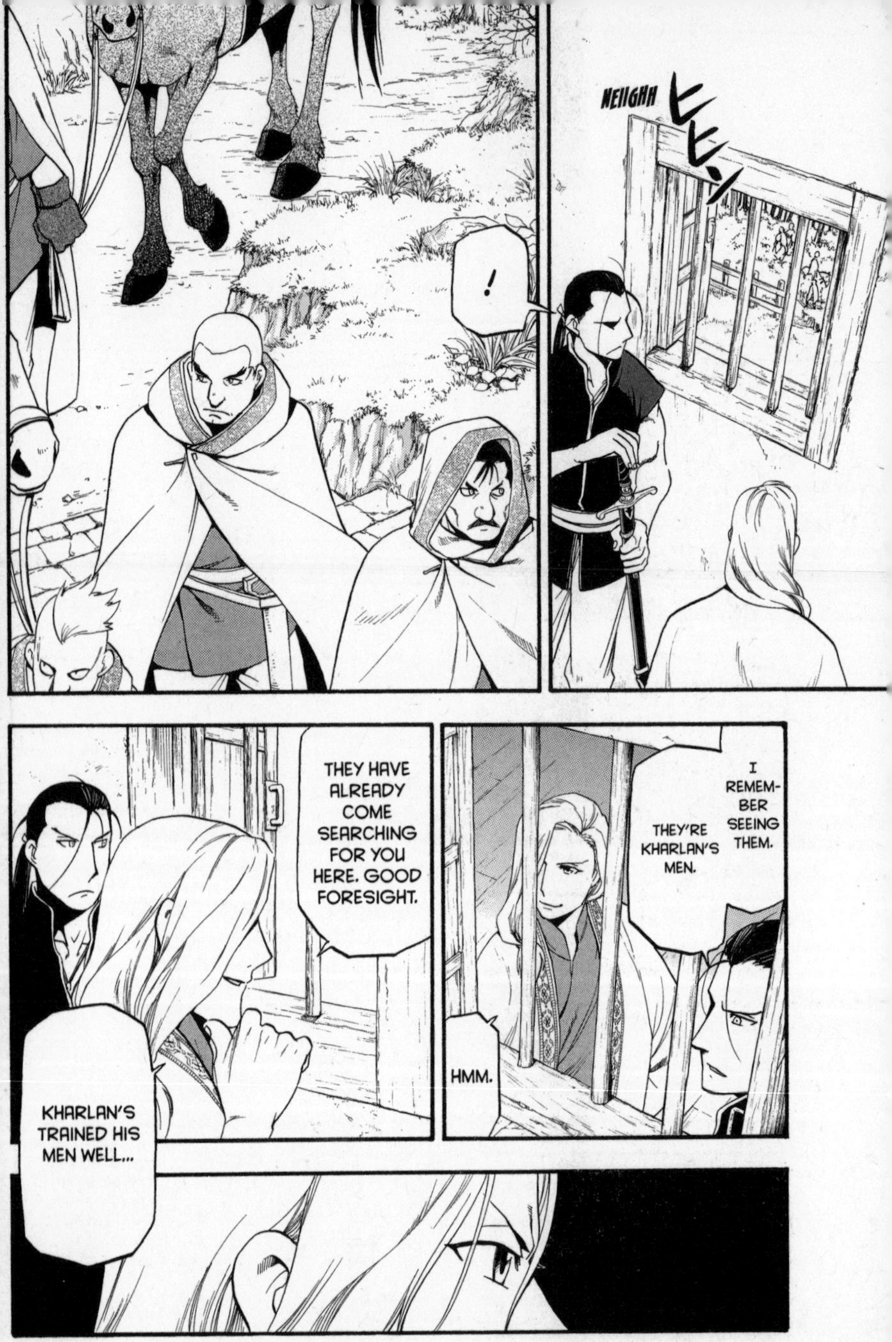
NEIIGHH
ヒヒン
!
I REMEMBER SEEING THEM.
THEY'RE KHARLAN'S MEN.
HMM.
THEY HAVE ALREADY COME SEARCHING FOR YOU HERE. GOOD FORESIGHT.
KHARLAN'S TRAINED HIS MEN WELL...

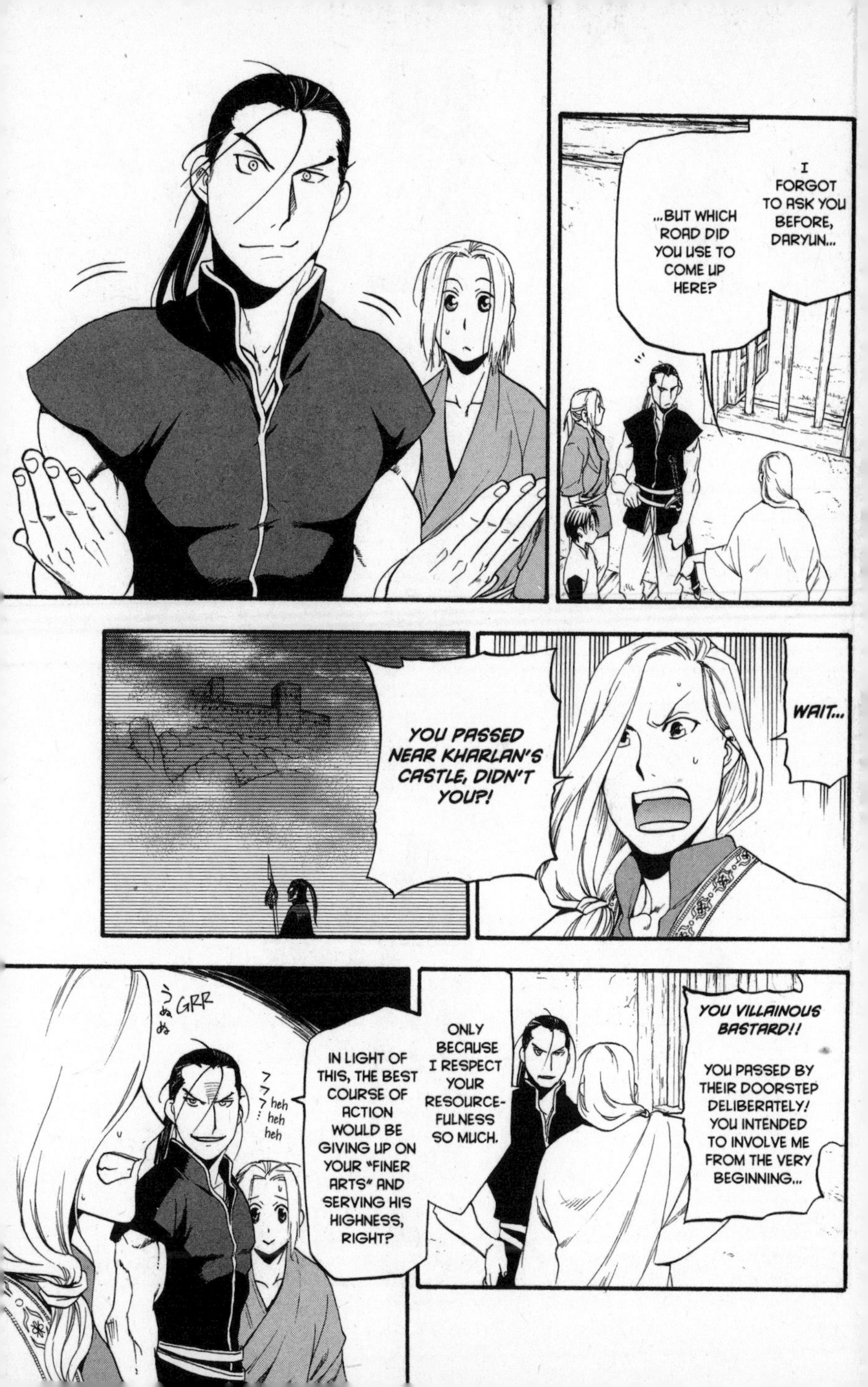
I FORGOT TO ASK YOU BEFORE, DARYUN...
...BUT WHICH ROAD DID YOU USE TO COME UP HERE?
WAIT...
YOU PASSED NEAR KHARLAN'S CASTLE, DIDN'T YOU?!
YOU VILLAINOUS BASTARD!!
YOU PASSED BY THEIR DOORSTEP DELIBERATELY! YOU INTENDED TO INVOLVE ME FROM THE VERY BEGINNING...
ONLY BECAUSE I RESPECT YOUR RESOURCE-FULNESS SO MUCH.
IN LIGHT OF THIS, THE BEST COURSE OF ACTION WOULD BE GIVING UP ON YOUR "FINER ARTS" AND SERVING HIS HIGHNESS, RIGHT?
うぬぬ GRR
フフフ… heh heh heh

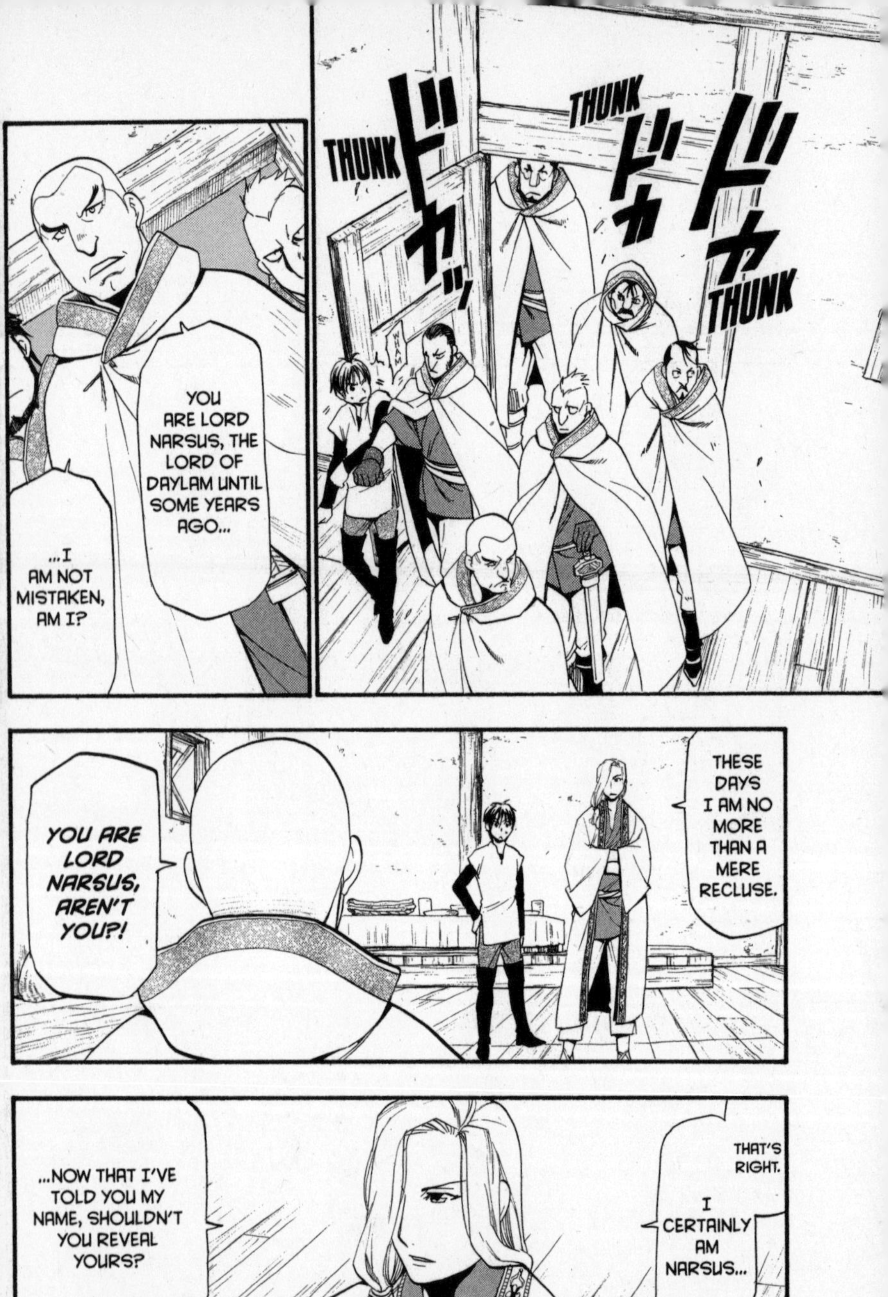
THUNK
ドガッ
THUNK
ドカ
ドカ
THUNK
WHAM
YOU ARE LORD NARSUS, THE LORD OF DAYLAM UNTIL SOME YEARS AGO...
...I AM NOT MISTAKEN, AM I?
THESE DAYS I AM NO MORE THAN A MERE RECLUSE.
YOU ARE LORD NARSUS, AREN'T YOU?!
THAT'S RIGHT.
I CERTAINLY AM NARSUS...
...NOW THAT I'VE TOLD YOU MY NAME, SHOULDN'T YOU REVEAL YOURS?

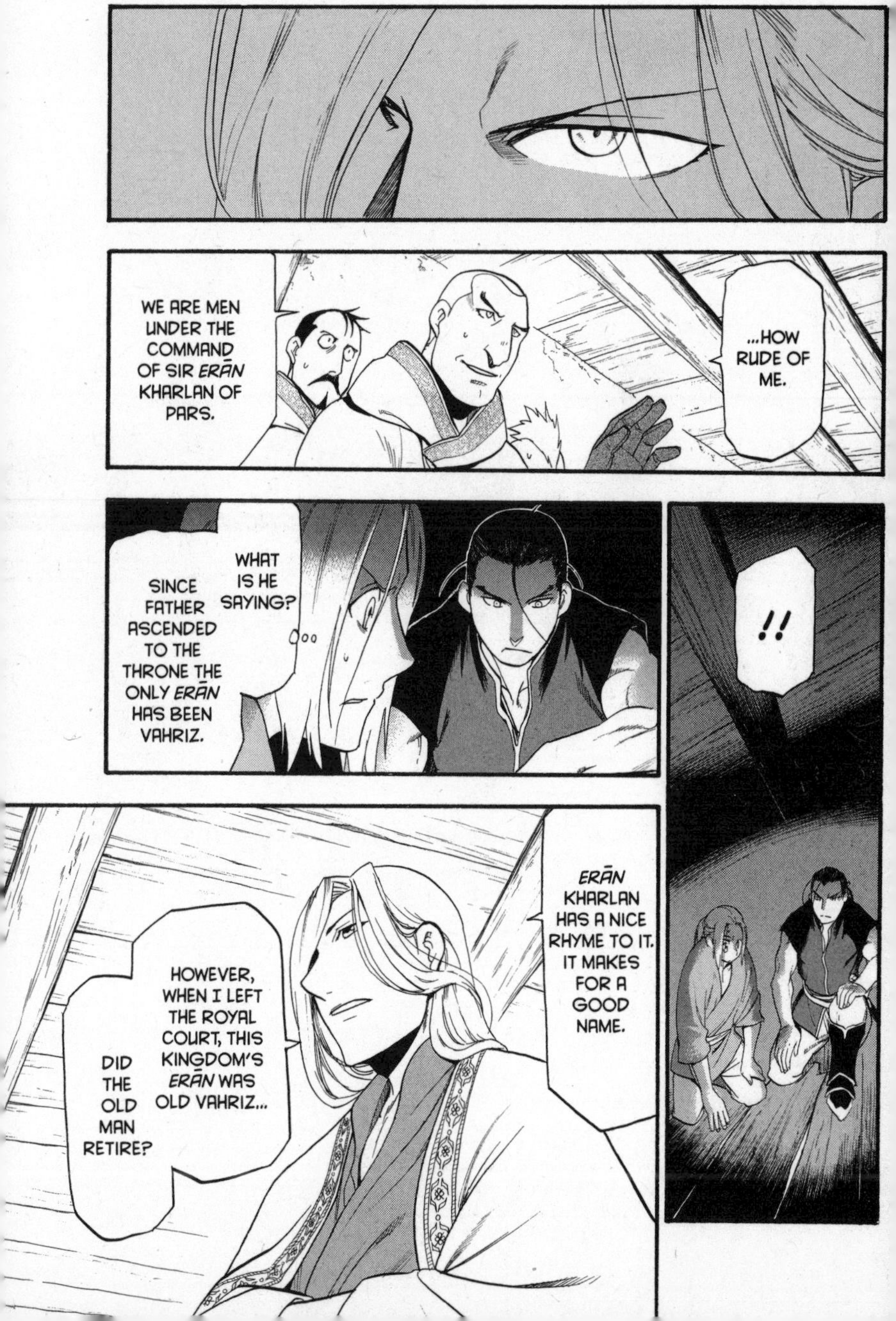
...HOW RUDE OF ME.
WE ARE MEN UNDER THE COMMAND OF SIR *ERĀN* KHARLAN OF PARS.
!!
WHAT IS HE SAYING?
SINCE FATHER ASCENDED TO THE THRONE THE ONLY *ERĀN* HAS BEEN VAHRIZ.
ERĀN KHARLAN HAS A NICE RHYME TO IT. IT MAKES FOR A GOOD NAME.
HOWEVER, WHEN I LEFT THE ROYAL COURT, THIS KINGDOM'S *ERĀN* WAS OLD VAHRIZ...
DID THE OLD MAN RETIRE?

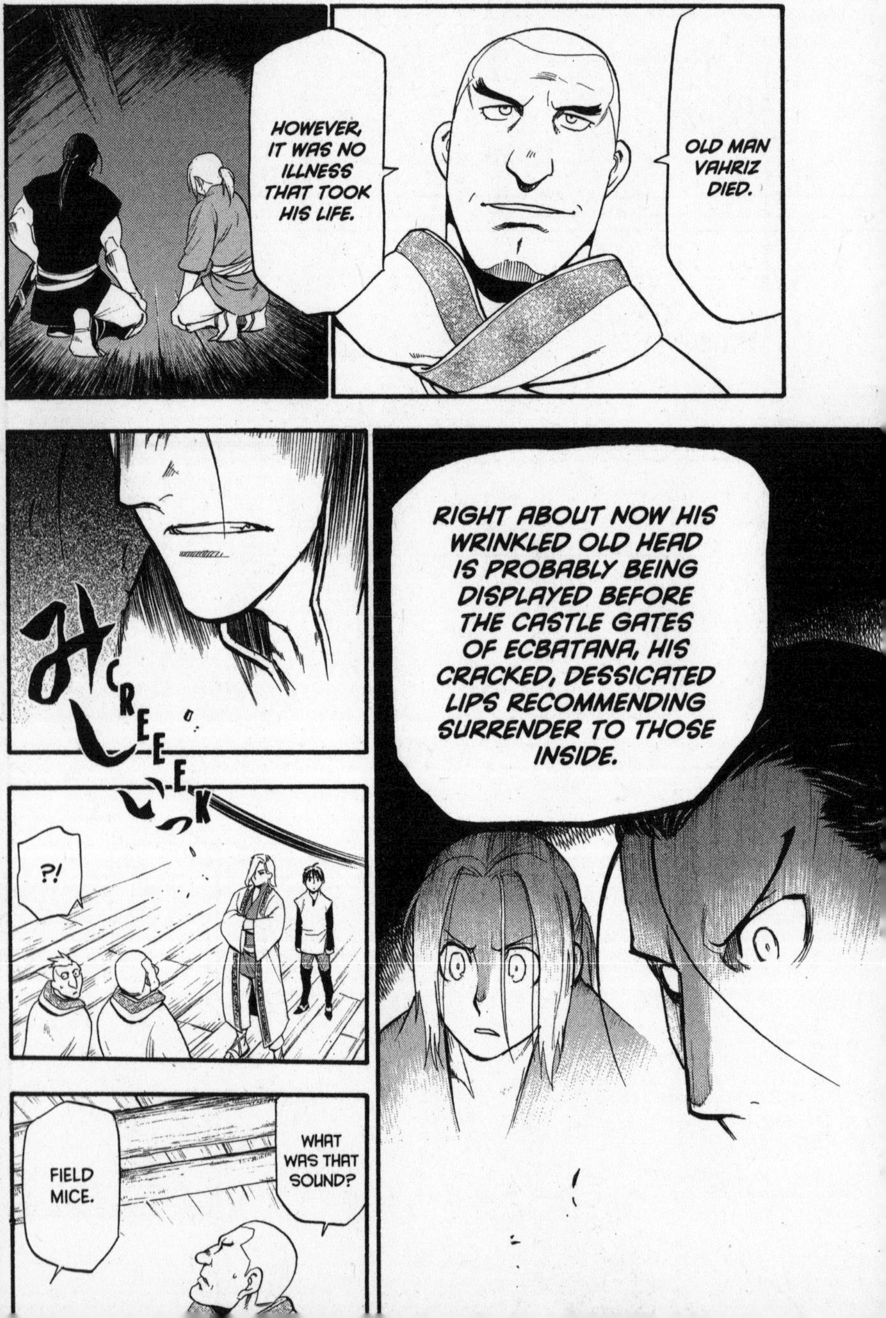
OLD MAN VAHRIZ DIED.
HOWEVER, IT WAS NO ILLNESS THAT TOOK HIS LIFE.
RIGHT ABOUT NOW HIS WRINKLED OLD HEAD IS PROBABLY BEING DISPLAYED BEFORE THE CASTLE GATES OF ECBATANA, HIS CRACKED, DESSICATED LIPS RECOMMENDING SURRENDER TO THOSE INSIDE.
CREEEEK
?!
WHAT WAS THAT SOUND?
FIELD MICE.

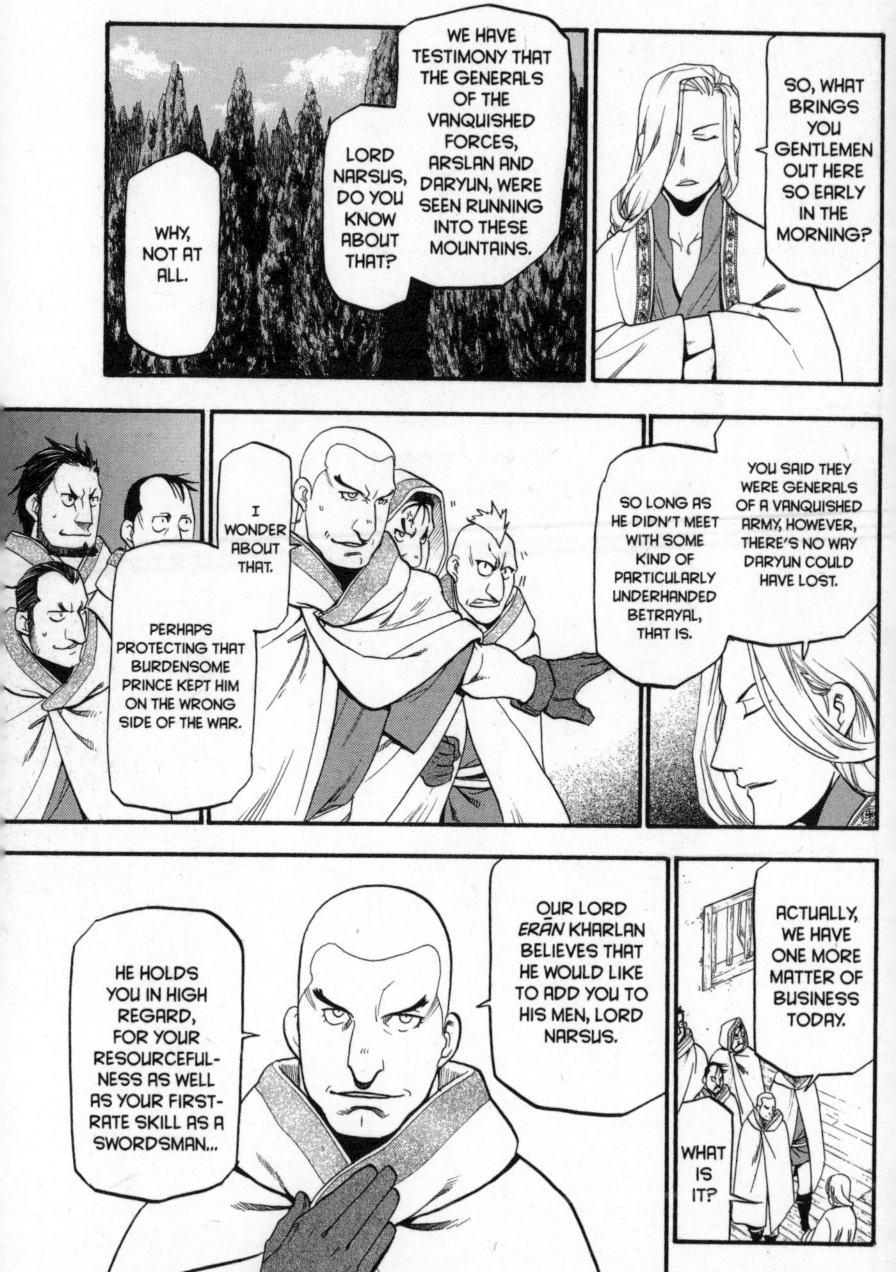
SO, WHAT BRINGS YOU GENTLEMEN OUT HERE SO EARLY IN THE MORNING?
WE HAVE TESTIMONY THAT THE GENERALS OF THE VANQUISHED FORCES, ARSLAN AND DARYUN, WERE SEEN RUNNING INTO THESE MOUNTAINS.
LORD NARSUS, DO YOU KNOW ABOUT THAT?
WHY, NOT AT ALL.
YOU SAID THEY WERE GENERALS OF A VANQUISHED ARMY, HOWEVER, THERE'S NO WAY DARYUN COULD HAVE LOST.
SO LONG AS HE DIDN'T MEET WITH SOME KIND OF PARTICULARLY UNDERHANDED BETRAYAL, THAT IS.
I WONDER ABOUT THAT.
PERHAPS PROTECTING THAT BURDENSOME PRINCE KEPT HIM ON THE WRONG SIDE OF THE WAR.
ACTUALLY, WE HAVE ONE MORE MATTER OF BUSINESS TODAY.
WHAT IS IT?
OUR LORD *ERĀN* KHARLAN BELIEVES THAT HE WOULD LIKE TO ADD YOU TO HIS MEN, LORD NARSUS.
HE HOLDS YOU IN HIGH REGARD, FOR YOUR RESOURCEFUL-NESS AS WELL AS YOUR FIRST-RATE SKILL AS A SWORDSMAN...

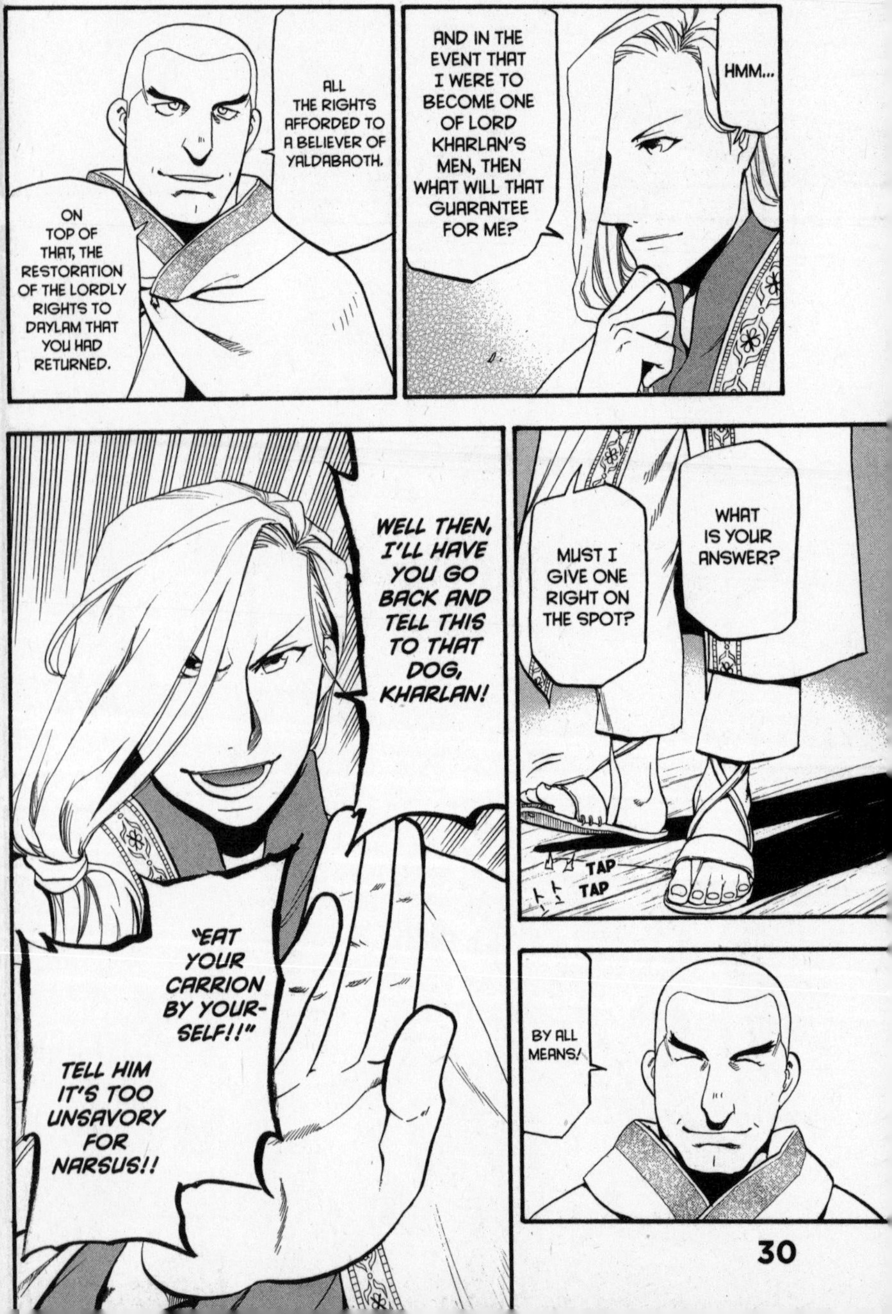
HMM...
AND IN THE EVENT THAT I WERE TO BECOME ONE OF LORD KHARLAN'S MEN, THEN WHAT WILL THAT GUARANTEE FOR ME?
ALL THE RIGHTS AFFORDED TO A BELIEVER OF YALDABAOTH.
ON TOP OF THAT, THE RESTORATION OF THE LORDLY RIGHTS TO DAYLAM THAT YOU HAD RETURNED.
WHAT IS YOUR ANSWER?
MUST I GIVE ONE RIGHT ON THE SPOT?
TAP
TAP
BY ALL MEANS!
WELL THEN, I'LL HAVE YOU GO BACK AND TELL THIS TO THAT DOG, KHARLAN!
"EAT YOUR CARRION BY YOUR-SELF!!"
TELL HIM IT'S TOO UNSAVORY FOR NARSUS!!

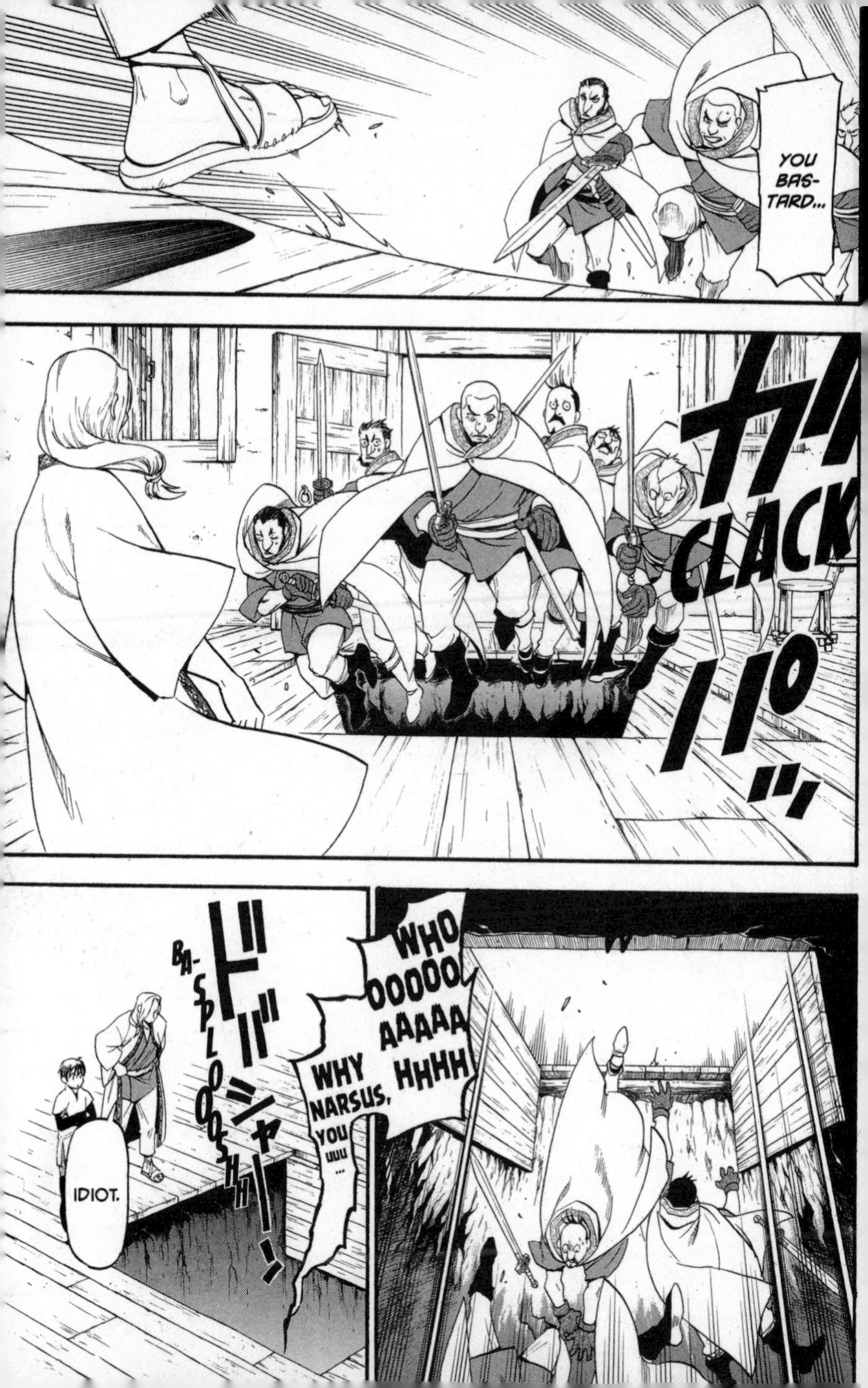
YOU BASTARD...
CLACK
WHOOOOOOAAAAAHHHH
WHY NARSUS, YOU uuu ...
BA-SPLOOOSHH
IDIOT.

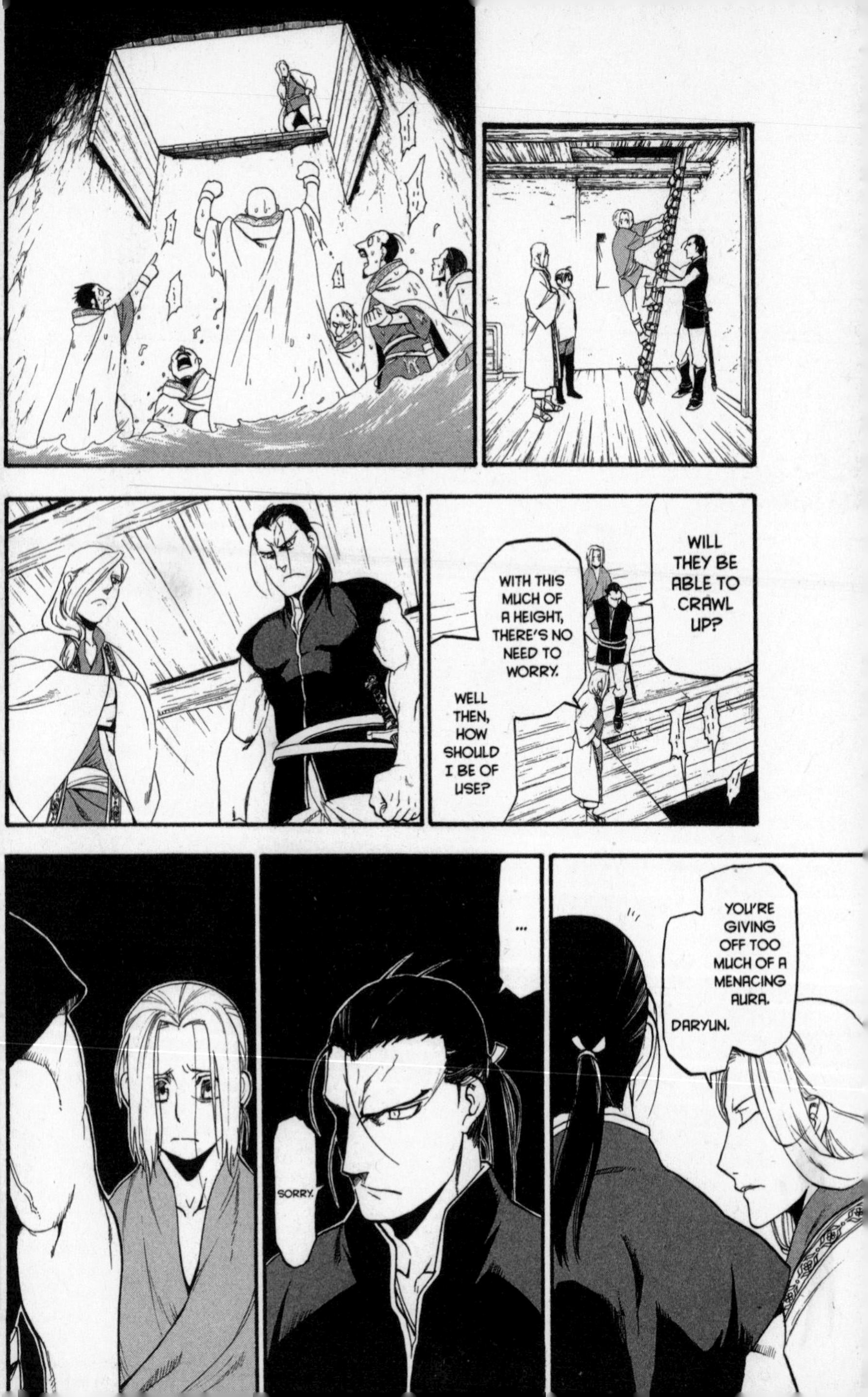
WILL THEY BE ABLE TO CRAWL UP?
WITH THIS MUCH OF A HEIGHT, THERE'S NO NEED TO WORRY.
WELL THEN, HOW SHOULD I BE OF USE?
YOU'RE GIVING OFF TOO MUCH OF A MENACING AURA.
DARYUN.
...
SORRY.

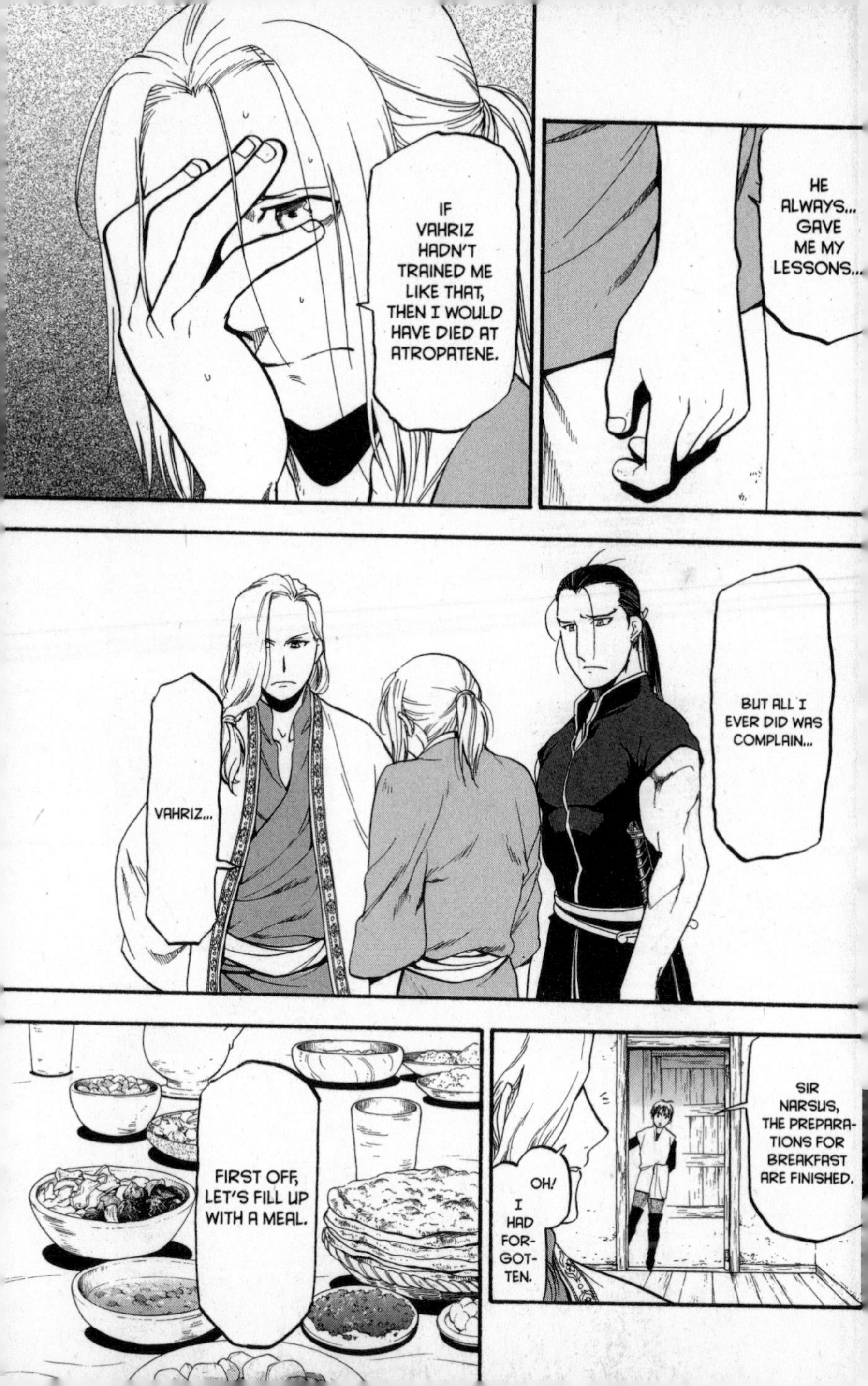
HE ALWAYS... GAVE ME MY LESSONS...
IF VAHRIZ HADN'T TRAINED ME LIKE THAT, THEN I WOULD HAVE DIED AT ATROPATENE.
BUT ALL I EVER DID WAS COMPLAIN...
VAHRIZ...
SIR NARSUS, THE PREPARATIONS FOR BREAKFAST ARE FINISHED.
OH! I HAD FOR-GOT-TEN.
FIRST OFF, LET'S FILL UP WITH A MEAL.

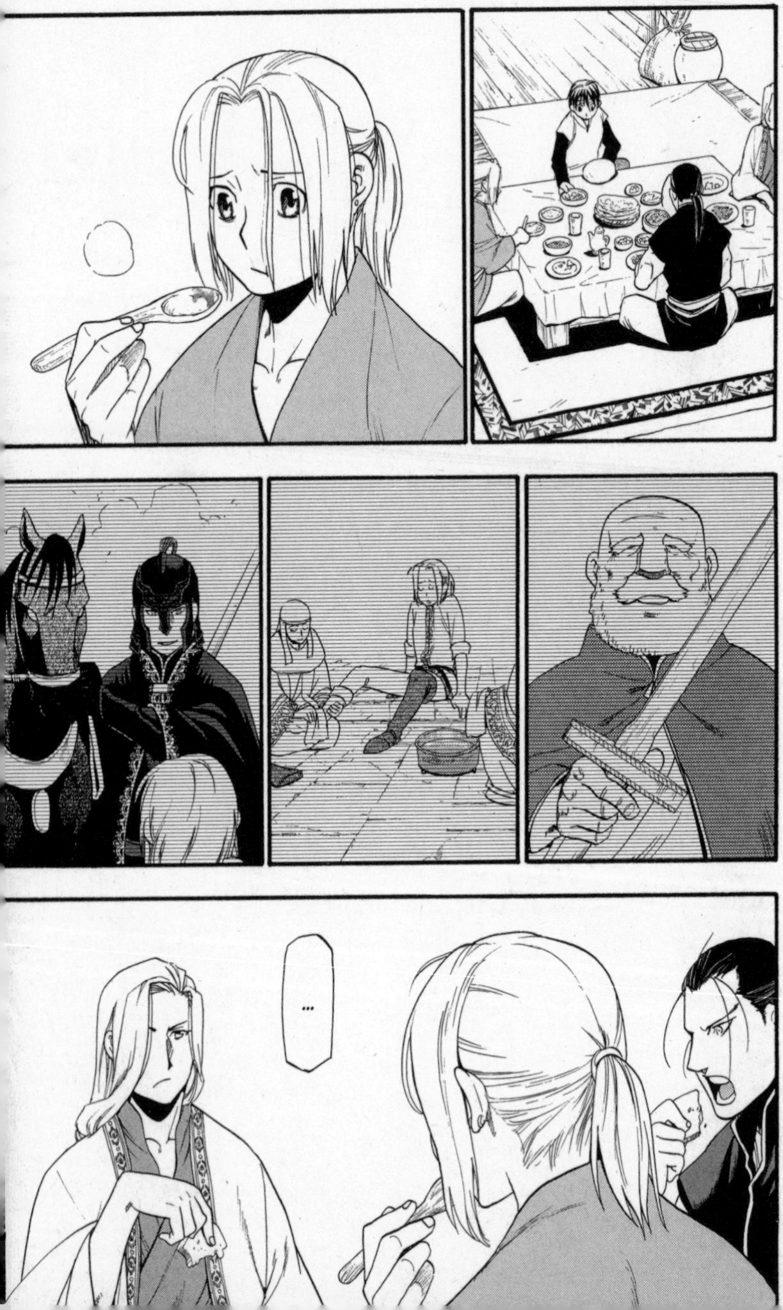
...

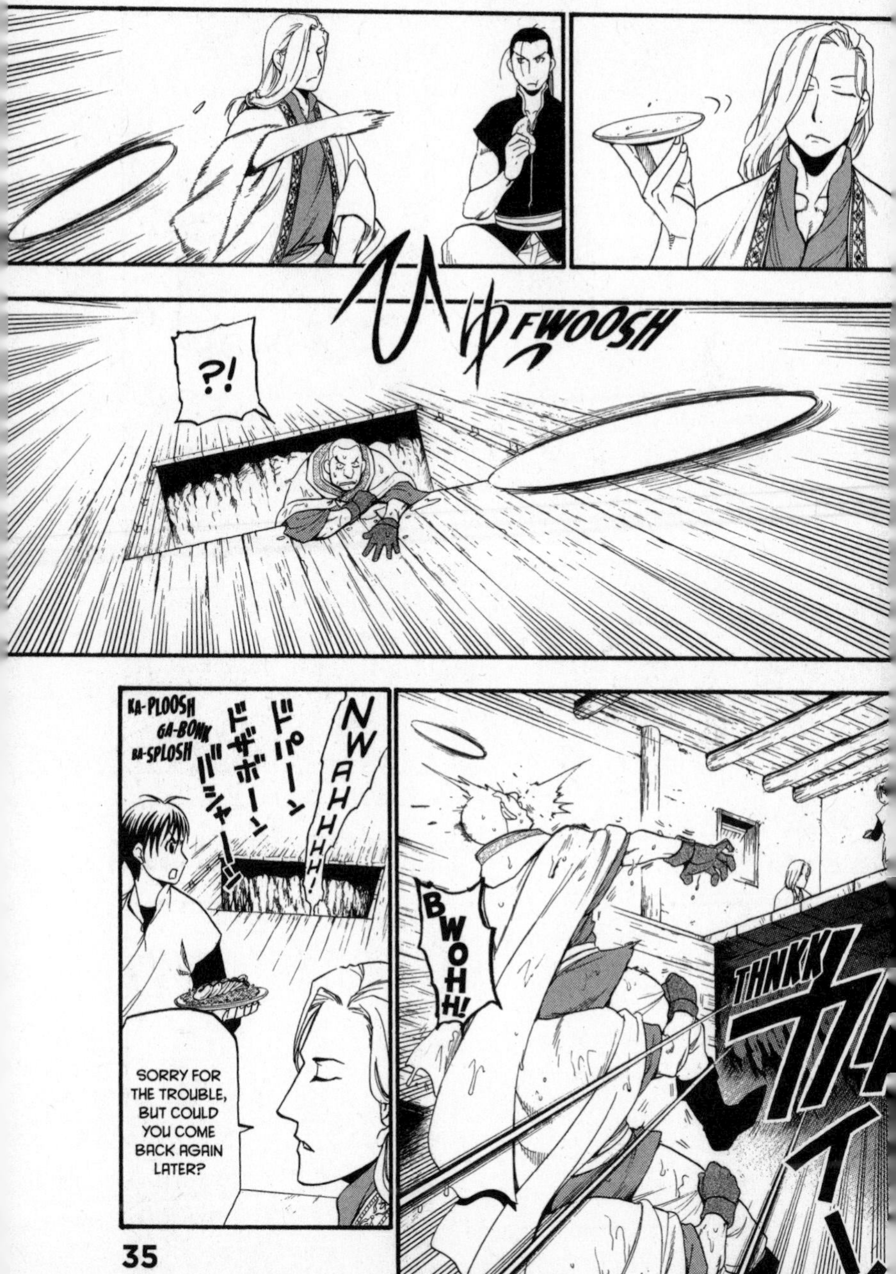
ひゅっ
FWOOSH
?!
BWOHH!
THNKK
NWAHHHHH!
ドパーン
ドザボーン
バシャーン
KA-PLOOSH
GA-BONK
BA-SPLOSH
SORRY FOR THE TROUBLE, BUT COULD YOU COME BACK AGAIN LATER?

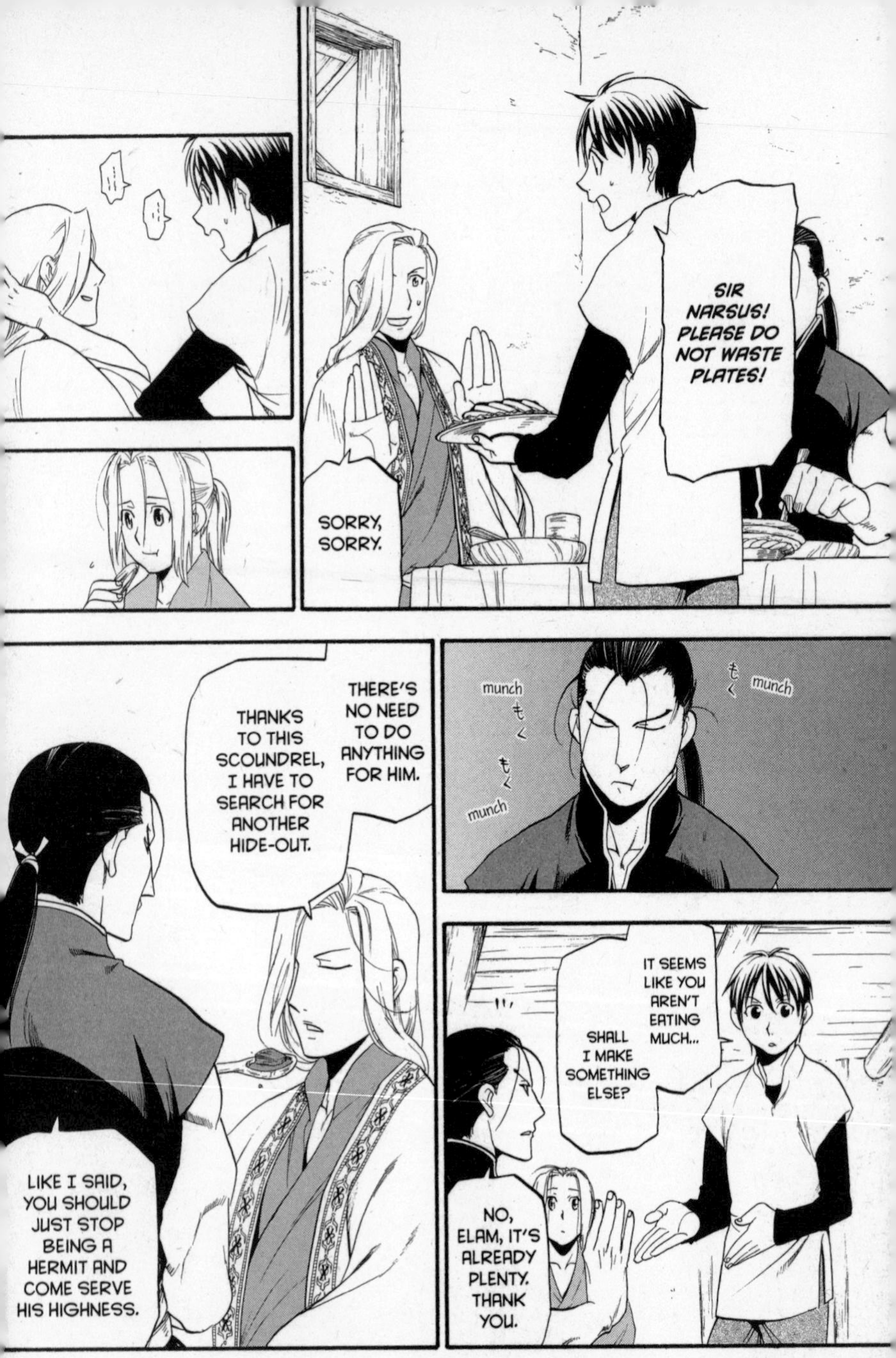
SIR NARSUS! PLEASE DO NOT WASTE PLATES!
SORRY, SORRY.
…
…
munch
もく
munch
もく
もく
munch
IT SEEMS LIKE YOU AREN'T EATING MUCH...
SHALL I MAKE SOMETHING ELSE?
!!
NO, ELAM, IT'S ALREADY PLENTY. THANK YOU.
THERE'S NO NEED TO DO ANYTHING FOR HIM.
THANKS TO THIS SCOUNDREL, I HAVE TO SEARCH FOR ANOTHER HIDE-OUT.
LIKE I SAID, YOU SHOULD JUST STOP BEING A HERMIT AND COME SERVE HIS HIGHNESS.

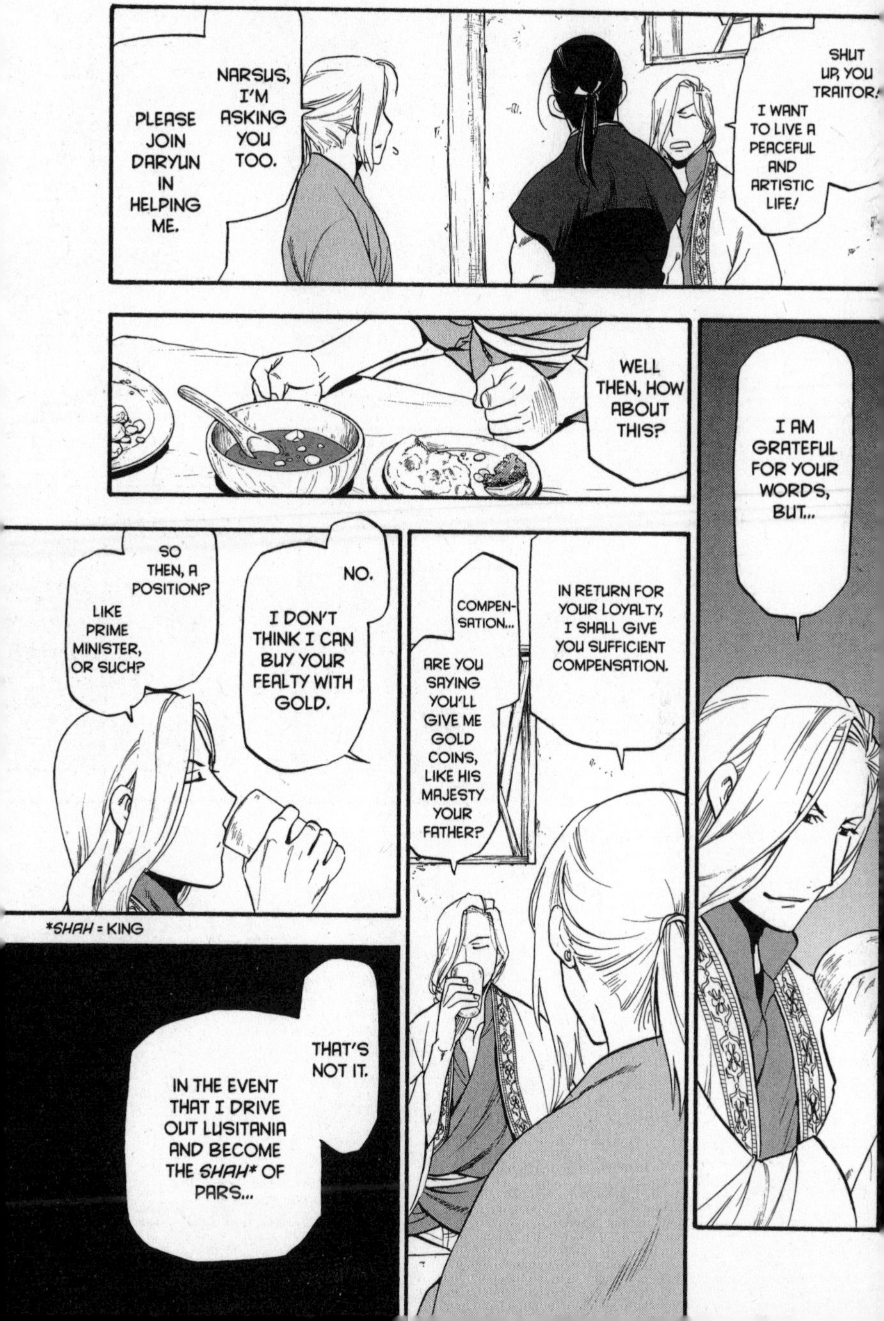
SHUT UP, YOU TRAITOR! I WANT TO LIVE A PEACEFUL AND ARTISTIC LIFE!
NARSUS, I'M ASKING YOU TOO. PLEASE JOIN DARYUN IN HELPING ME.
I AM GRATEFUL FOR YOUR WORDS, BUT...
WELL THEN, HOW ABOUT THIS?
IN RETURN FOR YOUR LOYALTY, I SHALL GIVE YOU SUFFICIENT COMPENSATION.
COMPENSATION...
ARE YOU SAYING YOU'LL GIVE ME GOLD COINS, LIKE HIS MAJESTY YOUR FATHER?
NO.
I DON'T THINK I CAN BUY YOUR FEALTY WITH GOLD.
SO THEN, A POSITION?
LIKE PRIME MINISTER, OR SUCH?
THAT'S NOT IT.
IN THE EVENT THAT I DRIVE OUT LUSITANIA AND BECOME THE *SHAH** OF PARS...

**SHAH* = KING

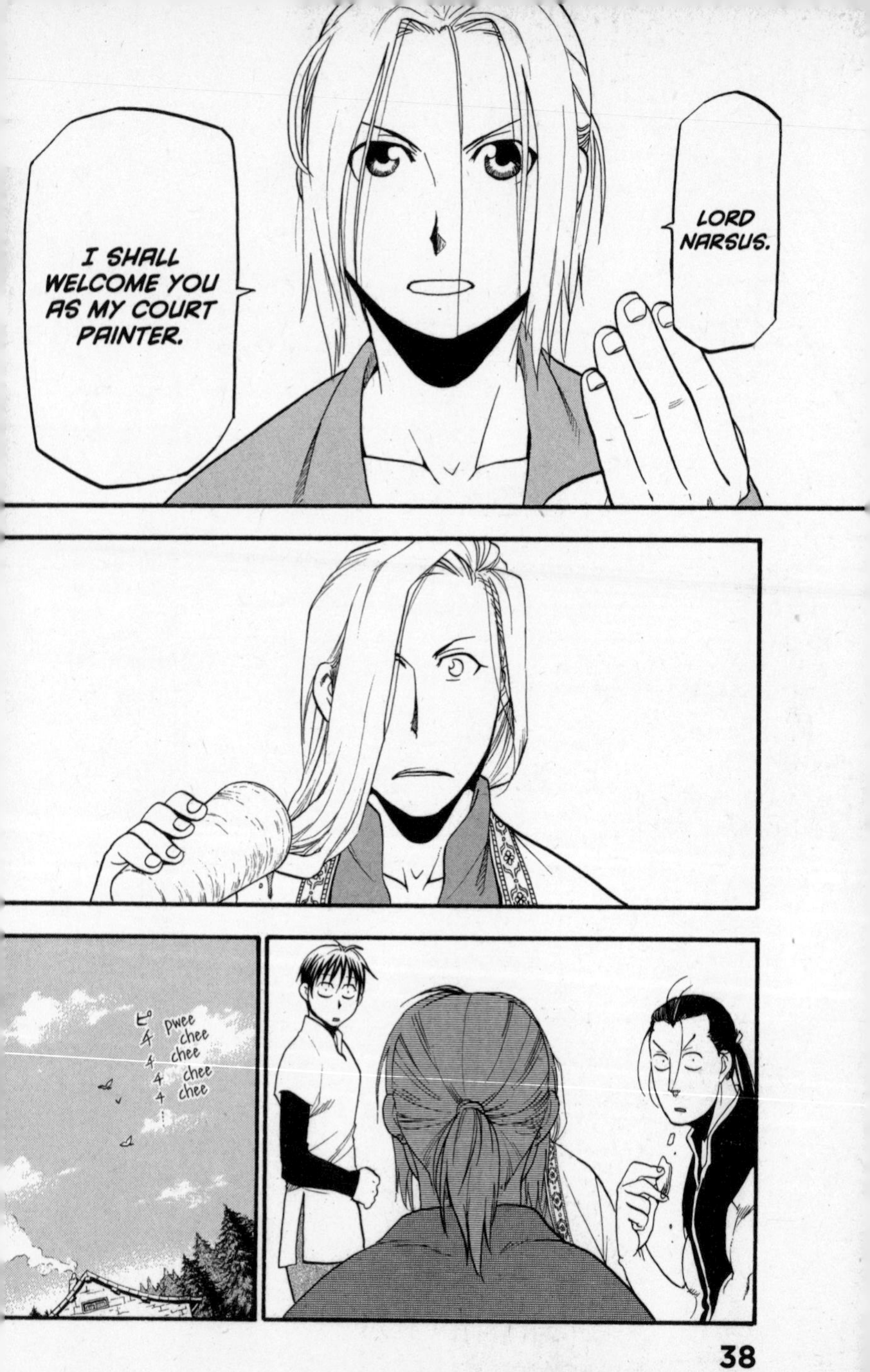
LORD NARSUS.
I SHALL WELCOME YOU AS MY COURT PAINTER.
pwee chee chee chee chee

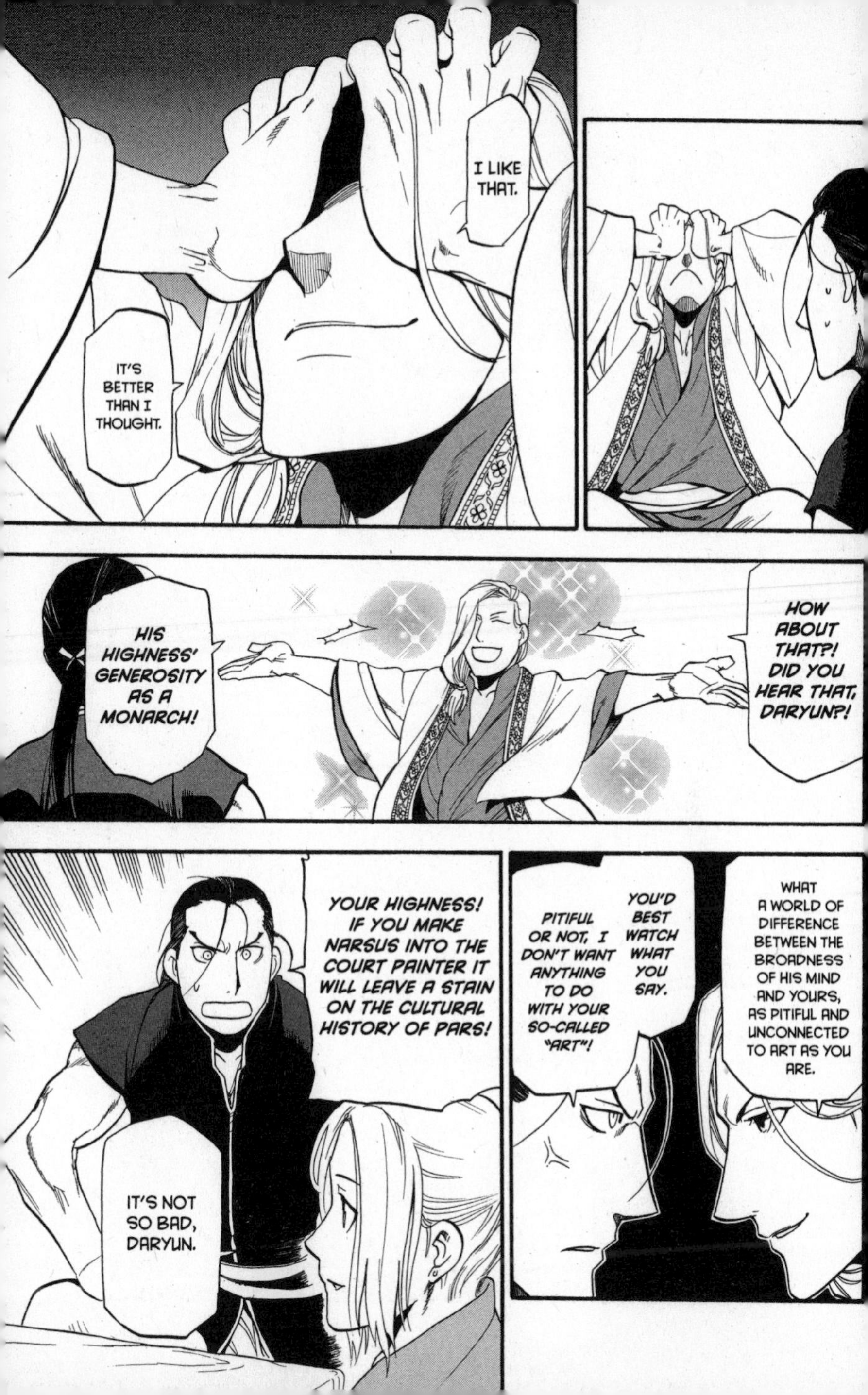
I LIKE THAT.
IT'S BETTER THAN I THOUGHT.
HOW ABOUT THAT?! DID YOU HEAR THAT, DARYUN?!
HIS HIGHNESS' GENEROSITY AS A MONARCH!
WHAT A WORLD OF DIFFERENCE BETWEEN THE BROADNESS OF HIS MIND AND YOURS, AS PITIFUL AND UNCONNECTED TO ART AS YOU ARE.
YOU'D BEST WATCH WHAT YOU SAY.
PITIFUL OR NOT, I DON'T WANT ANYTHING TO DO WITH YOUR SO-CALLED "ART"!
YOUR HIGHNESS! IF YOU MAKE NARSUS INTO THE COURT PAINTER IT WILL LEAVE A STAIN ON THE CULTURAL HISTORY OF PARS!
IT'S NOT SO BAD, DARYUN.

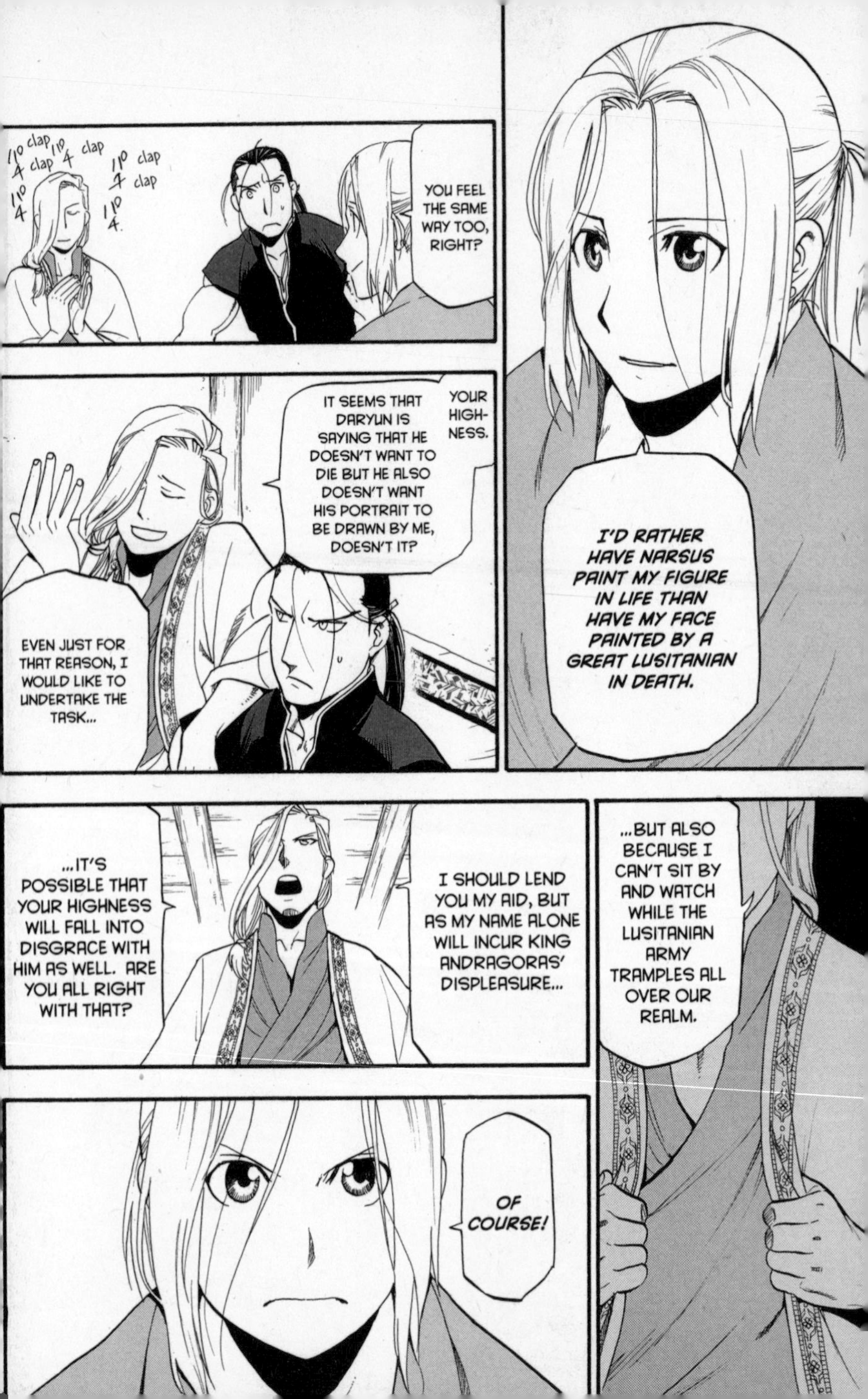
I'D RATHER HAVE NARSUS PAINT MY FIGURE IN LIFE THAN HAVE MY FACE PAINTED BY A GREAT LUSITANIAN IN DEATH.
YOU FEEL THE SAME WAY TOO, RIGHT?
clap
clap
clap
clap
YOUR HIGHNESS.
IT SEEMS THAT DARYUN IS SAYING THAT HE DOESN'T WANT TO DIE BUT HE ALSO DOESN'T WANT HIS PORTRAIT TO BE DRAWN BY ME, DOESN'T IT?
EVEN JUST FOR THAT REASON, I WOULD LIKE TO UNDERTAKE THE TASK...
...BUT ALSO BECAUSE I CAN'T SIT BY AND WATCH WHILE THE LUSITANIAN ARMY TRAMPLES ALL OVER OUR REALM.
I SHOULD LEND YOU MY AID, BUT AS MY NAME ALONE WILL INCUR KING ANDRAGORAS' DISPLEASURE...
...IT'S POSSIBLE THAT YOUR HIGHNESS WILL FALL INTO DISGRACE WITH HIM AS WELL. ARE YOU ALL RIGHT WITH THAT?
OF COURSE!

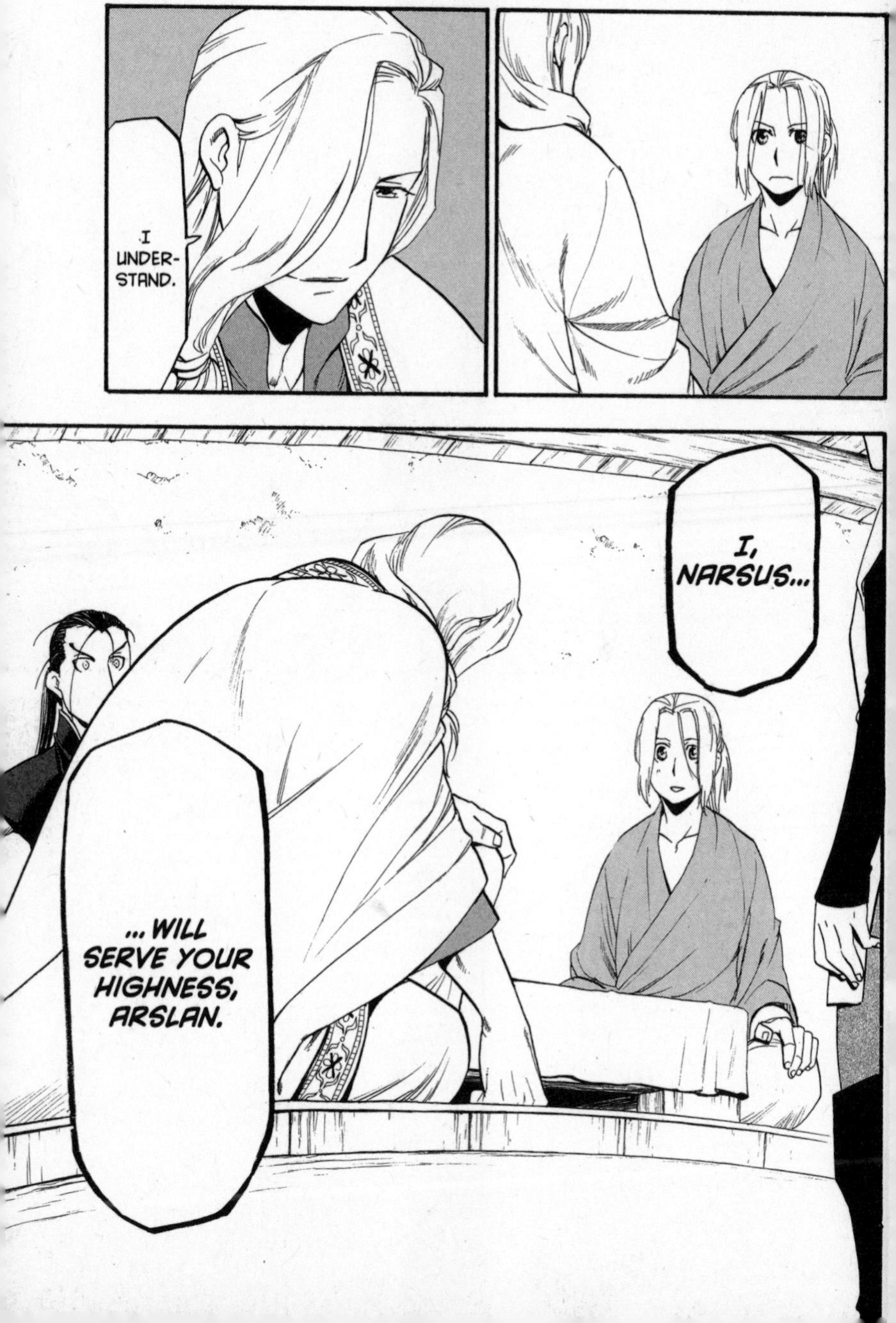
I UNDER-STAND.
I, NARSUS...
...WILL SERVE YOUR HIGHNESS, ARSLAN.

THE HEROIC LEGEND OF
ARSLAN

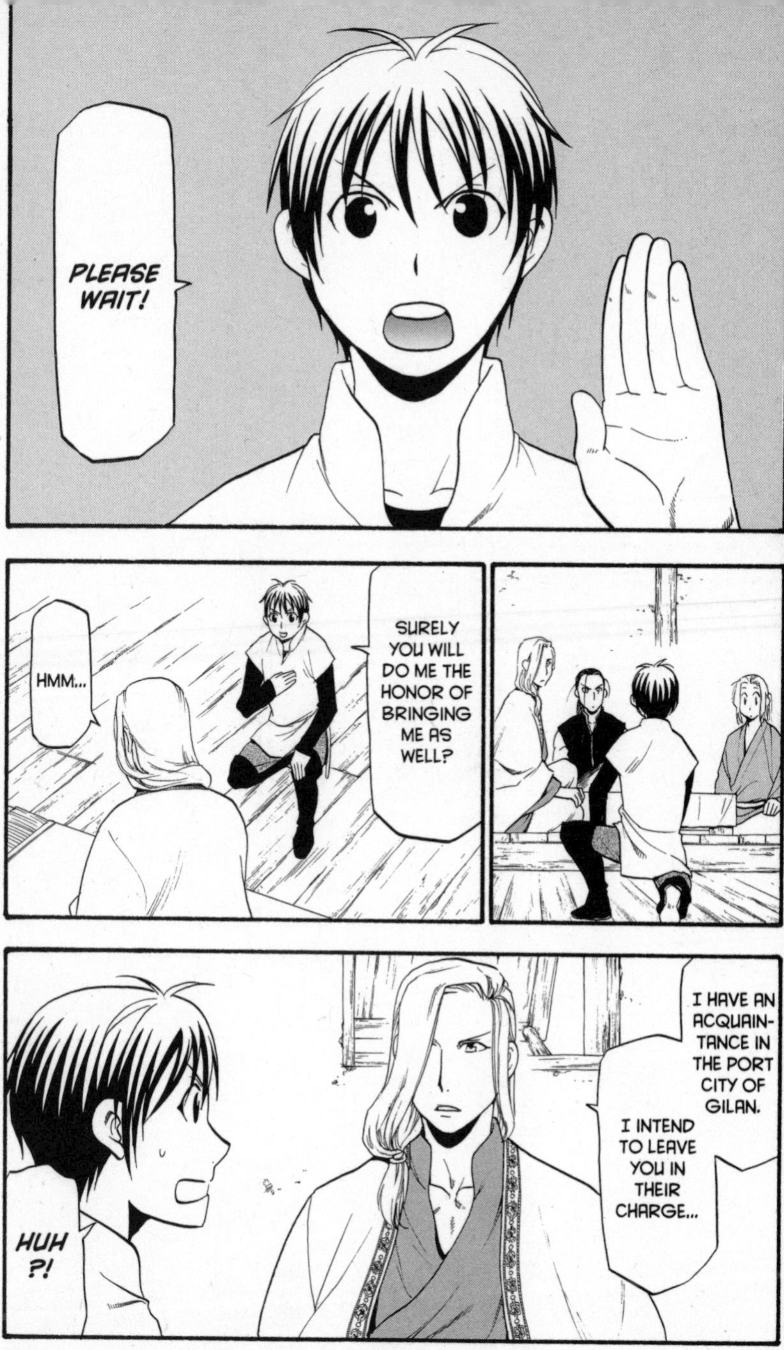
PLEASE WAIT!
SURELY YOU WILL DO ME THE HONOR OF BRINGING ME AS WELL?
HMM...
I HAVE AN ACQUAINTANCE IN THE PORT CITY OF GILAN.
I INTEND TO LEAVE YOU IN THEIR CHARGE...
HUH?!

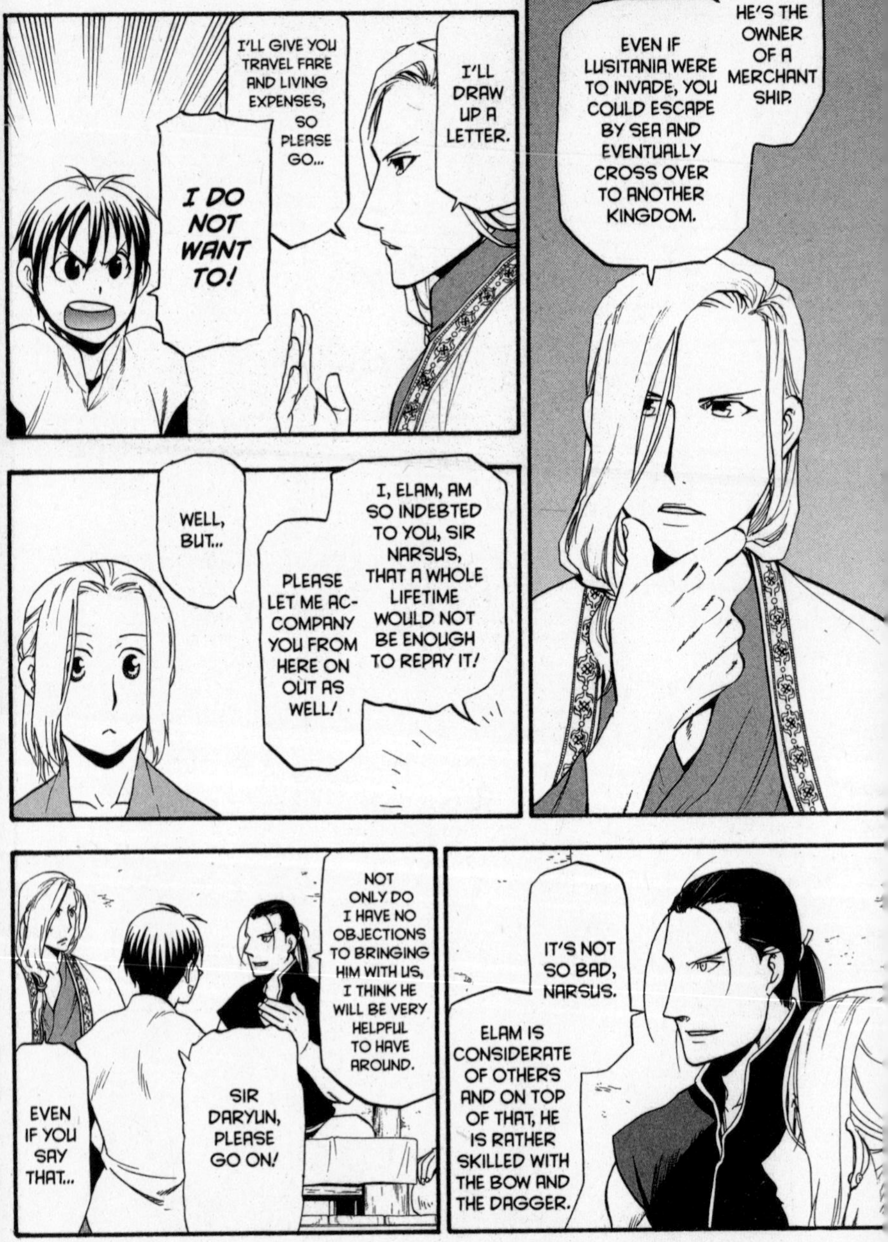
HE'S THE OWNER OF A MERCHANT SHIP.
EVEN IF LUSITANIA WERE TO INVADE, YOU COULD ESCAPE BY SEA AND EVENTUALLY CROSS OVER TO ANOTHER KINGDOM.
I'LL DRAW UP A LETTER.
I'LL GIVE YOU TRAVEL FARE AND LIVING EXPENSES, SO PLEASE GO...
I DO NOT WANT TO!
I, ELAM, AM SO INDEBTED TO YOU, SIR NARSUS, THAT A WHOLE LIFETIME WOULD NOT BE ENOUGH TO REPAY IT!
PLEASE LET ME AC-COMPANY YOU FROM HERE ON OUT AS WELL!
WELL, BUT...
IT'S NOT SO BAD, NARSUS.
ELAM IS CONSIDERATE OF OTHERS AND ON TOP OF THAT, HE IS RATHER SKILLED WITH THE BOW AND THE DAGGER.
NOT ONLY DO I HAVE NO OBJECTIONS TO BRINGING HIM WITH US, I THINK HE WILL BE VERY HELPFUL TO HAVE AROUND.
SIR DARYUN, PLEASE GO ON!
EVEN IF YOU SAY THAT...

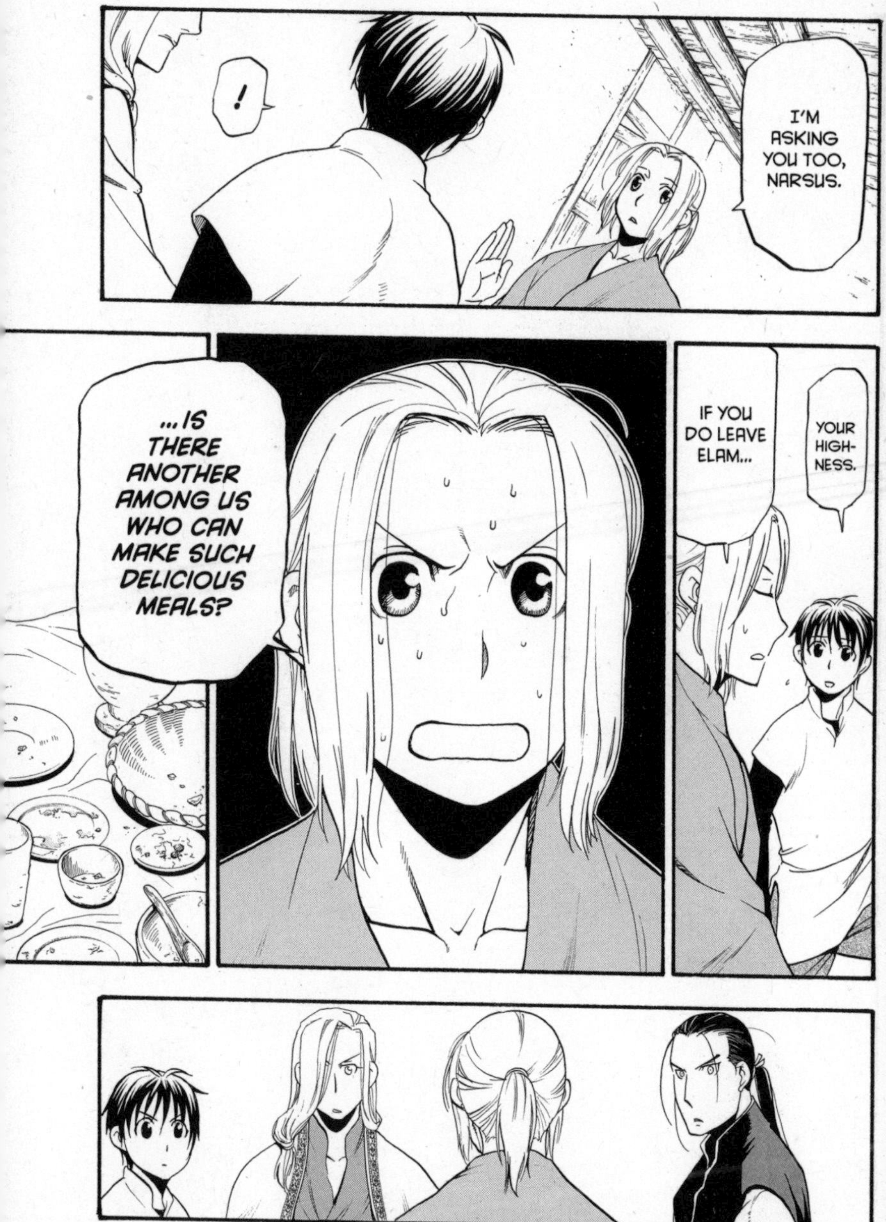
I'M ASKING YOU TOO, NARSUS.
!
YOUR HIGHNESS.
IF YOU DO LEAVE ELAM...
...IS THERE ANOTHER AMONG US WHO CAN MAKE SUCH DELICIOUS MEALS?

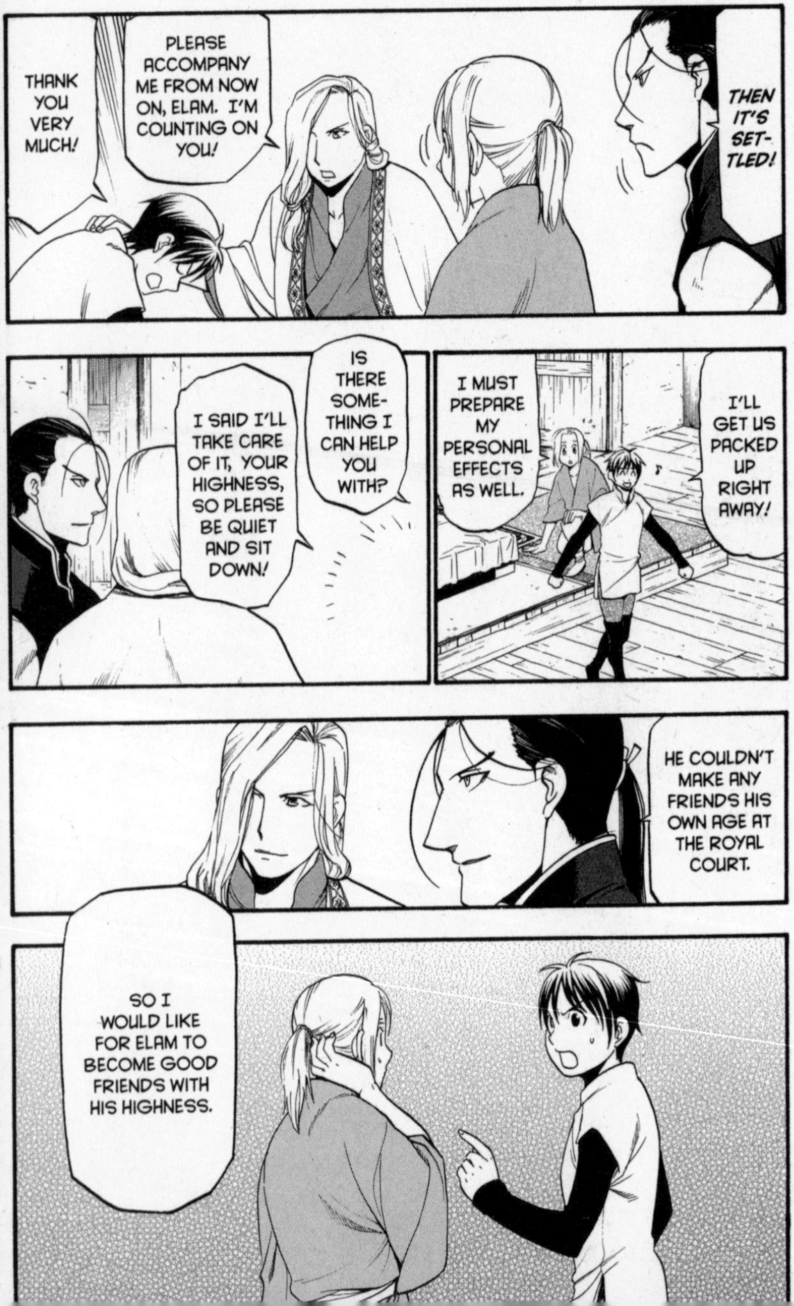
THEN IT'S SET-TLED!
PLEASE ACCOMPANY ME FROM NOW ON, ELAM. I'M COUNTING ON YOU!
THANK YOU VERY MUCH!
I'LL GET US PACKED UP RIGHT AWAY!
I MUST PREPARE MY PERSONAL EFFECTS AS WELL.
IS THERE SOME-THING I CAN HELP YOU WITH?
I SAID I'LL TAKE CARE OF IT, YOUR HIGHNESS, SO PLEASE BE QUIET AND SIT DOWN!
HE COULDN'T MAKE ANY FRIENDS HIS OWN AGE AT THE ROYAL COURT.
SO I WOULD LIKE FOR ELAM TO BECOME GOOD FRIENDS WITH HIS HIGHNESS.

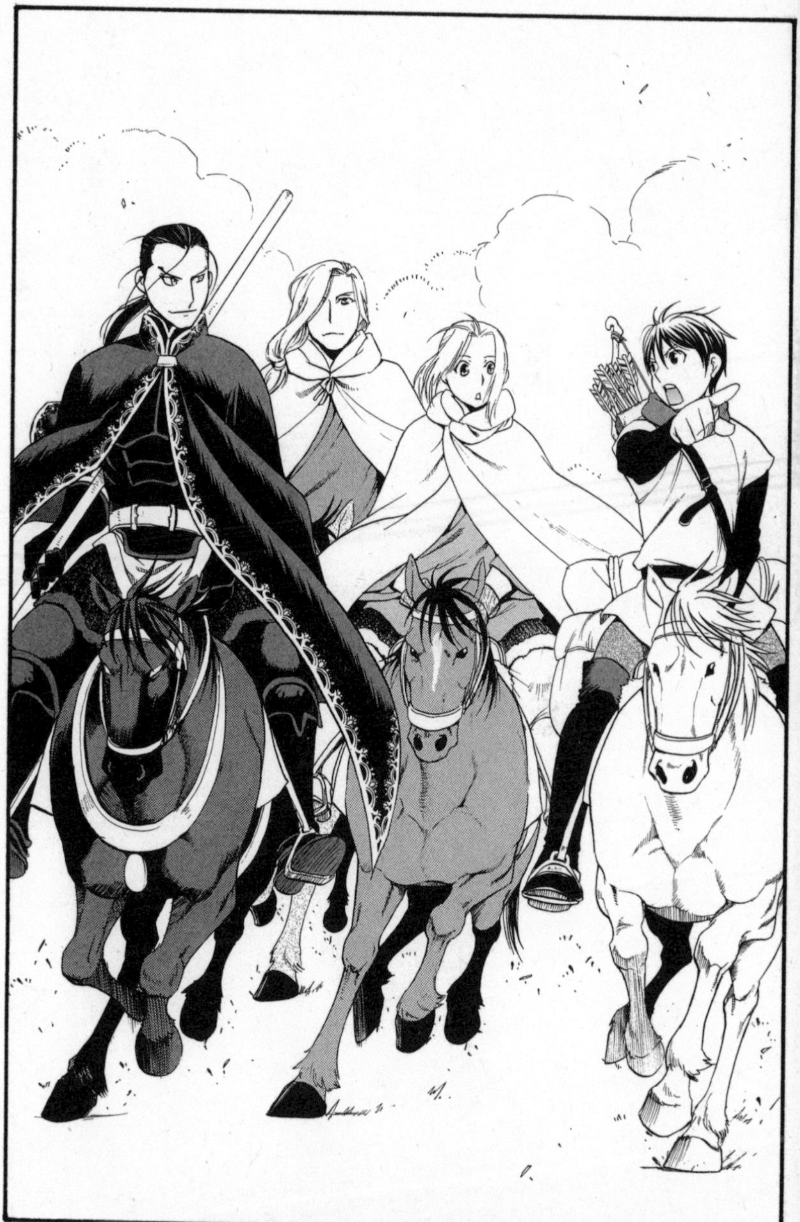

Chapter 6: One Arrow of Salvation

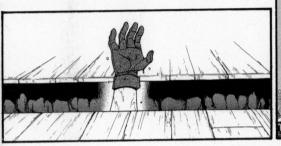

SPLOSH

HFFF

HAA

HAA

THE
HORSES
...

HFFF

HAA

HAA

HFFF

HAA

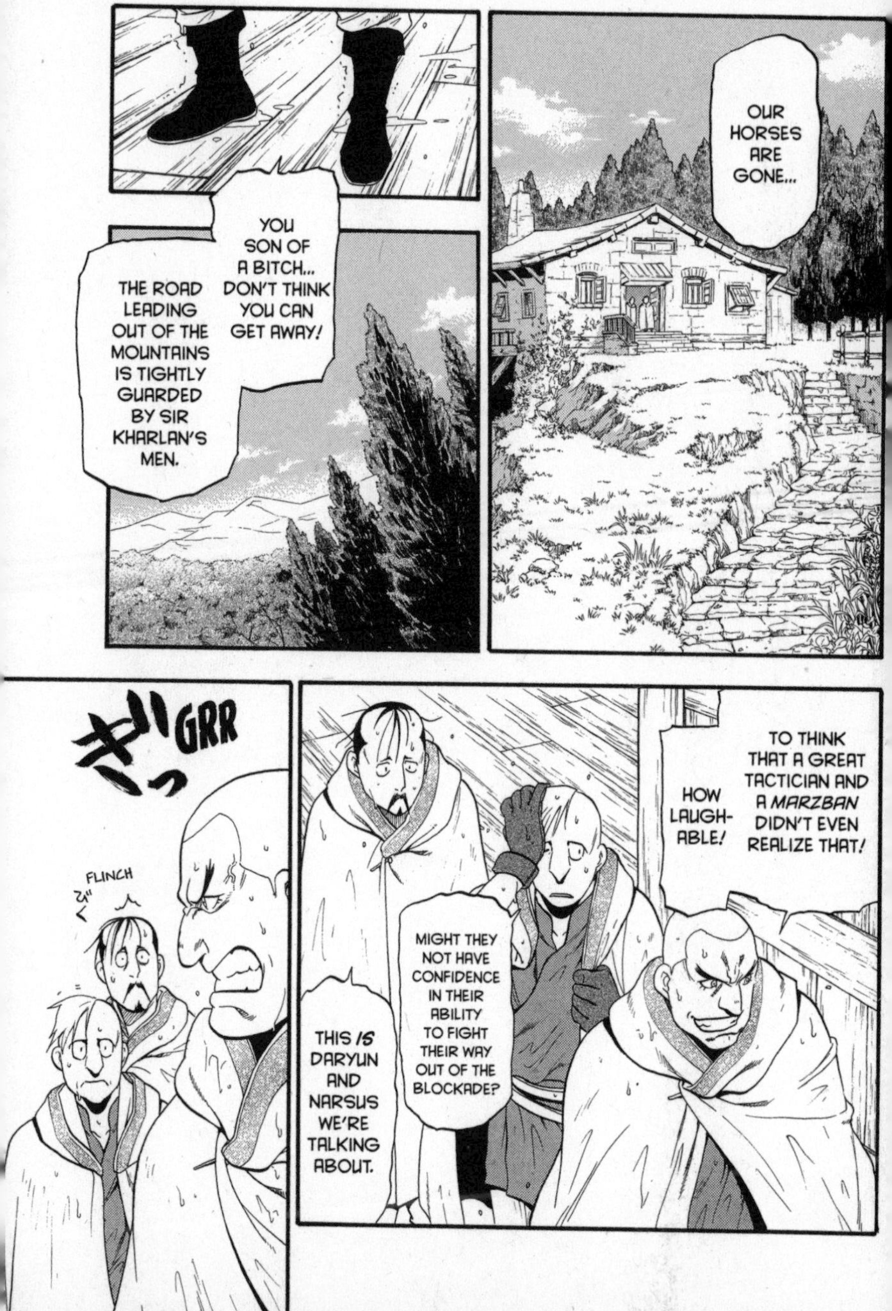
OUR HORSES ARE GONE...
YOU SON OF A BITCH... DON'T THINK YOU CAN GET AWAY!
THE ROAD LEADING OUT OF THE MOUNTAINS IS TIGHTLY GUARDED BY SIR KHARLAN'S MEN.
TO THINK THAT A GREAT TACTICIAN AND A *MARZBAN* DIDN'T EVEN REALIZE THAT!
HOW LAUGH-ABLE!
MIGHT THEY NOT HAVE CONFIDENCE IN THEIR ABILITY TO FIGHT THEIR WAY OUT OF THE BLOCKADE?
THIS *IS* DARYUN AND NARSUS WE'RE TALKING ABOUT.
GRR
FLINCH

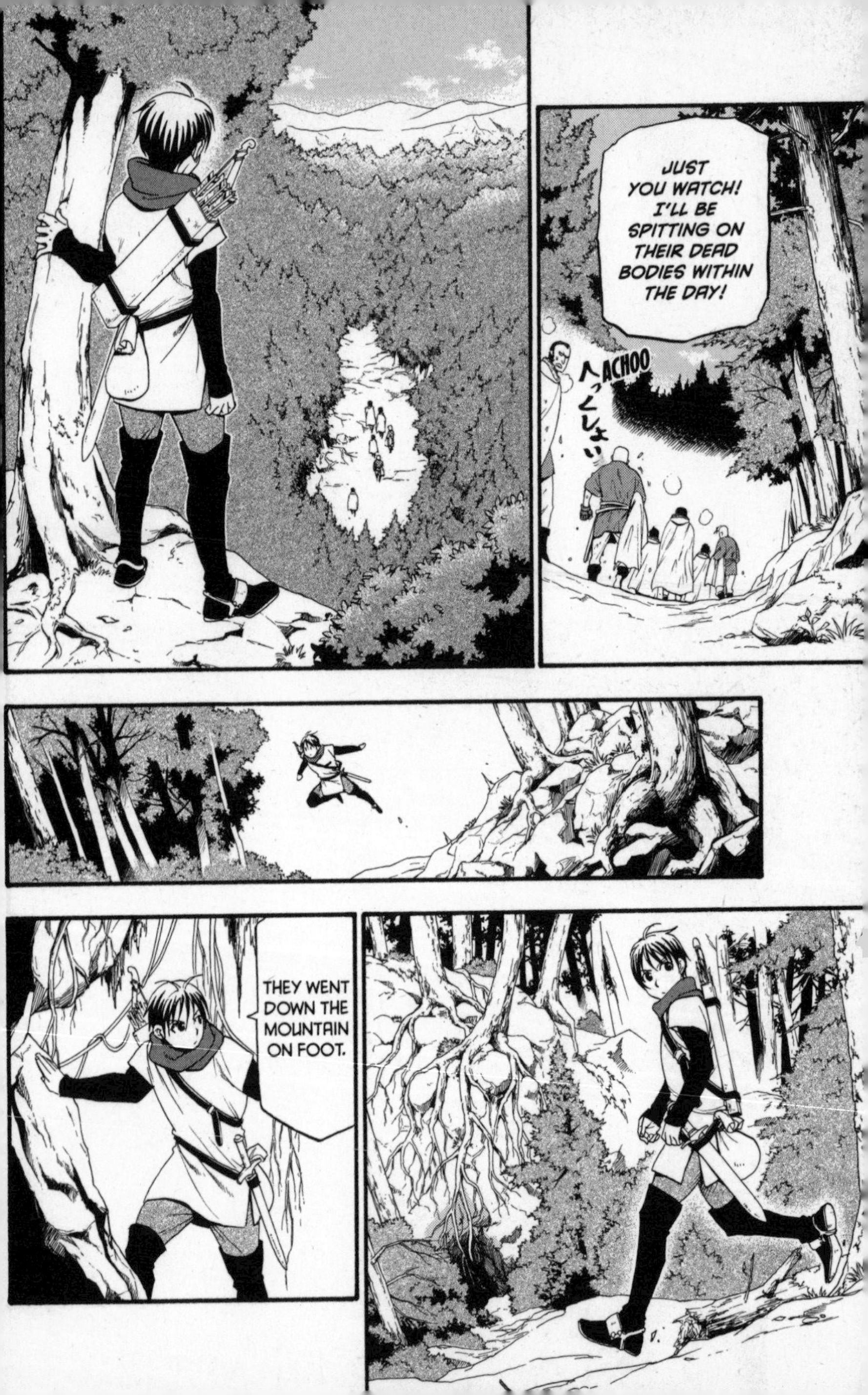
JUST YOU WATCH! I'LL BE SPITTING ON THEIR DEAD BODIES WITHIN THE DAY!
ACHOO
へっくしょい
THEY WENT DOWN THE MOUNTAIN ON FOOT.

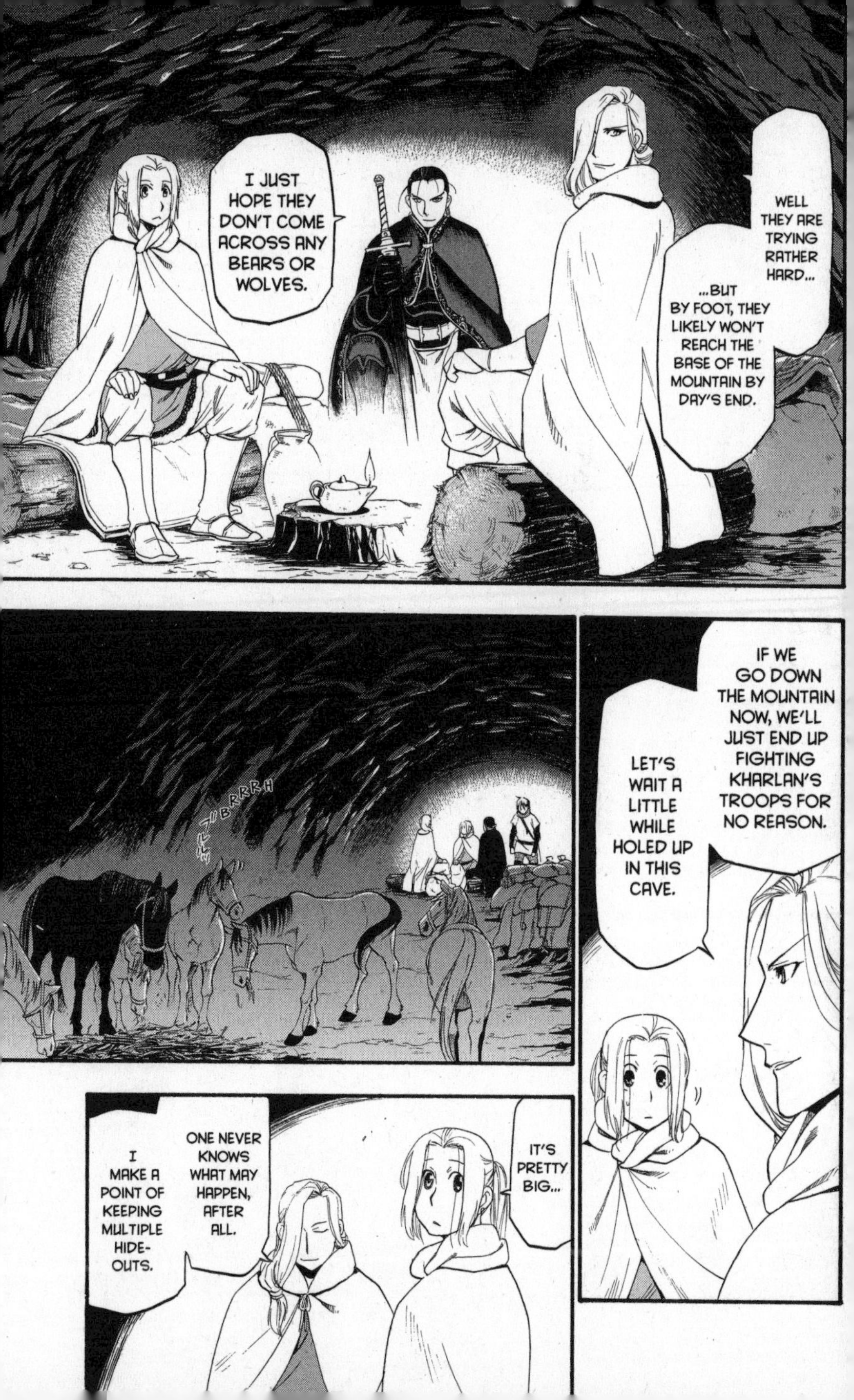
WELL THEY ARE TRYING RATHER HARD...
...BUT BY FOOT, THEY LIKELY WON'T REACH THE BASE OF THE MOUNTAIN BY DAY'S END.
I JUST HOPE THEY DON'T COME ACROSS ANY BEARS OR WOLVES.
IF WE GO DOWN THE MOUNTAIN NOW, WE'LL JUST END UP FIGHTING KHARLAN'S TROOPS FOR NO REASON.
LET'S WAIT A LITTLE WHILE HOLED UP IN THIS CAVE.
BRRRH
IT'S PRETTY BIG...
ONE NEVER KNOWS WHAT MAY HAPPEN, AFTER ALL.
I MAKE A POINT OF KEEPING MULTIPLE HIDE-OUTS.

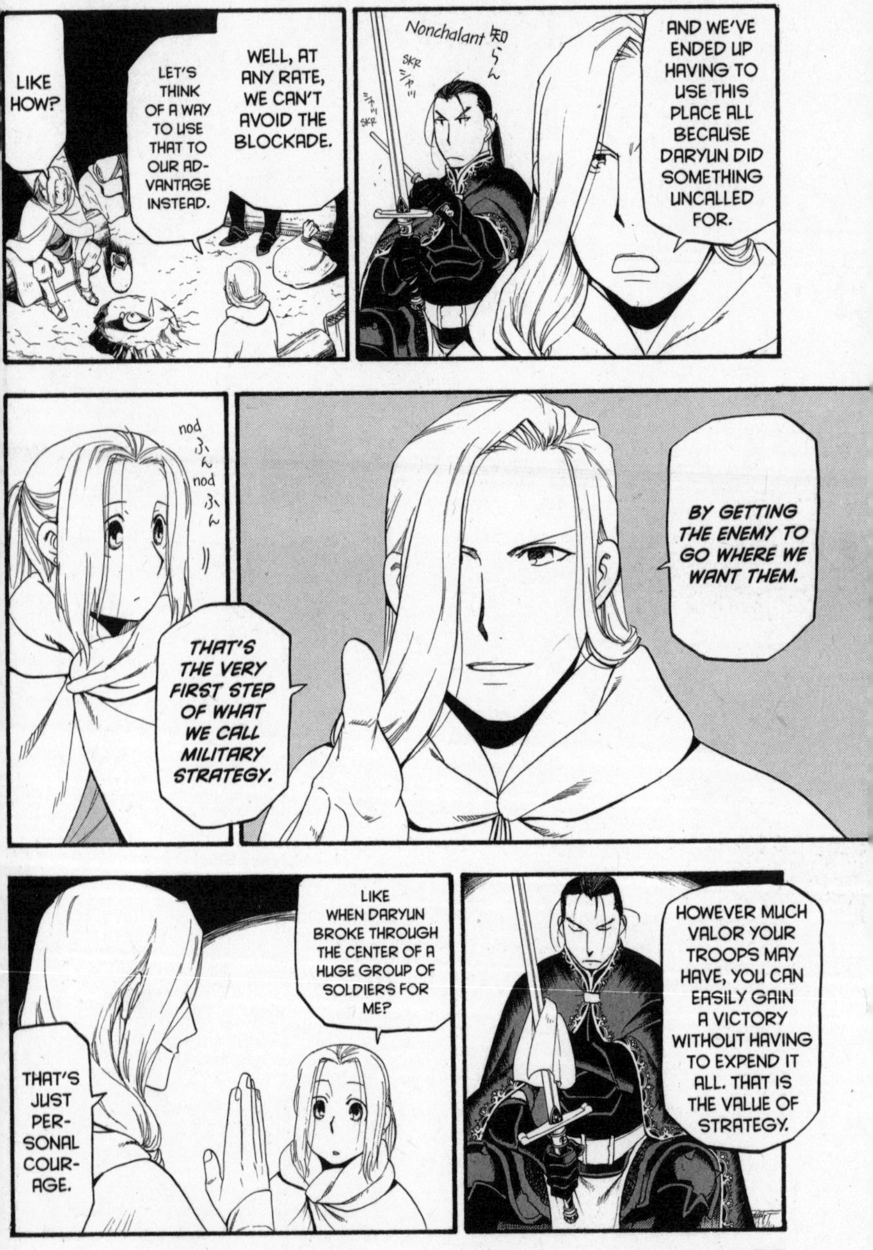
AND WE'VE ENDED UP HAVING TO USE THIS PLACE ALL BECAUSE DARYUN DID SOMETHING UNCALLED FOR.
Nonchalant 知らん
SKR シャッ
SKR シャッ
WELL, AT ANY RATE, WE CAN'T AVOID THE BLOCKADE.
LET'S THINK OF A WAY TO USE THAT TO OUR ADVANTAGE INSTEAD.
LIKE HOW?
BY GETTING THE ENEMY TO GO WHERE WE WANT THEM.
THAT'S THE VERY FIRST STEP OF WHAT WE CALL MILITARY STRATEGY.
nod ふん nod ふん
HOWEVER MUCH VALOR YOUR TROOPS MAY HAVE, YOU CAN EASILY GAIN A VICTORY WITHOUT HAVING TO EXPEND IT ALL. THAT IS THE VALUE OF STRATEGY.
LIKE WHEN DARYUN BROKE THROUGH THE CENTER OF A HUGE GROUP OF SOLDIERS FOR ME?
THAT'S JUST PERSONAL COURAGE.

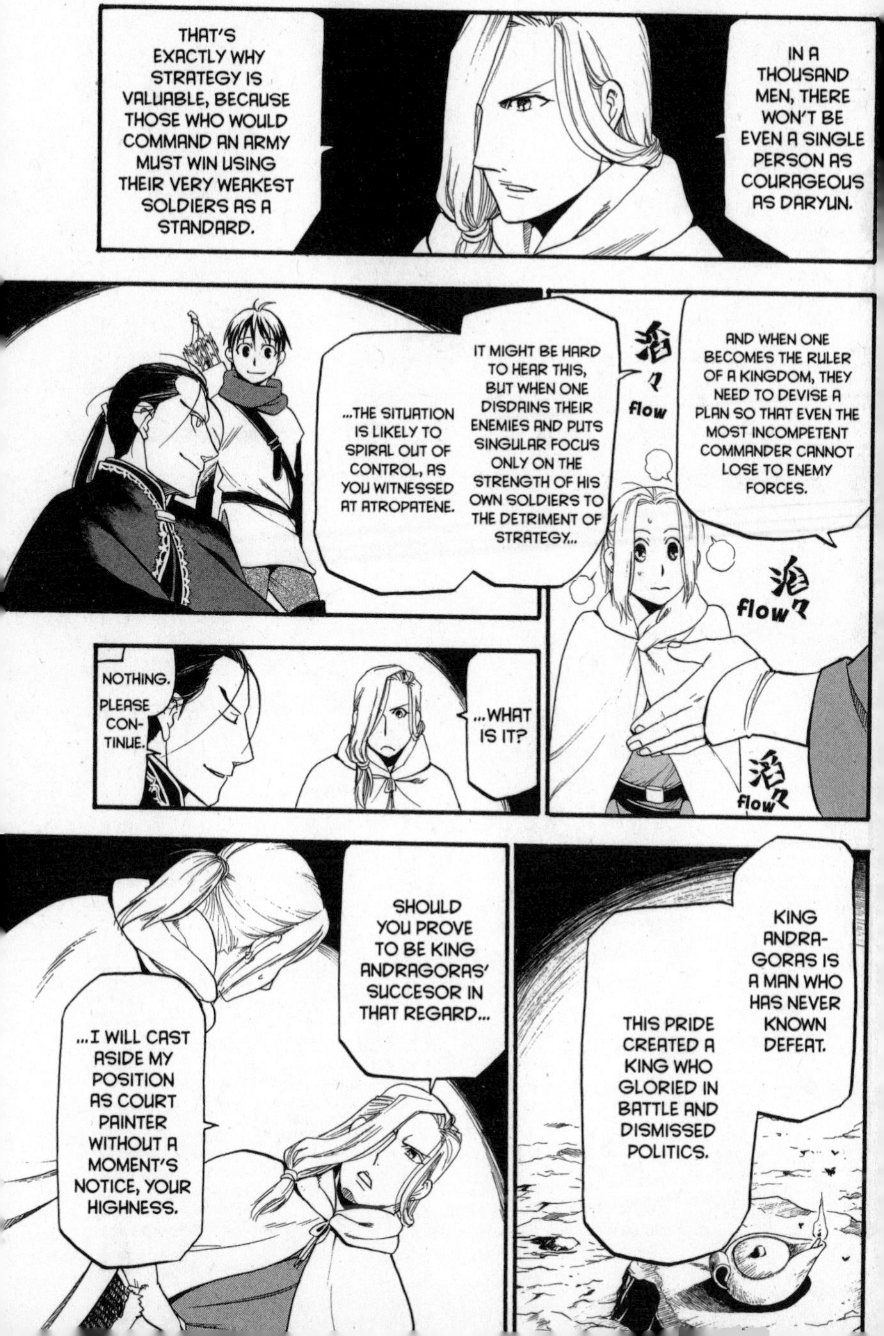
IN A THOUSAND MEN, THERE WON'T BE EVEN A SINGLE PERSON AS COURAGEOUS AS DARYUN.
THAT'S EXACTLY WHY STRATEGY IS VALUABLE, BECAUSE THOSE WHO WOULD COMMAND AN ARMY MUST WIN USING THEIR VERY WEAKEST SOLDIERS AS A STANDARD.
AND WHEN ONE BECOMES THE RULER OF A KINGDOM, THEY NEED TO DEVISE A PLAN SO THAT EVEN THE MOST INCOMPETENT COMMANDER CANNOT LOSE TO ENEMY FORCES.
滔々 flow
滔々 flow
滔々 flow
IT MIGHT BE HARD TO HEAR THIS, BUT WHEN ONE DISDAINS THEIR ENEMIES AND PUTS SINGULAR FOCUS ONLY ON THE STRENGTH OF HIS OWN SOLDIERS TO THE DETRIMENT OF STRATEGY...
...THE SITUATION IS LIKELY TO SPIRAL OUT OF CONTROL, AS YOU WITNESSED AT ATROPATENE.
...WHAT IS IT?
NOTHING.
PLEASE CONTINUE.
KING ANDRAGORAS IS A MAN WHO HAS NEVER KNOWN DEFEAT.
THIS PRIDE CREATED A KING WHO GLORIED IN BATTLE AND DISMISSED POLITICS.
SHOULD YOU PROVE TO BE KING ANDRAGORAS' SUCCESOR IN THAT REGARD...
...I WILL CAST ASIDE MY POSITION AS COURT PAINTER WITHOUT A MOMENT'S NOTICE, YOUR HIGHNESS.

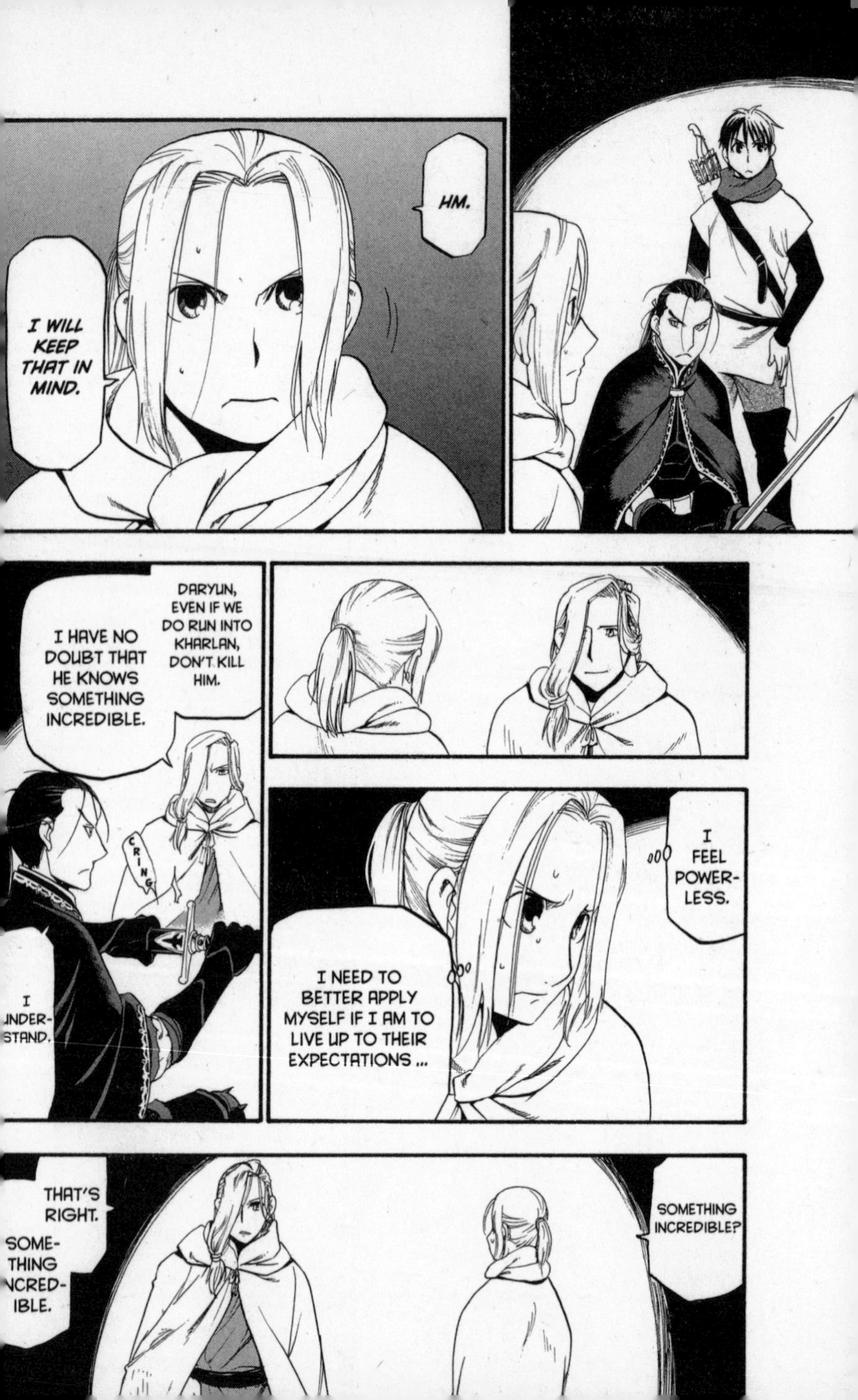
HM.
I WILL KEEP THAT IN MIND.
I FEEL POWER-LESS.
I NEED TO BETTER APPLY MYSELF IF I AM TO LIVE UP TO THEIR EXPECTATIONS ...
DARYUN, EVEN IF WE DO RUN INTO KHARLAN, DON'T KILL HIM.
I HAVE NO DOUBT THAT HE KNOWS SOMETHING INCREDIBLE.
CRING
I UNDER-STAND.
SOMETHING INCREDIBLE?
THAT'S RIGHT.
SOME-THING INCRED-IBLE.

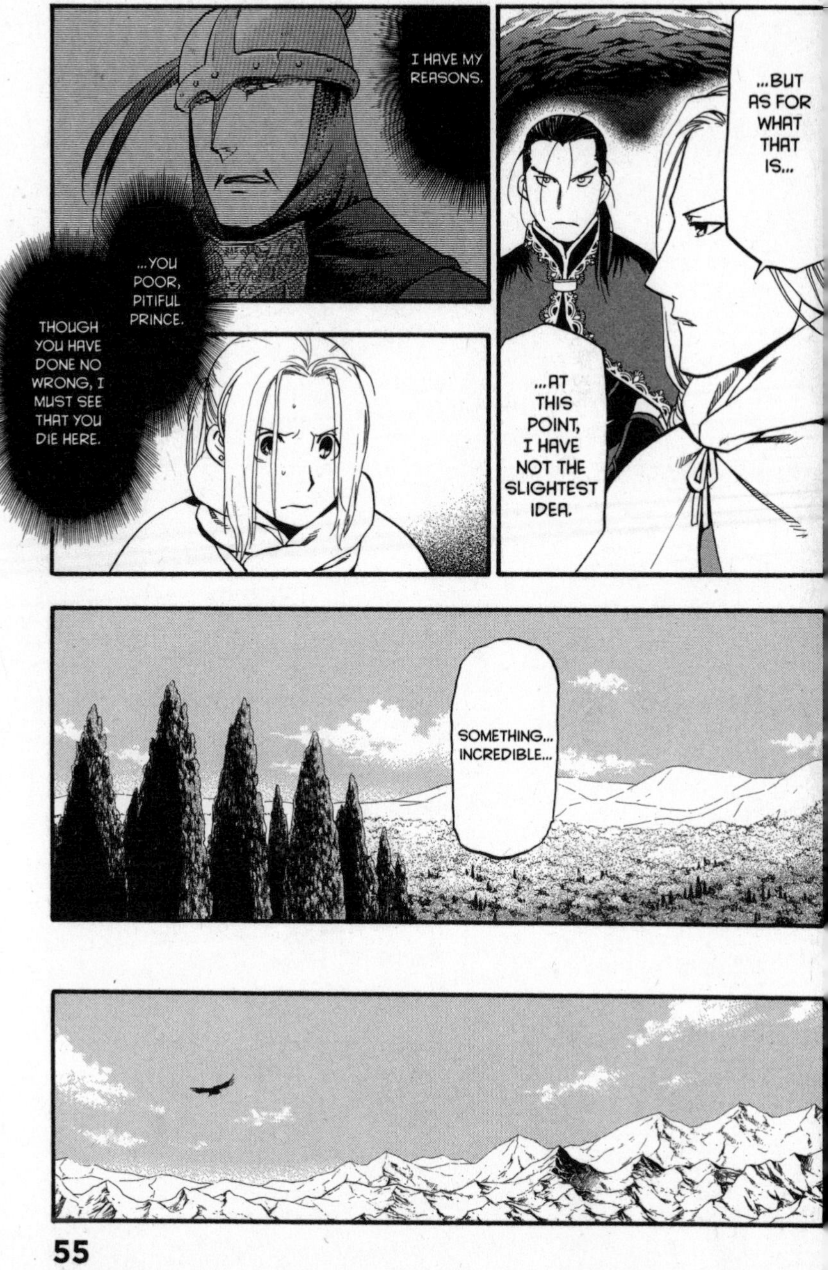
...BUT AS FOR WHAT THAT IS...
...AT THIS POINT, I HAVE NOT THE SLIGHTEST IDEA.
I HAVE MY REASONS.
...YOU POOR, PITIFUL PRINCE.
THOUGH YOU HAVE DONE NO WRONG, I MUST SEE THAT YOU DIE HERE.
SOMETHING... INCREDIBLE...

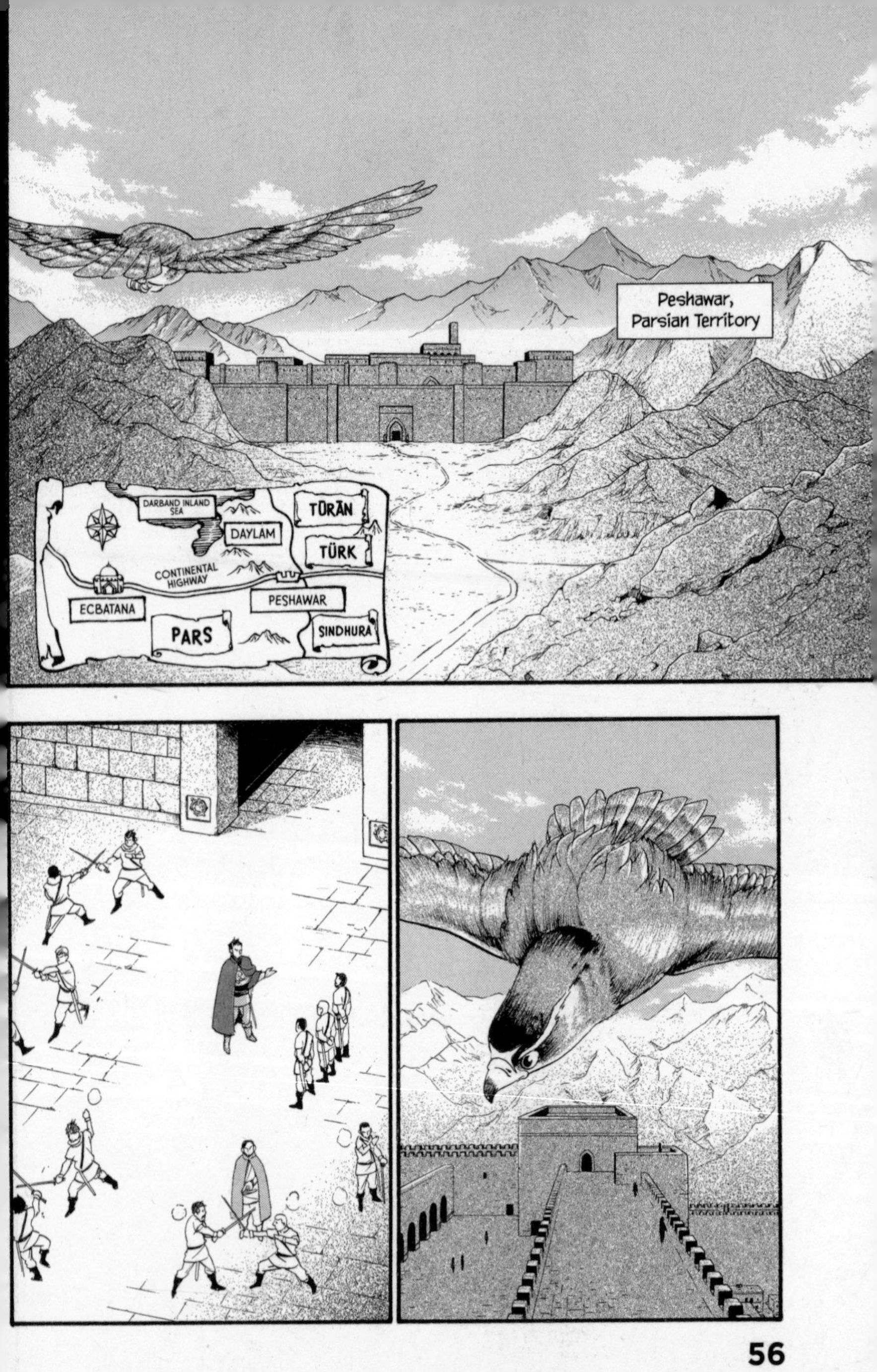
Peshawar, Parsian Territory
DARBAND INLAND SEA
DAYLAM
TŪRĀN
TÜRK
CONTINENTAL HIGHWAY
ECBATANA
PESHAWAR
PARS
SINDHURA

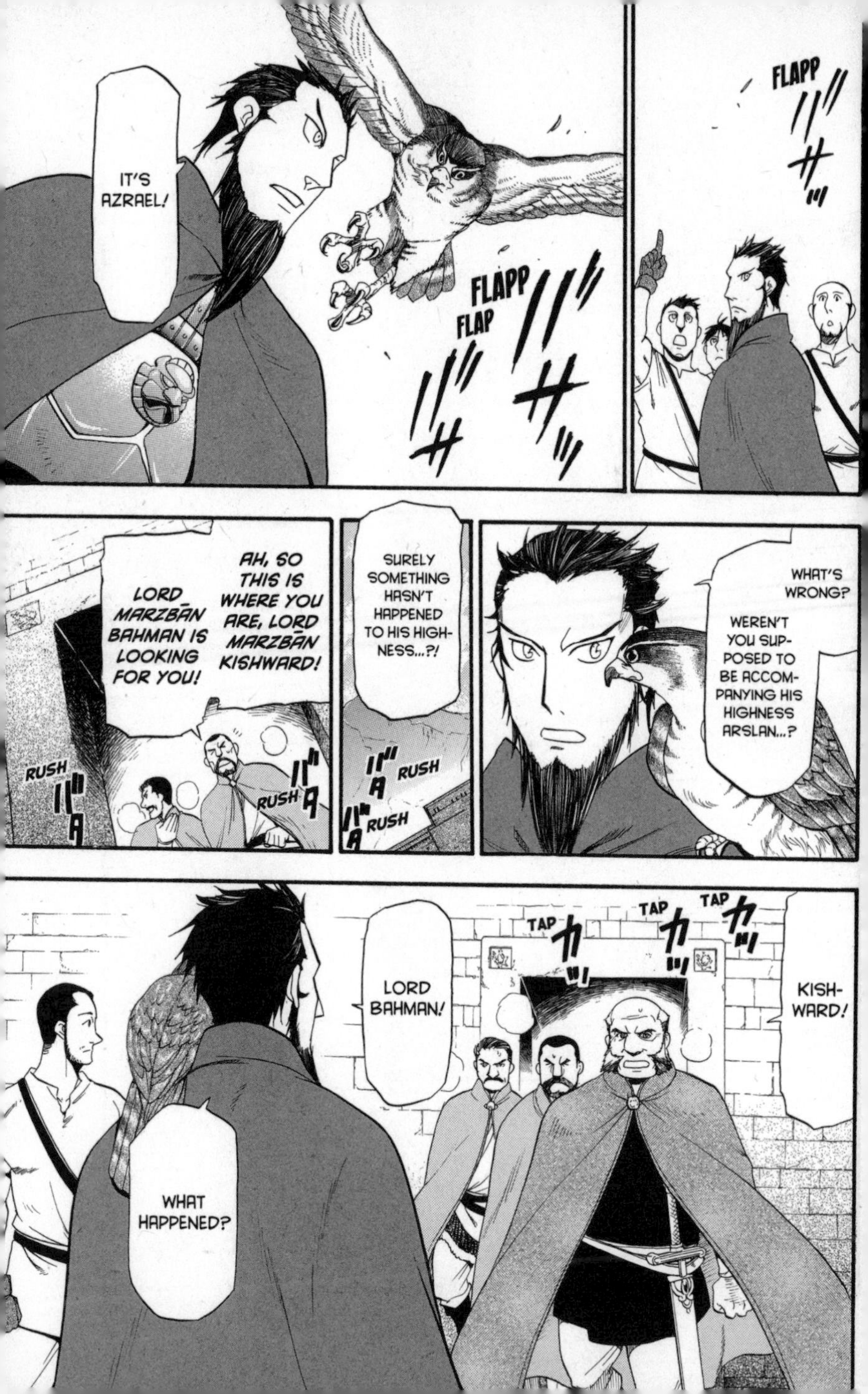
FLAPP
IT'S AZRAEL!
FLAPP
FLAP
WHAT'S WRONG?
WEREN'T YOU SUPPOSED TO BE ACCOMPANYING HIS HIGHNESS ARSLAN...?
SURELY SOMETHING HASN'T HAPPENED TO HIS HIGHNESS...?!
RUSH
RUSH
AH, SO THIS IS WHERE YOU ARE, LORD MARZBĀN KISHWARD!
LORD MARZBĀN BAHMAN IS LOOKING FOR YOU!
RUSH
RUSH
KISHWARD!
TAP
TAP
TAP
LORD BAHMAN!
WHAT HAPPENED?

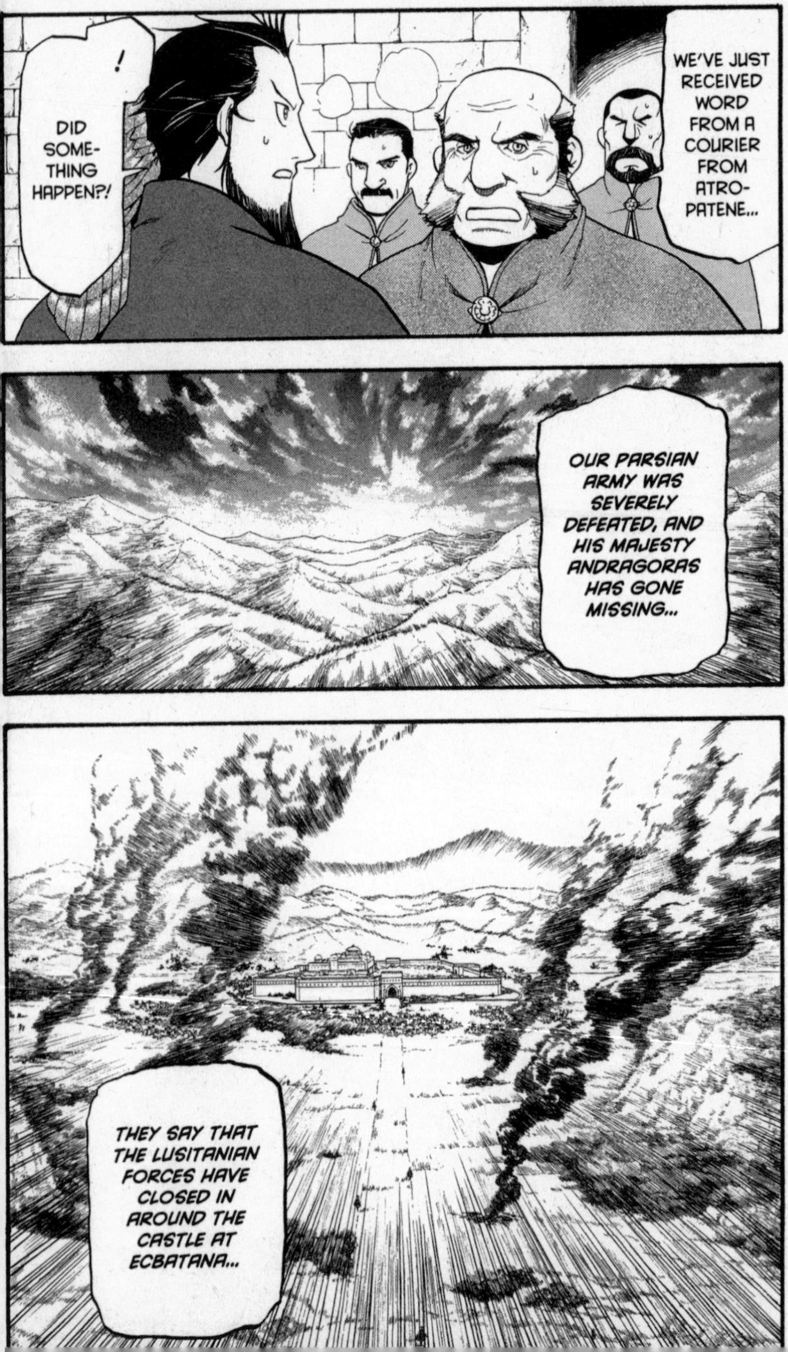
WE'VE JUST RECEIVED WORD FROM A COURIER FROM ATRO-PATENE...
!
DID SOME-THING HAPPEN?!
OUR PARSIAN ARMY WAS SEVERELY DEFEATED, AND HIS MAJESTY ANDRAGORAS HAS GONE MISSING...
THEY SAY THAT THE LUSITANIAN FORCES HAVE CLOSED IN AROUND THE CASTLE AT ECBATANA...

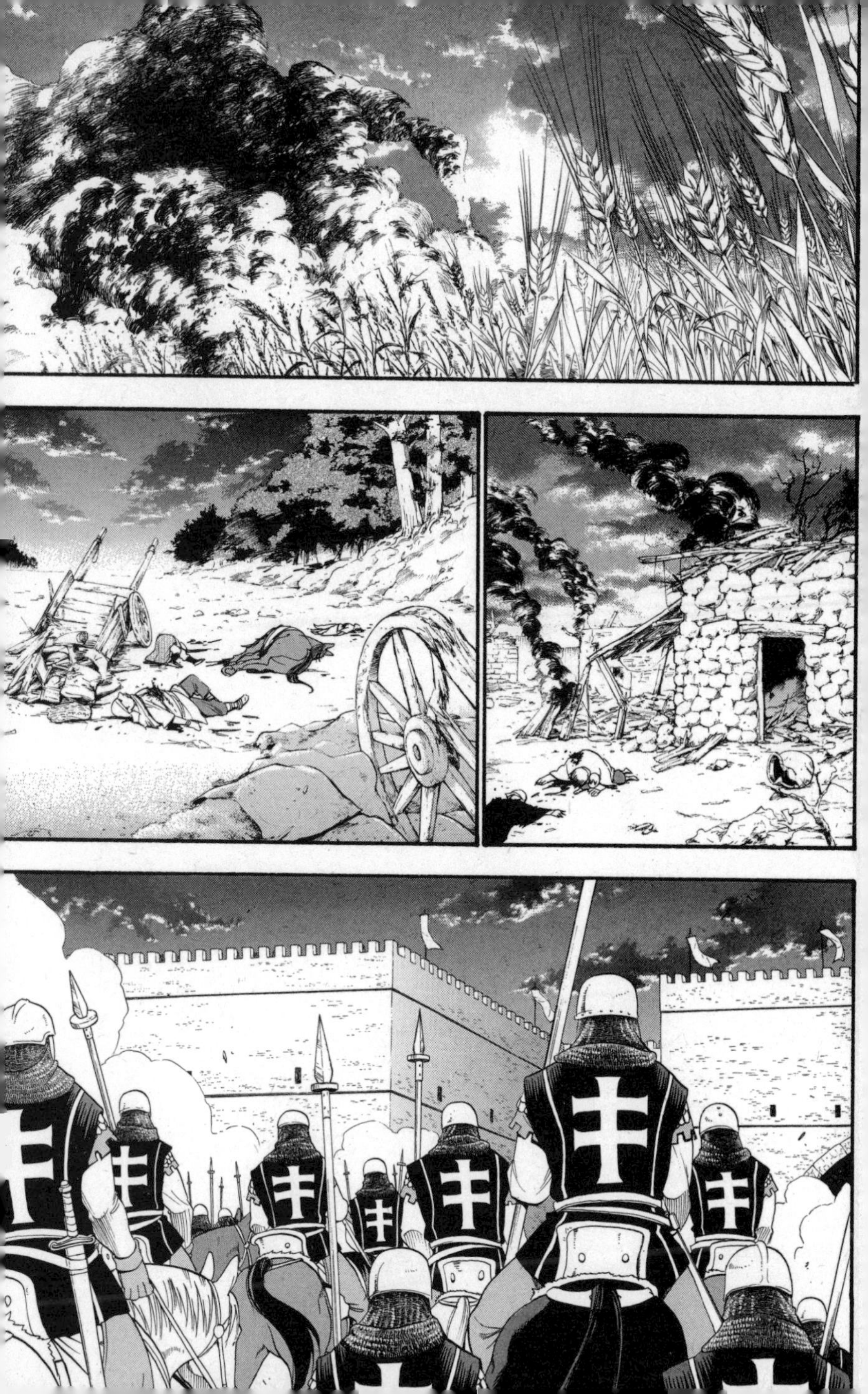

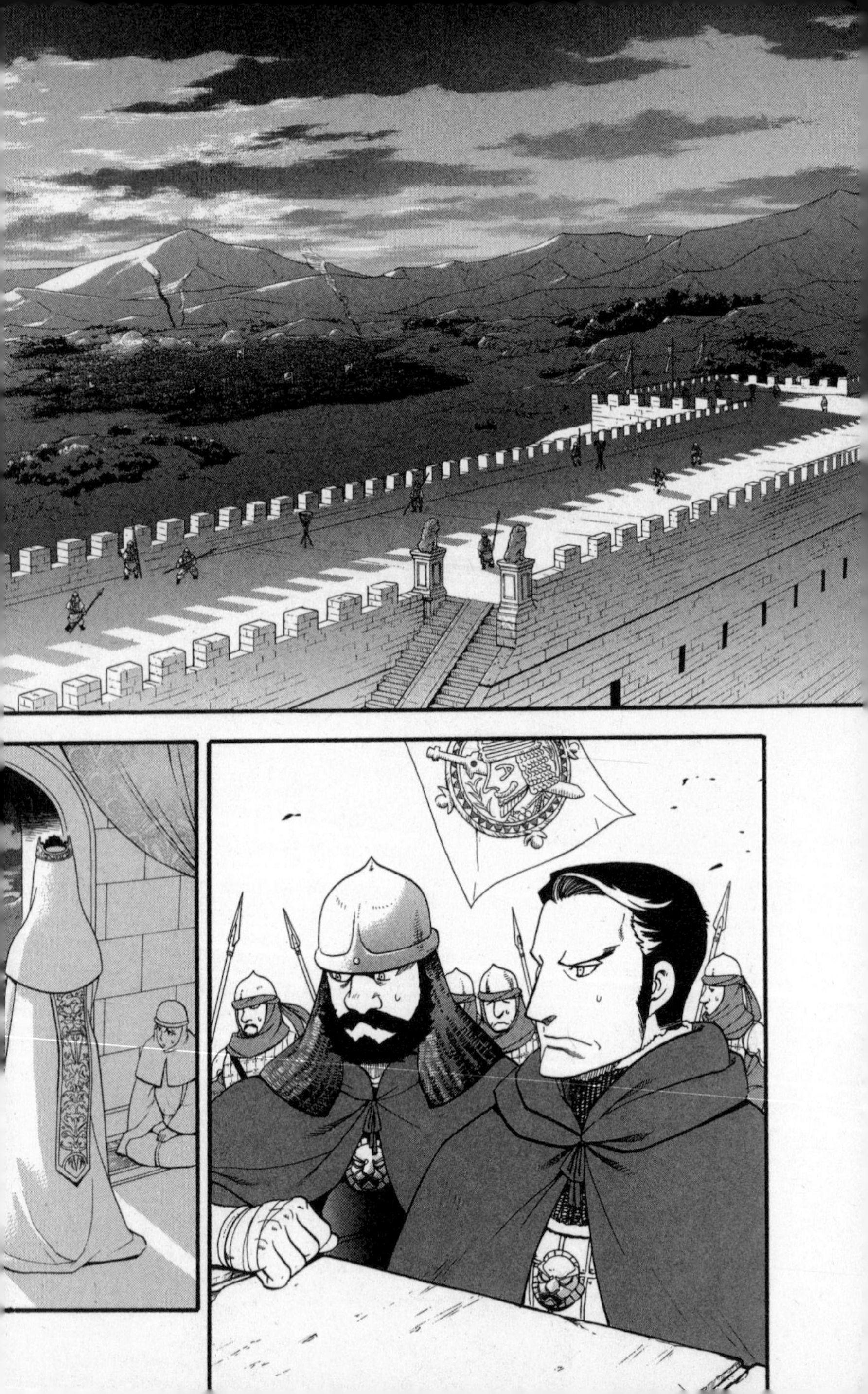

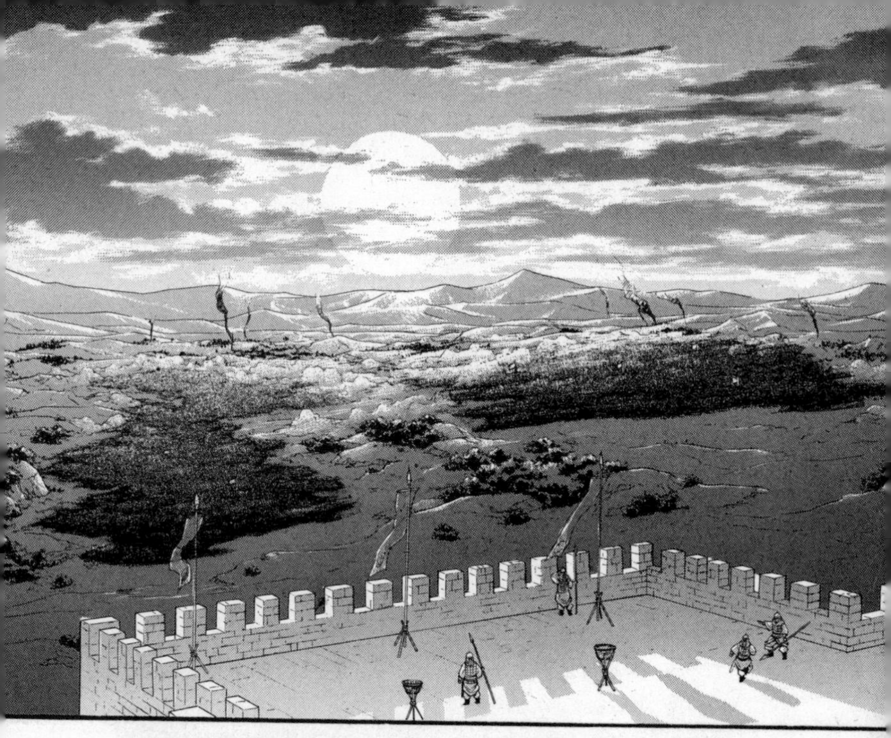

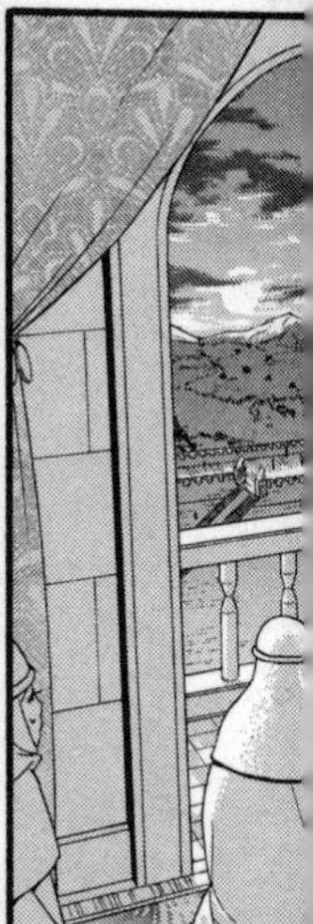

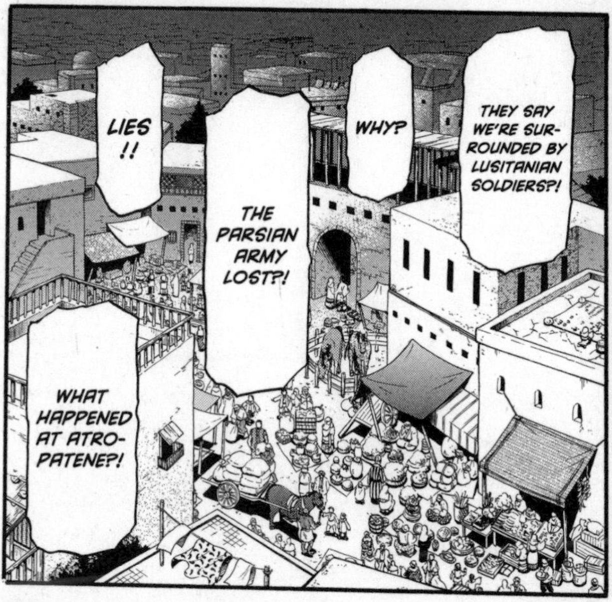
THEY SAY WE'RE SUR-ROUNDED BY LUSITANIAN SOLDIERS?!
WHY?
THE PARSIAN ARMY LOST?!
LIES !!
WHAT HAPPENED AT ATRO-PATENE?!

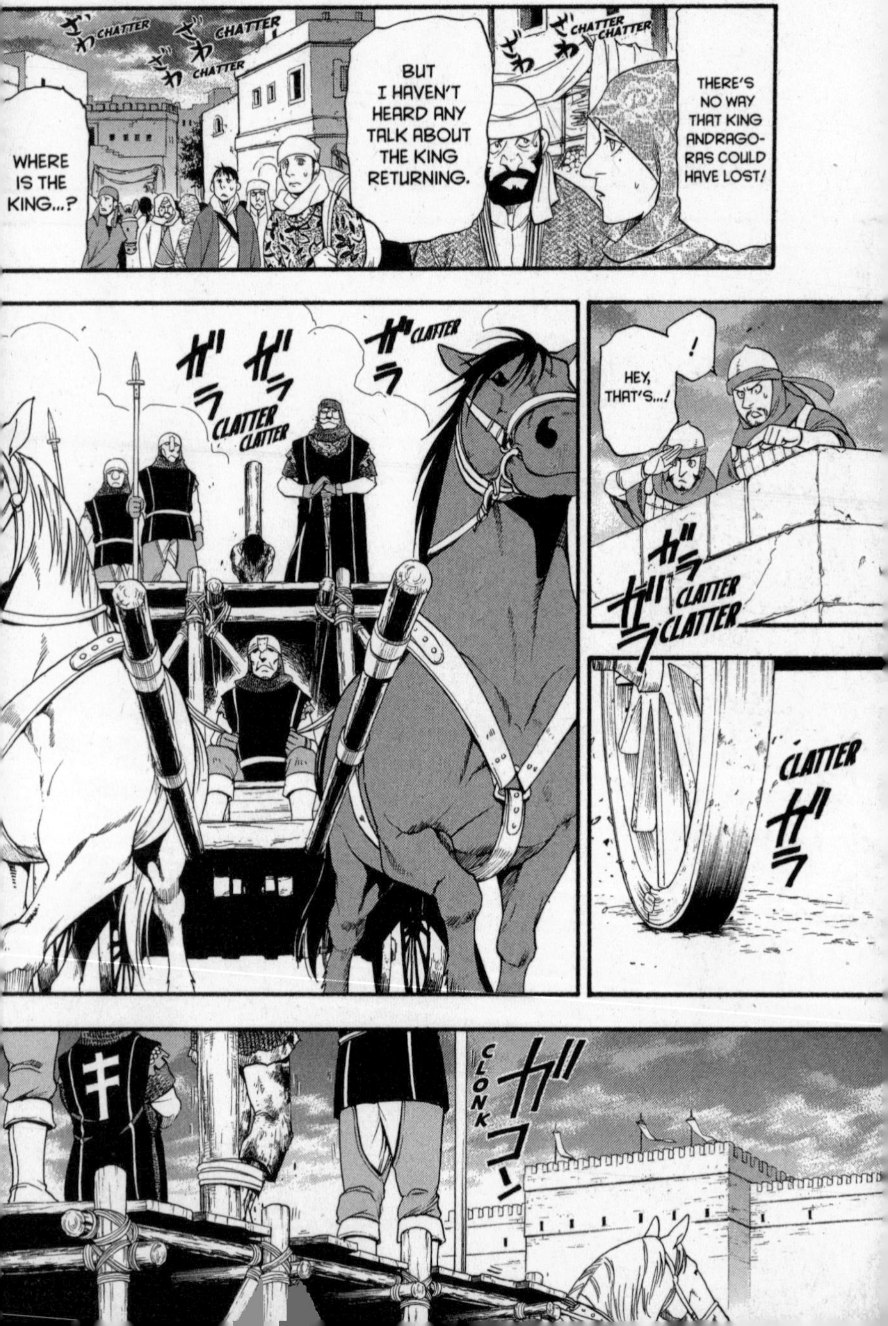
THERE'S NO WAY THAT KING ANDRAGORAS COULD HAVE LOST!
ざわ CHATTER ざわ CHATTER
BUT I HAVEN'T HEARD ANY TALK ABOUT THE KING RETURNING.
ざわ CHATTER ざわ CHATTER ざわ CHATTER
WHERE IS THE KING...?
!
HEY, THAT'S...!
ガラ ガラ CLATTER CLATTER
CLATTER ガラ
ガラ CLATTER
ガラ ガラ CLATTER CLATTER
CLONK ガコーン

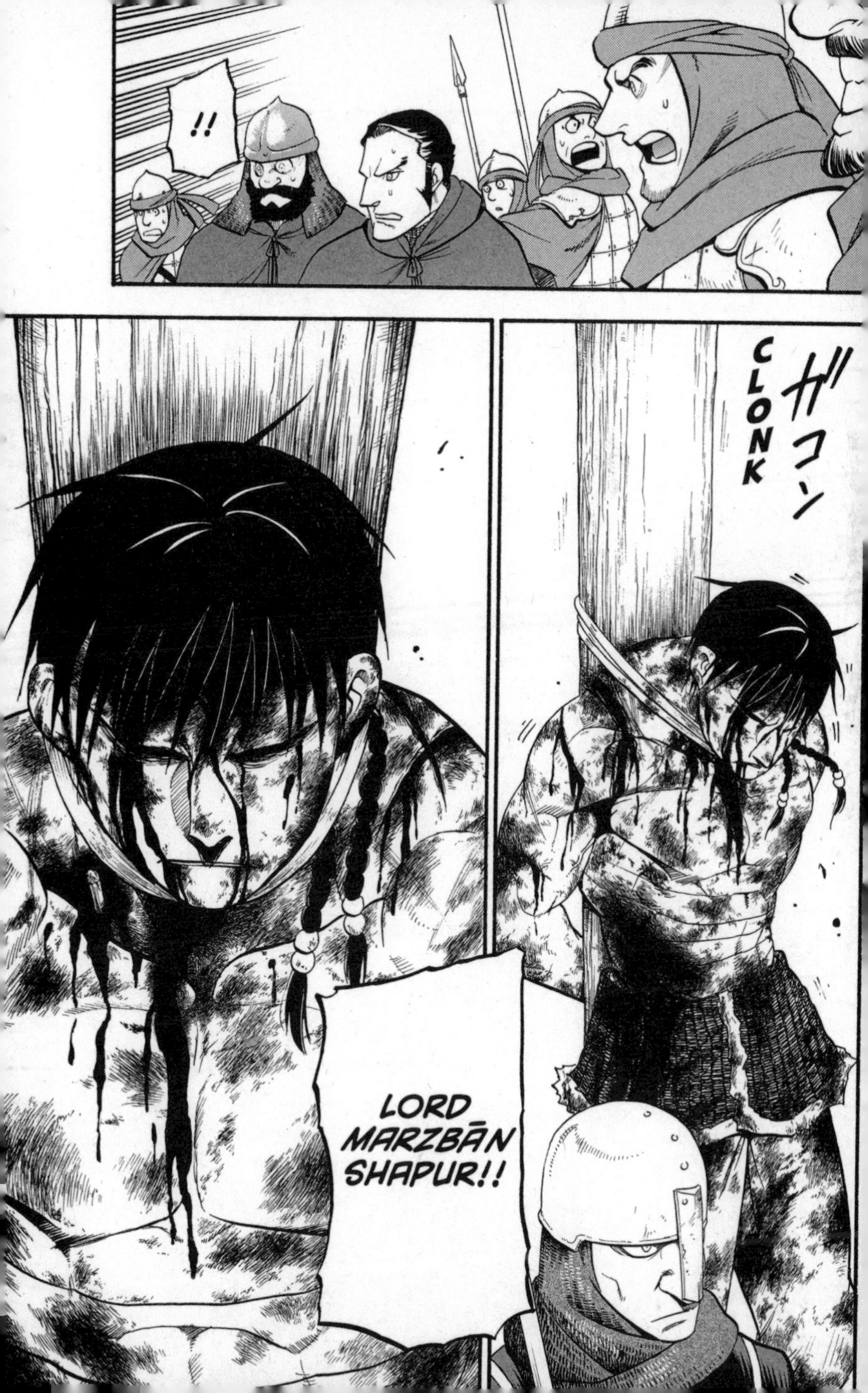
!!
ガコン
CLONK
LORD MARZBĀN SHAPUR!!

BLOODY HELL...

LORD SHA-PUR...

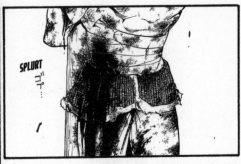

SPLURT

DRIP

DRIP

HEAR ME!!

YOU HEATHENS IN THE CASTLE WHO DO NOT FEAR GOD!!

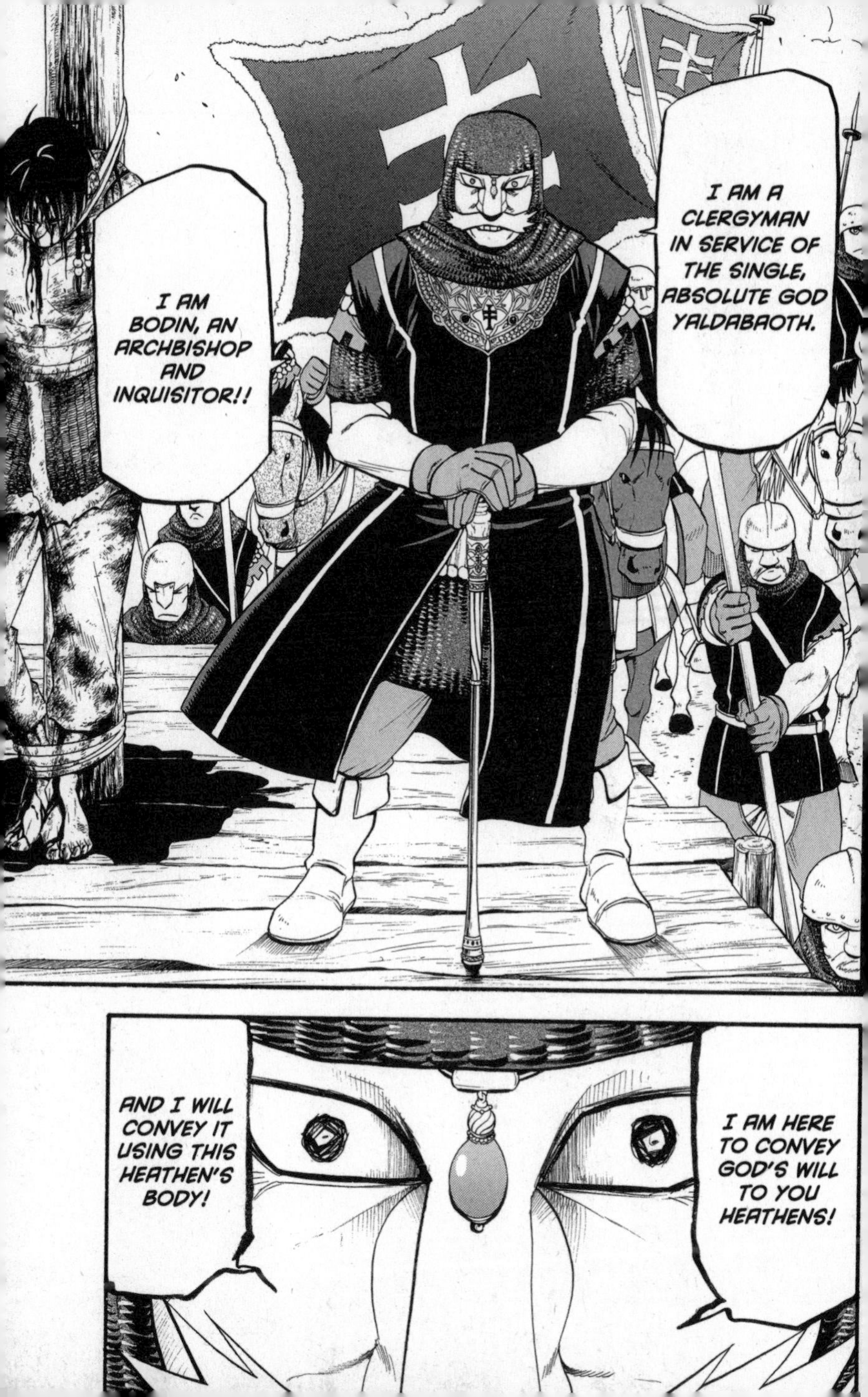
I AM A CLERGYMAN IN SERVICE OF THE SINGLE, ABSOLUTE GOD YALDABAOTH.
I AM BODIN, AN ARCHBISHOP AND INQUISITOR!!
I AM HERE TO CONVEY GOD'S WILL TO YOU HEATHENS!
AND I WILL CONVEY IT USING THIS HEATHEN'S BODY!

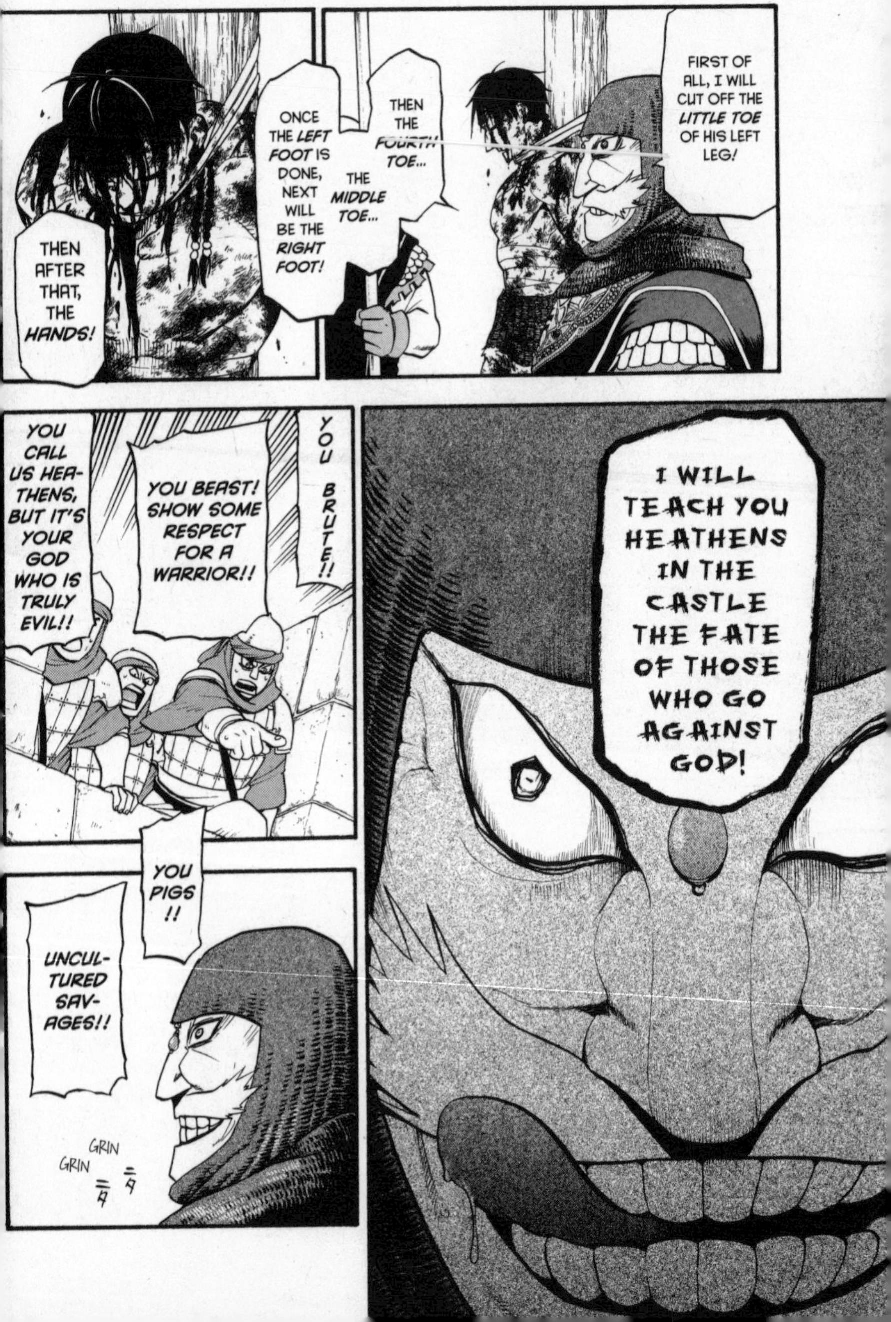

FIRST OF ALL, I WILL CUT OFF THE *LITTLE TOE* OF HIS LEFT LEG!
THEN THE *FOURTH* TOE...
THE *MIDDLE* TOE...
ONCE THE *LEFT FOOT* IS DONE, NEXT WILL BE THE *RIGHT FOOT!*
THEN AFTER THAT, THE *HANDS!*
I WILL TEACH YOU HEATHENS IN THE CASTLE THE FATE OF THOSE WHO GO AGAINST GOD!
YOU BRUTE!!
YOU BEAST! SHOW SOME RESPECT FOR A WARRIOR!!
YOU CALL US HEA-THENS, BUT IT'S YOUR GOD WHO IS TRULY EVIL!!
YOU PIGS!!
UNCUL-TURED SAV-AGES!!
GRIN
GRIN

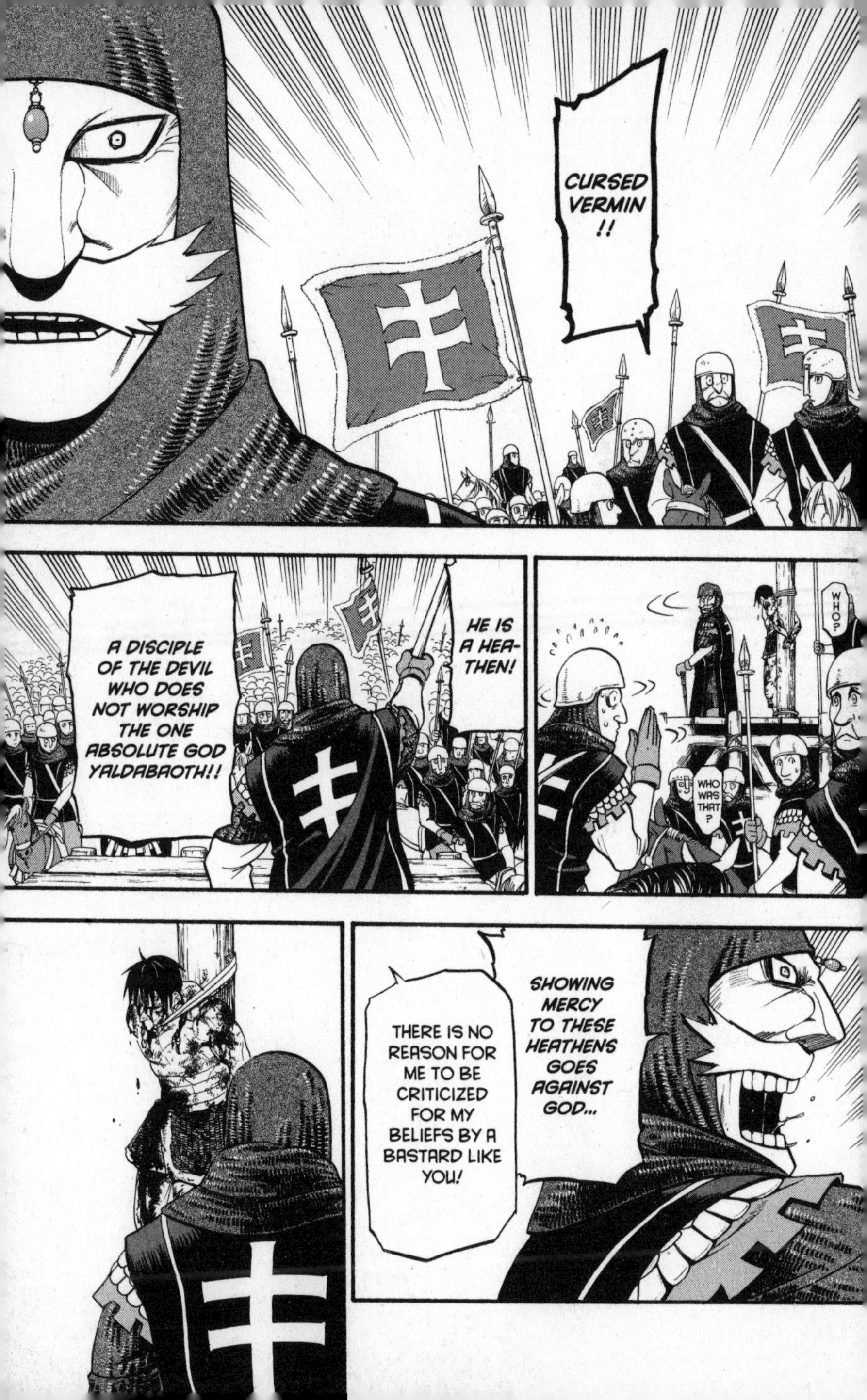
CURSED VERMIN !!
WHO?
WHO WAS THAT?
HE IS A HEA-THEN!
A DISCIPLE OF THE DEVIL WHO DOES NOT WORSHIP THE ONE ABSOLUTE GOD YALDABAOTH!!
SHOWING MERCY TO THESE HEATHENS GOES AGAINST GOD...
THERE IS NO REASON FOR ME TO BE CRITICIZED FOR MY BELIEFS BY A BASTARD LIKE YOU!

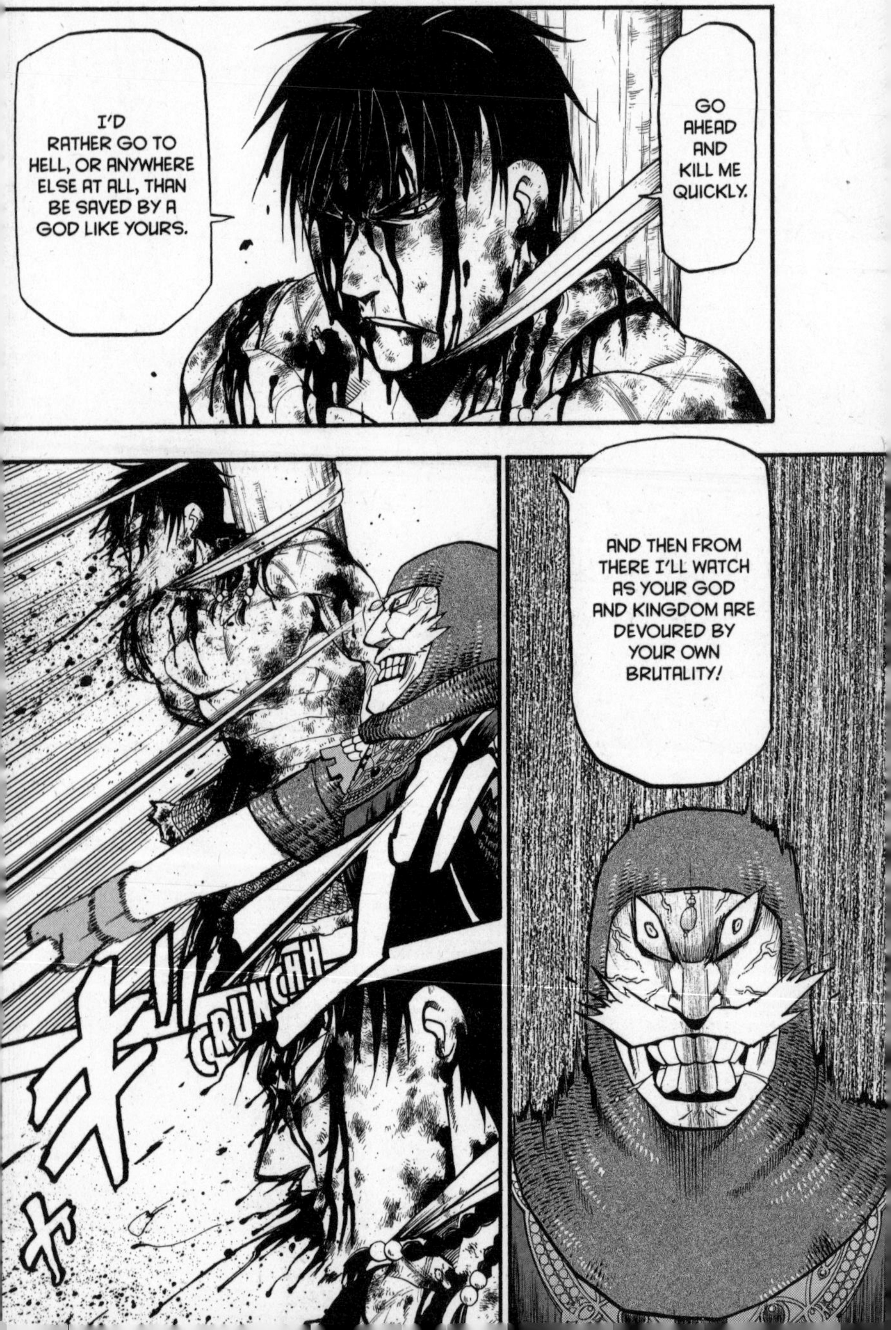
GO AHEAD AND KILL ME QUICKLY.
I'D RATHER GO TO HELL, OR ANYWHERE ELSE AT ALL, THAN BE SAVED BY A GOD LIKE YOURS.
AND THEN FROM THERE I'LL WATCH AS YOUR GOD AND KINGDOM ARE DEVOURED BY YOUR OWN BRUTALITY!
CRUNCHH

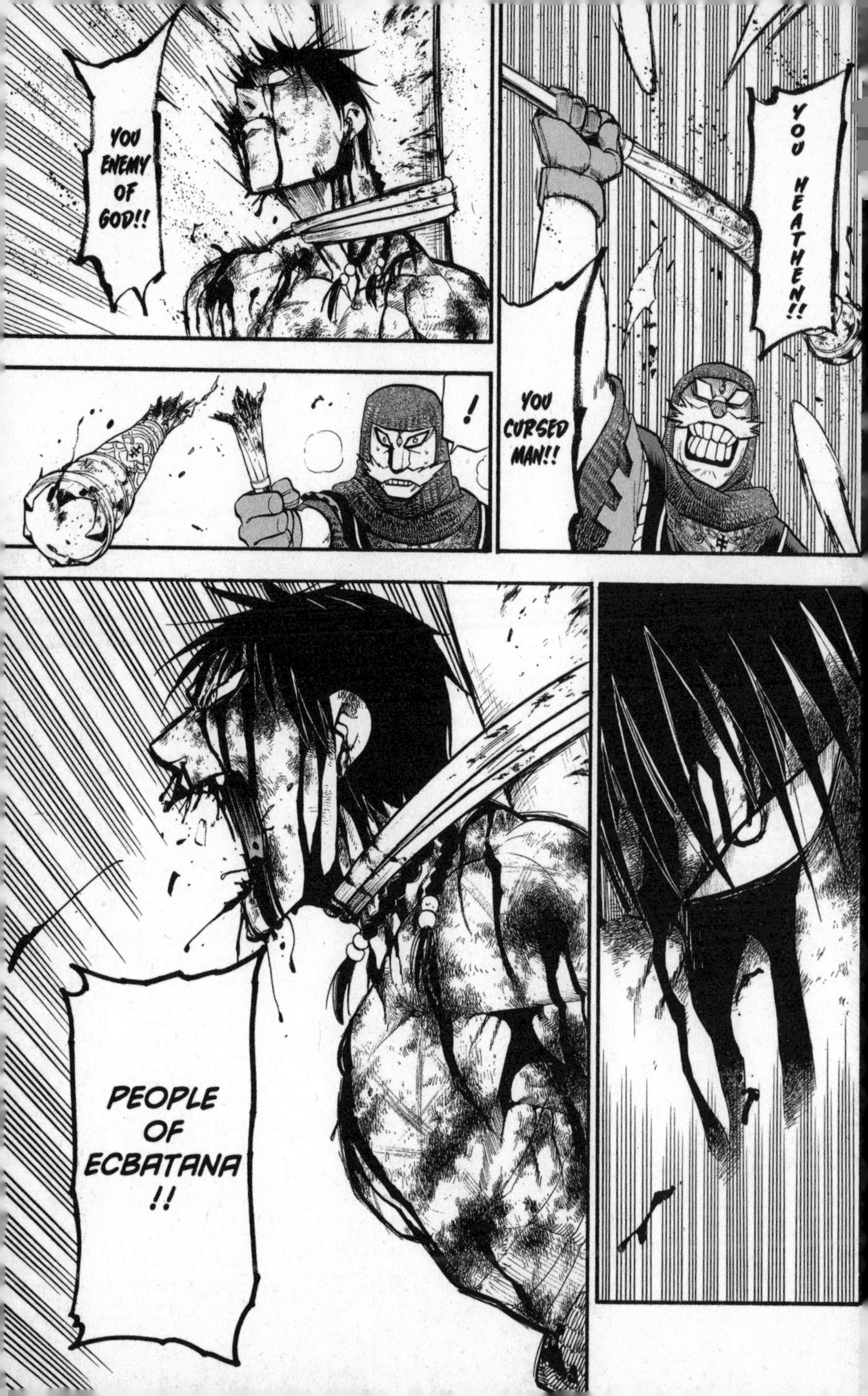
YOU HEATHEN!!
YOU CURSED MAN!!
YOU ENEMY OF GOD!!
!
PEOPLE OF ECBATANA !!

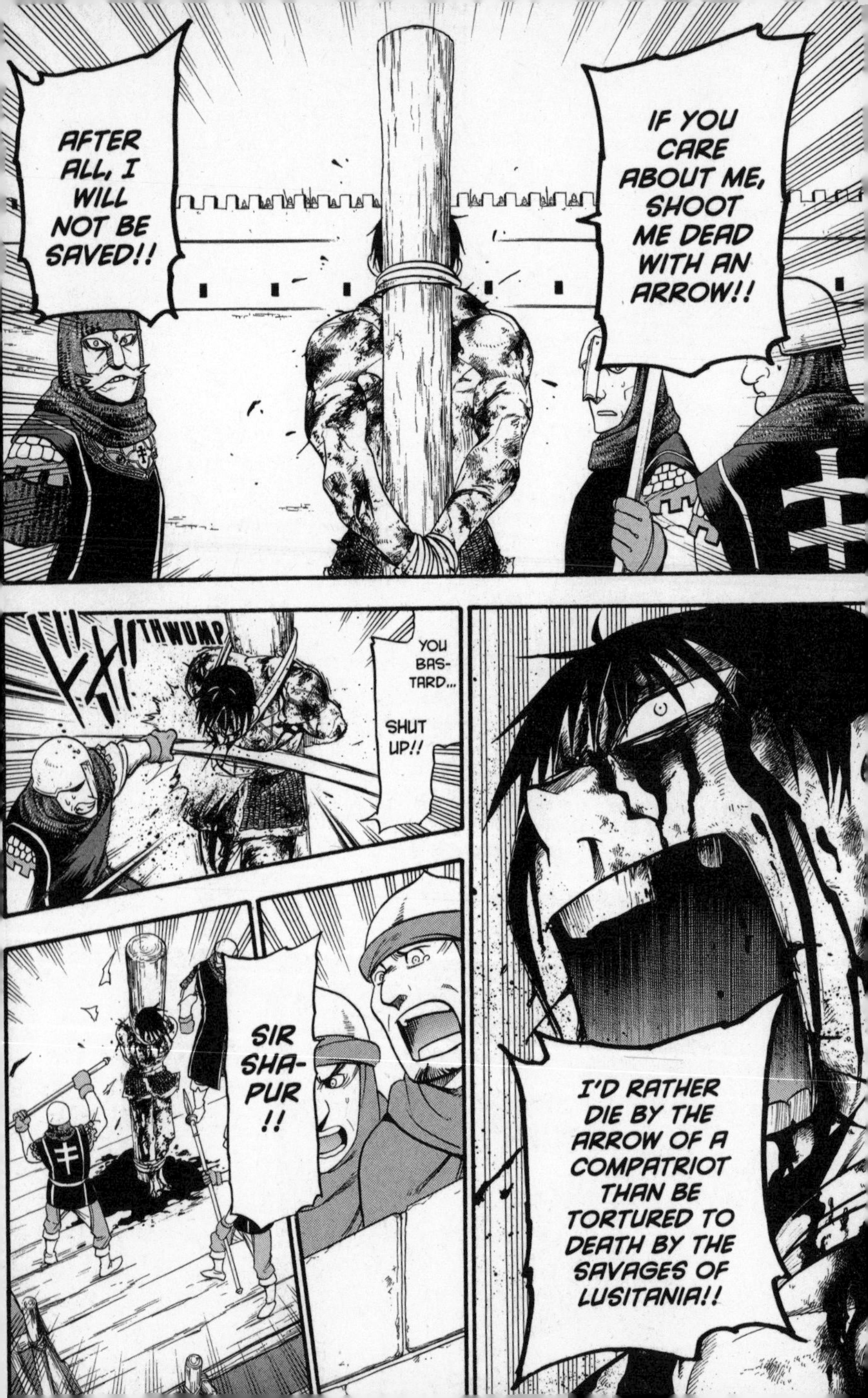
IF YOU CARE ABOUT ME, SHOOT ME DEAD WITH AN ARROW!!
AFTER ALL, I WILL NOT BE SAVED!!
I'D RATHER DIE BY THE ARROW OF A COMPATRIOT THAN BE TORTURED TO DEATH BY THE SAVAGES OF LUSITANIA!!
THWUMP
YOU BAS-TARD...
SHUT UP!!
SIR SHA-PUR!!

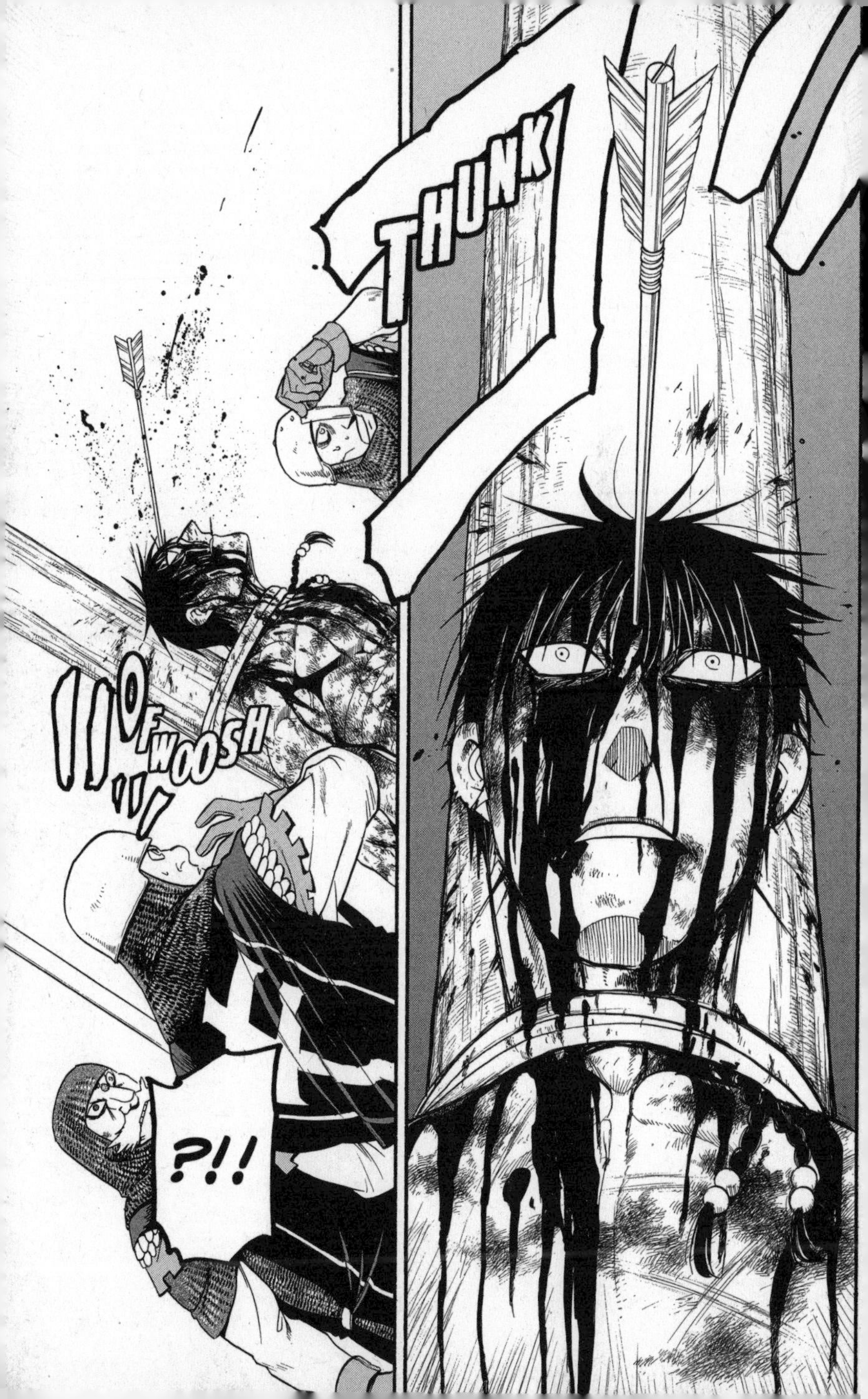
THUNK
FWOOSH
?!!

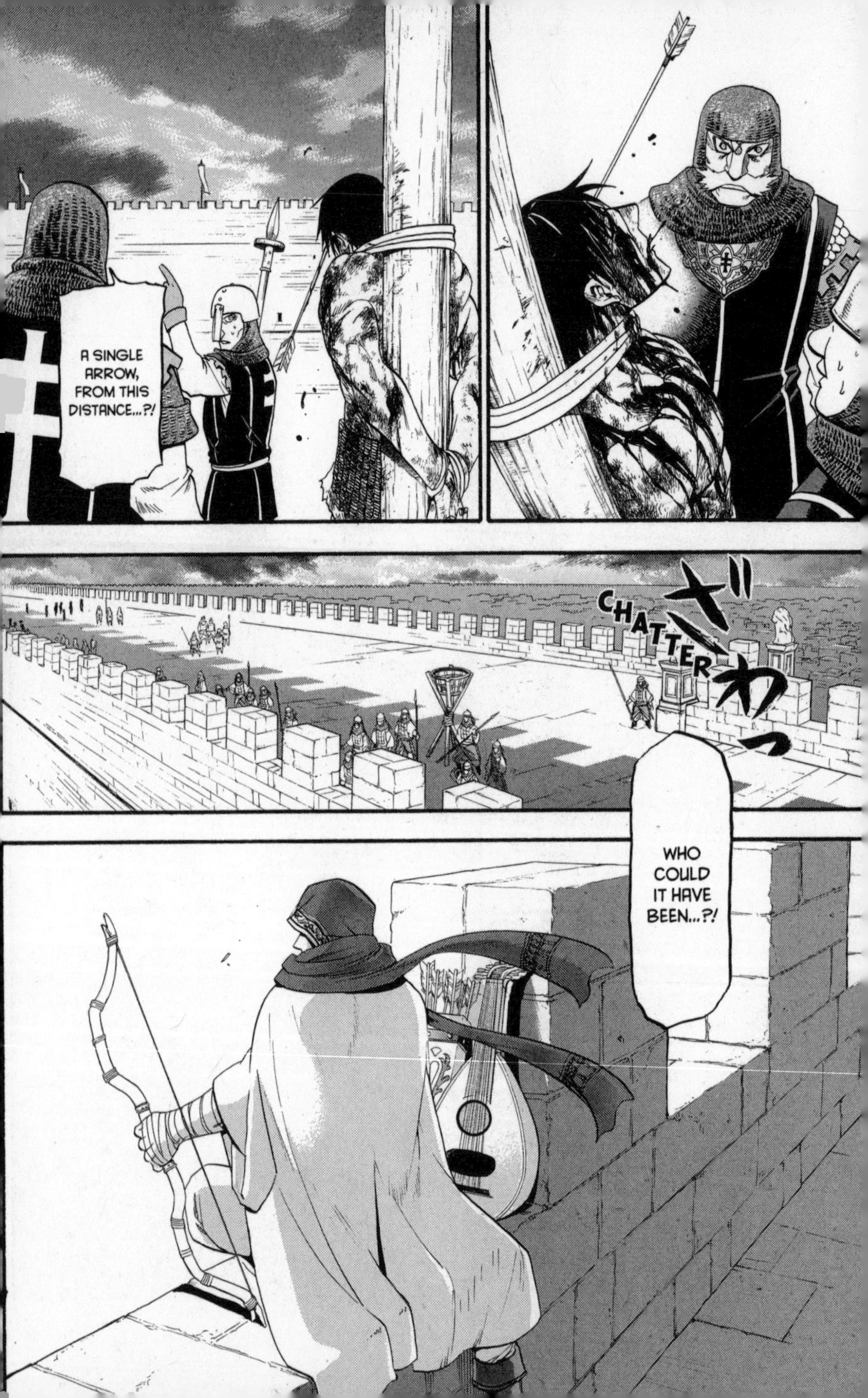
A SINGLE ARROW, FROM THIS DISTANCE...?!
ざわっ
CHATTER
WHO COULD IT HAVE BEEN...?!

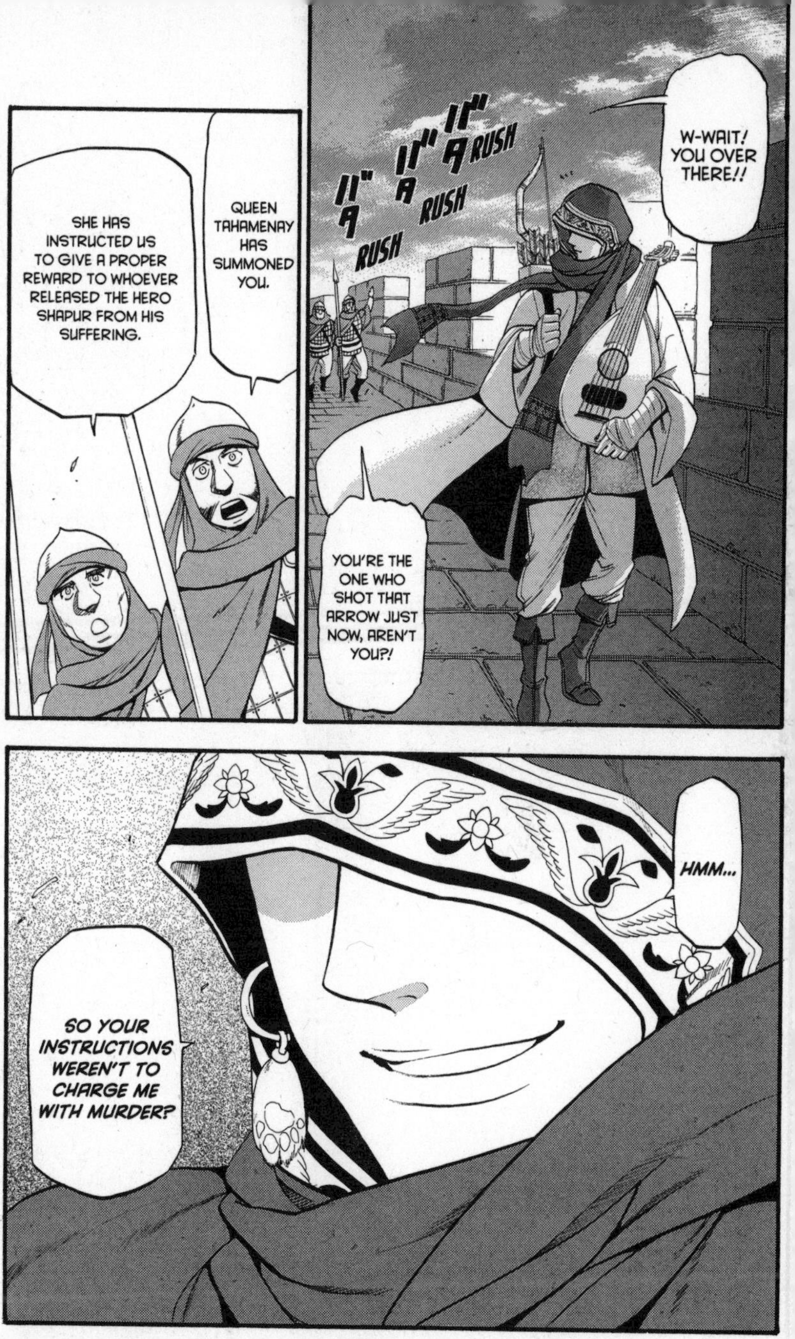
W-WAIT! YOU OVER THERE!!
RUSH
RUSH
RUSH
YOU'RE THE ONE WHO SHOT THAT ARROW JUST NOW, AREN'T YOU?!
QUEEN TAHAMENAY HAS SUMMONED YOU.
SHE HAS INSTRUCTED US TO GIVE A PROPER REWARD TO WHOEVER RELEASED THE HERO SHAPUR FROM HIS SUFFERING.
HMM...
SO YOUR INSTRUCTIONS WEREN'T TO CHARGE ME WITH MURDER?

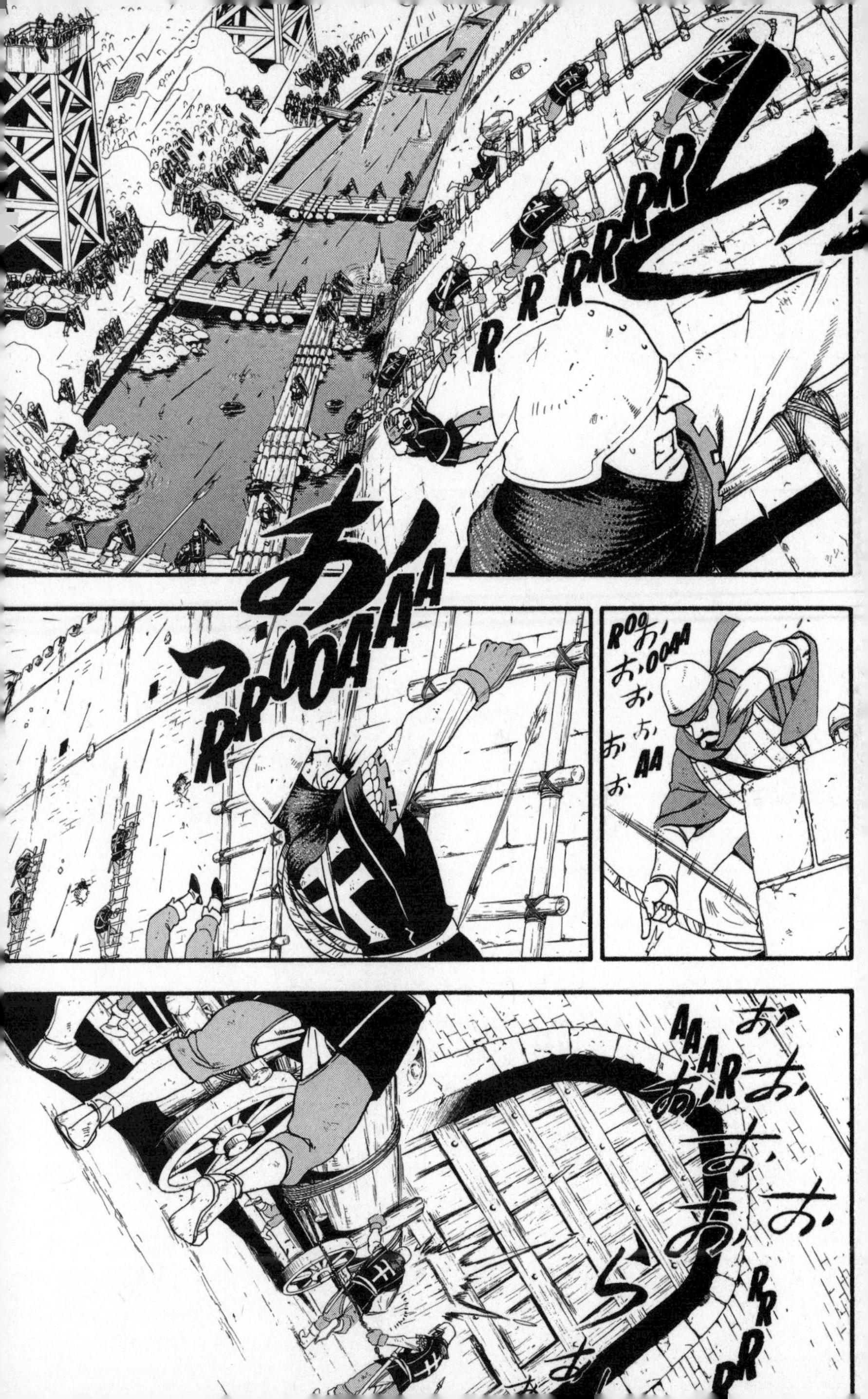
RRRRRRRRRR
おおっ
RROOOAAA
ROOおOOAA
おおおおAA
AAAR
RRRR

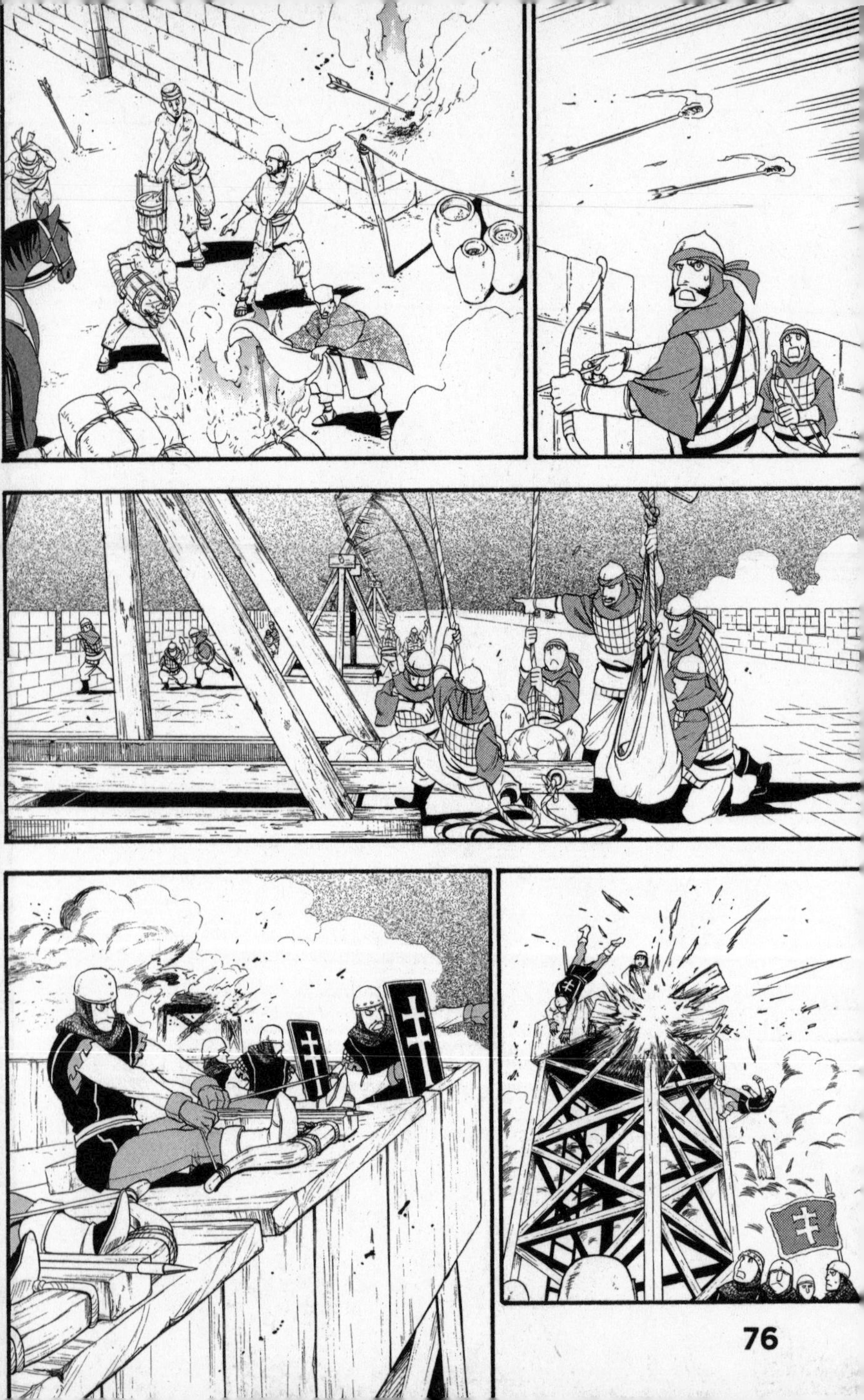

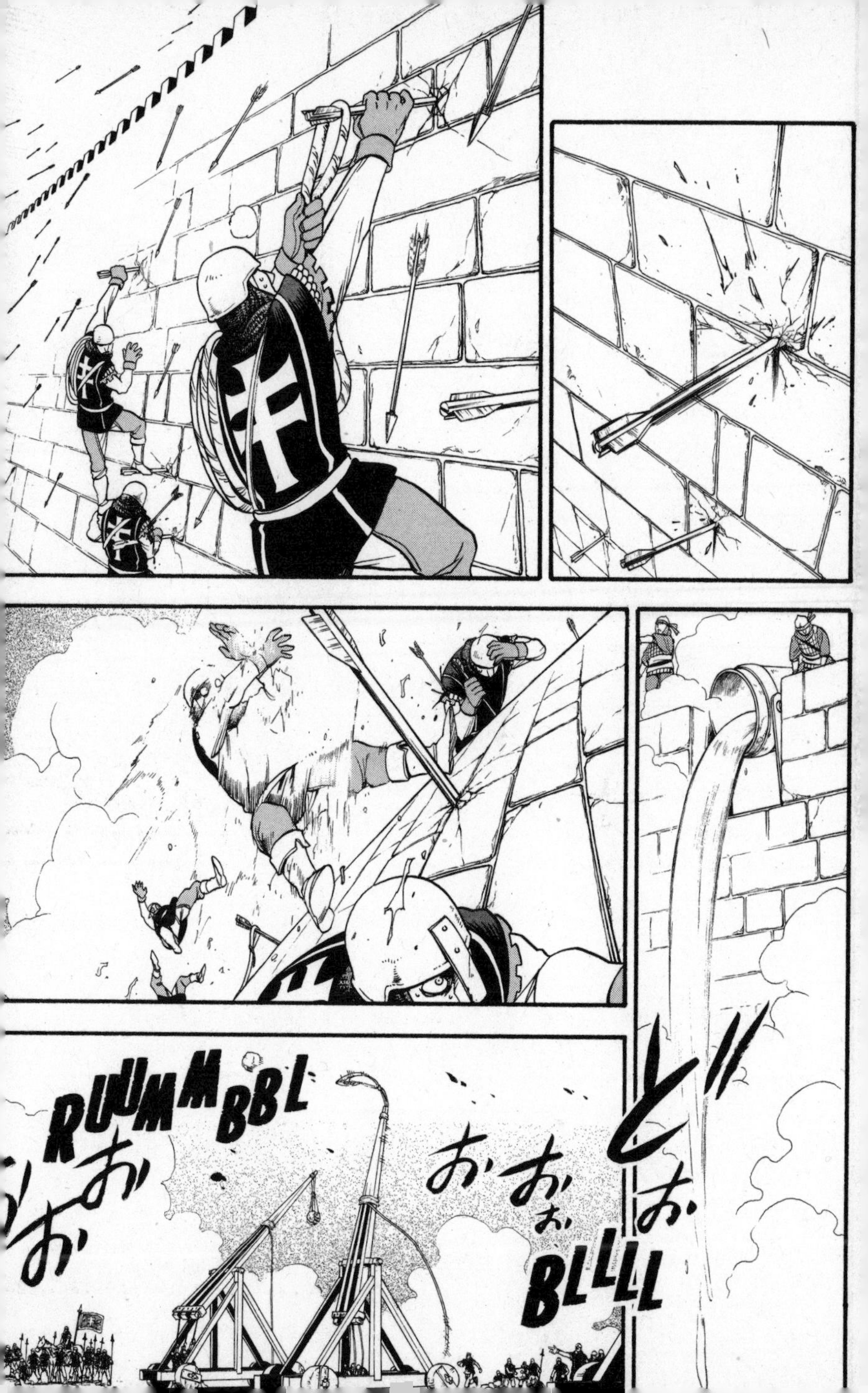
ど!!
お
BLLLLL
おおぉ
RUUMMBBL
おお

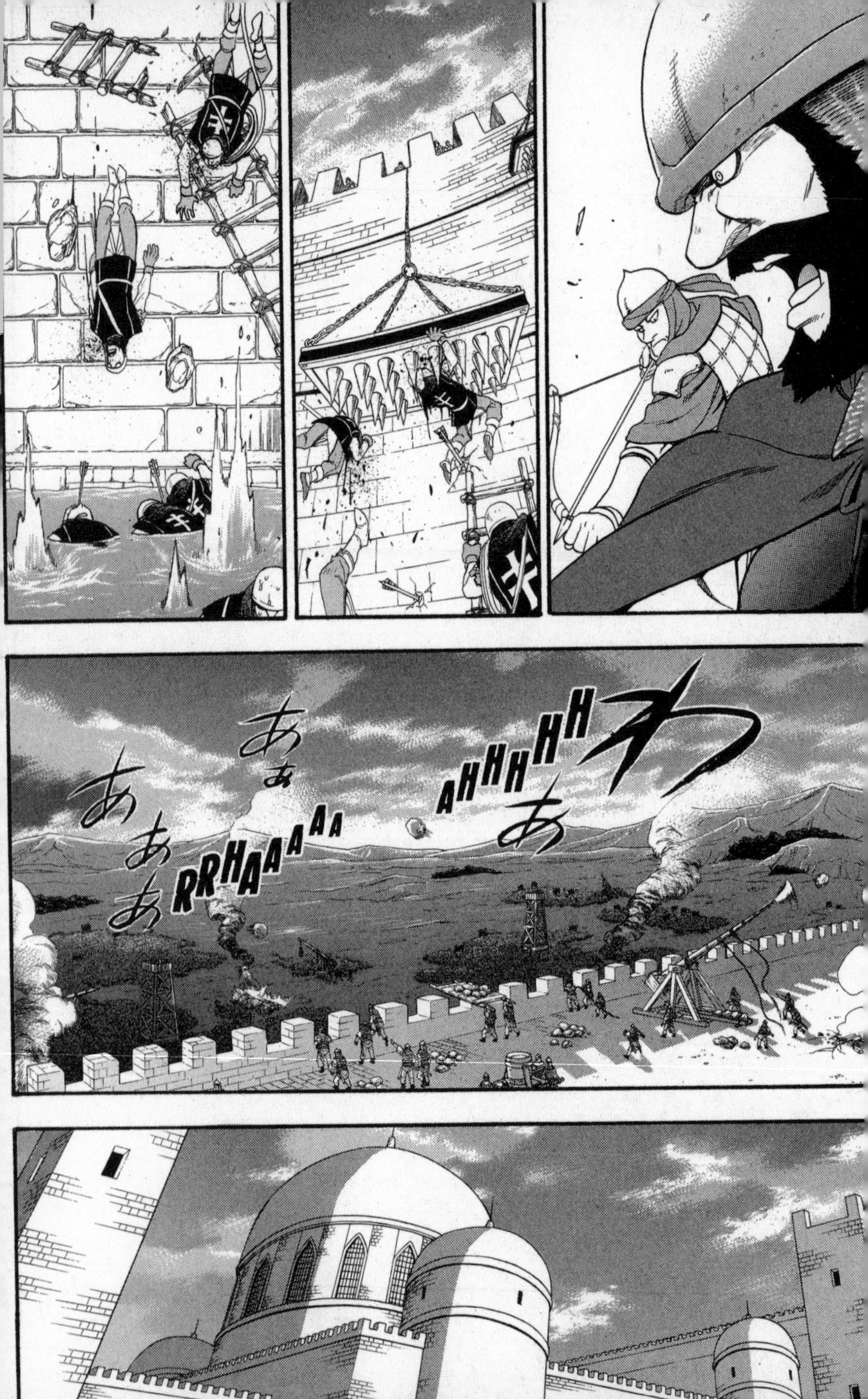
わっ
あ
AHHHHH
ああ
あああ
RRHAAAAA

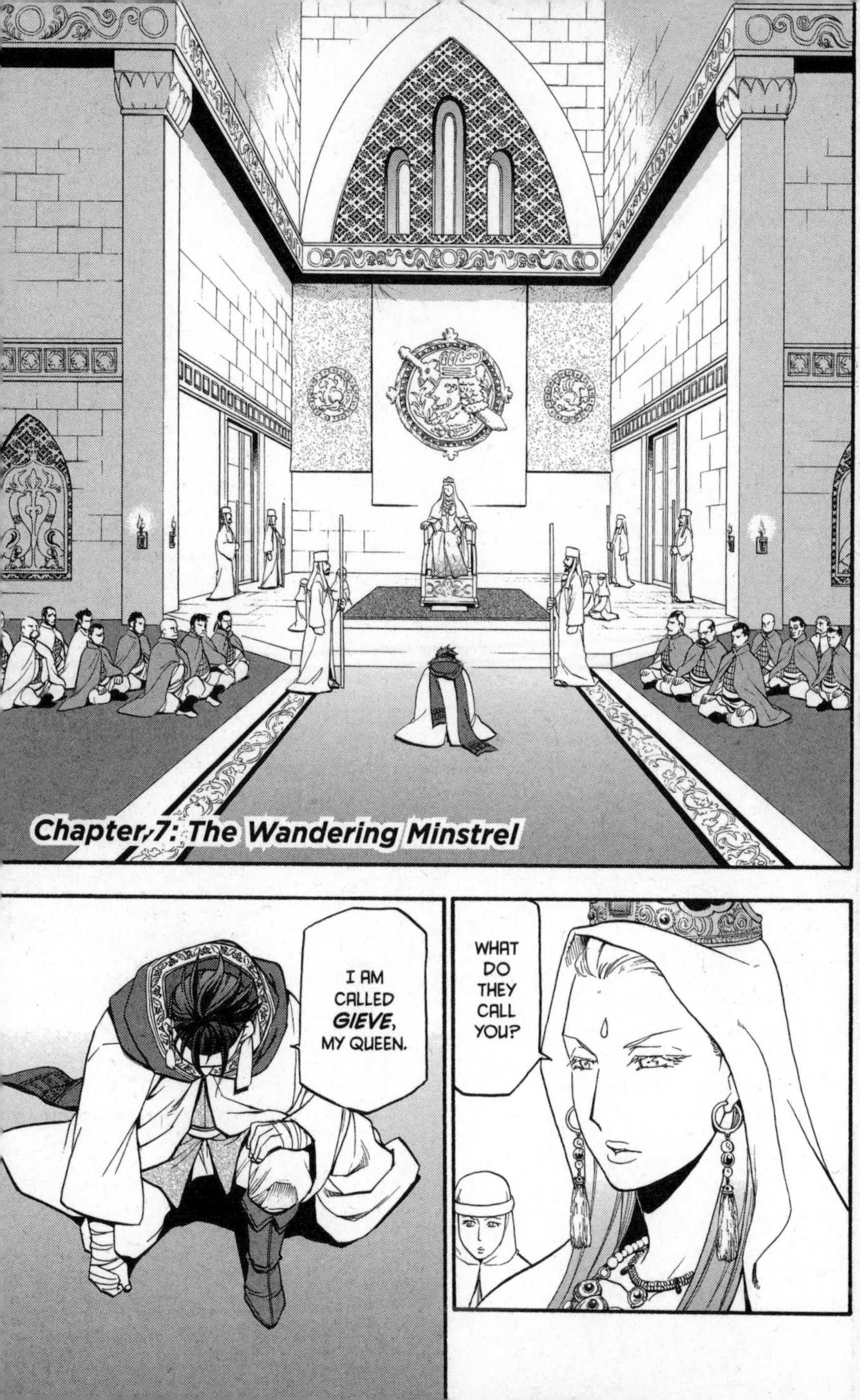
Chapter 7: The Wandering Minstrel
WHAT DO THEY CALL YOU?
I AM CALLED GIEVE, MY QUEEN.

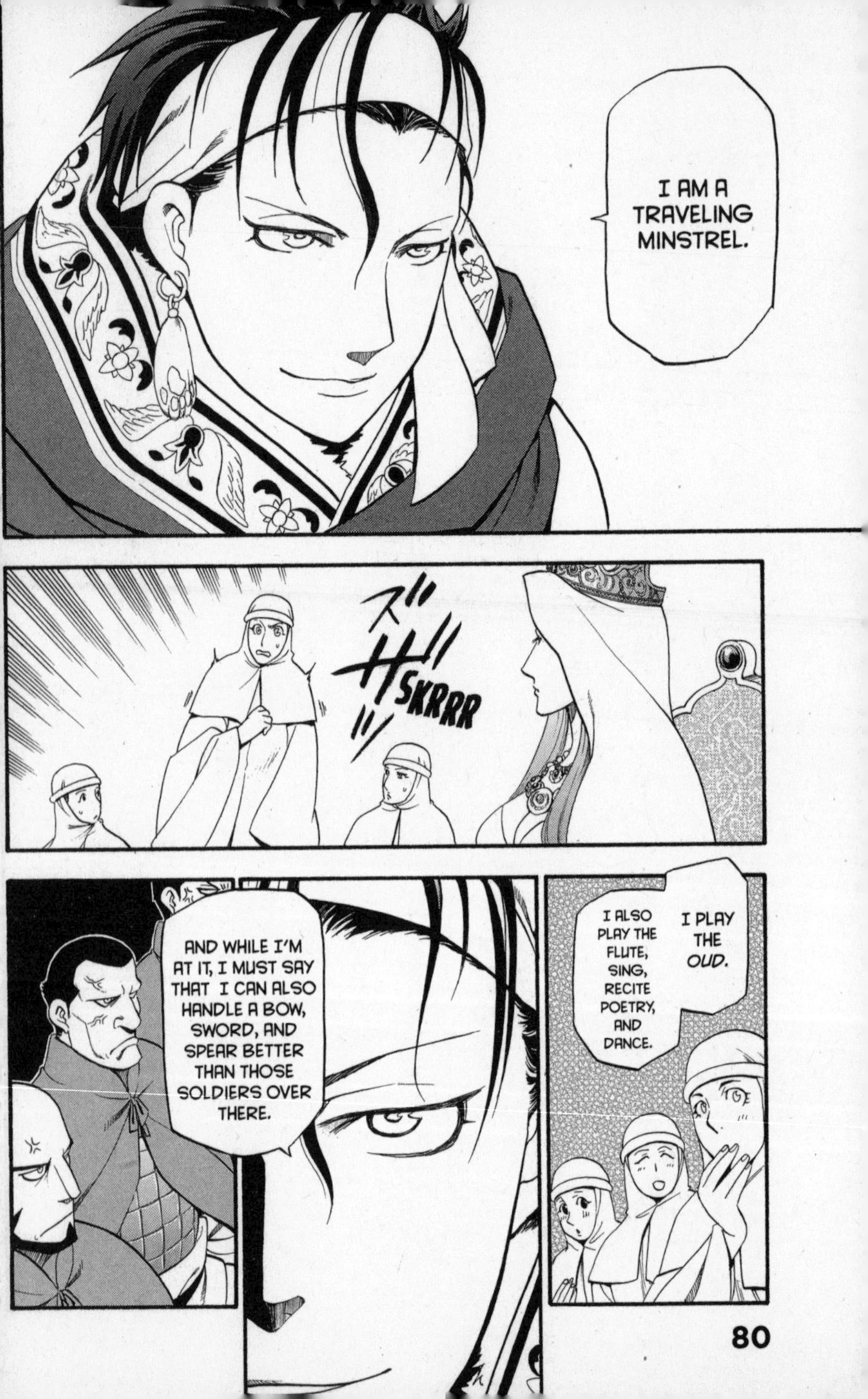
I AM A TRAVELING MINSTREL.
ズザ
SKRRR
I PLAY THE *OUD*.
I ALSO PLAY THE FLUTE, SING, RECITE POETRY, AND DANCE.
AND WHILE I'M AT IT, I MUST SAY THAT I CAN ALSO HANDLE A BOW, SWORD, AND SPEAR BETTER THAN THOSE SOLDIERS OVER THERE.

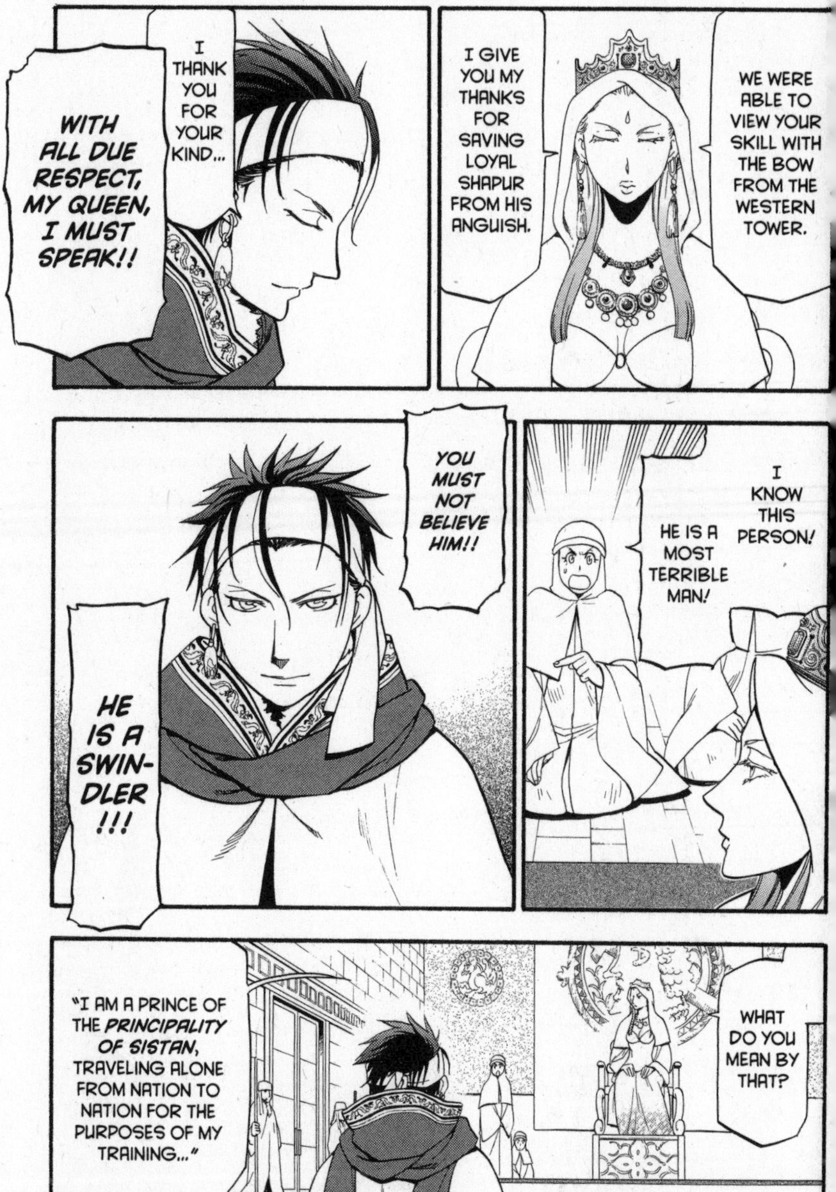

WE WERE ABLE TO VIEW YOUR SKILL WITH THE BOW FROM THE WESTERN TOWER.
I GIVE YOU MY THANKS FOR SAVING LOYAL SHAPUR FROM HIS ANGUISH.
I THANK YOU FOR YOUR KIND...
WITH ALL DUE RESPECT, MY QUEEN, I MUST SPEAK!!
I KNOW THIS PERSON!
HE IS A MOST TERRIBLE MAN!
YOU MUST NOT BELIEVE HIM!!
HE IS A SWIN-DLER!!!
WHAT DO YOU MEAN BY THAT?
"I AM A PRINCE OF THE PRINCIPALITY OF SISTAN, TRAVELING ALONE FROM NATION TO NATION FOR THE PURPOSES OF MY TRAINING..."

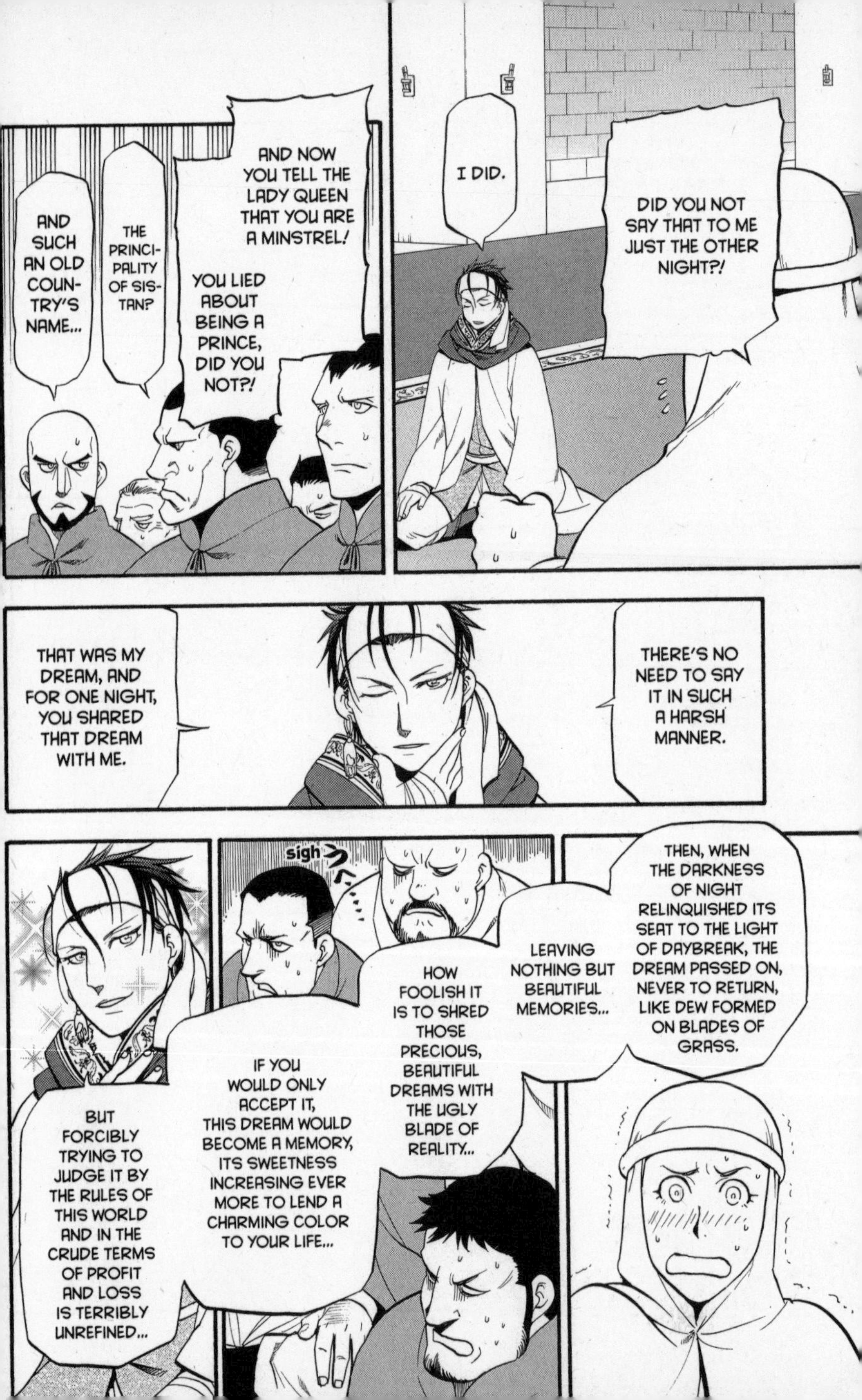

DID YOU NOT SAY THAT TO ME JUST THE OTHER NIGHT?!
I DID.
AND NOW YOU TELL THE LADY QUEEN THAT YOU ARE A MINSTREL!
YOU LIED ABOUT BEING A PRINCE, DID YOU NOT?!
THE PRINCIPALITY OF SISTAN?
AND SUCH AN OLD COUNTRY'S NAME...
THERE'S NO NEED TO SAY IT IN SUCH A HARSH MANNER.
THAT WAS MY DREAM, AND FOR ONE NIGHT, YOU SHARED THAT DREAM WITH ME.
THEN, WHEN THE DARKNESS OF NIGHT RELINQUISHED ITS SEAT TO THE LIGHT OF DAYBREAK, THE DREAM PASSED ON, NEVER TO RETURN, LIKE DEW FORMED ON BLADES OF GRASS.
LEAVING NOTHING BUT BEAUTIFUL MEMORIES...
sigh
HOW FOOLISH IT IS TO SHRED THOSE PRECIOUS, BEAUTIFUL DREAMS WITH THE UGLY BLADE OF REALITY...
IF YOU WOULD ONLY ACCEPT IT, THIS DREAM WOULD BECOME A MEMORY, ITS SWEETNESS INCREASING EVER MORE TO LEND A CHARMING COLOR TO YOUR LIFE...
BUT FORCIBLY TRYING TO JUDGE IT BY THE RULES OF THIS WORLD AND IN THE CRUDE TERMS OF PROFIT AND LOSS IS TERRIBLY UNREFINED...

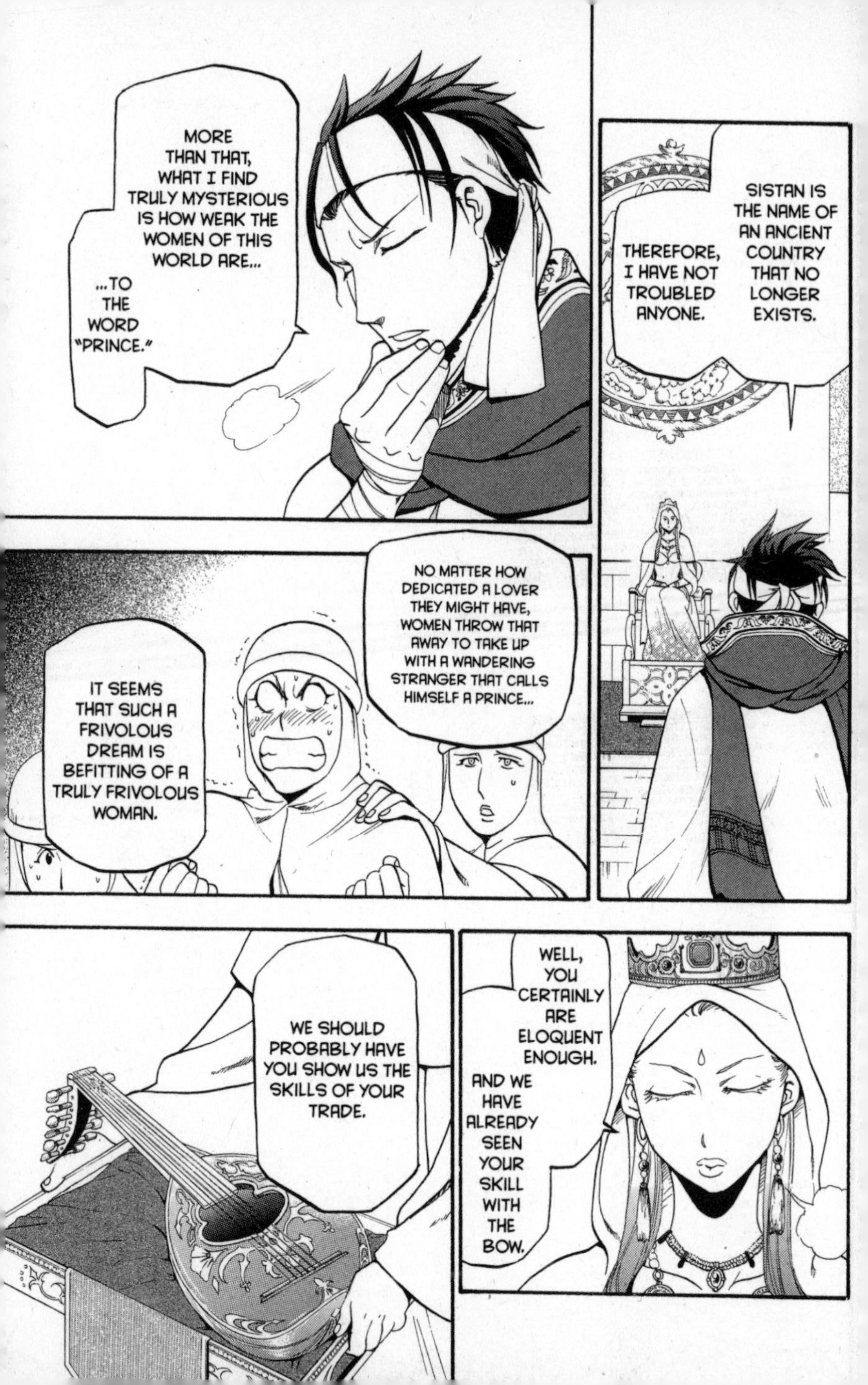
SISTAN IS THE NAME OF AN ANCIENT COUNTRY THAT NO LONGER EXISTS.
THEREFORE, I HAVE NOT TROUBLED ANYONE.
MORE THAN THAT, WHAT I FIND TRULY MYSTERIOUS IS HOW WEAK THE WOMEN OF THIS WORLD ARE...
...TO THE WORD "PRINCE."
NO MATTER HOW DEDICATED A LOVER THEY MIGHT HAVE, WOMEN THROW THAT AWAY TO TAKE UP WITH A WANDERING STRANGER THAT CALLS HIMSELF A PRINCE...
IT SEEMS THAT SUCH A FRIVOLOUS DREAM IS BEFITTING OF A TRULY FRIVOLOUS WOMAN.
WELL, YOU CERTAINLY ARE ELOQUENT ENOUGH.
AND WE HAVE ALREADY SEEN YOUR SKILL WITH THE BOW.
WE SHOULD PROBABLY HAVE YOU SHOW US THE SKILLS OF YOUR TRADE.

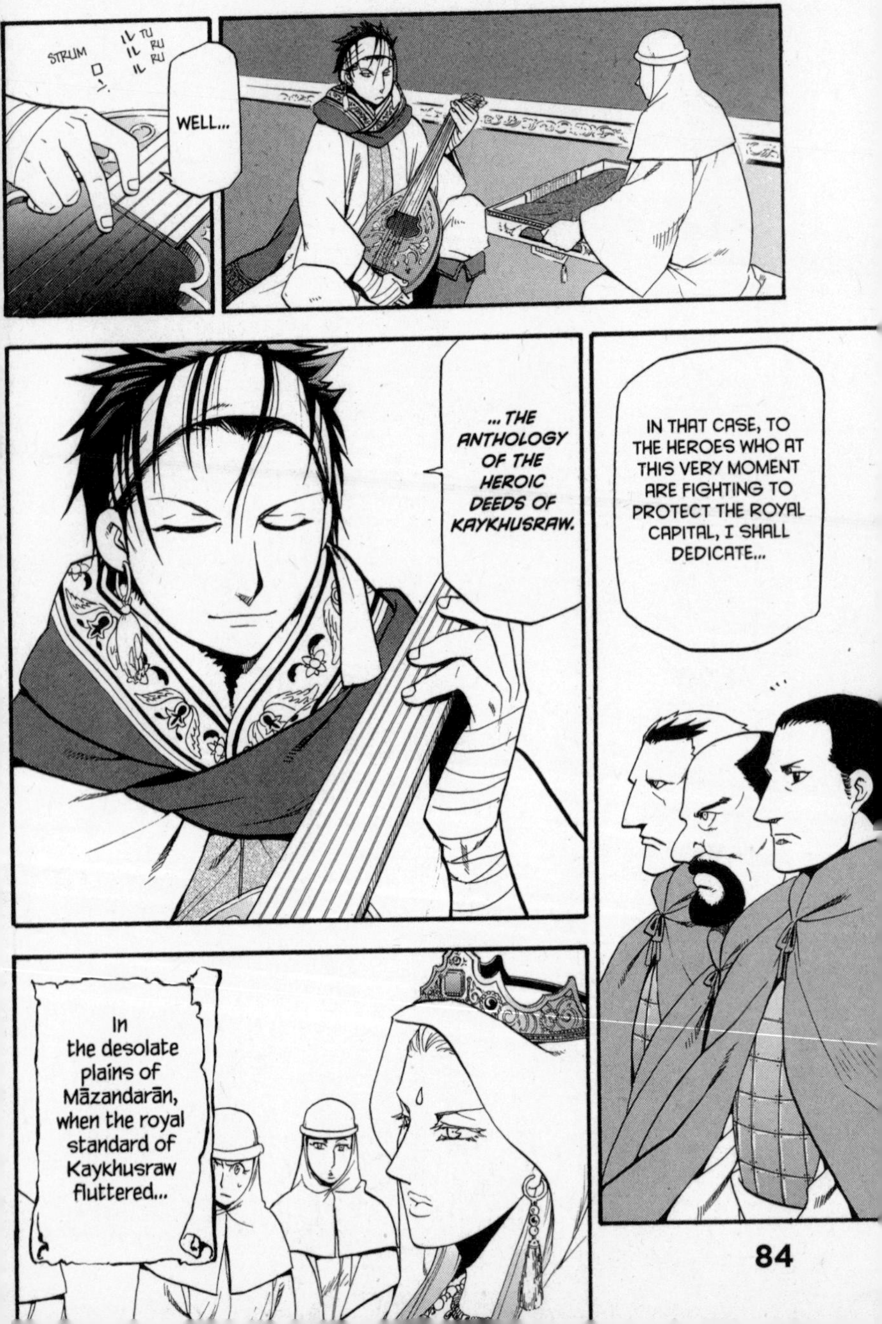
STRUM
TU RU RU
WELL...
IN THAT CASE, TO THE HEROES WHO AT THIS VERY MOMENT ARE FIGHTING TO PROTECT THE ROYAL CAPITAL, I SHALL DEDICATE...
...THE ANTHOLOGY OF THE HEROIC DEEDS OF KAYKHUSRAW.
...
In the desolate plains of Māzandarān, when the royal standard of Kaykhusraw fluttered...

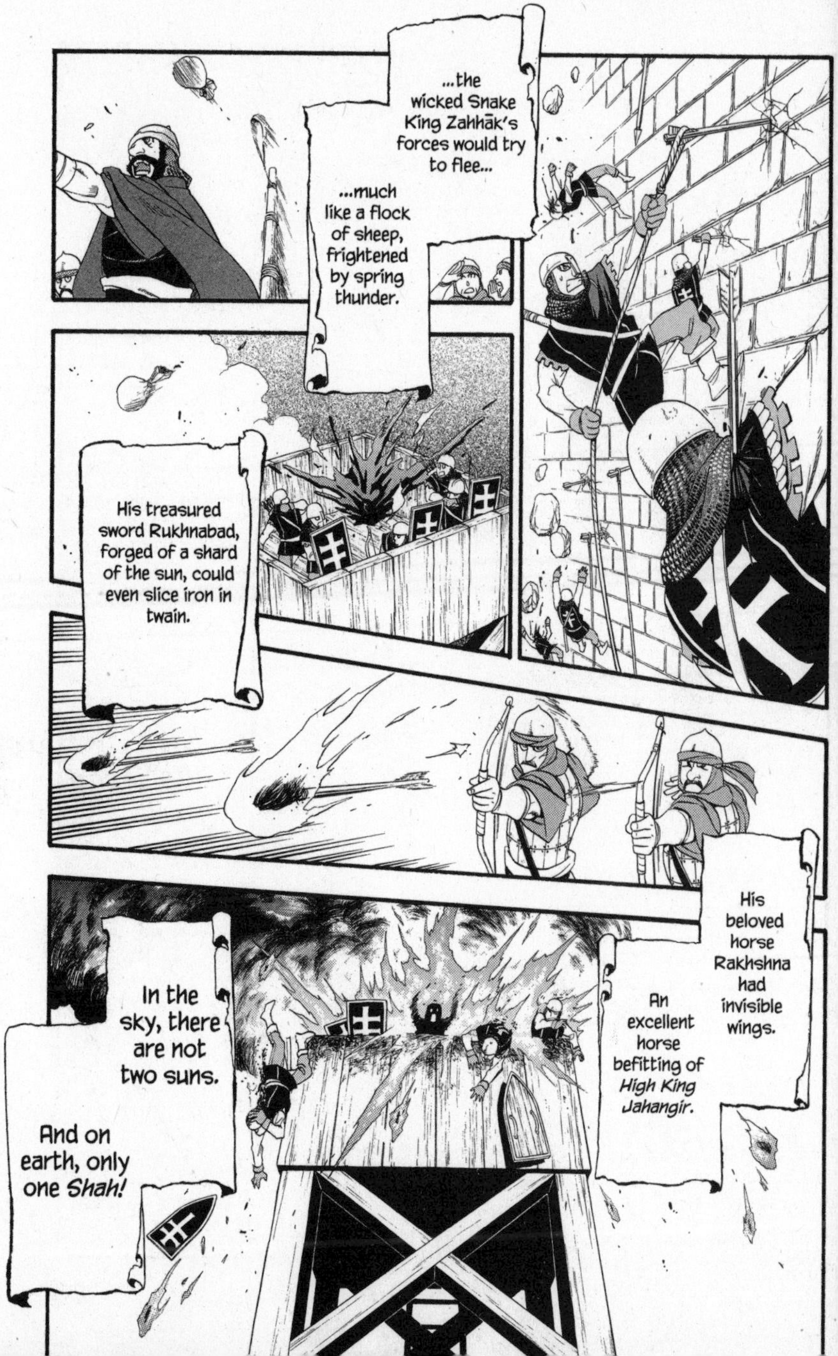
...the wicked Snake King Zahhāk's forces would try to flee...
...much like a flock of sheep, frightened by spring thunder.
His treasured sword Rukhnabad, forged of a shard of the sun, could even slice iron in twain.
His beloved horse Rakhshna had invisible wings.
An excellent horse befitting of *High King Jahangir*.
In the sky, there are not two suns.
And on earth, only one *Shah!*

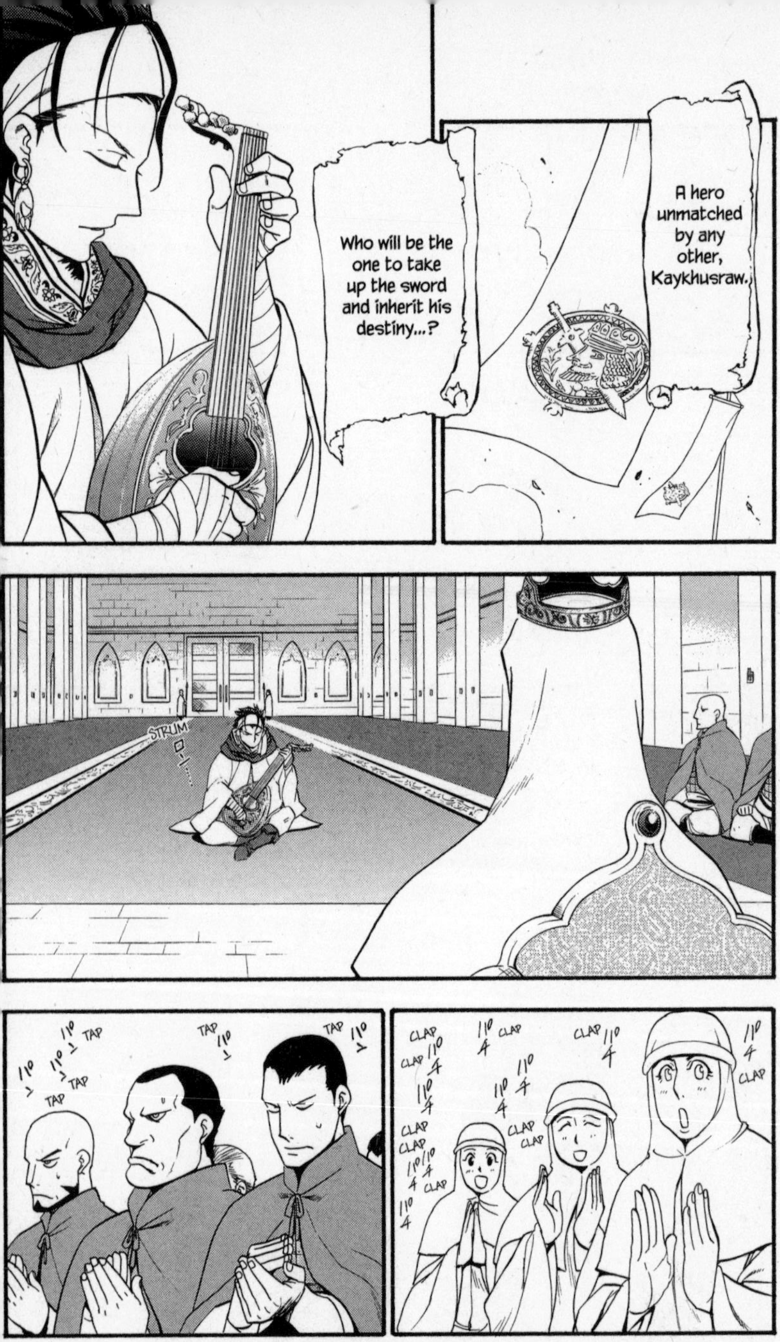
A hero unmatched by any other, Kaykhusraw.
Who will be the one to take up the sword and inherit his destiny...?
STRUM
CLAP CLAP CLAP CLAP CLAP CLAP CLAP CLAP CLAP
TAP TAP TAP TAP TAP

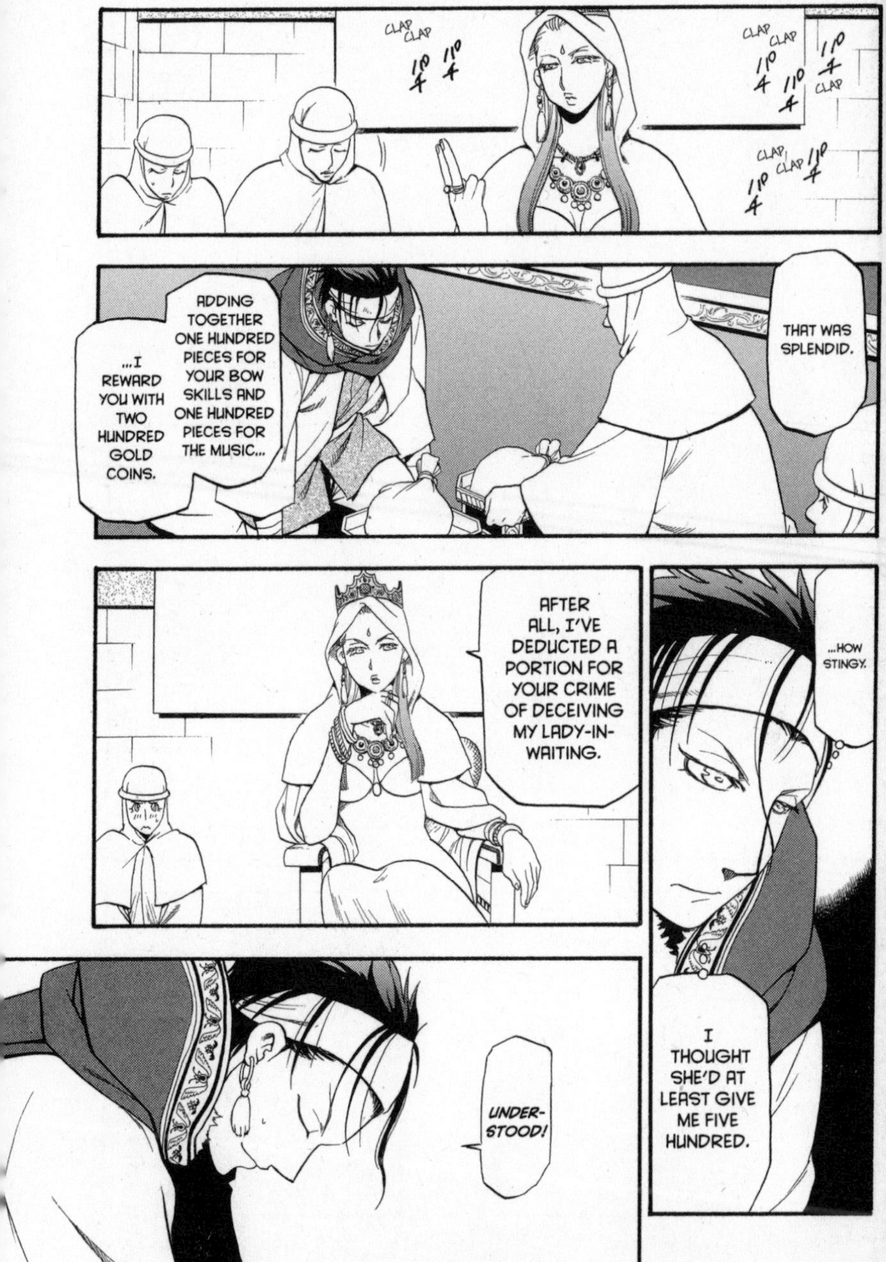
CLAP CLAP
CLAP CLAP
CLAP
CLAP, CLAP
CLAP CLAP
THAT WAS SPLENDID.
ADDING TOGETHER ONE HUNDRED PIECES FOR YOUR BOW SKILLS AND ONE HUNDRED PIECES FOR THE MUSIC...
...I REWARD YOU WITH TWO HUNDRED GOLD COINS.
...HOW STINGY.
I THOUGHT SHE'D AT LEAST GIVE ME FIVE HUNDRED.
AFTER ALL, I'VE DEDUCTED A PORTION FOR YOUR CRIME OF DECEIVING MY LADY-IN-WAITING.
UNDER-STOOD!

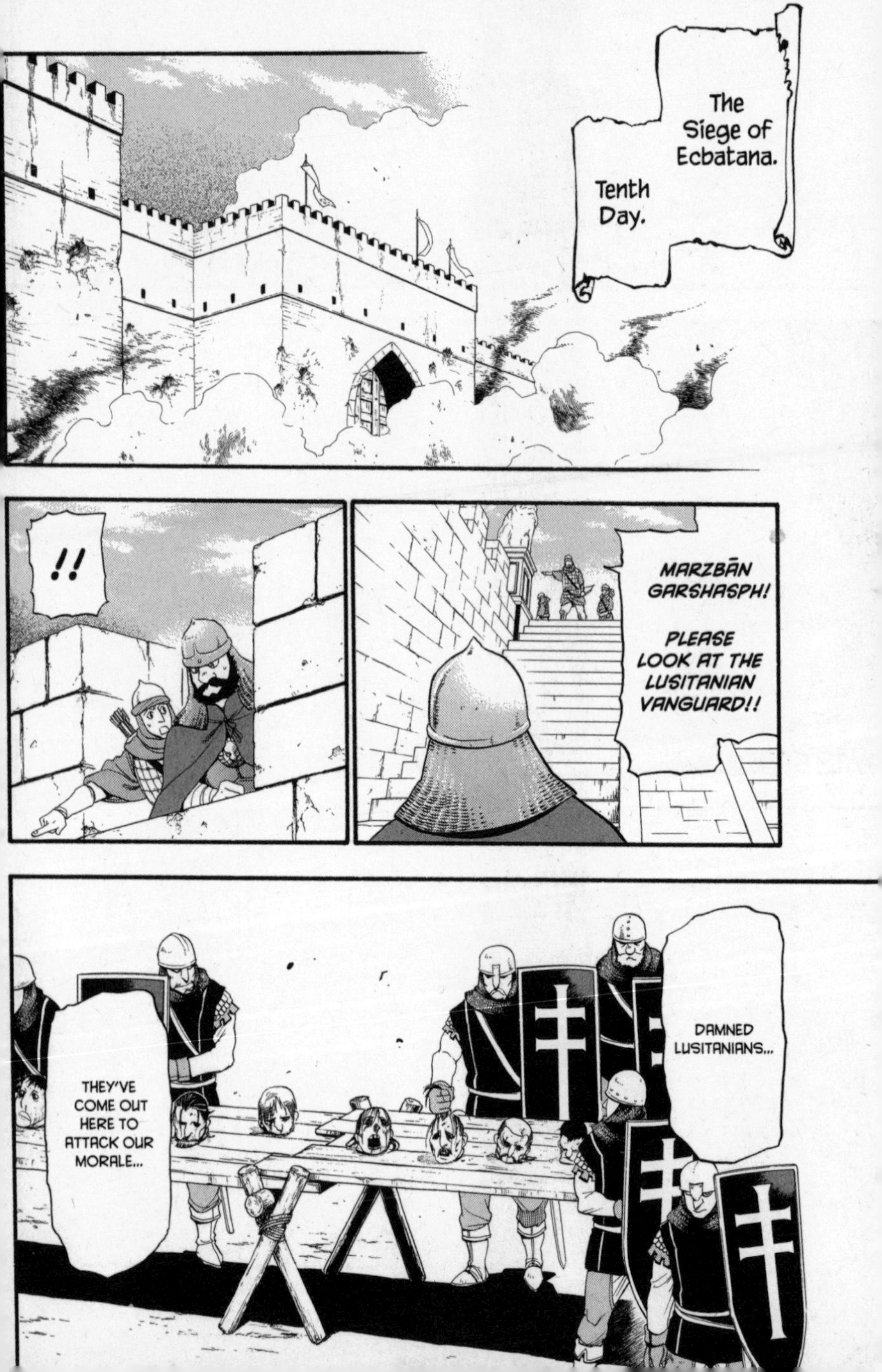
The Siege of Ecbatana.
Tenth Day.
MARZBĀN GARSHASPH!
PLEASE LOOK AT THE LUSITANIAN VANGUARD!!
!!
DAMNED LUSITANIANS...
THEY'VE COME OUT HERE TO ATTACK OUR MORALE...

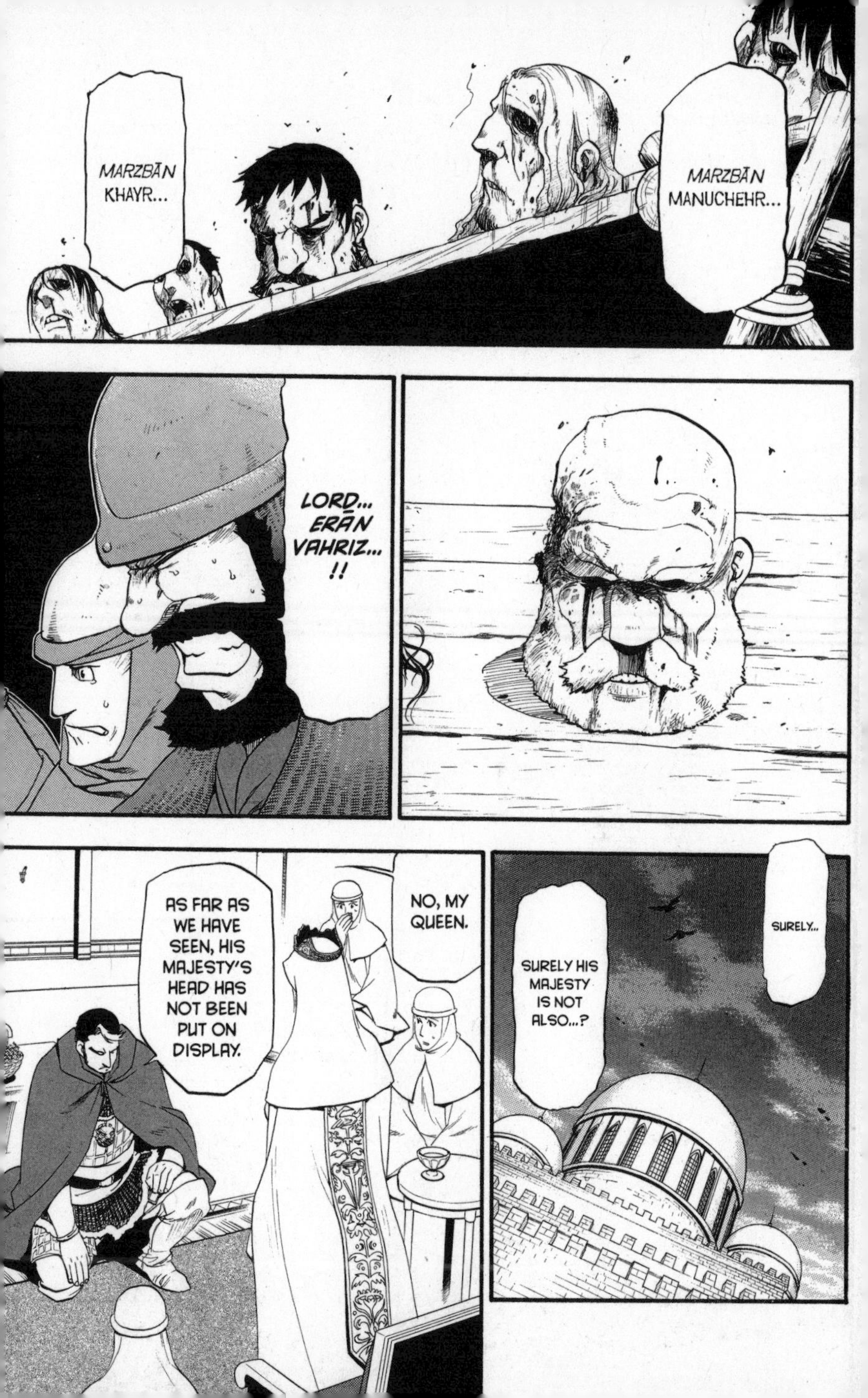
MARZBĀN MANUCHEHR...
MARZBĀN KHAYR...
LORD... ERĀN VAHRIZ... !!
SURELY...
SURELY HIS MAJESTY IS NOT ALSO...?
NO, MY QUEEN.
AS FAR AS WE HAVE SEEN, HIS MAJESTY'S HEAD HAS NOT BEEN PUT ON DISPLAY.

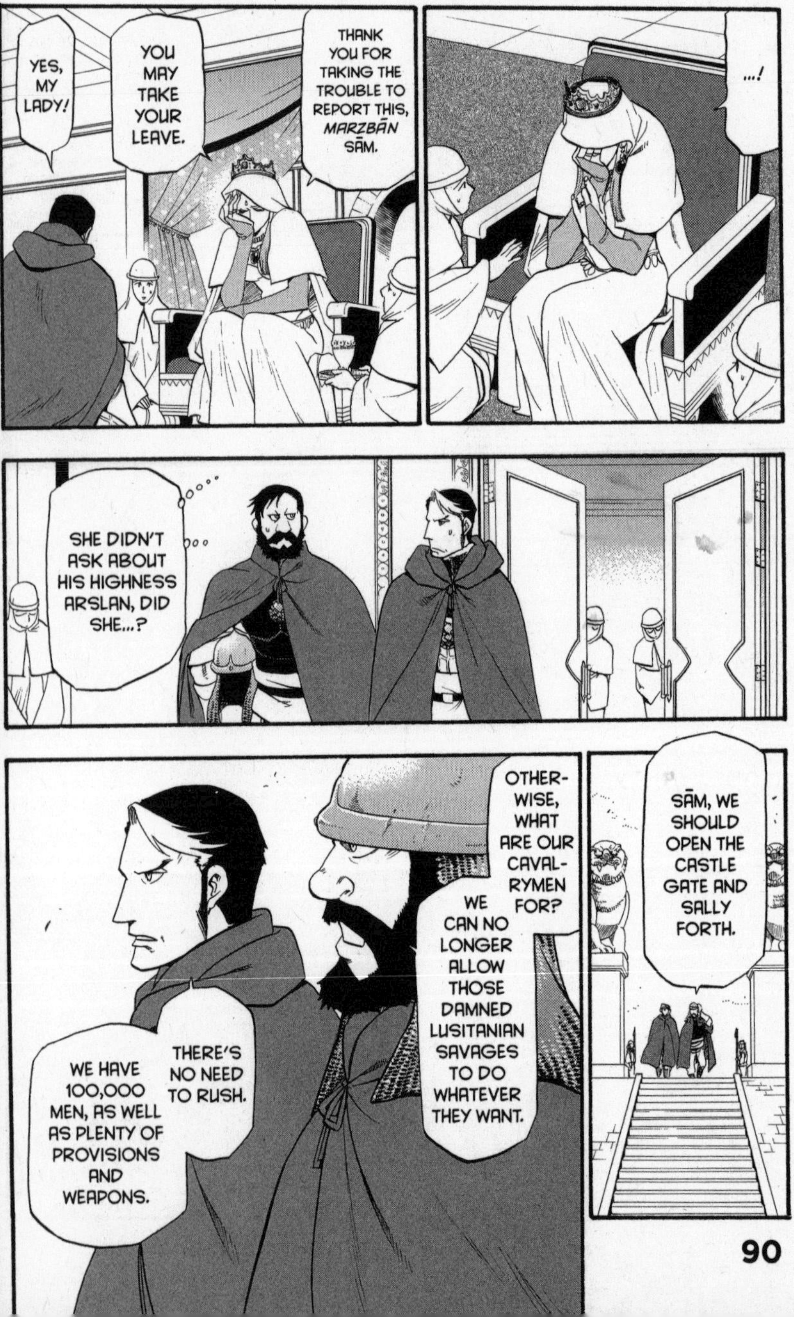
...!
THANK YOU FOR TAKING THE TROUBLE TO REPORT THIS, *MARZBĀN* SĀM.
YOU MAY TAKE YOUR LEAVE.
YES, MY LADY!
SHE DIDN'T ASK ABOUT HIS HIGHNESS ARSLAN, DID SHE...?
SĀM, WE SHOULD OPEN THE CASTLE GATE AND SALLY FORTH.
WE CAN NO LONGER ALLOW THOSE DAMNED LUSITANIAN SAVAGES TO DO WHATEVER THEY WANT.
OTHERWISE, WHAT ARE OUR CAVALRYMEN FOR?
THERE'S NO NEED TO RUSH.
WE HAVE 100,000 MEN, AS WELL AS PLENTY OF PROVISIONS AND WEAPONS.

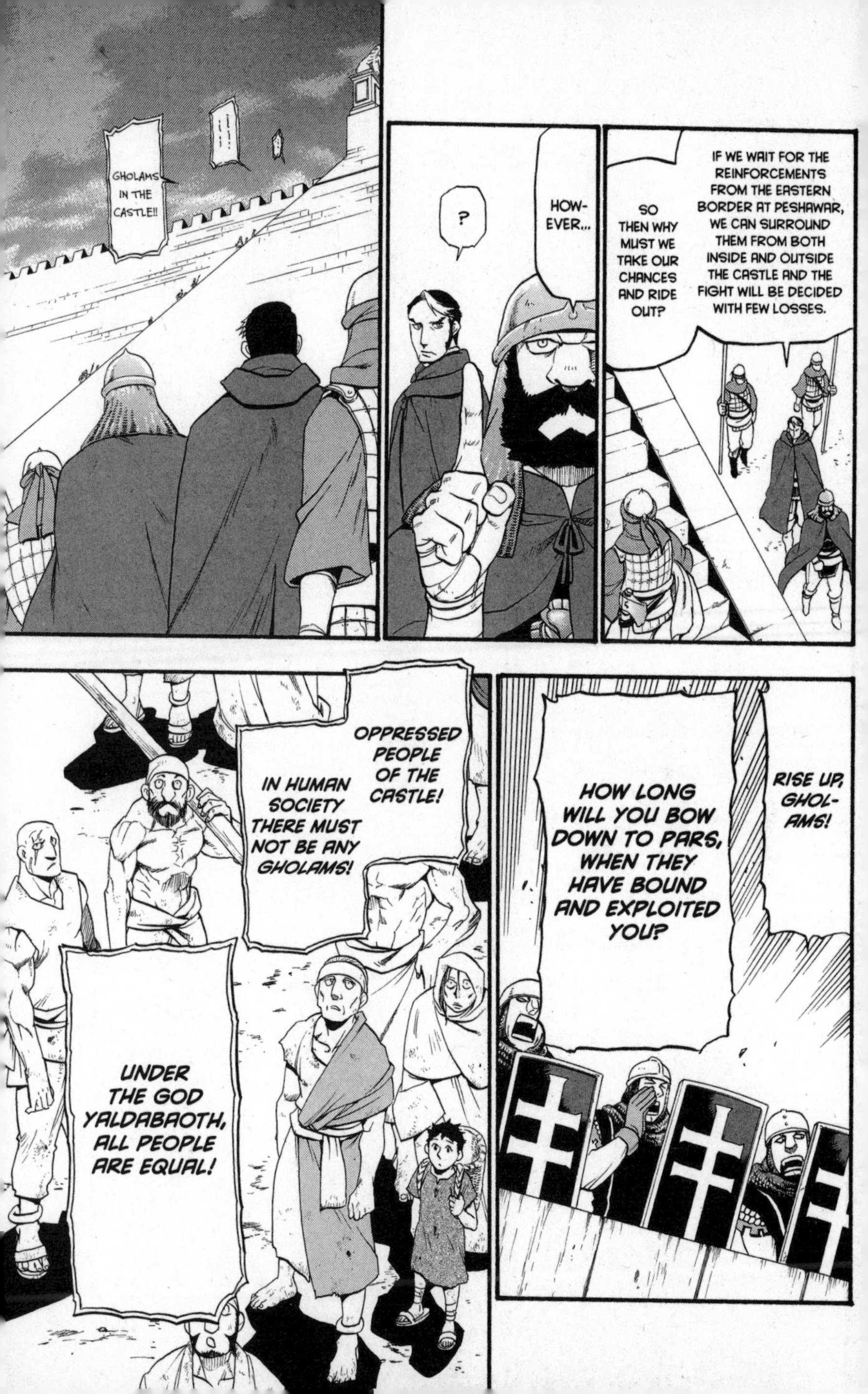
IF WE WAIT FOR THE REINFORCEMENTS FROM THE EASTERN BORDER AT PESHAWAR, WE CAN SURROUND THEM FROM BOTH INSIDE AND OUTSIDE THE CASTLE AND THE FIGHT WILL BE DECIDED WITH FEW LOSSES.
SO THEN WHY MUST WE TAKE OUR CHANCES AND RIDE OUT?
HOW-EVER...
?
GHOLAMS IN THE CASTLE!!
RISE UP, GHOL-AMS!
HOW LONG WILL YOU BOW DOWN TO PARS, WHEN THEY HAVE BOUND AND EXPLOITED YOU?
OPPRESSED PEOPLE OF THE CASTLE!
IN HUMAN SOCIETY THERE MUST NOT BE ANY GHOLAMS!
UNDER THE GOD YALDABAOTH, ALL PEOPLE ARE EQUAL!

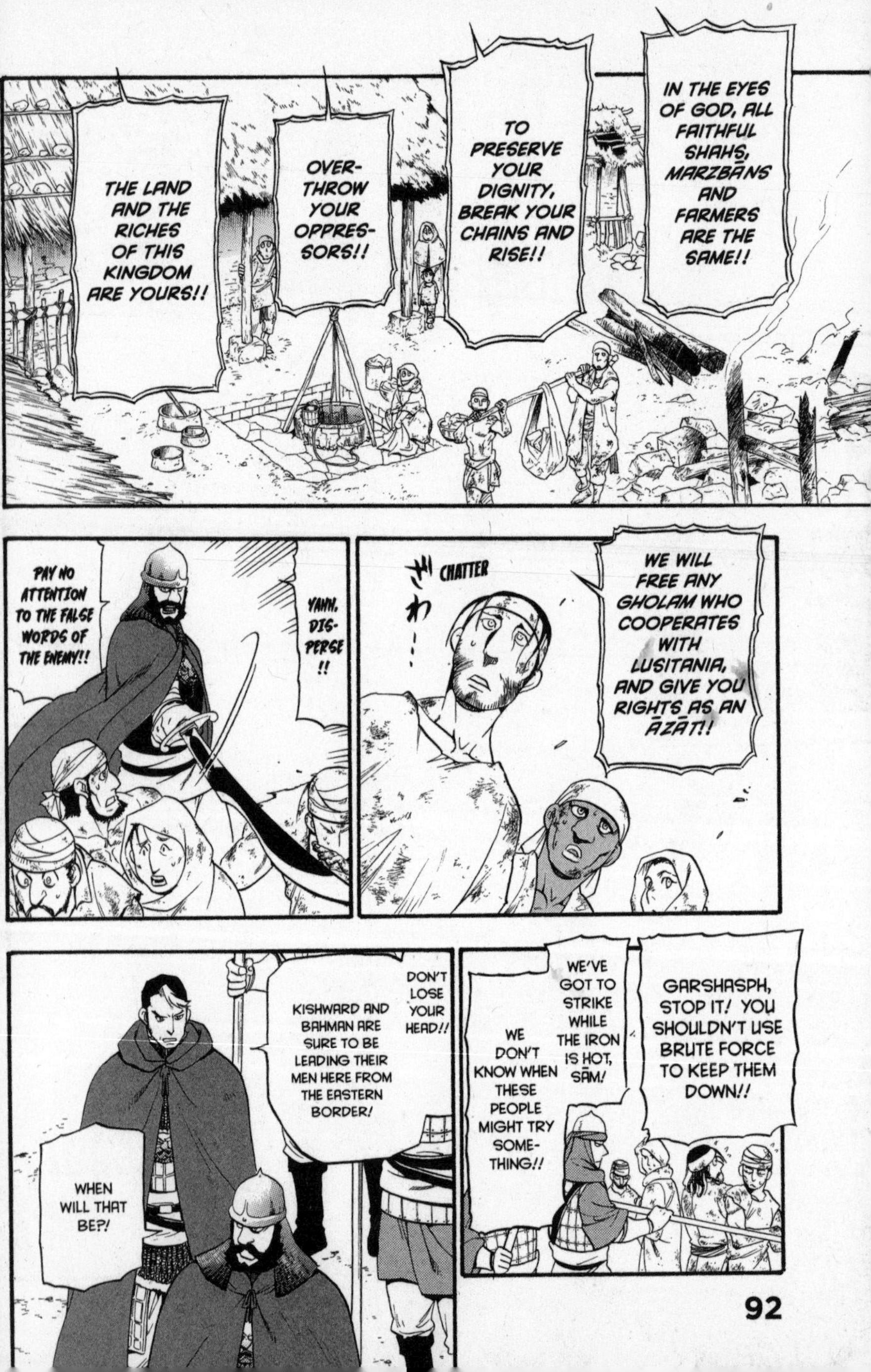
IN THE EYES OF GOD, ALL FAITHFUL SHAHS, MARZBĀNS AND FARMERS ARE THE SAME!!
TO PRESERVE YOUR DIGNITY, BREAK YOUR CHAINS AND RISE!!
OVER-THROW YOUR OPPRES-SORS!!
THE LAND AND THE RICHES OF THIS KINGDOM ARE YOURS!!
WE WILL FREE ANY GHOLAM WHO COOPERATES WITH LUSITANIA, AND GIVE YOU RIGHTS AS AN ĀZĀT!!
ざわ…
CHATTER
YAHN, DIS-PERSE!!
PAY NO ATTENTION TO THE FALSE WORDS OF THE ENEMY!!
GARSHASPH, STOP IT! YOU SHOULDN'T USE BRUTE FORCE TO KEEP THEM DOWN!!
WE'VE GOT TO STRIKE WHILE THE IRON IS HOT, SĀM!
WE DON'T KNOW WHEN THESE PEOPLE MIGHT TRY SOME-THING!!
DON'T LOSE YOUR HEAD!!
KISHWARD AND BAHMAN ARE SURE TO BE LEADING THEIR MEN HERE FROM THE EASTERN BORDER!
WHEN WILL THAT BE?!

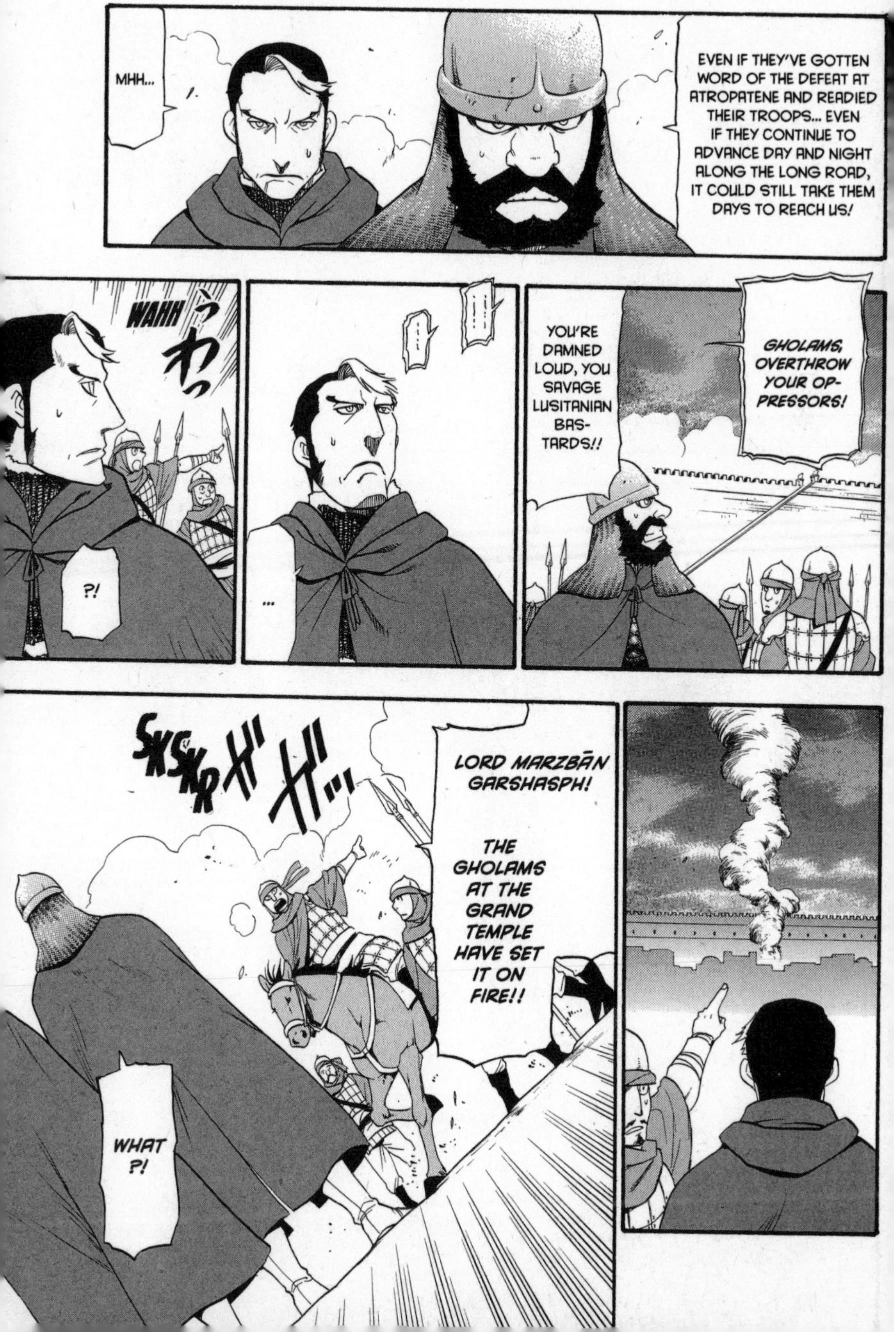
EVEN IF THEY'VE GOTTEN WORD OF THE DEFEAT AT ATROPATENE AND READIED THEIR TROOPS... EVEN IF THEY CONTINUE TO ADVANCE DAY AND NIGHT ALONG THE LONG ROAD, IT COULD STILL TAKE THEM DAYS TO REACH US!
MHH...
GHOLAMS, OVERTHROW YOUR OPPRESSORS!
YOU'RE DAMNED LOUD, YOU SAVAGE LUSITANIAN BASTARDS!!
...
WAHH
?!
LORD MARZBĀN GARSHASPH!
THE GHOLAMS AT THE GRAND TEMPLE HAVE SET IT ON FIRE!!
SKSKR
WHAT?!

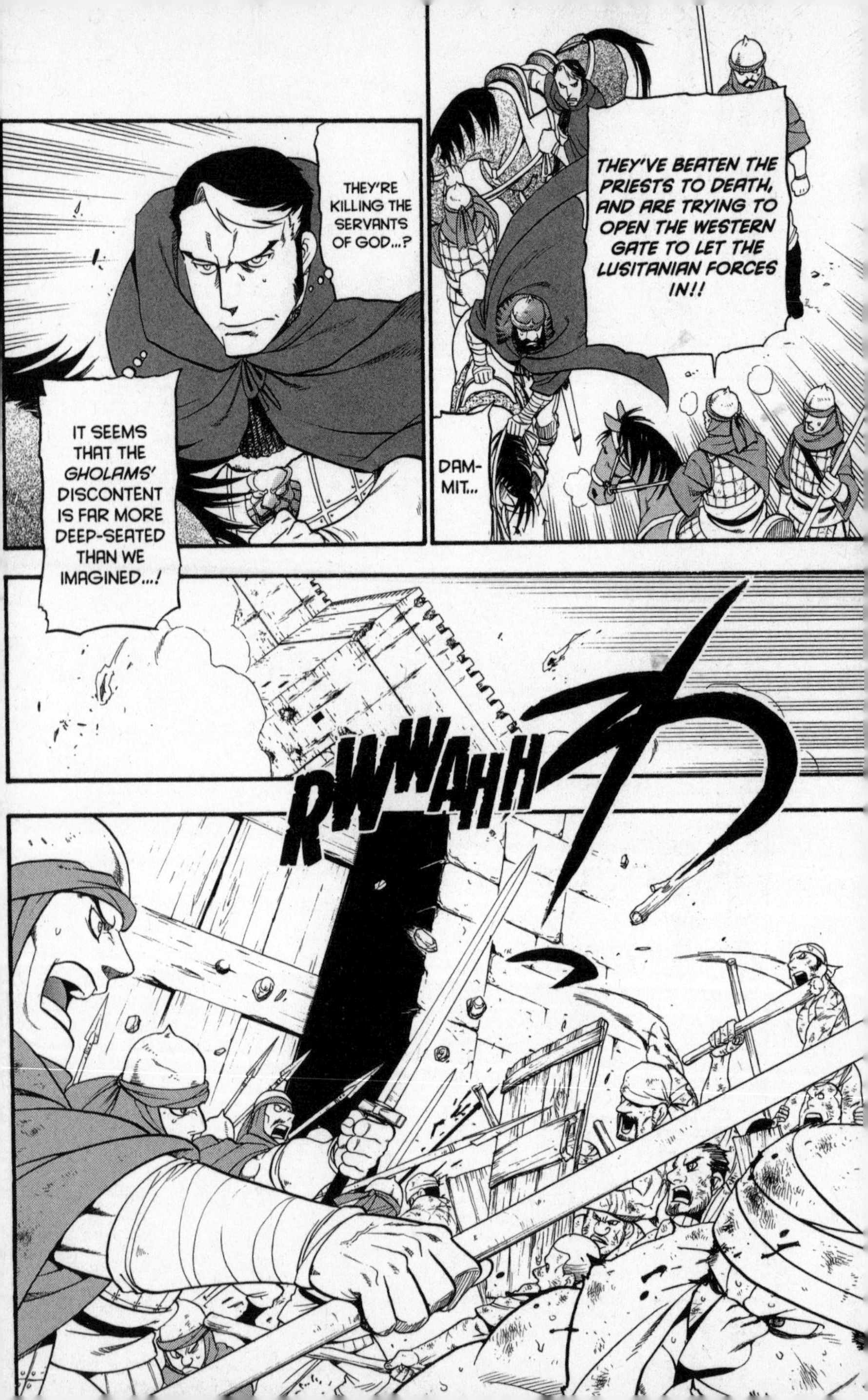

THEY'VE BEATEN THE PRIESTS TO DEATH, AND ARE TRYING TO OPEN THE WESTERN GATE TO LET THE LUSITANIAN FORCES IN!!
DAM-MIT...
THEY'RE KILLING THE SERVANTS OF GOD...?
IT SEEMS THAT THE *GHOLAMS'* DISCONTENT IS FAR MORE DEEP-SEATED THAN WE IMAGINED...!
RWWAHH

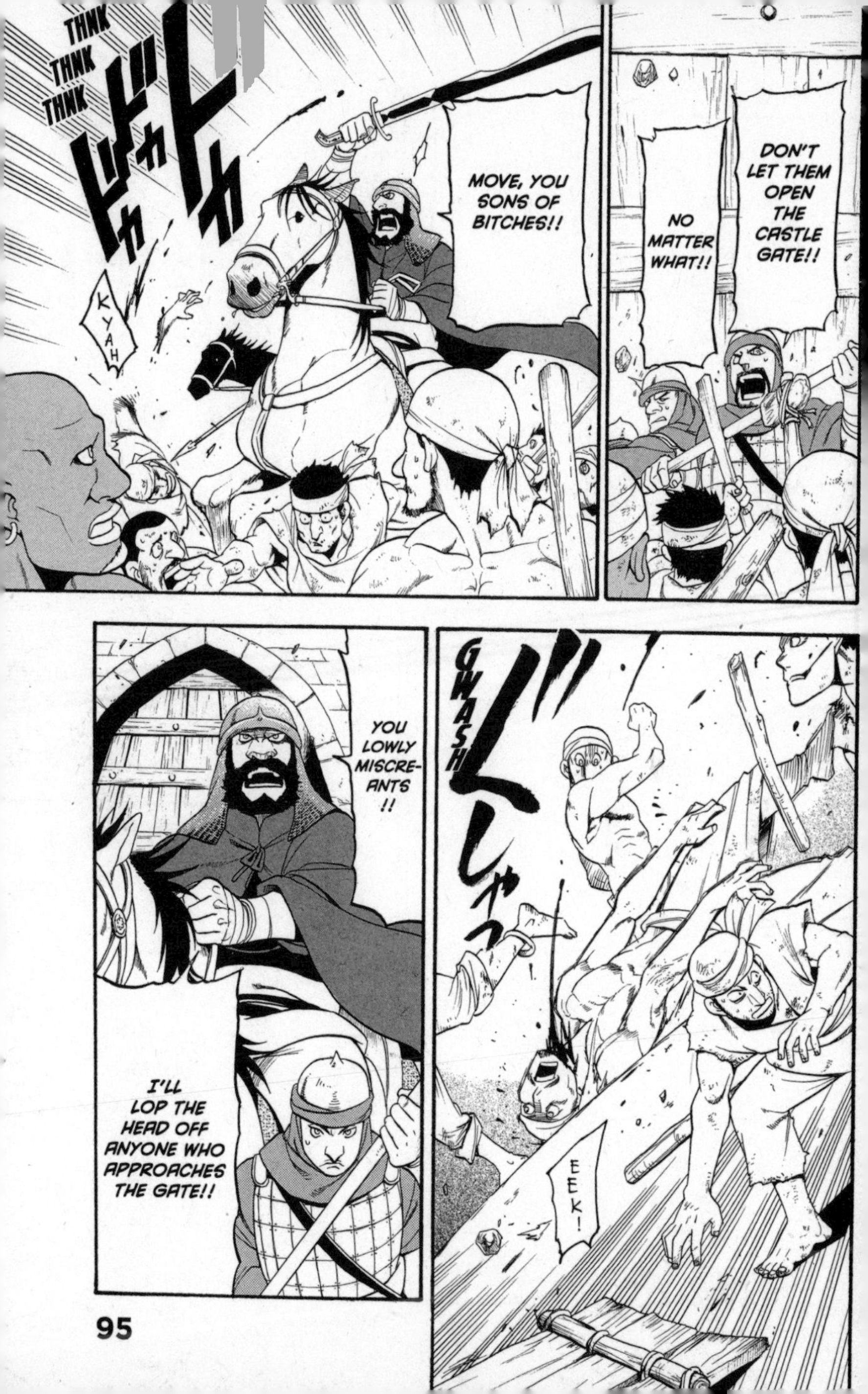
DON'T LET THEM OPEN THE CASTLE GATE!!
NO MATTER WHAT!!
MOVE, YOU SONS OF BITCHES!!
THNK THNK THNK
ドカドカ
KYAH
GWASH
ドしゃっ
EEK!
YOU LOWLY MISCREANTS!!
I'LL LOP THE HEAD OFF ANYONE WHO APPROACHES THE GATE!!

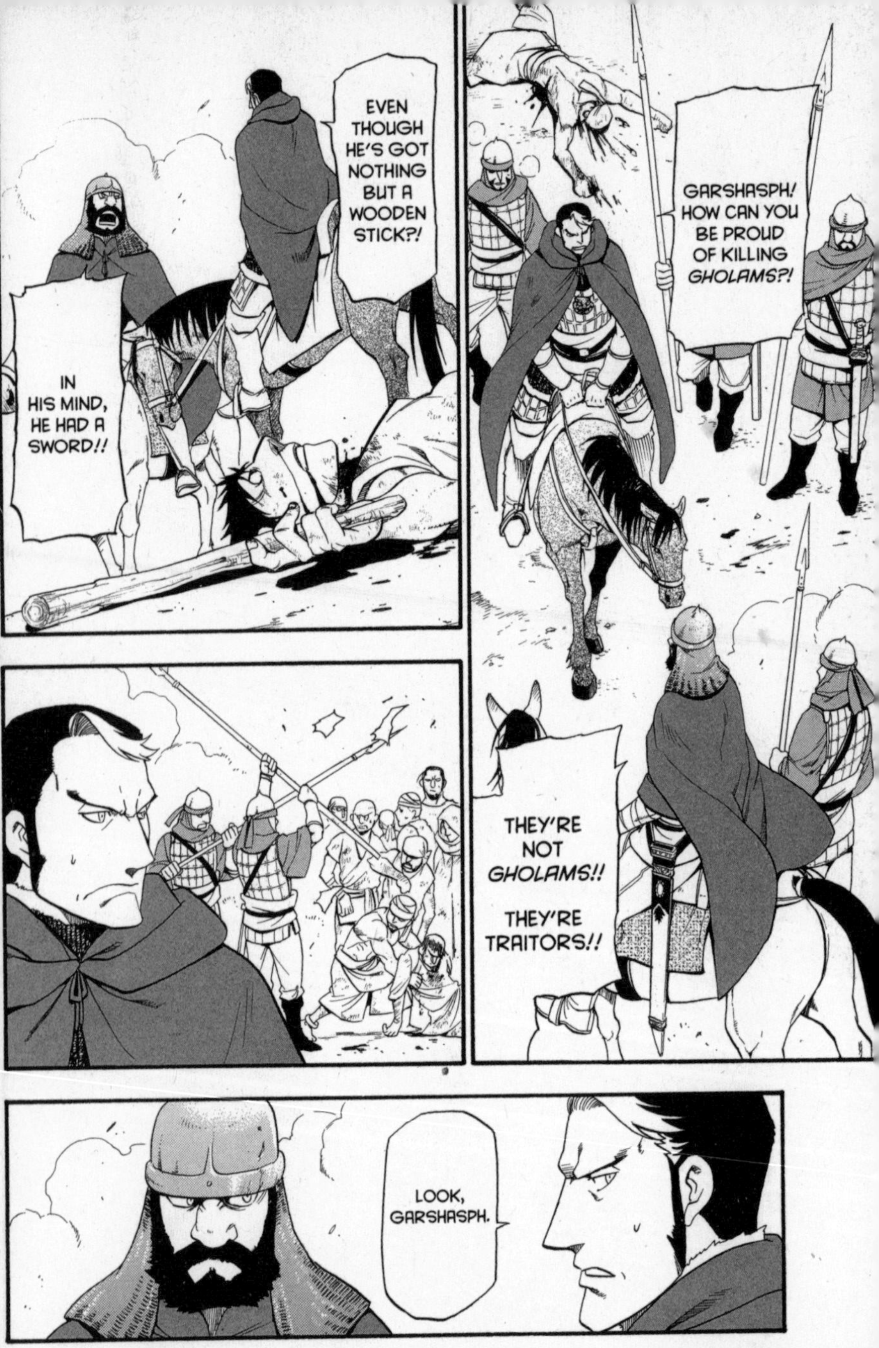
GARSHASPH! HOW CAN YOU BE PROUD OF KILLING *GHOLAMS?!*
THEY'RE NOT *GHOLAMS!!* THEY'RE TRAITORS!!
EVEN THOUGH HE'S GOT NOTHING BUT A WOODEN STICK?!
IN HIS MIND, HE HAD A SWORD!!
LOOK, GARSHASPH.

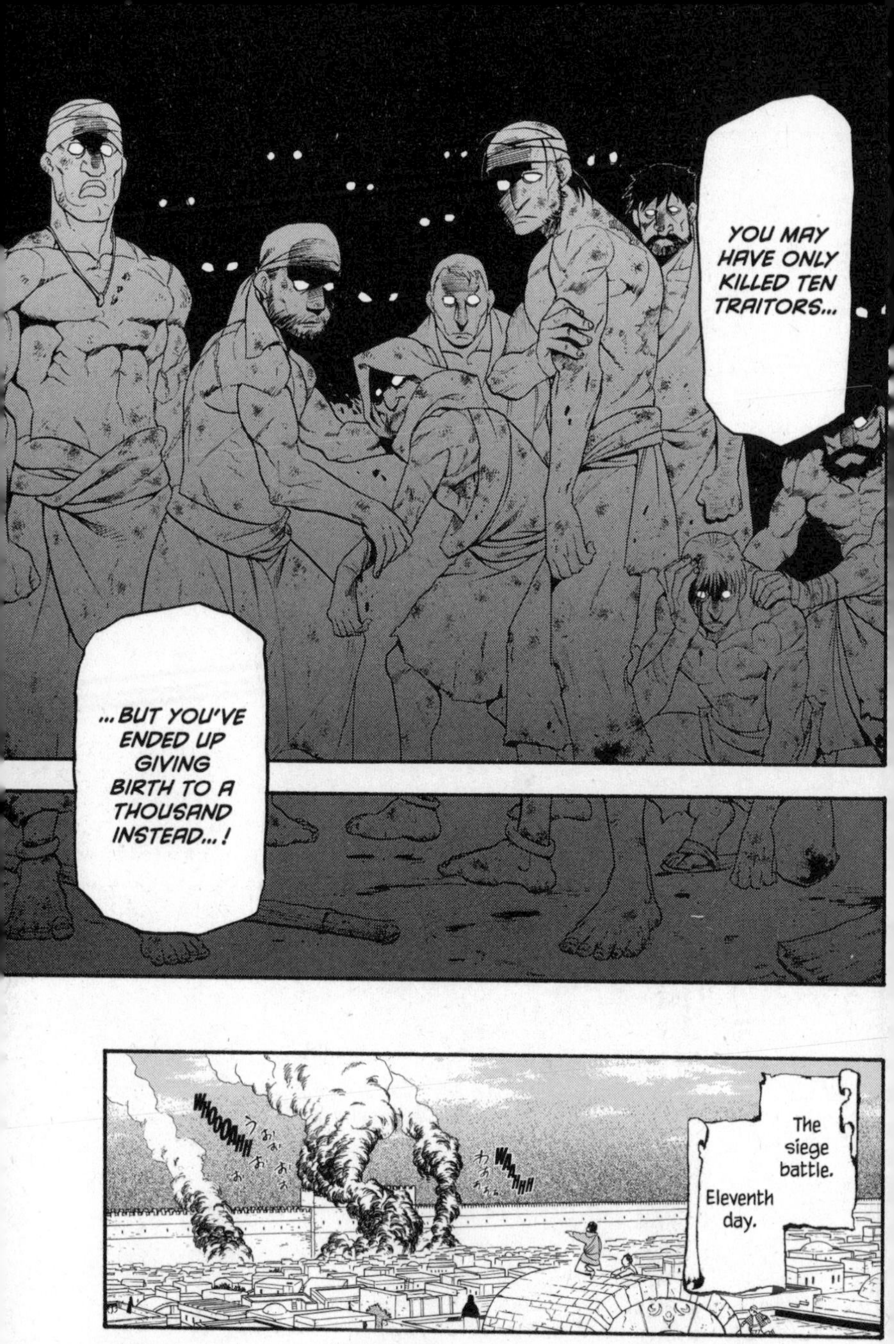
YOU MAY HAVE ONLY KILLED TEN TRAITORS...
...BUT YOU'VE ENDED UP GIVING BIRTH TO A THOUSAND INSTEAD...!
The siege battle.
Eleventh day.
WAAHHH
WHOOOAHH

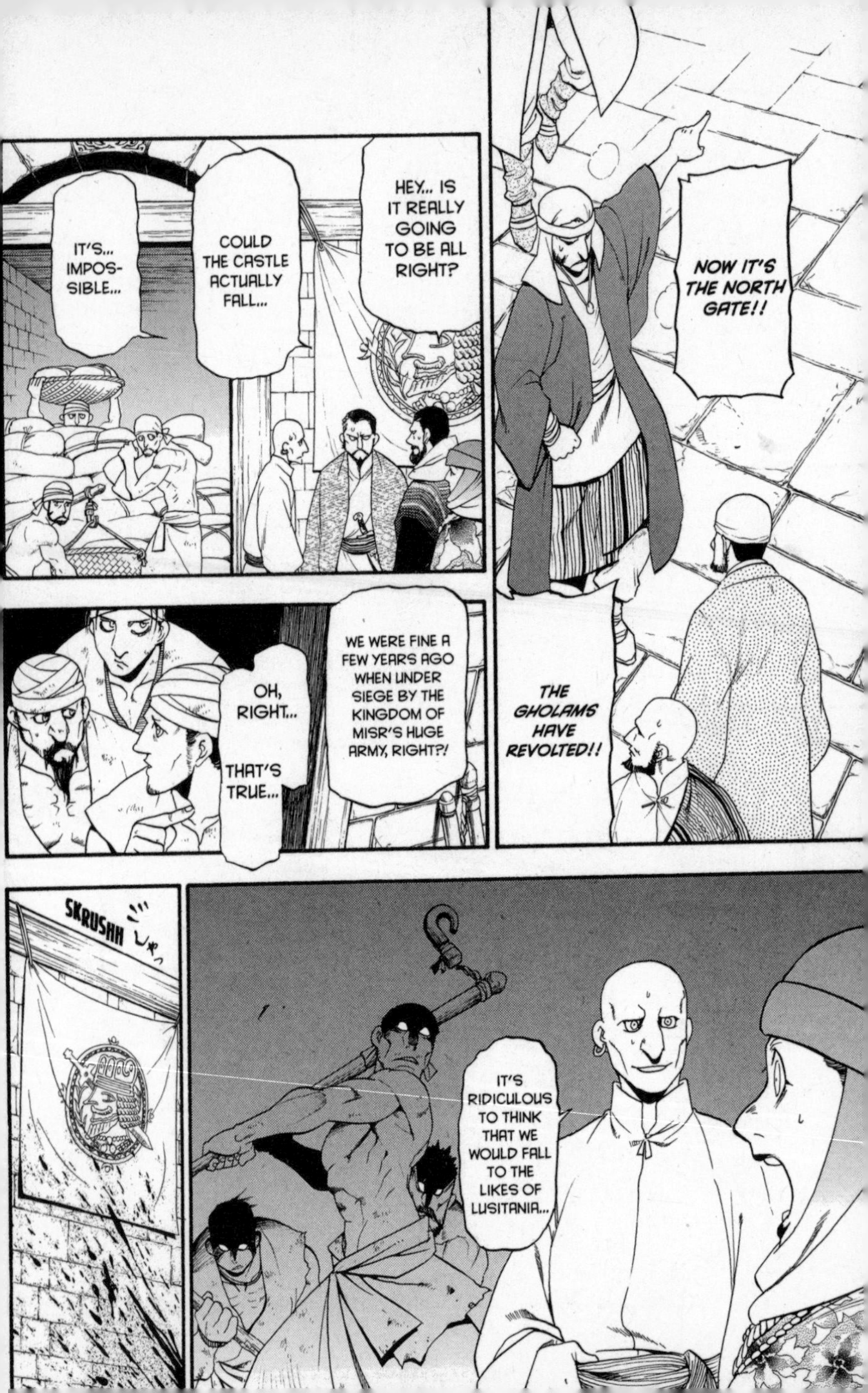
NOW IT'S THE NORTH GATE!!
THE GHOLAMS HAVE REVOLTED!!
HEY... IS IT REALLY GOING TO BE ALL RIGHT?
COULD THE CASTLE ACTUALLY FALL...
IT'S... IMPOSSIBLE...
WE WERE FINE A FEW YEARS AGO WHEN UNDER SIEGE BY THE KINGDOM OF MISR'S HUGE ARMY, RIGHT?!
OH, RIGHT...
THAT'S TRUE...
IT'S RIDICULOUS TO THINK THAT WE WOULD FALL TO THE LIKES OF LUSITANIA...
SKRUSHH

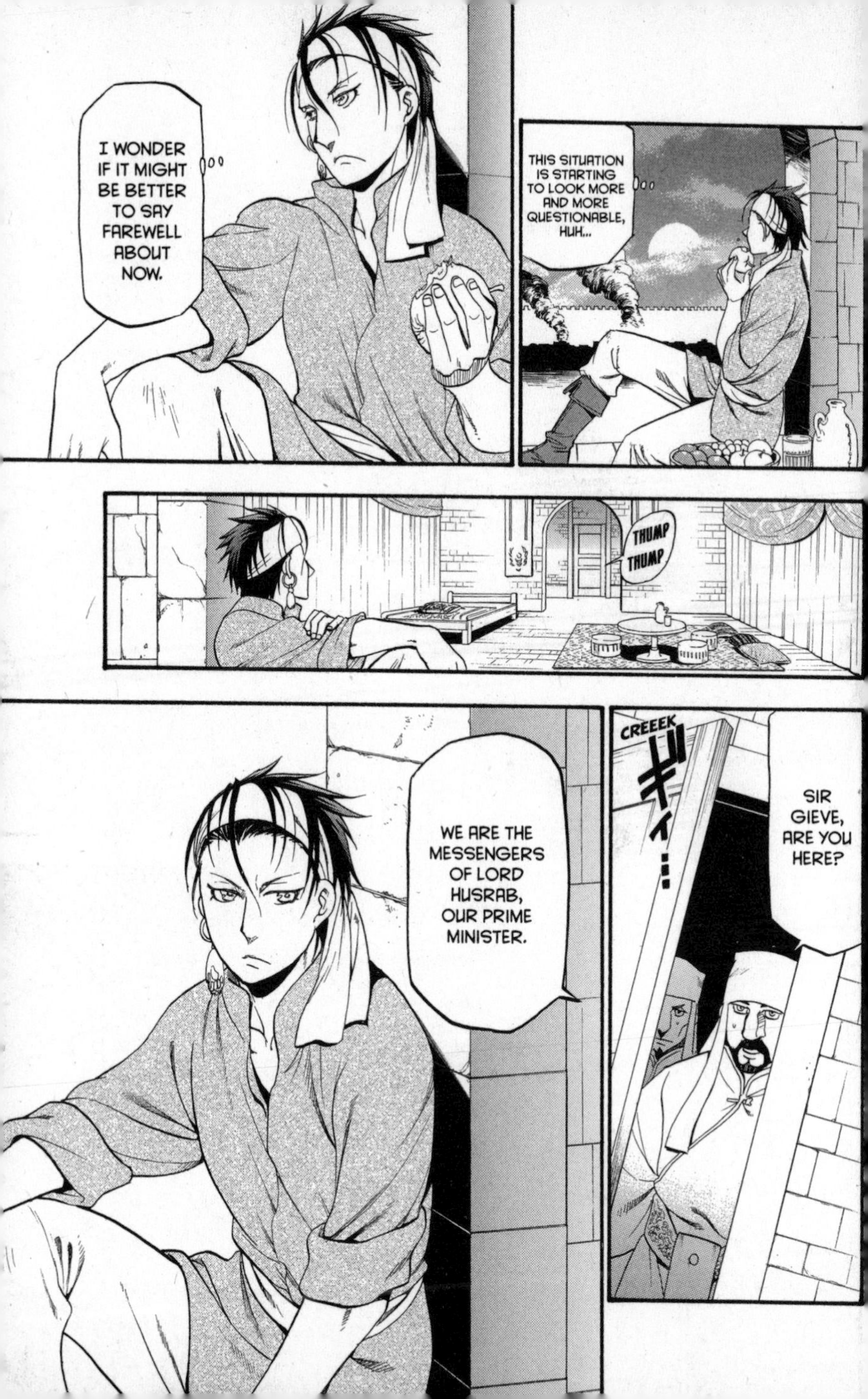
THIS SITUATION IS STARTING TO LOOK MORE AND MORE QUESTIONABLE, HUH...
I WONDER IF IT MIGHT BE BETTER TO SAY FAREWELL ABOUT NOW.
THUMP THUMP
CREEEK
SIR GIEVE, ARE YOU HERE?
WE ARE THE MESSENGERS OF LORD HUSRAB, OUR PRIME MINISTER.

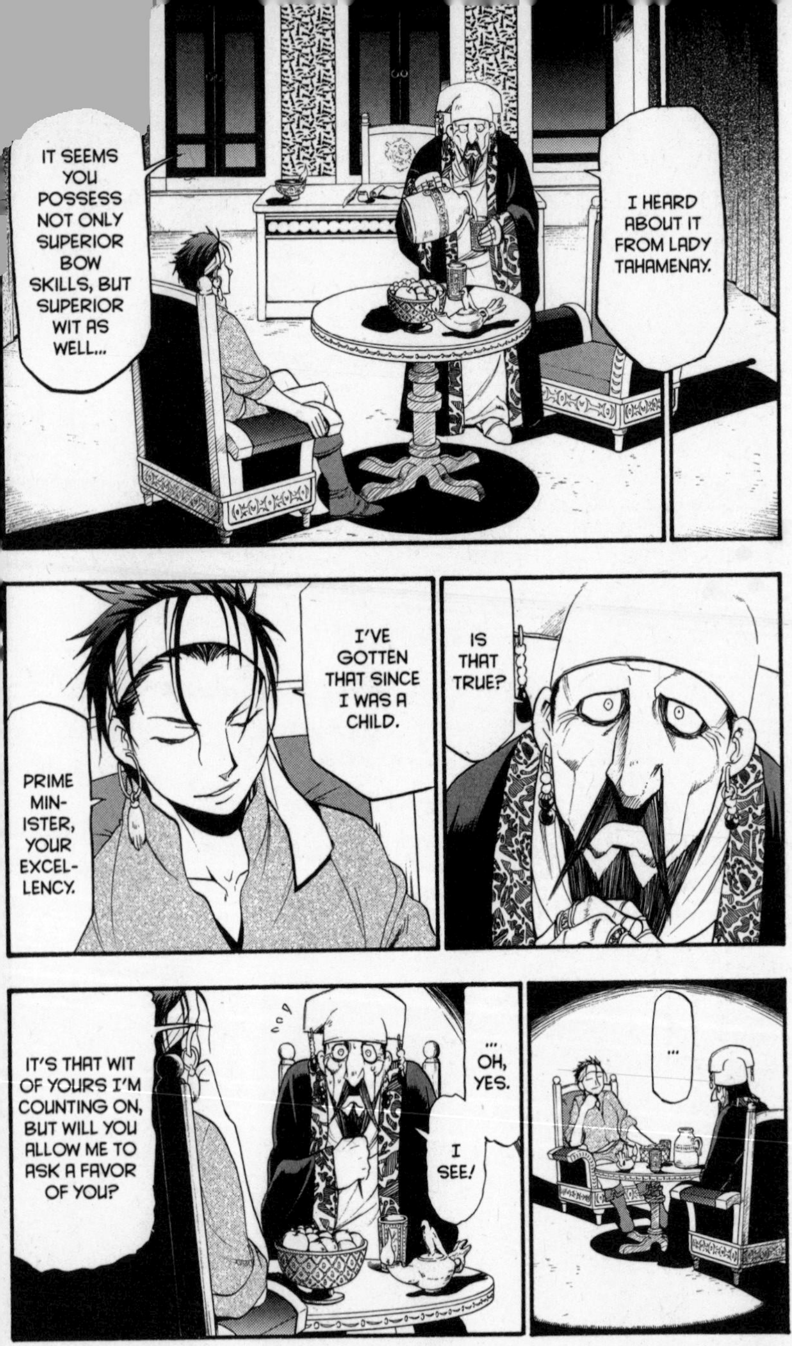
I HEARD ABOUT IT FROM LADY TAHAMENAY.
IT SEEMS YOU POSSESS NOT ONLY SUPERIOR BOW SKILLS, BUT SUPERIOR WIT AS WELL...
IS THAT TRUE?
I'VE GOTTEN THAT SINCE I WAS A CHILD.
PRIME MIN-ISTER, YOUR EXCEL-LENCY.
...
...OH, YES.
I SEE!
IT'S THAT WIT OF YOURS I'M COUNTING ON, BUT WILL YOU ALLOW ME TO ASK A FAVOR OF YOU?

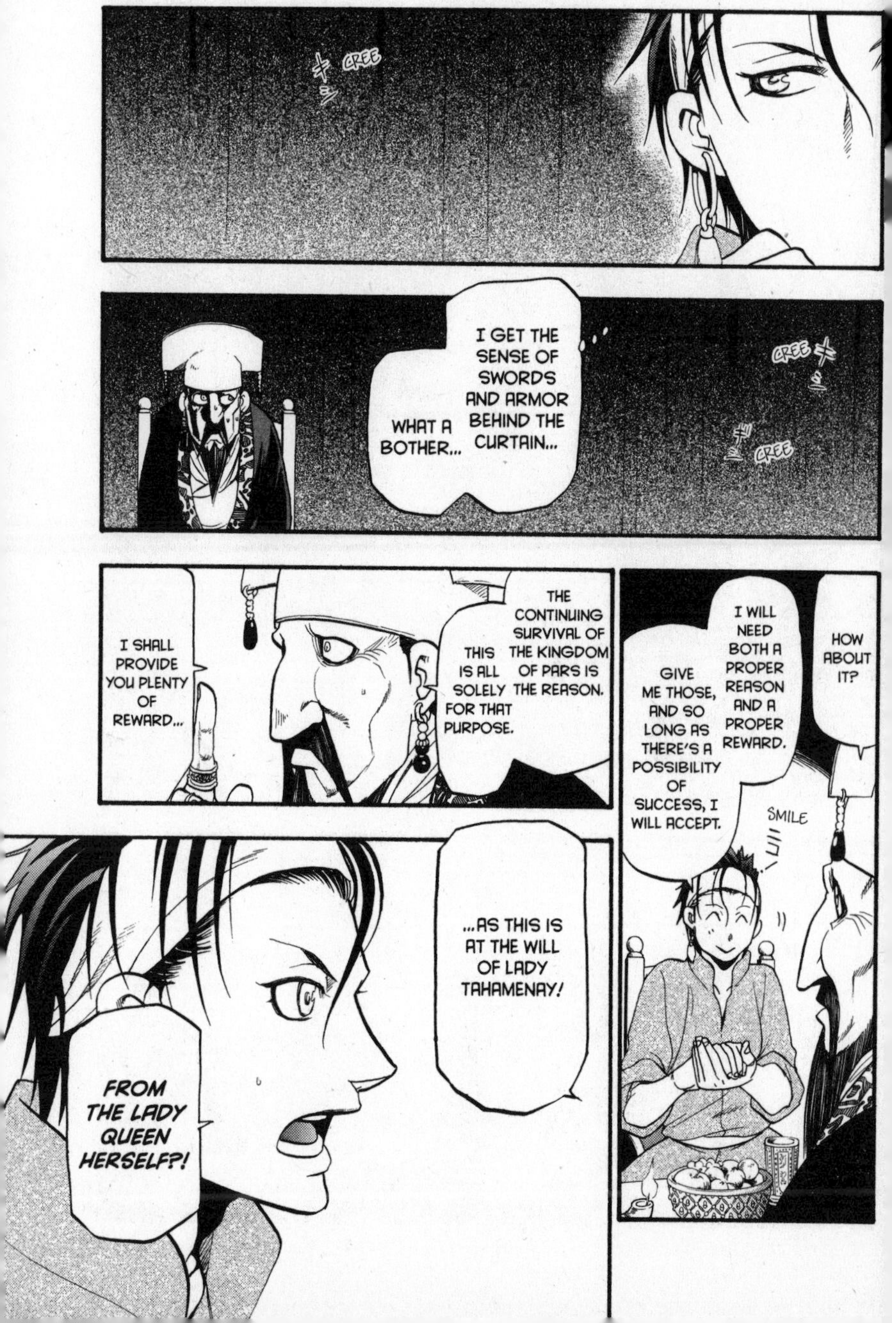
CREE
CREE
CREE
I GET THE SENSE OF SWORDS AND ARMOR BEHIND THE CURTAIN...
WHAT A BOTHER...
HOW ABOUT IT?
I WILL NEED BOTH A PROPER REASON AND A PROPER REWARD.
GIVE ME THOSE, AND SO LONG AS THERE'S A POSSIBILITY OF SUCCESS, I WILL ACCEPT.
SMILE
THE CONTINUING SURVIVAL OF THE KINGDOM OF PARS IS THE REASON.
THIS IS ALL SOLELY FOR THAT PURPOSE.
I SHALL PROVIDE YOU PLENTY OF REWARD...
...AS THIS IS AT THE WILL OF LADY TAHAMENAY!
FROM THE LADY QUEEN HERSELF?!

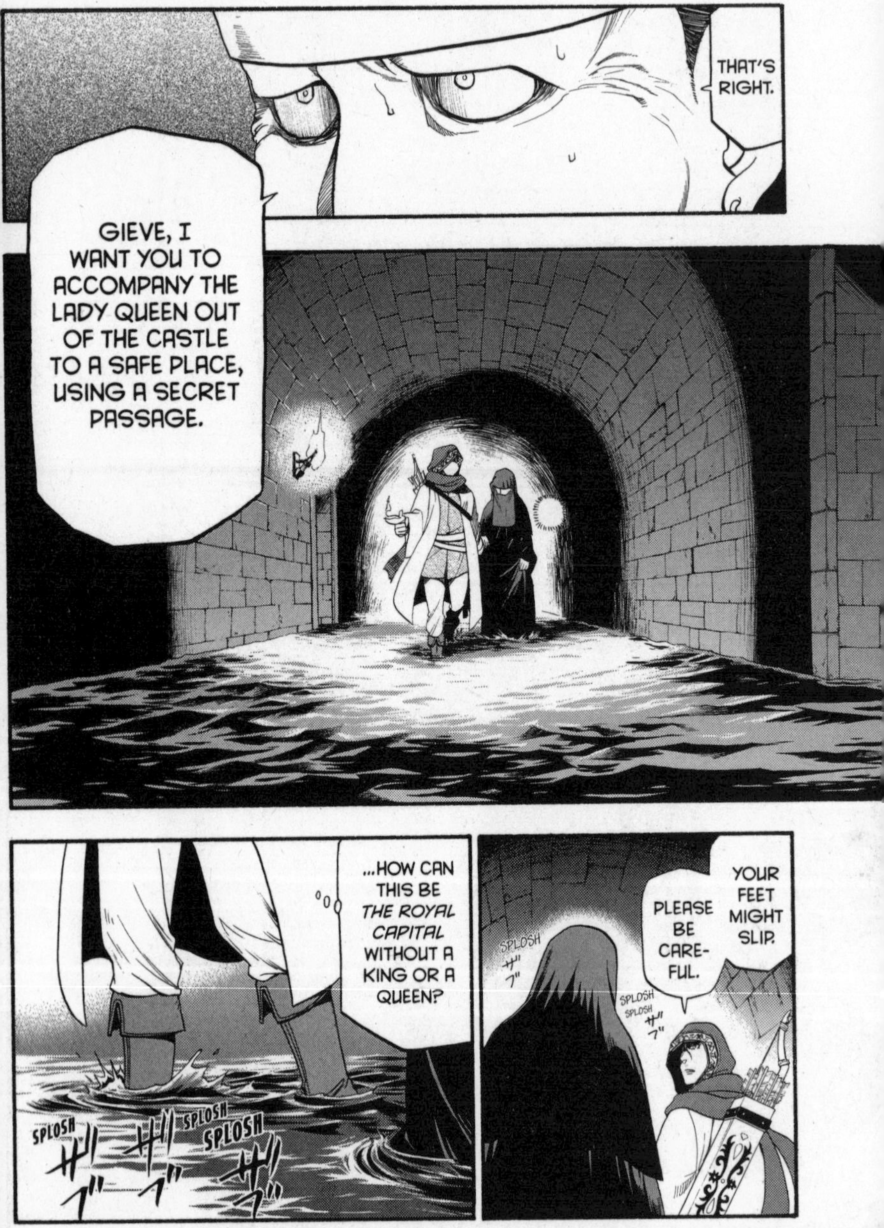

THAT'S RIGHT.
GIEVE, I WANT YOU TO ACCOMPANY THE LADY QUEEN OUT OF THE CASTLE TO A SAFE PLACE, USING A SECRET PASSAGE.
YOUR FEET MIGHT SLIP.
PLEASE BE CARE-FUL.
SPLOSH
SPLOSH SPLOSH
...HOW CAN THIS BE *THE ROYAL CAPITAL* WITHOUT A KING OR A QUEEN?
SPLOSH
SPLOSH
SPLOSH

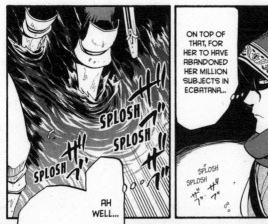

ON TOP OF THAT, FOR HER TO HAVE ABANDONED HER MILLION SUBJECTS IN ECBATANA...

SPLOSH
SPLOSH
SPLOSH

SPLOSH
SPLOSH

AH WELL...

AREN'T THERE PROPER KINGS ANYWHERE...?

THE HEROIC LEGEND OF
ARSLAN

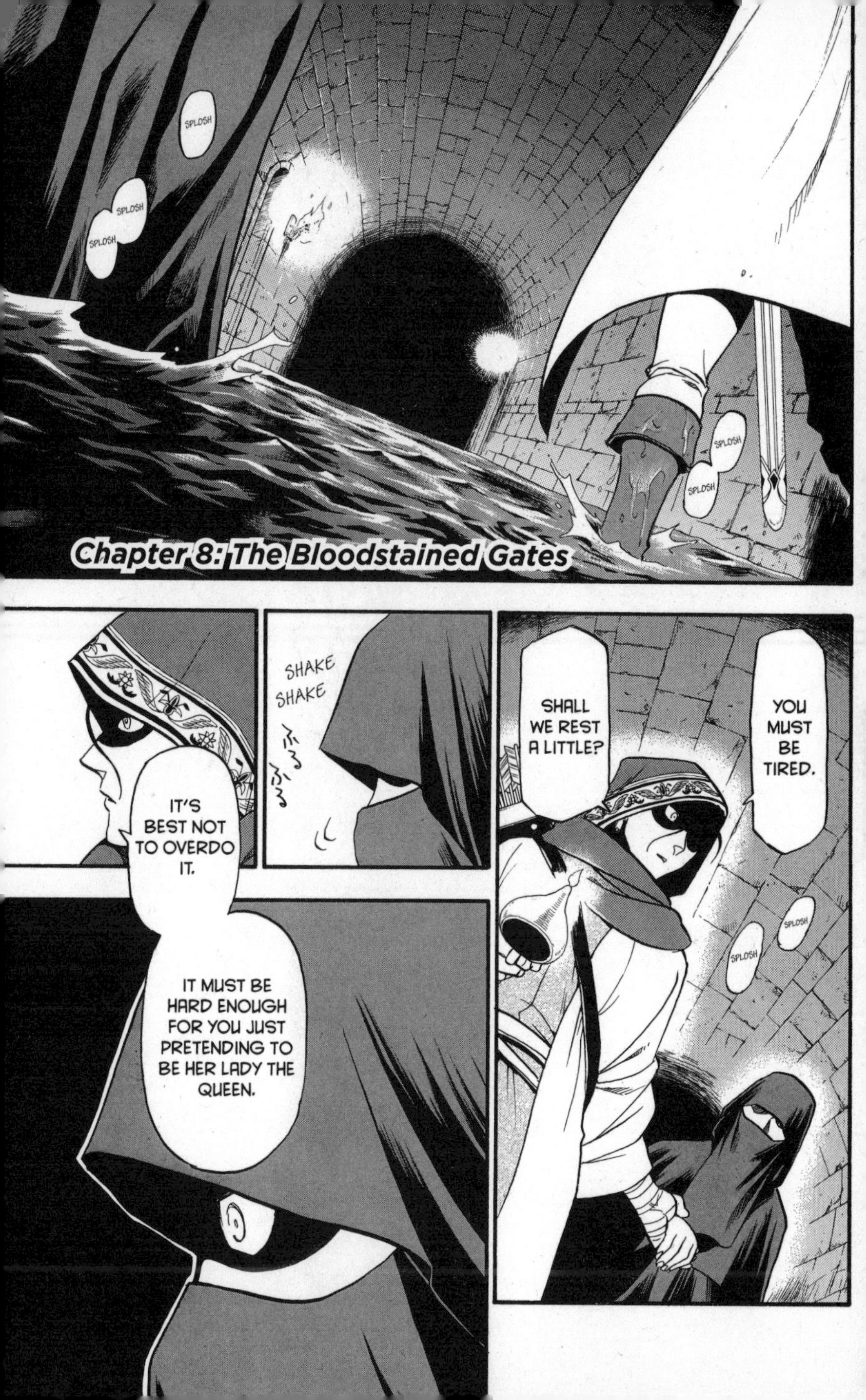
SPLOSH
SPLOSH
SPLOSH
SPLOSH
SPLOSH
Chapter 8: The Bloodstained Gates
YOU MUST BE TIRED.
SHALL WE REST A LITTLE?
SPLOSH
SPLOSH
SHAKE SHAKE
ぶるぶる
IT'S BEST NOT TO OVERDO IT.
IT MUST BE HARD ENOUGH FOR YOU JUST PRETENDING TO BE HER LADY THE QUEEN.

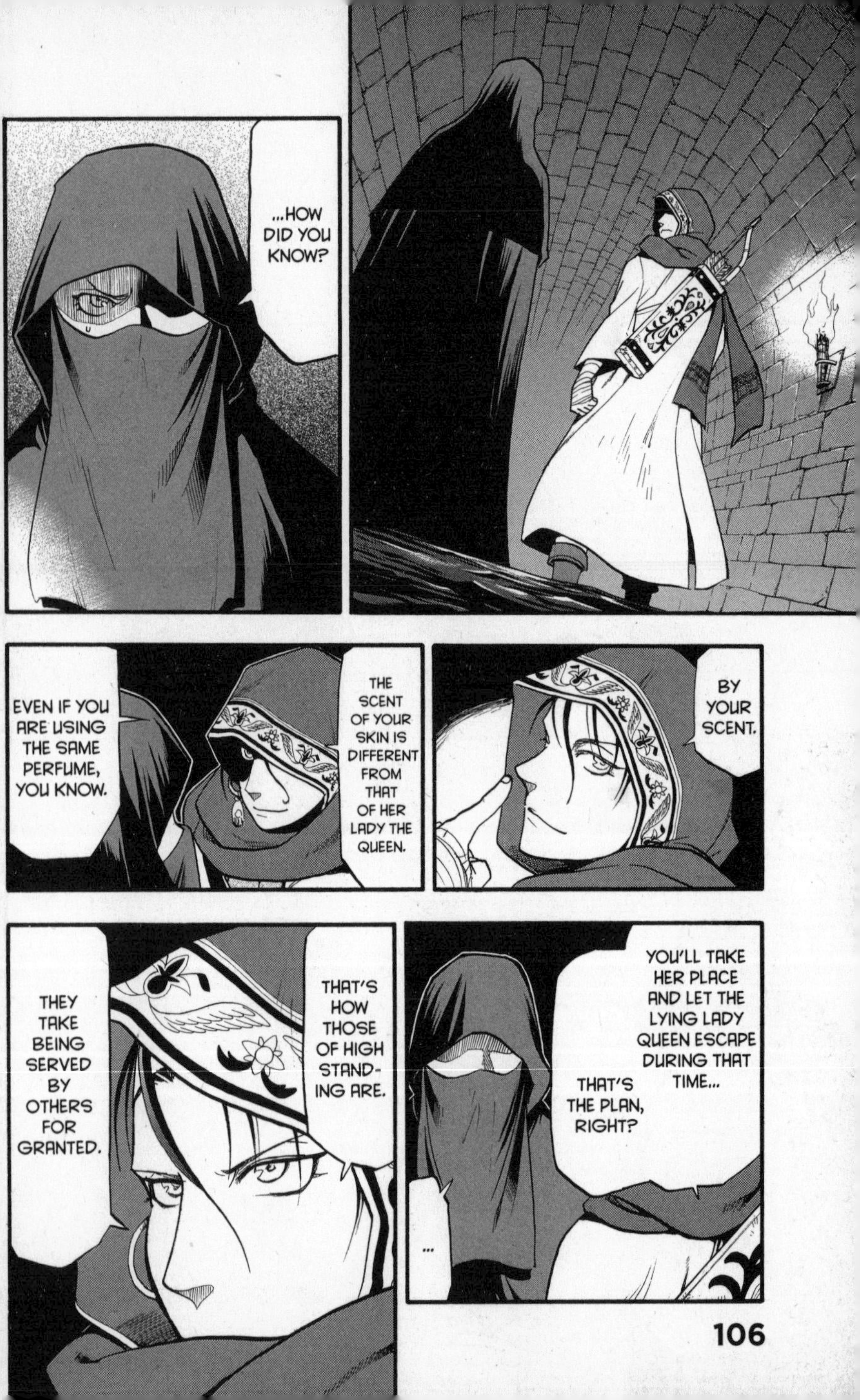
...HOW DID YOU KNOW?
BY YOUR SCENT.
THE SCENT OF YOUR SKIN IS DIFFERENT FROM THAT OF HER LADY THE QUEEN.
EVEN IF YOU ARE USING THE SAME PERFUME, YOU KNOW.
YOU'LL TAKE HER PLACE AND LET THE LYING LADY QUEEN ESCAPE DURING THAT TIME...
THAT'S THE PLAN, RIGHT?
...
THAT'S HOW THOSE OF HIGH STANDING ARE.
THEY TAKE BEING SERVED BY OTHERS FOR GRANTED.

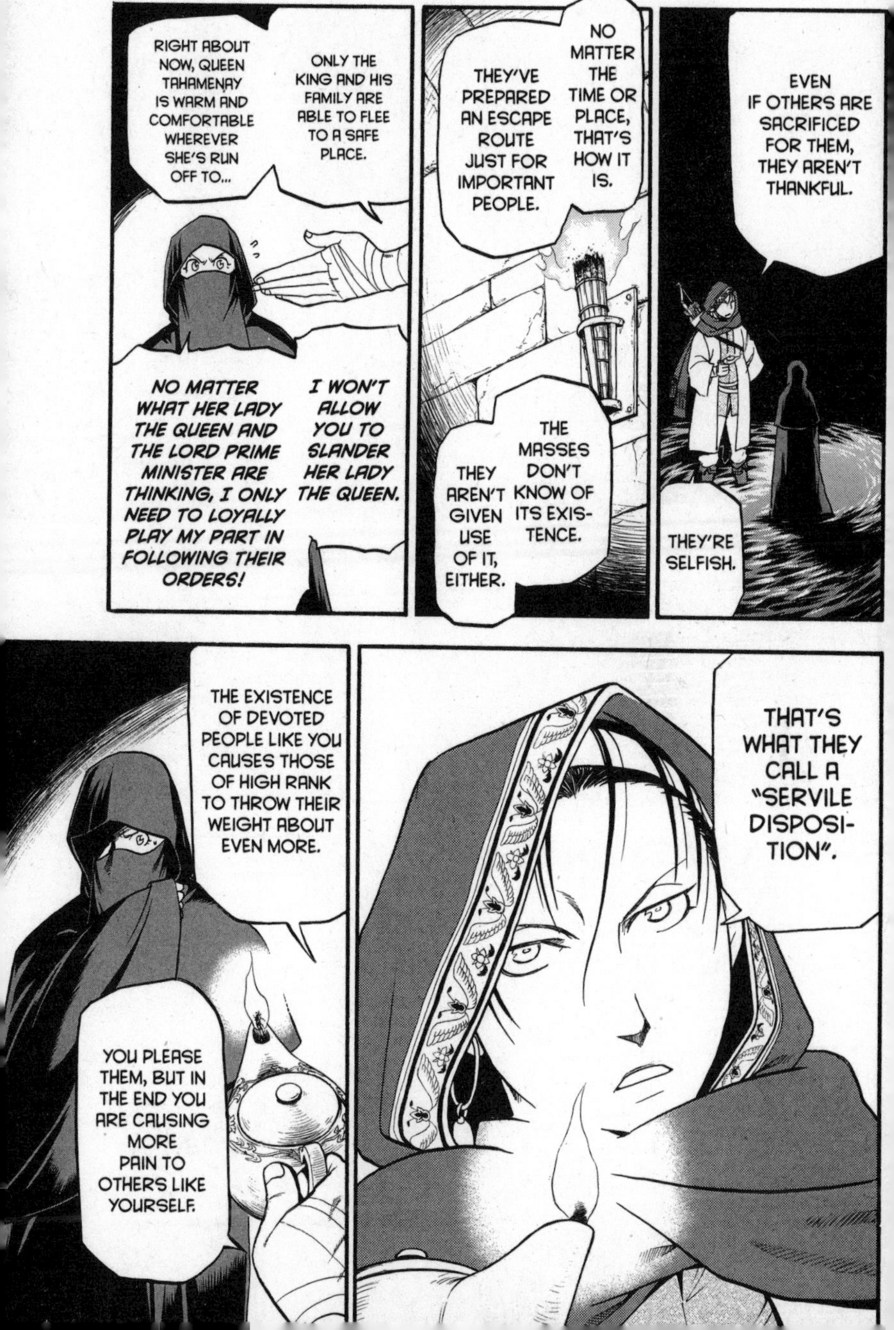
EVEN IF OTHERS ARE SACRIFICED FOR THEM, THEY AREN'T THANKFUL.
THEY'RE SELFISH.
NO MATTER THE TIME OR PLACE, THAT'S HOW IT IS.
THEY'VE PREPARED AN ESCAPE ROUTE JUST FOR IMPORTANT PEOPLE.
THE MASSES DON'T KNOW OF ITS EXISTENCE.
THEY AREN'T GIVEN USE OF IT, EITHER.
RIGHT ABOUT NOW, QUEEN TAHAMENAY IS WARM AND COMFORTABLE WHEREVER SHE'S RUN OFF TO...
ONLY THE KING AND HIS FAMILY ARE ABLE TO FLEE TO A SAFE PLACE.
NO MATTER WHAT HER LADY THE QUEEN AND THE LORD PRIME MINISTER ARE THINKING, I ONLY NEED TO LOYALLY PLAY MY PART IN FOLLOWING THEIR ORDERS!
I WON'T ALLOW YOU TO SLANDER HER LADY THE QUEEN.
THAT'S WHAT THEY CALL A "SERVILE DISPOSITION".
THE EXISTENCE OF DEVOTED PEOPLE LIKE YOU CAUSES THOSE OF HIGH RANK TO THROW THEIR WEIGHT ABOUT EVEN MORE.
YOU PLEASE THEM, BUT IN THE END YOU ARE CAUSING MORE PAIN TO OTHERS LIKE YOURSELF.

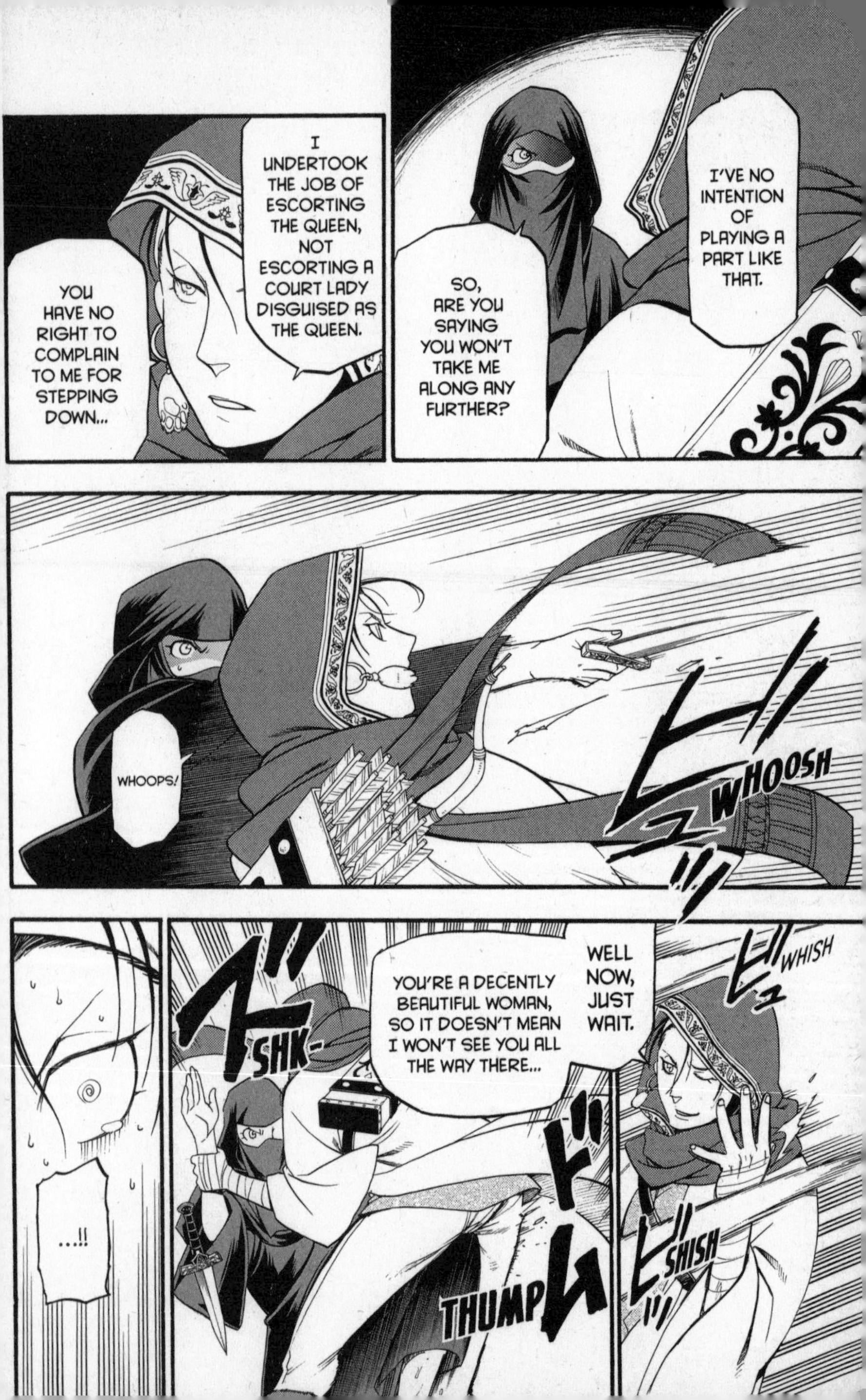
I'VE NO INTENTION OF PLAYING A PART LIKE THAT.
SO, ARE YOU SAYING YOU WON'T TAKE ME ALONG ANY FURTHER?
I UNDERTOOK THE JOB OF ESCORTING THE QUEEN, NOT ESCORTING A COURT LADY DISGUISED AS THE QUEEN.
YOU HAVE NO RIGHT TO COMPLAIN TO ME FOR STEPPING DOWN...
WHOOSH
WHOOPS!
WHISH
WELL NOW, JUST WAIT.
YOU'RE A DECENTLY BEAUTIFUL WOMAN, SO IT DOESN'T MEAN I WON'T SEE YOU ALL THE WAY THERE...
SHISH
THUMP
SHK-
...!!

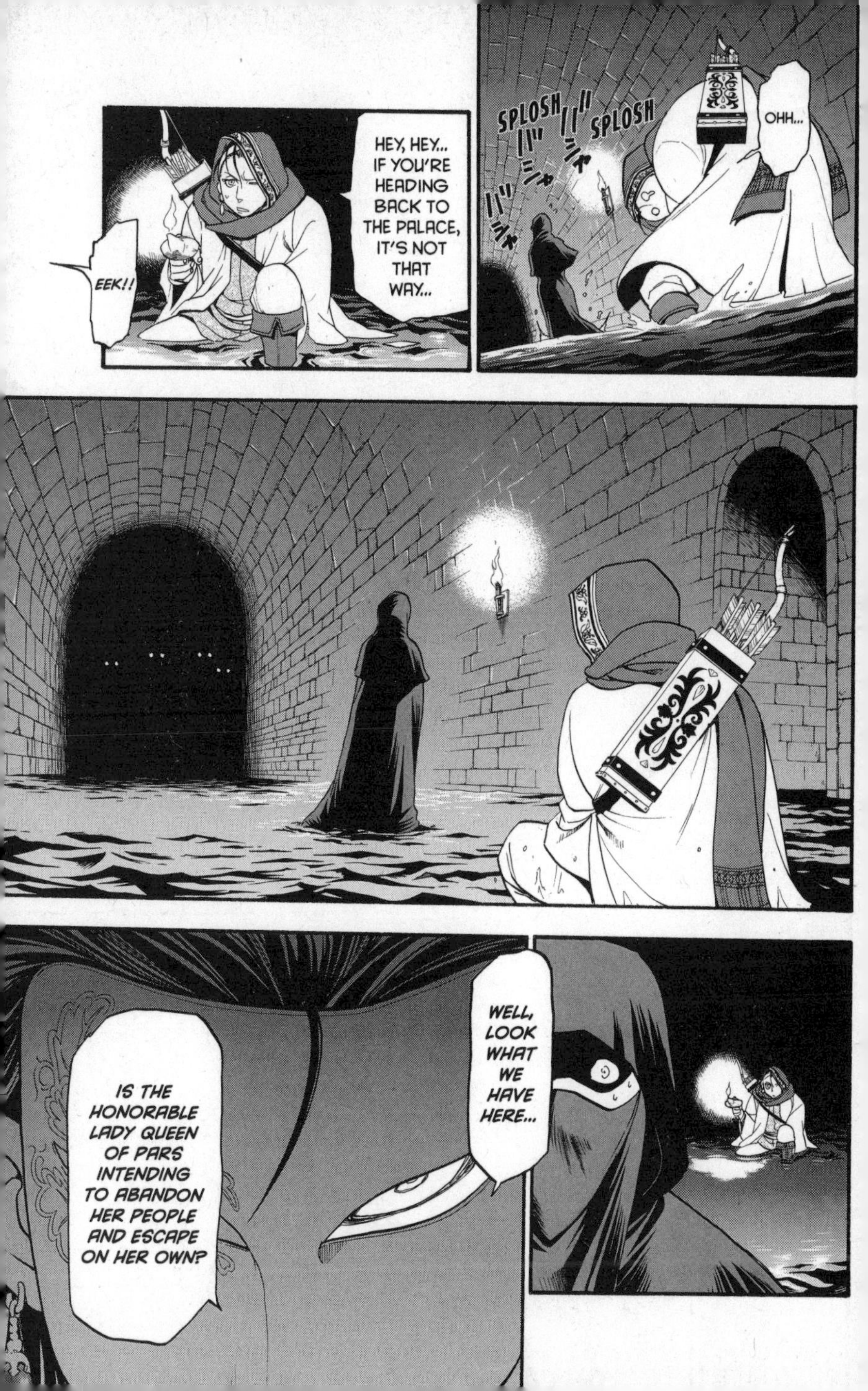

SPLOSH
SPLOSH
OHH...
HEY, HEY... IF YOU'RE HEADING BACK TO THE PALACE, IT'S NOT THAT WAY...
EEK!!
WELL, LOOK WHAT WE HAVE HERE...
IS THE HONORABLE LADY QUEEN OF PARS INTENDING TO ABANDON HER PEOPLE AND ESCAPE ON HER OWN?

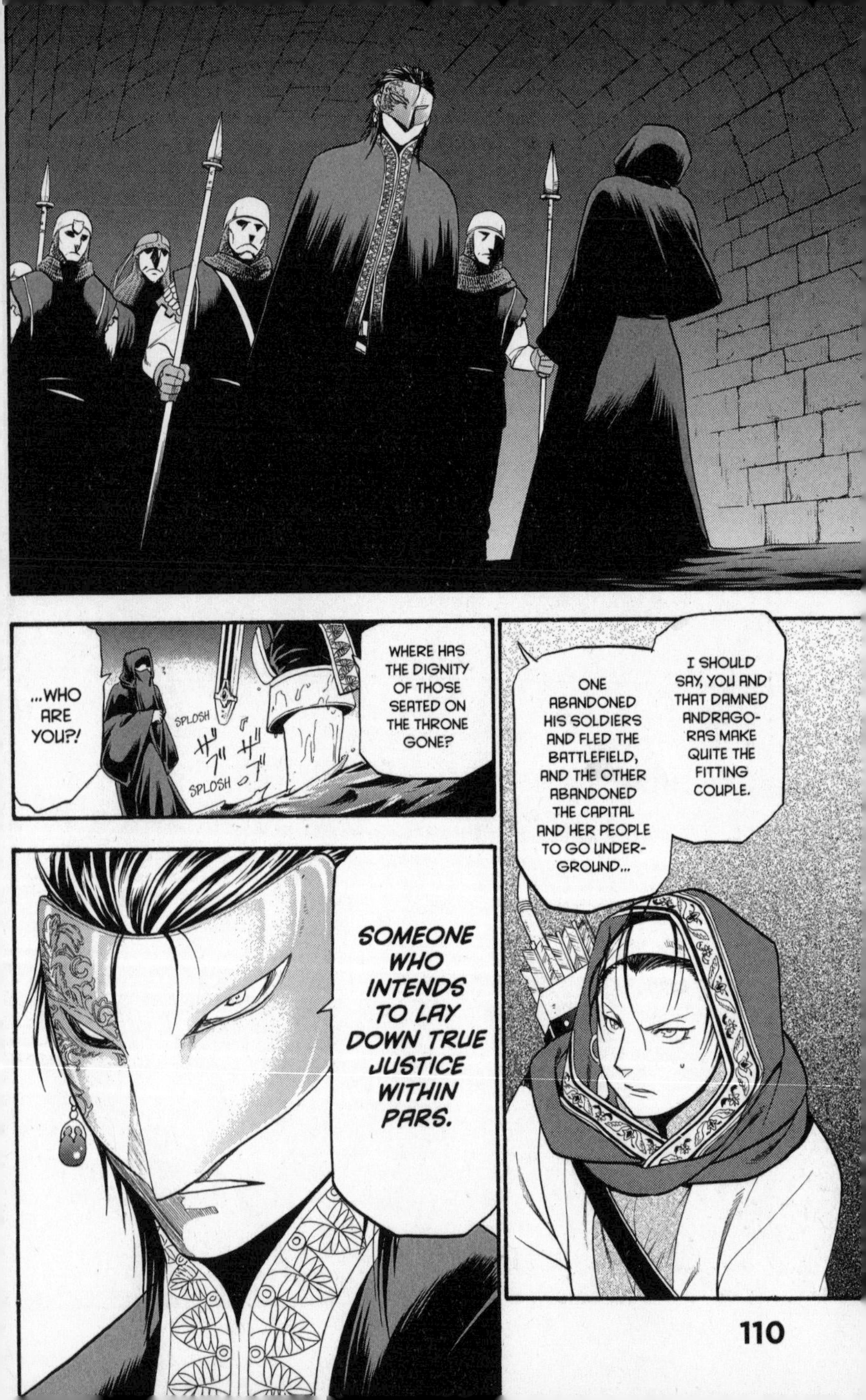

I SHOULD SAY, YOU AND THAT DAMNED ANDRAGO-RAS MAKE QUITE THE FITTING COUPLE.
ONE ABANDONED HIS SOLDIERS AND FLED THE BATTLEFIELD, AND THE OTHER ABANDONED THE CAPITAL AND HER PEOPLE TO GO UNDER-GROUND...
WHERE HAS THE DIGNITY OF THOSE SEATED ON THE THRONE GONE?
SPLOSH
SPLOSH
...WHO ARE YOU?!
SOMEONE WHO INTENDS TO LAY DOWN TRUE JUSTICE WITHIN PARS.

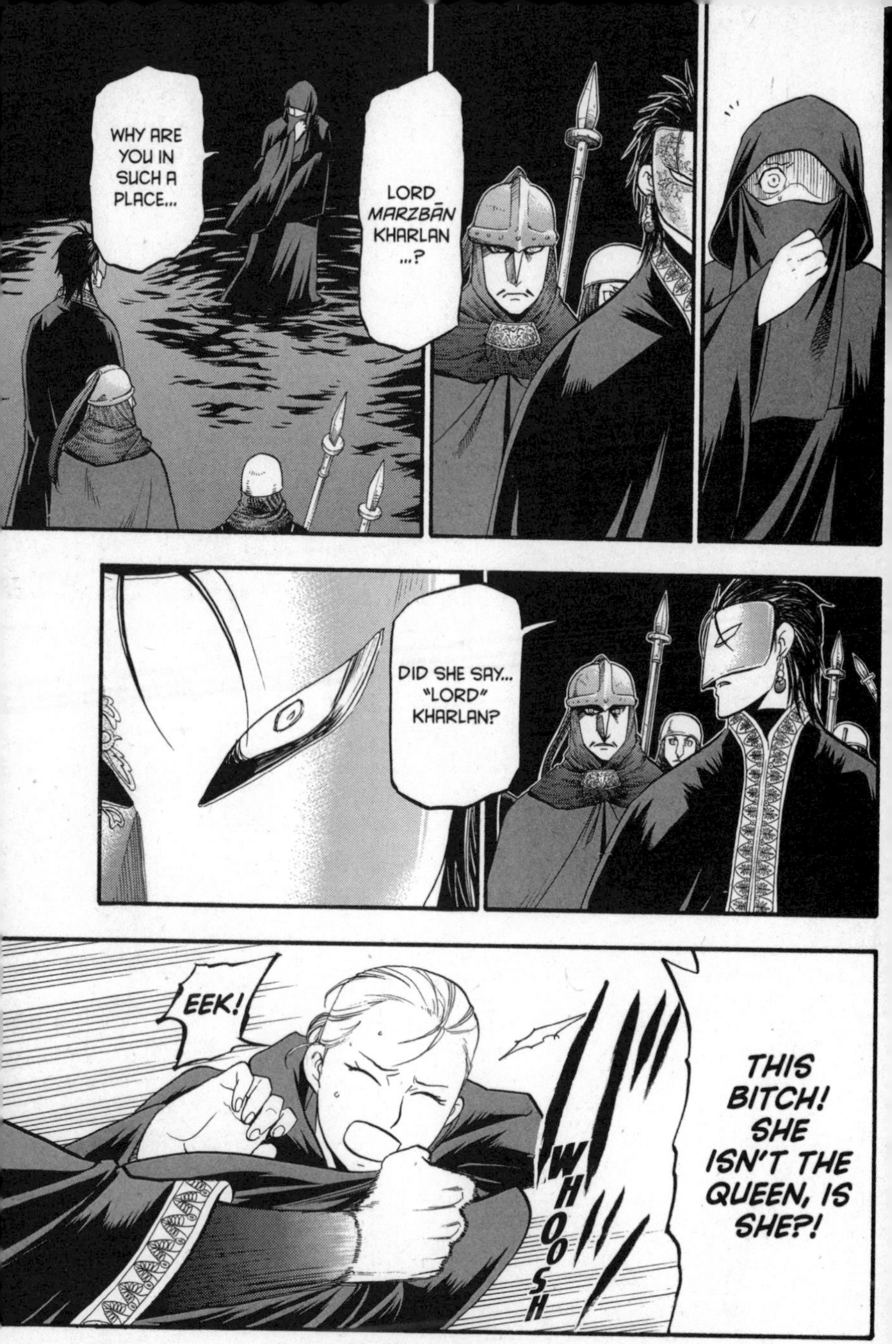
LORD MARZBĀN KHARLAN ...?
WHY ARE YOU IN SUCH A PLACE...
DID SHE SAY... "LORD" KHARLAN?
THIS BITCH! SHE ISN'T THE QUEEN, IS SHE?!
WHOOSH
EEK!

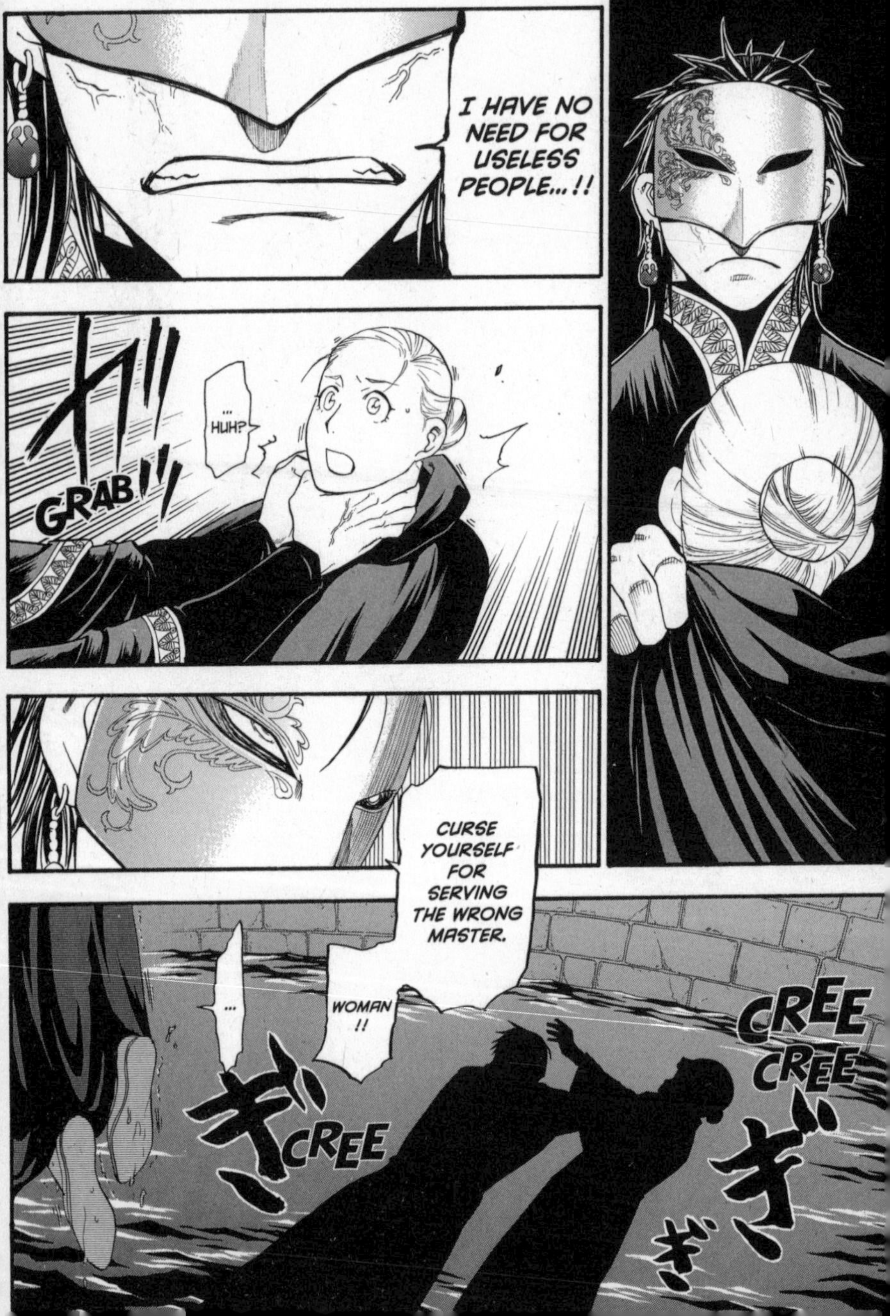
I HAVE NO NEED FOR USELESS PEOPLE...!!
... HUH?
GRAB!!
CURSE YOURSELF FOR SERVING THE WRONG MASTER.
CREE CREE
WOMAN !!
...
CREE

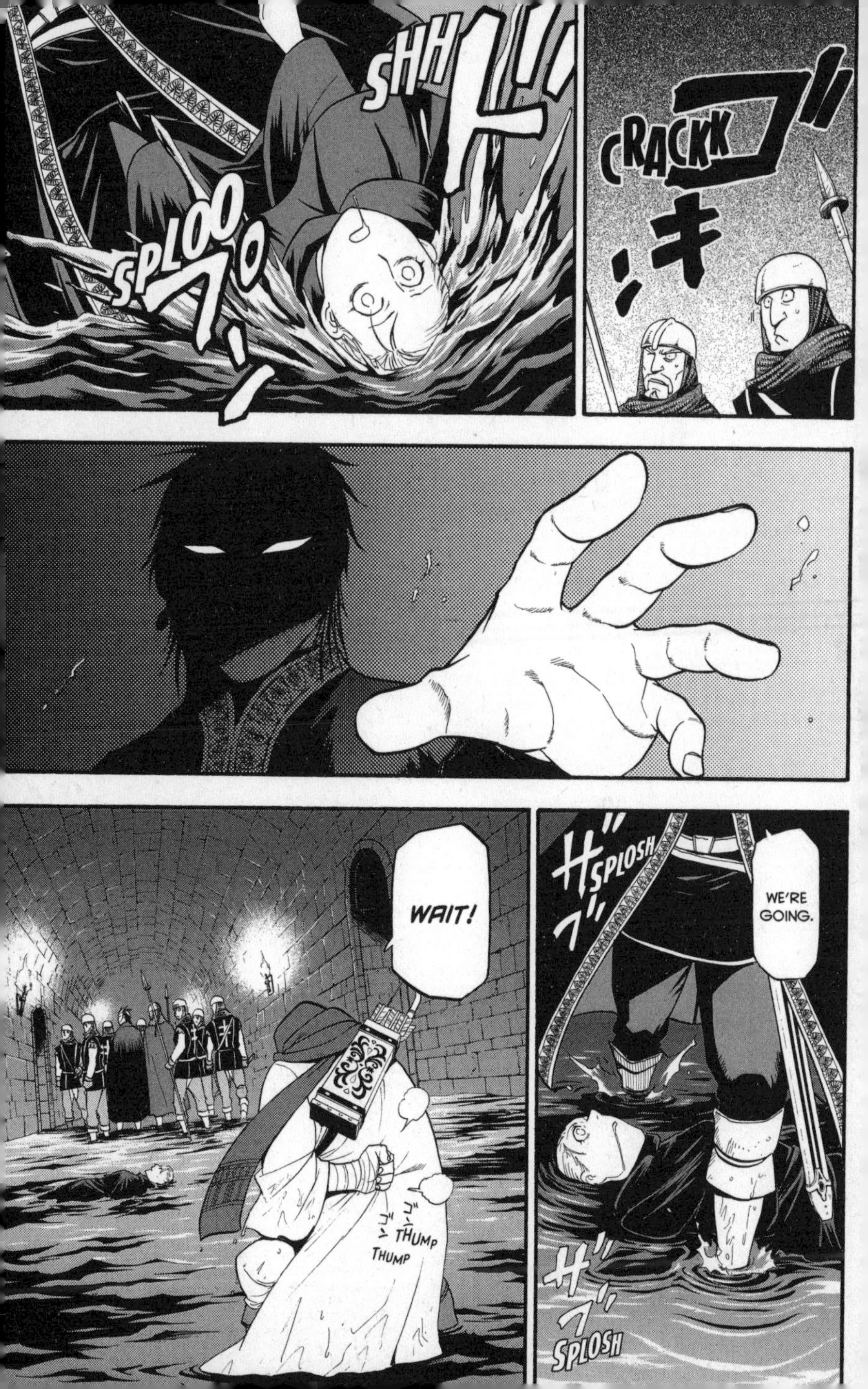
CRACKK
SHH
SPLOO
SPLOSH
WE'RE GOING.
SPLOSH
WAIT!
THUMP
THUMP

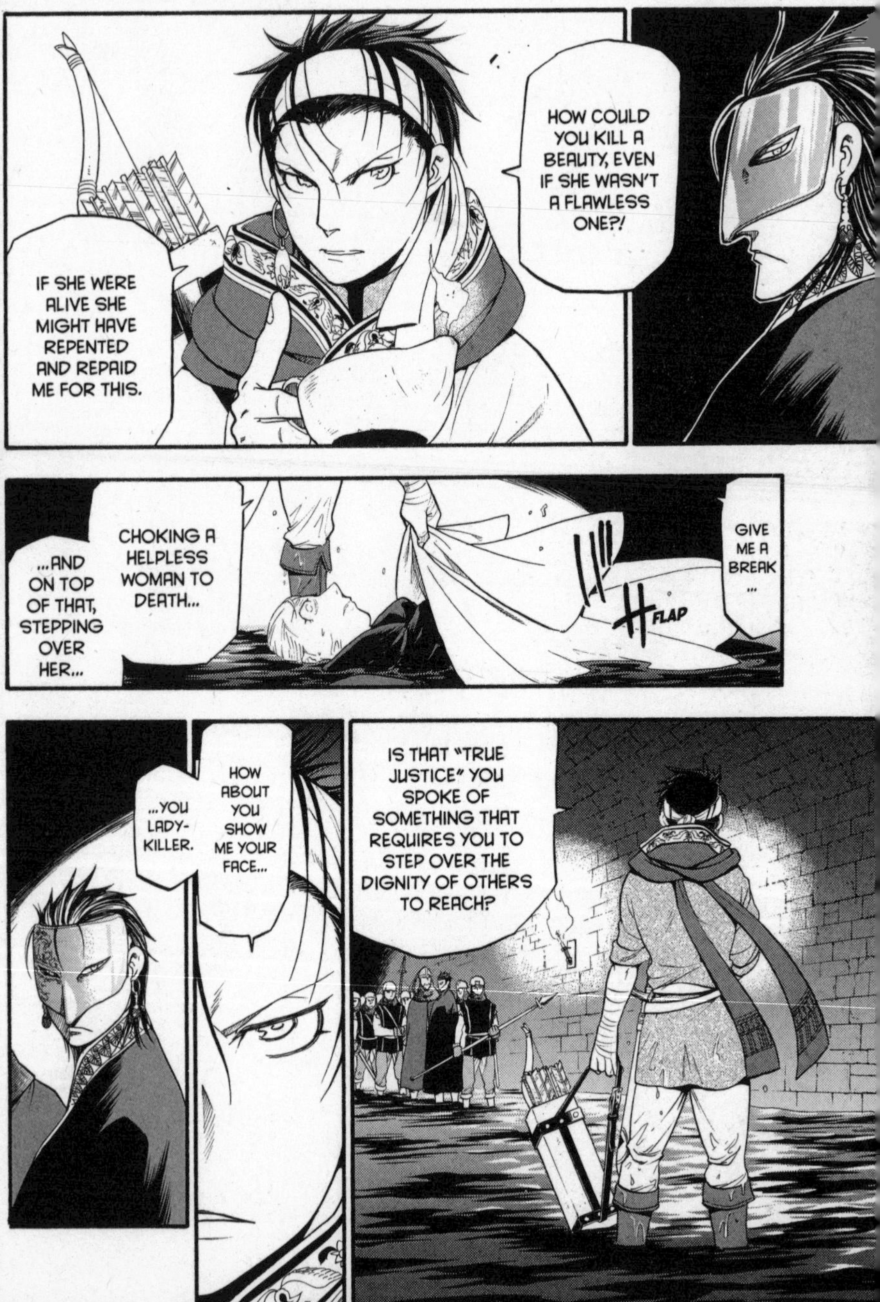
HOW COULD YOU KILL A BEAUTY, EVEN IF SHE WASN'T A FLAWLESS ONE?!
IF SHE WERE ALIVE SHE MIGHT HAVE REPENTED AND REPAID ME FOR THIS.
GIVE ME A BREAK...
FLAP
CHOKING A HELPLESS WOMAN TO DEATH...
...AND ON TOP OF THAT, STEPPING OVER HER...
IS THAT "TRUE JUSTICE" YOU SPOKE OF SOMETHING THAT REQUIRES YOU TO STEP OVER THE DIGNITY OF OTHERS TO REACH?
HOW ABOUT YOU SHOW ME YOUR FACE...
...YOU LADY-KILLER.

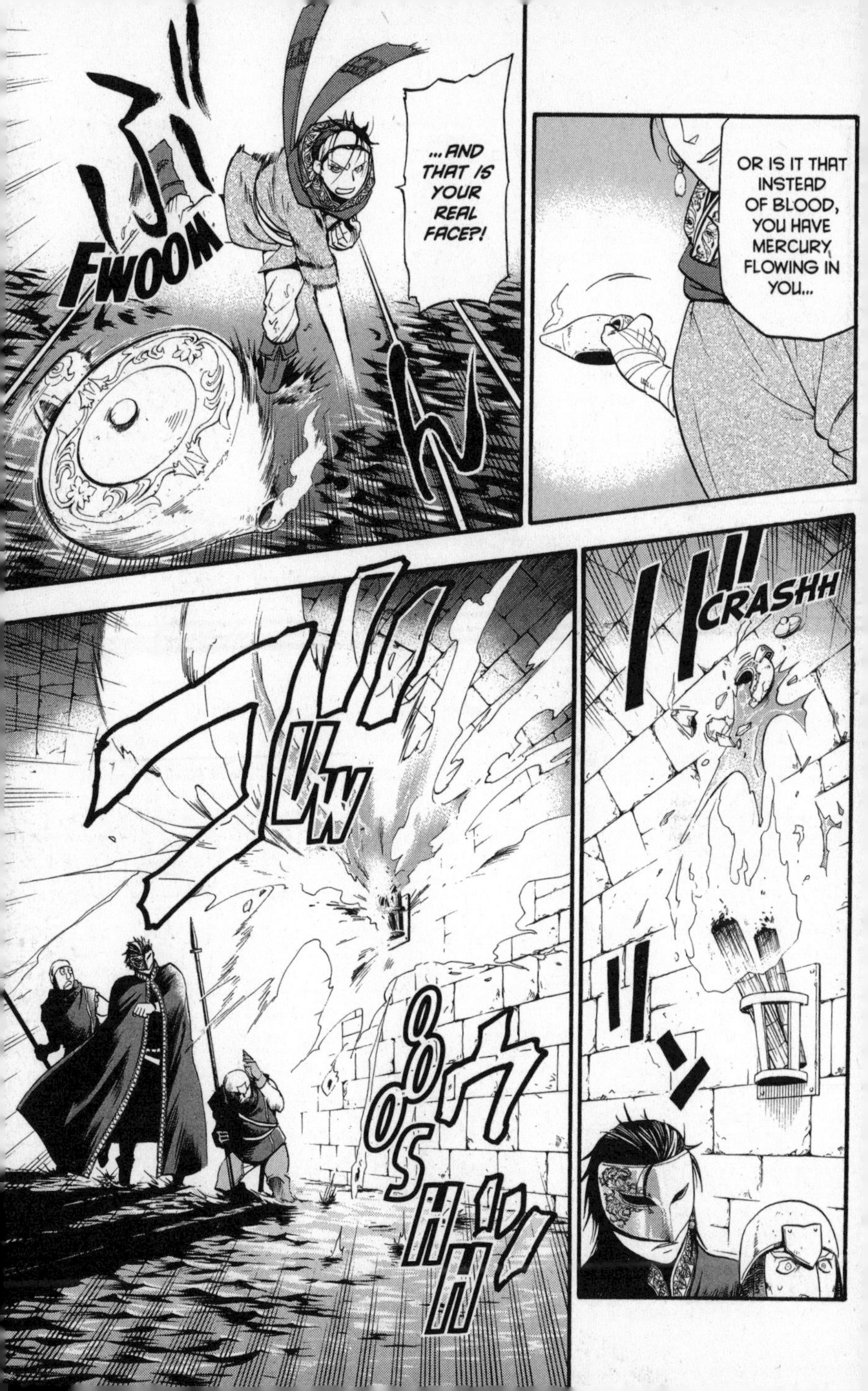
OR IS IT THAT INSTEAD OF BLOOD, YOU HAVE MERCURY FLOWING IN YOU...
...AND THAT IS YOUR REAL FACE?!
FWOOM
CRASHH
FWOOOSHH

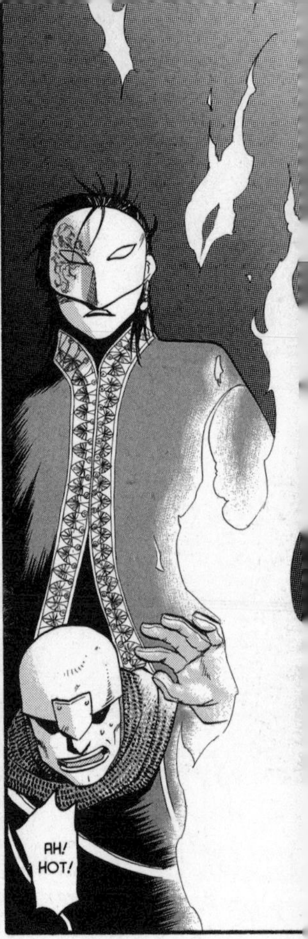
AH! HOT!
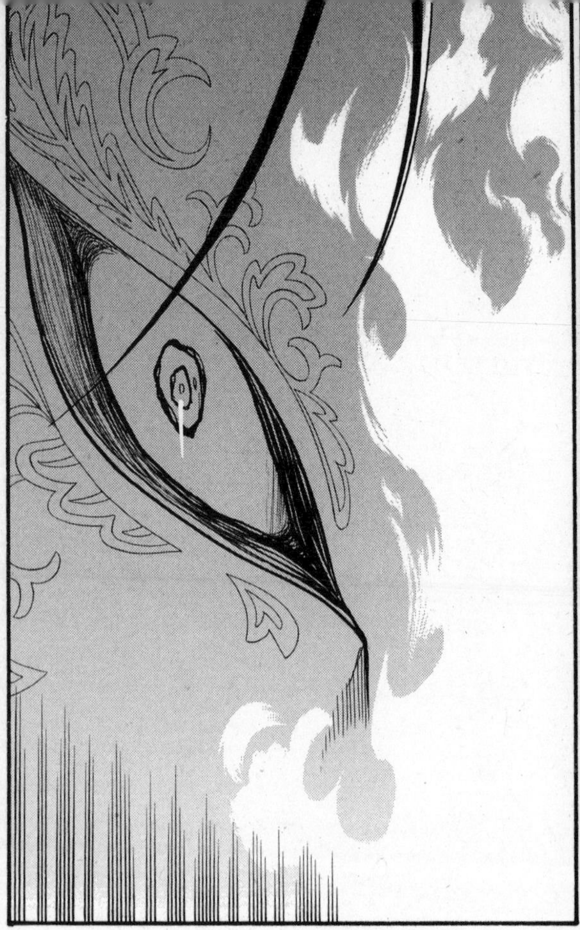
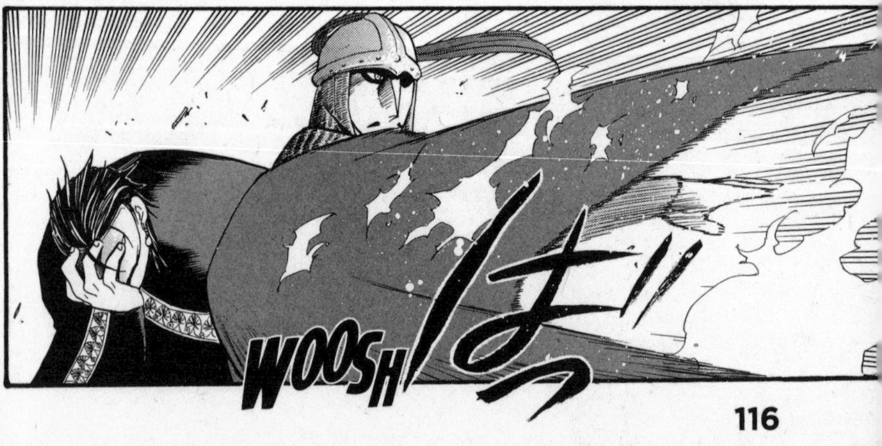
WOOSH
はっ

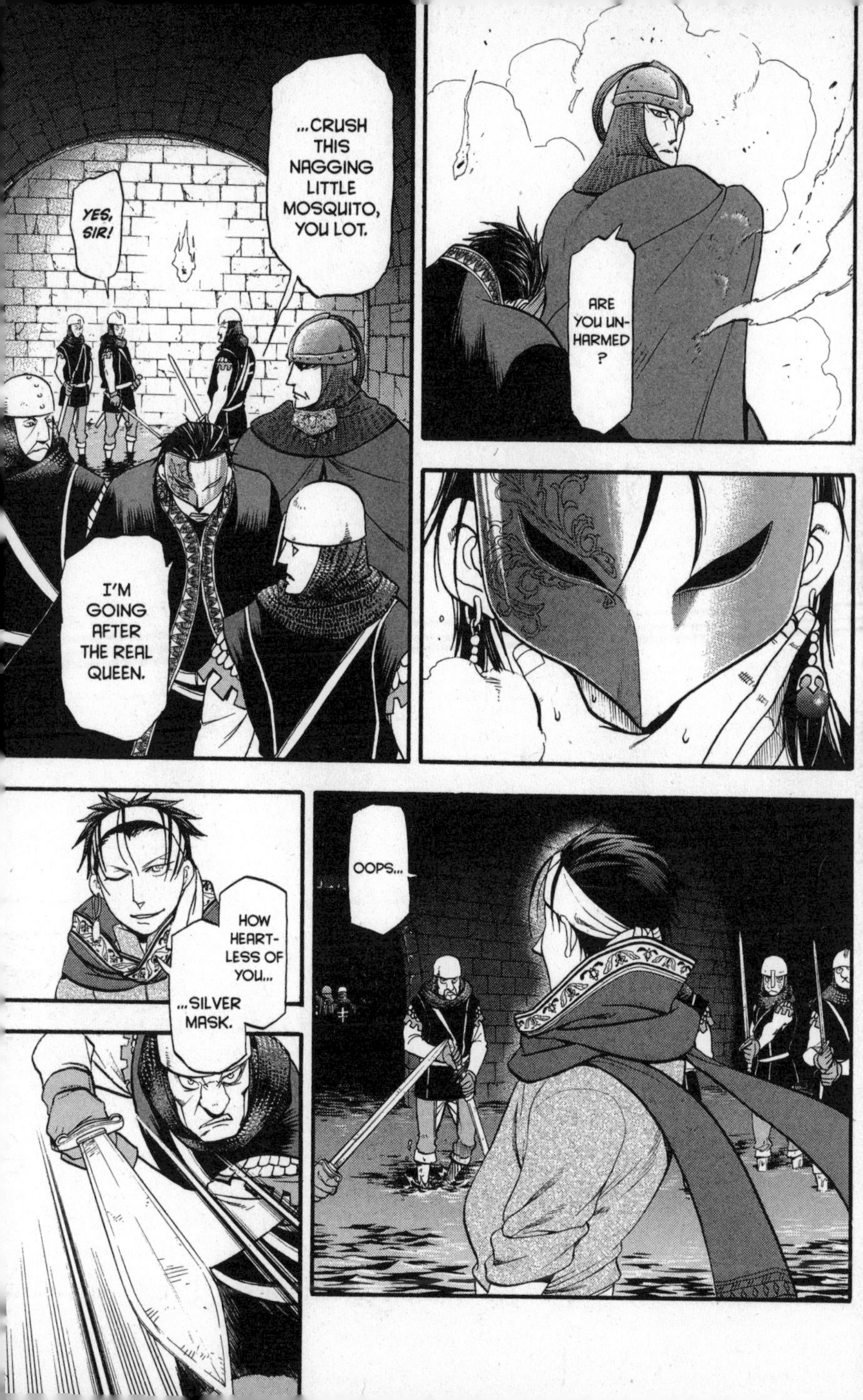
ARE YOU UNHARMED?
...CRUSH THIS NAGGING LITTLE MOSQUITO, YOU LOT.
YES, SIR!
I'M GOING AFTER THE REAL QUEEN.
OOPS...
HOW HEART-LESS OF YOU...
...SILVER MASK.

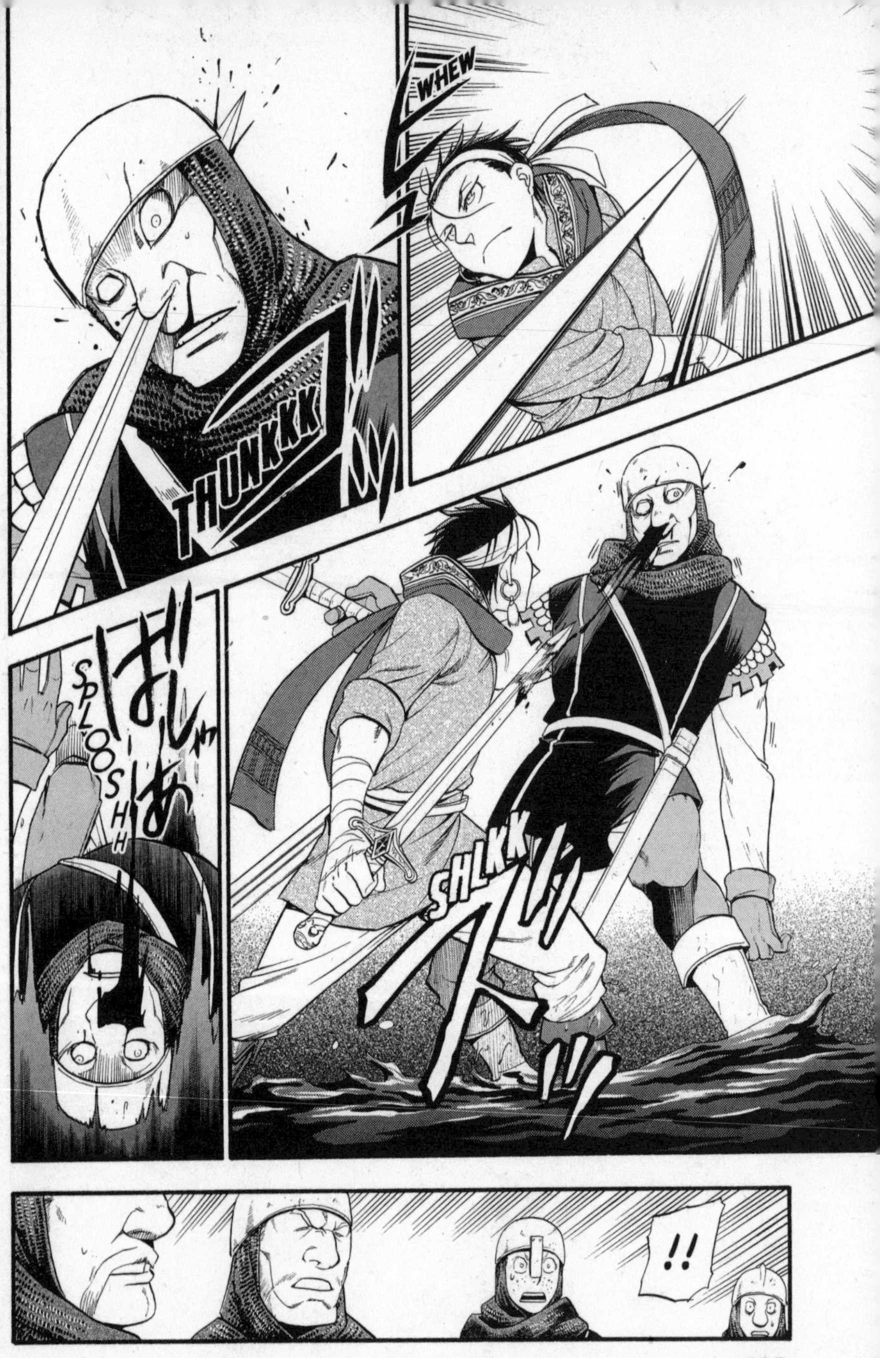

WHEW
THUNKKK
SHLKK
SPLOOSHH
ばしゃ
ばしゃ
!!

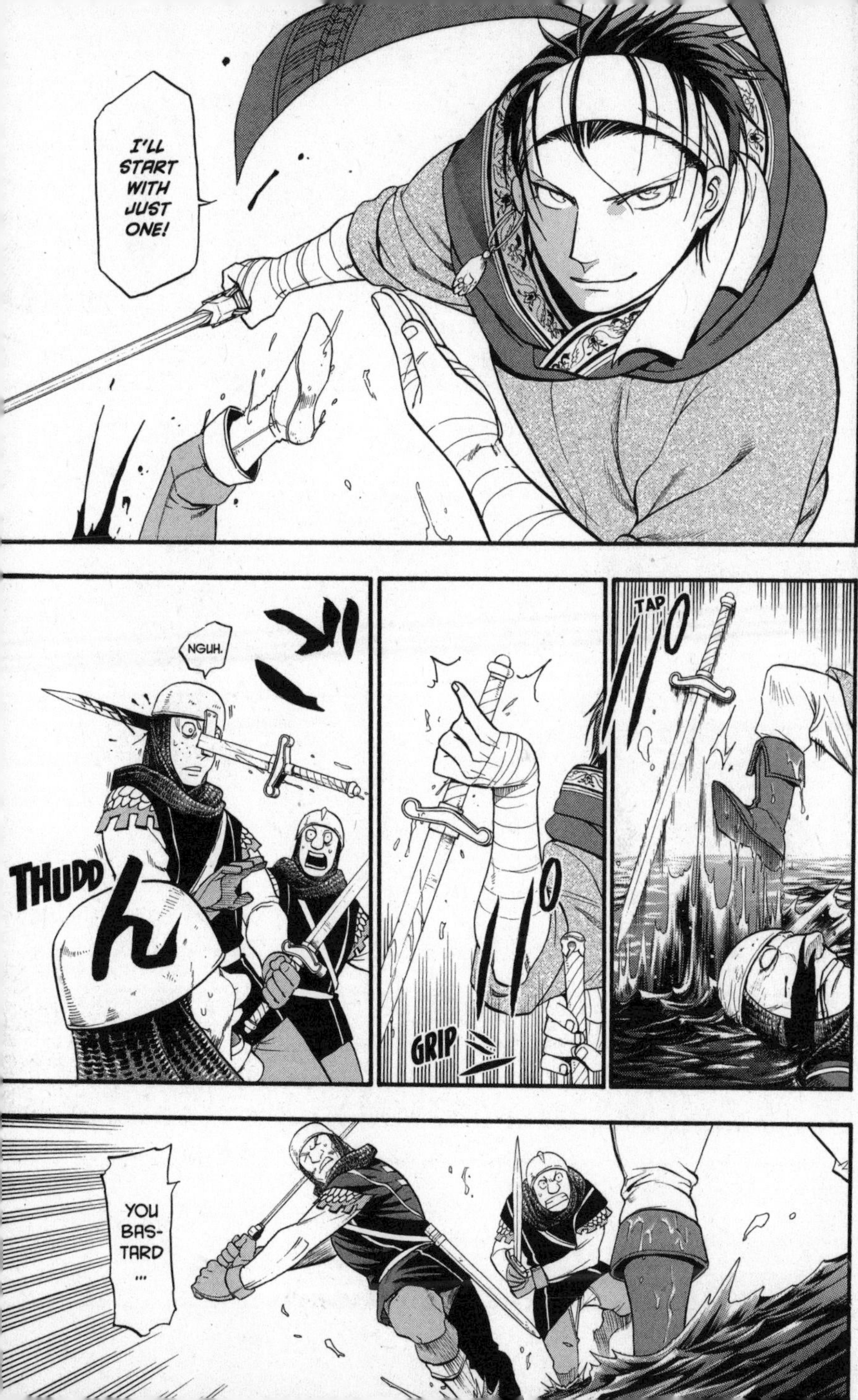
I'LL START WITH JUST ONE!
TAP
GRIP
NGUH.
THUDD
YOU BAS-TARD ...

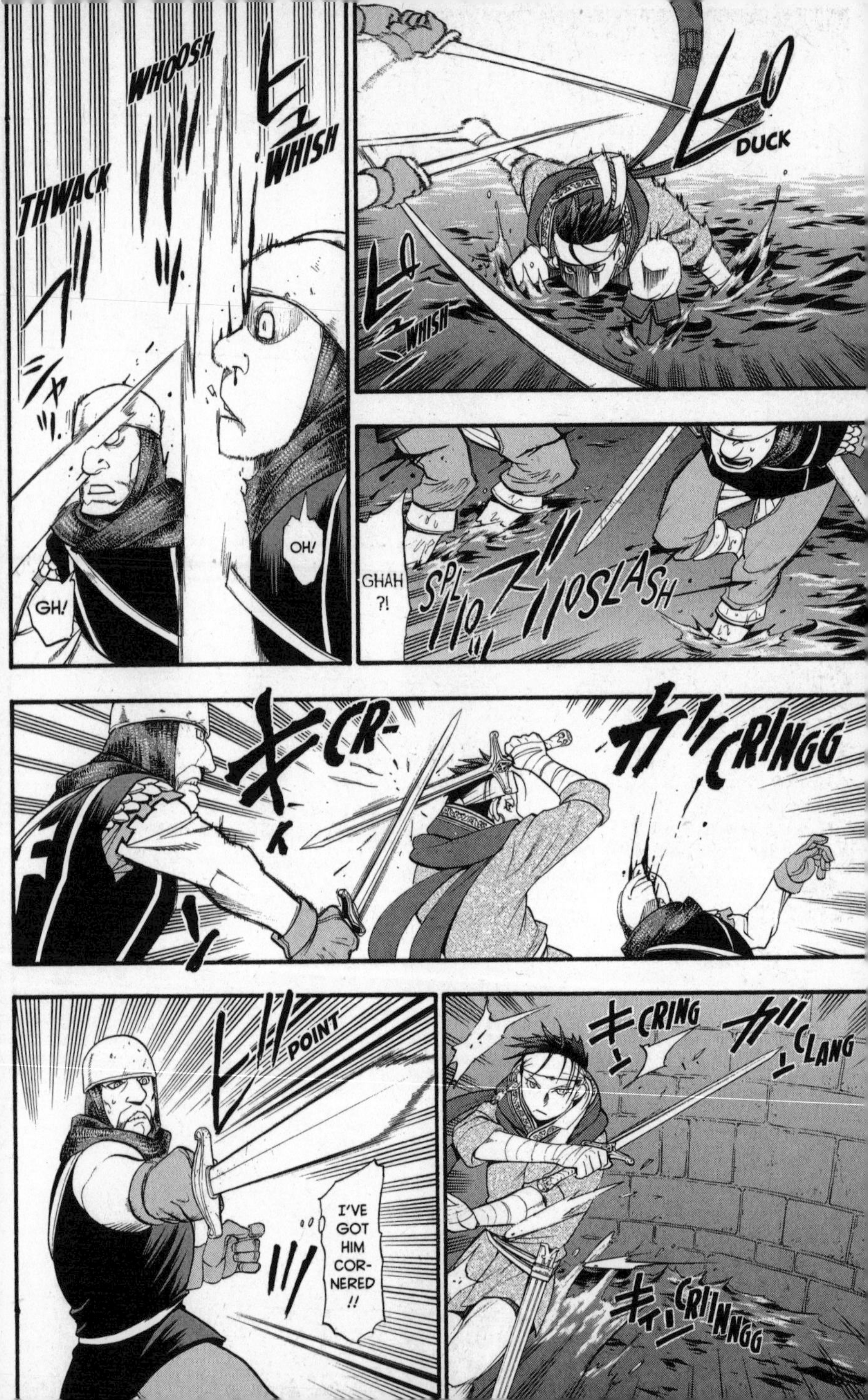
DUCK
WHISH
GHAH ?!
SPLOSLASH
WHISH
WHOOSH
THWACK
OH!
GH!
CRINGG
CR-K
CLANG
CRING
CRIINNGG
POINT
I'VE GOT HIM COR-NERED !!

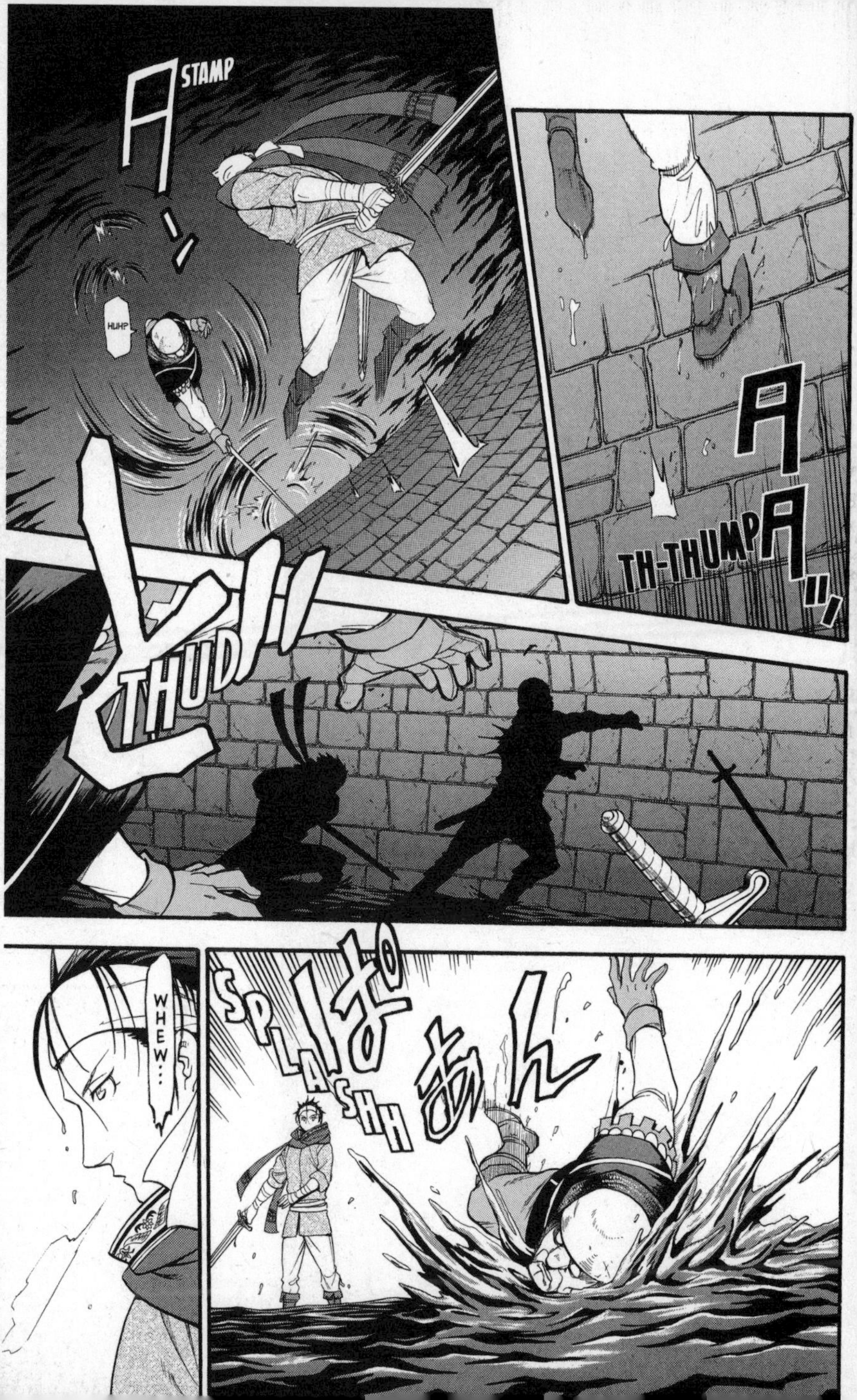
TH-THUMP
STAMP
HUH?
THUD
SPLASHH
WHEW...

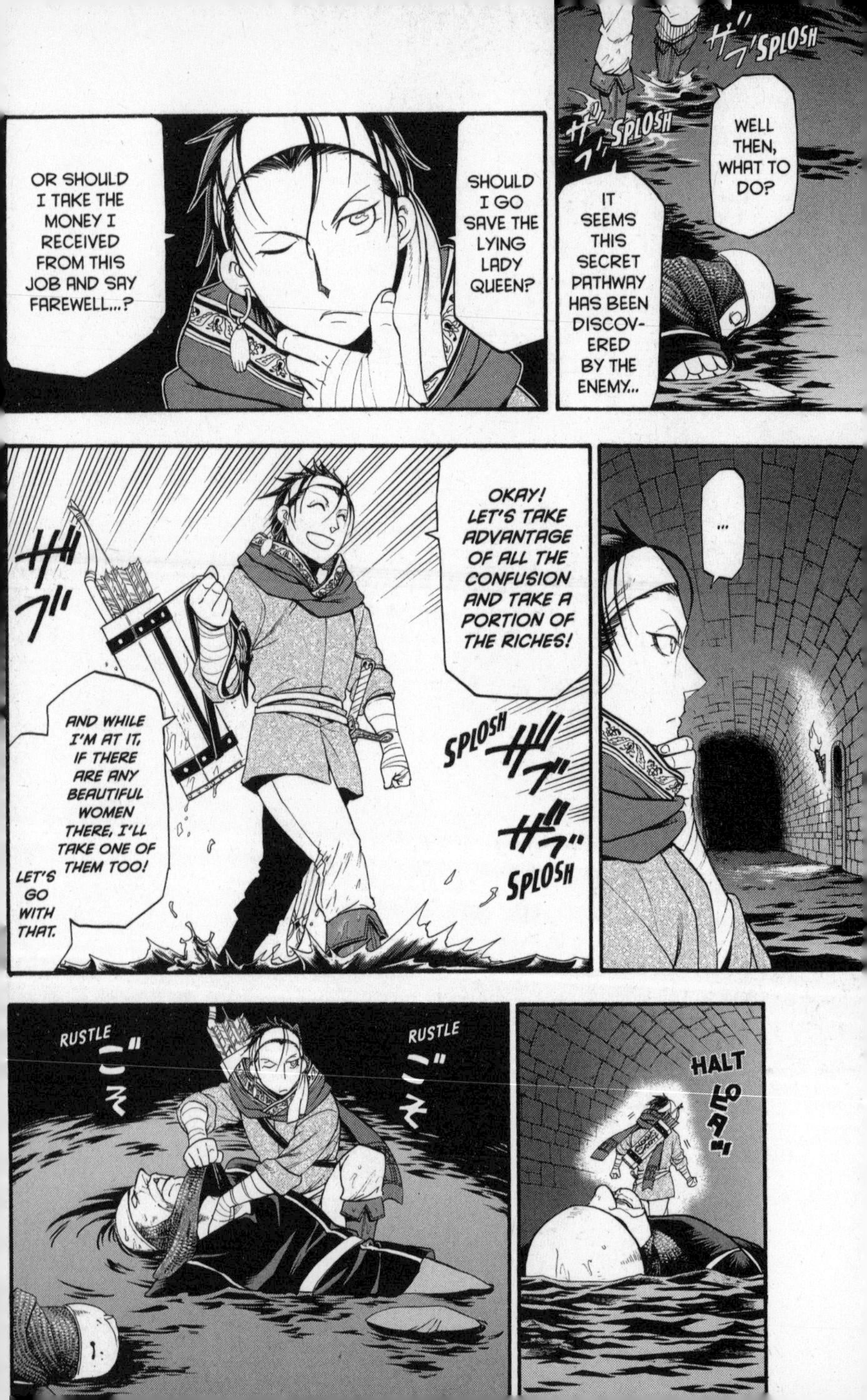

ザブ SPLOSH
ザブ SPLOSH
WELL THEN, WHAT TO DO?
IT SEEMS THIS SECRET PATHWAY HAS BEEN DISCOVERED BY THE ENEMY...
SHOULD I GO SAVE THE LYING LADY QUEEN?
OR SHOULD I TAKE THE MONEY I RECEIVED FROM THIS JOB AND SAY FAREWELL...?
...
SPLOSH ザブ
ザブ SPLOSH
OKAY! LET'S TAKE ADVANTAGE OF ALL THE CONFUSION AND TAKE A PORTION OF THE RICHES!
ザブ
AND WHILE I'M AT IT, IF THERE ARE ANY BEAUTIFUL WOMEN THERE, I'LL TAKE ONE OF THEM TOO!
LET'S GO WITH THAT.
HALT ピタッ
RUSTLE ごそ
RUSTLE ごそ

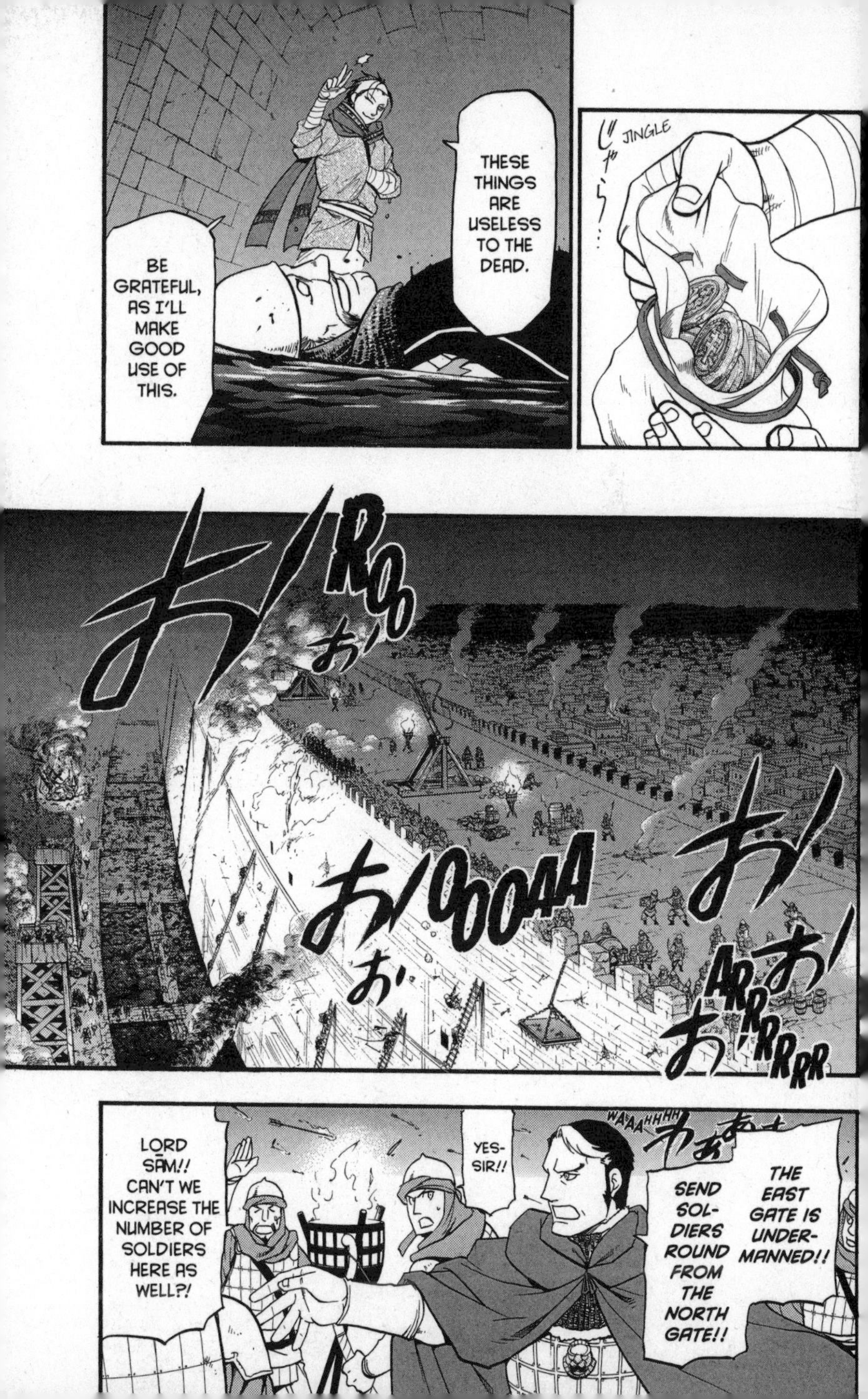
JINGLE
THESE THINGS ARE USELESS TO THE DEAD.
BE GRATEFUL, AS I'LL MAKE GOOD USE OF THIS.
ROOO
OOOAA
ARRRRRR
WAAAHHHH
THE EAST GATE IS UNDER-MANNED!!
SEND SOL-DIERS ROUND FROM THE NORTH GATE!!
YES-SIR!!
LORD SĀM!! CAN'T WE INCREASE THE NUMBER OF SOLDIERS HERE AS WELL?!

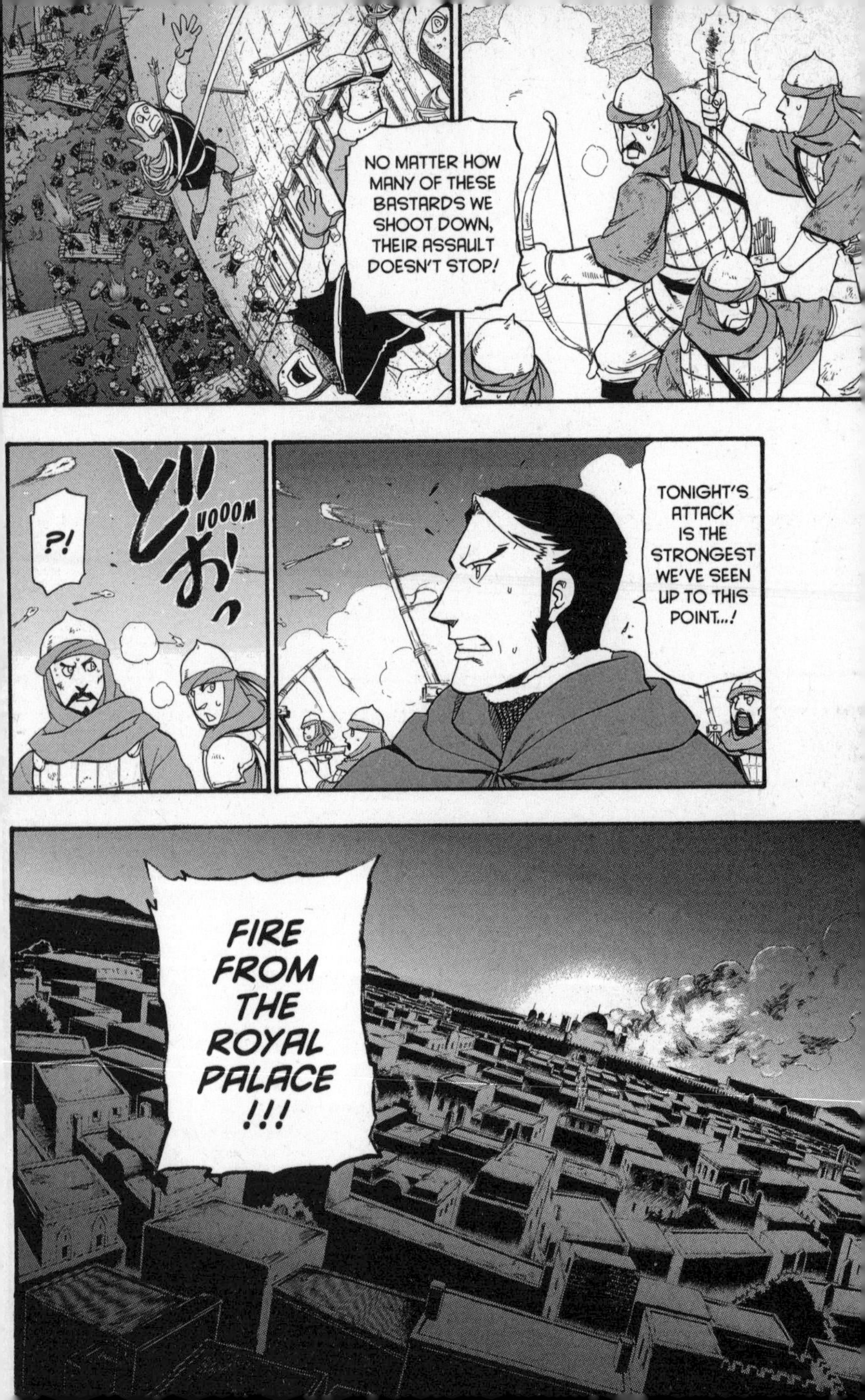
NO MATTER HOW MANY OF THESE BASTARDS WE SHOOT DOWN, THEIR ASSAULT DOESN'T STOP!
TONIGHT'S ATTACK IS THE STRONGEST WE'VE SEEN UP TO THIS POINT...!
どおっ
VOOOM
?!
FIRE FROM THE ROYAL PALACE!!!

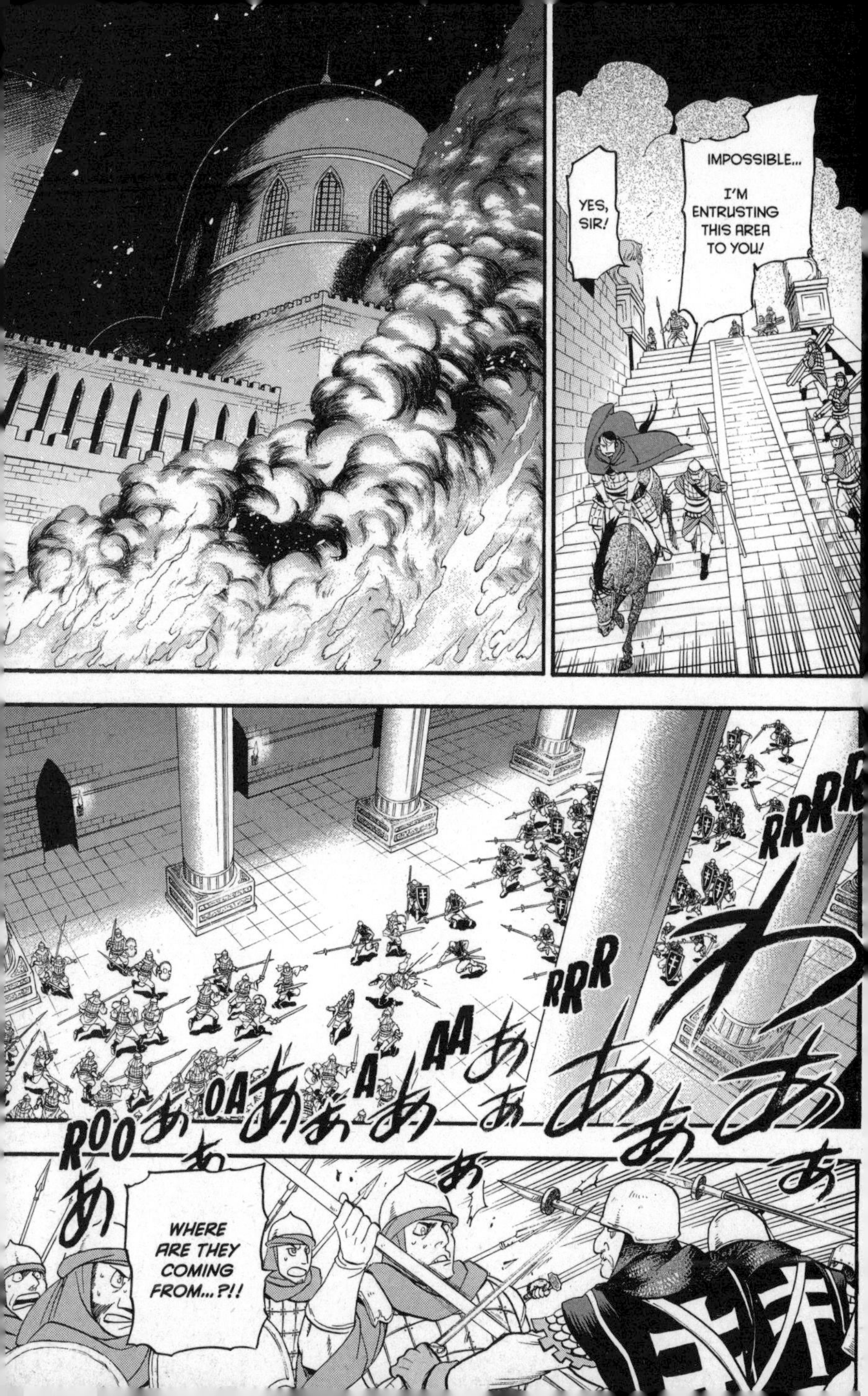

IMPOSSIBLE...
I'M ENTRUSTING THIS AREA TO YOU!
YES, SIR!
ROO
OA
A
AA
RRR
RRRR
WHERE ARE THEY COMING FROM...?!!

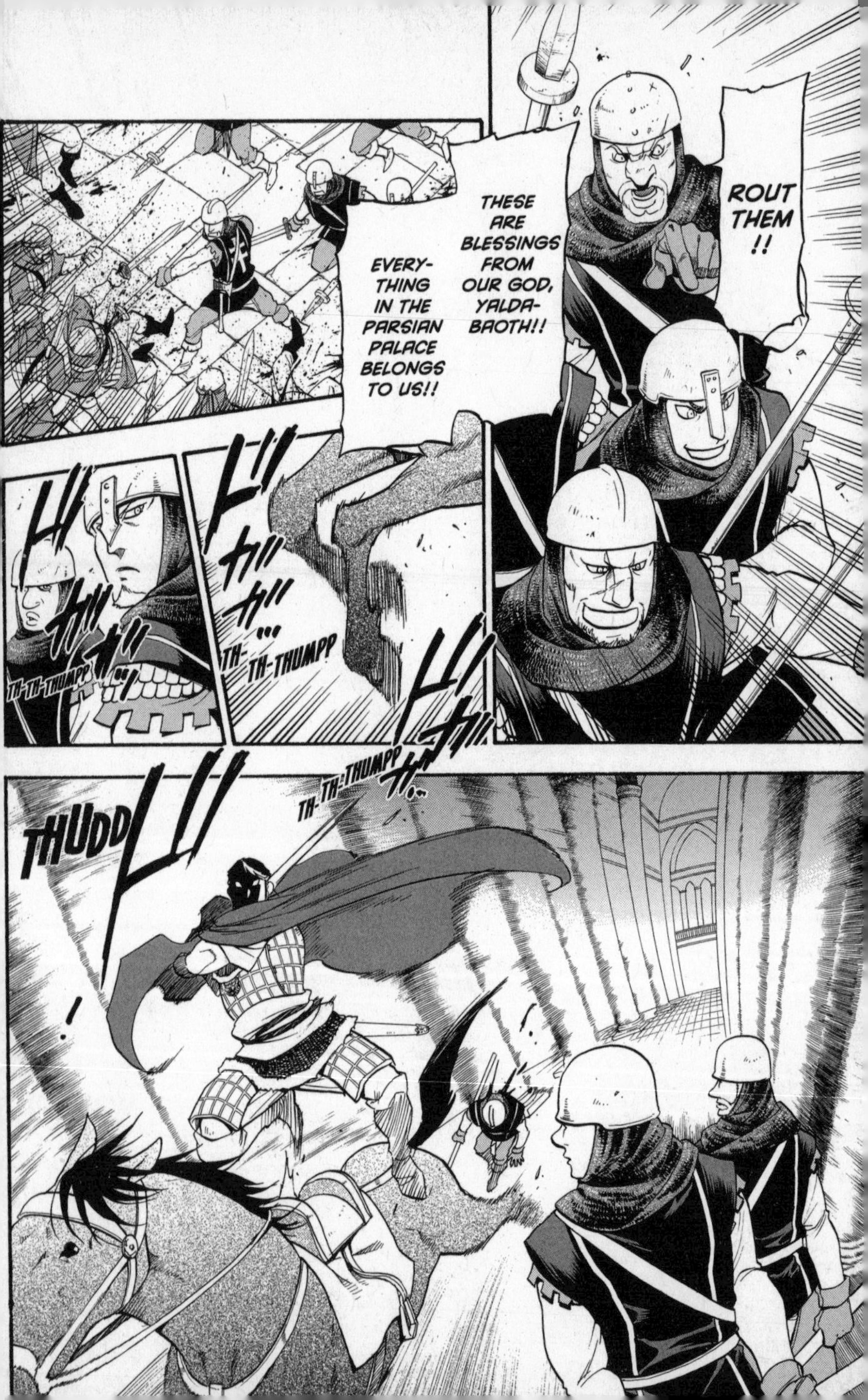
ROUT THEM !!
THESE ARE BLESSINGS FROM OUR GOD, YALDABAOTH!!
EVERYTHING IN THE PARSIAN PALACE BELONGS TO US!!
TH-TH-THUMPP
TH-TH-THUMPP
TH-TH-THUMPP
THUDD

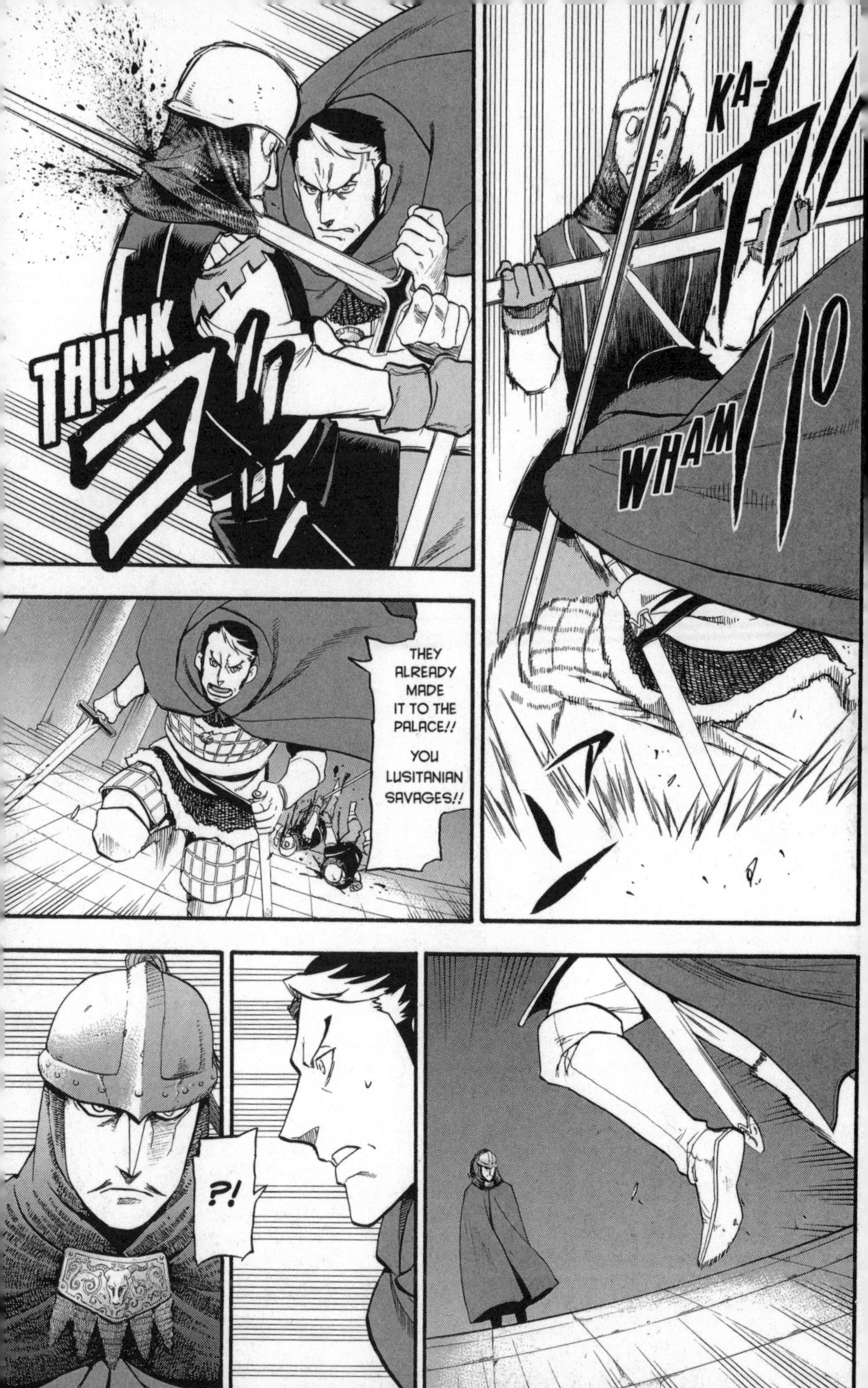
KA-
WHAM
THUNK
THEY ALREADY MADE IT TO THE PALACE!!
YOU LUSITANIAN SAVAGES!!
?!

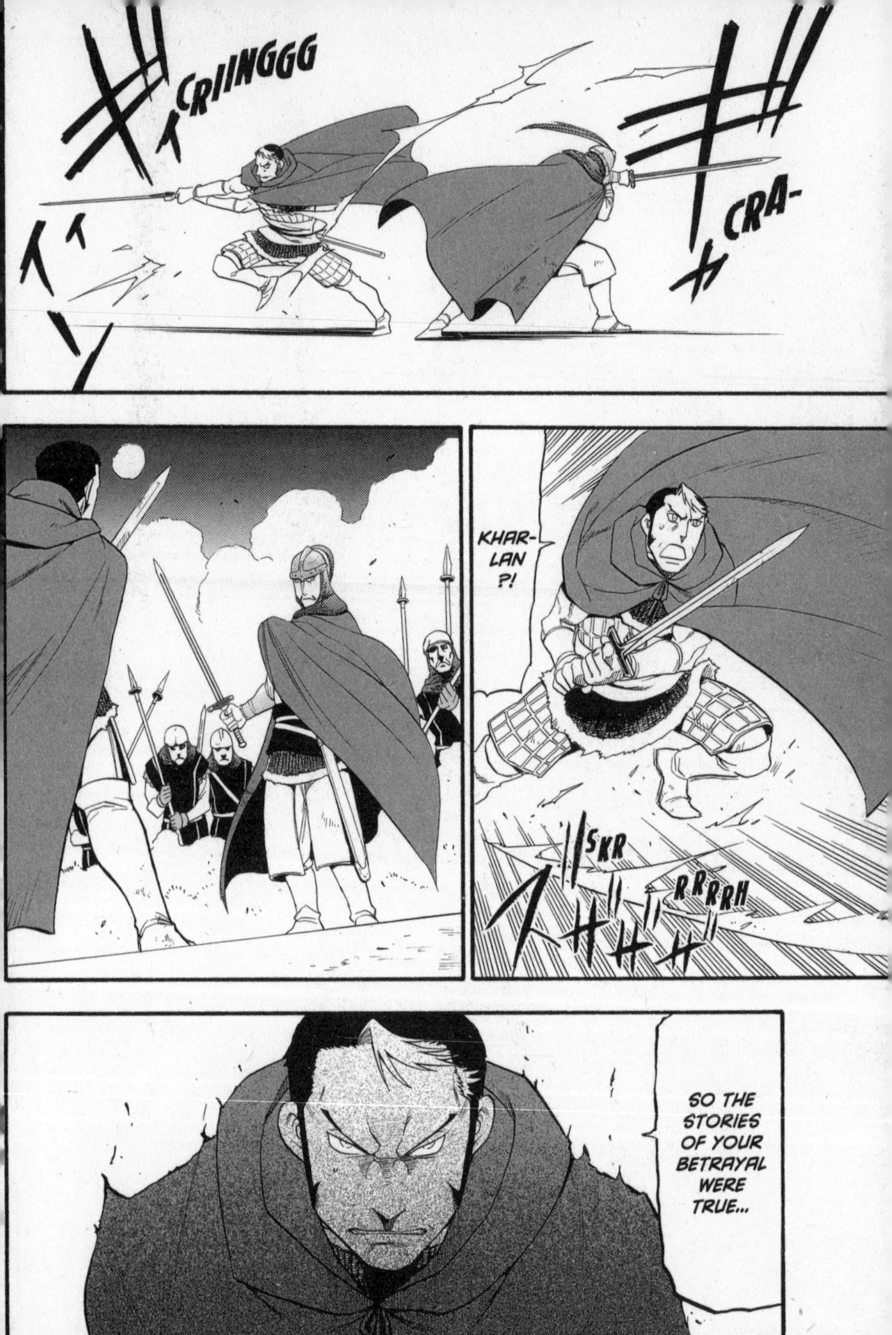

CRIINGGG
CRA-
KHAR-LAN?!
SKR
RRRRH
SO THE STORIES OF YOUR BETRAYAL WERE TRUE...

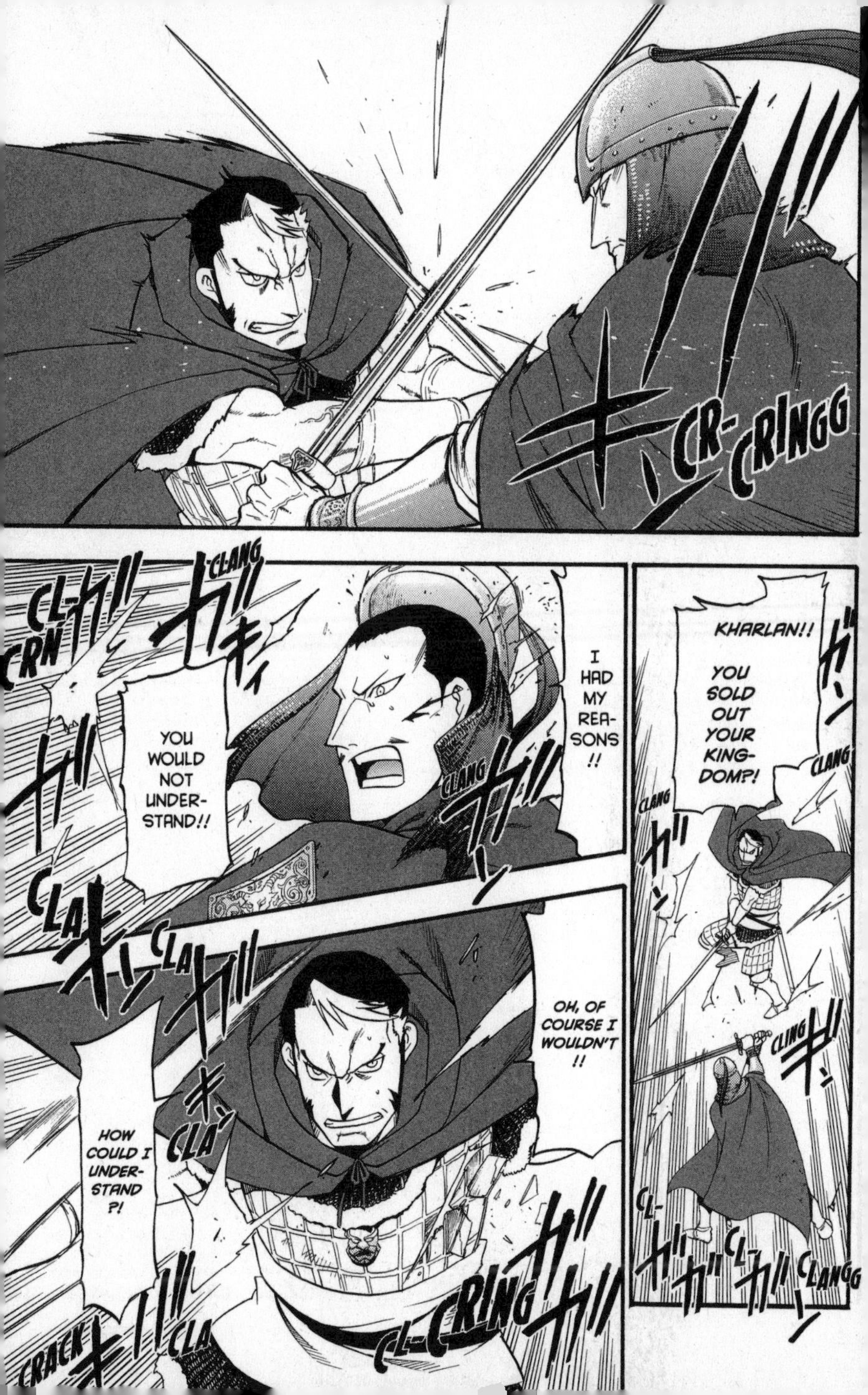
CR-CRINGG
KHARLAN!!
YOU SOLD OUT YOUR KING-DOM?!
CLANG
CLANG
CLING
CL-
CL-
CLANGG
CLANG
I HAD MY REA-SONS!!
YOU WOULD NOT UNDER-STAND!!
CL-CRN
CLANG
CLA
CLA
OH, OF COURSE I WOULDN'T!!
HOW COULD I UNDER-STAND?!
CLA
CL-CRING
CLA
CRACK

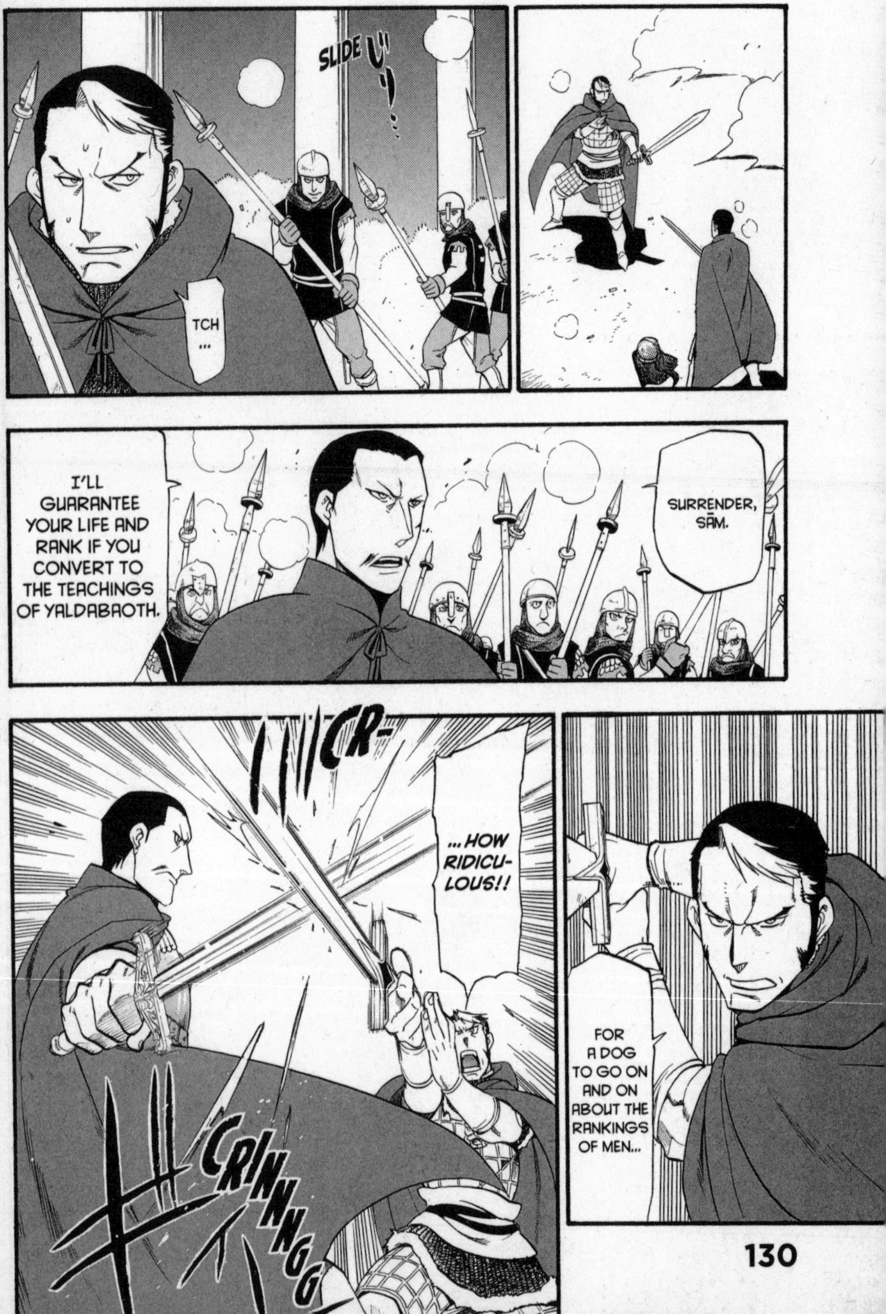

SLIDE
TCH ...
SURRENDER, SĀM.
I'LL GUARANTEE YOUR LIFE AND RANK IF YOU CONVERT TO THE TEACHINGS OF YALDABAOTH.
FOR A DOG TO GO ON AND ON ABOUT THE RANKINGS OF MEN...
...HOW RIDICULOUS!!
CR-
CRINNNGG

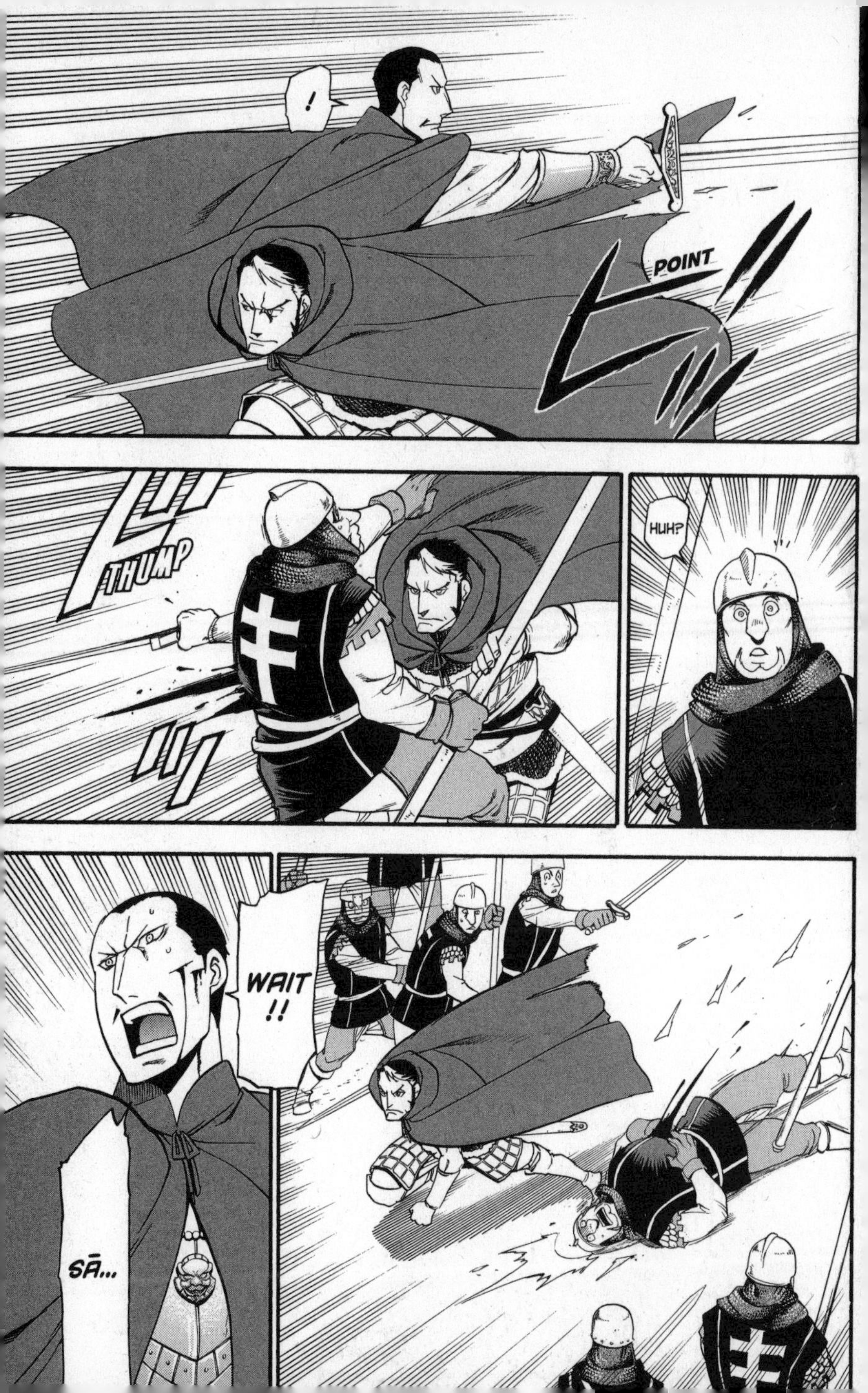
!
POINT
HUH?
THUMP
WAIT !!
SĀ...

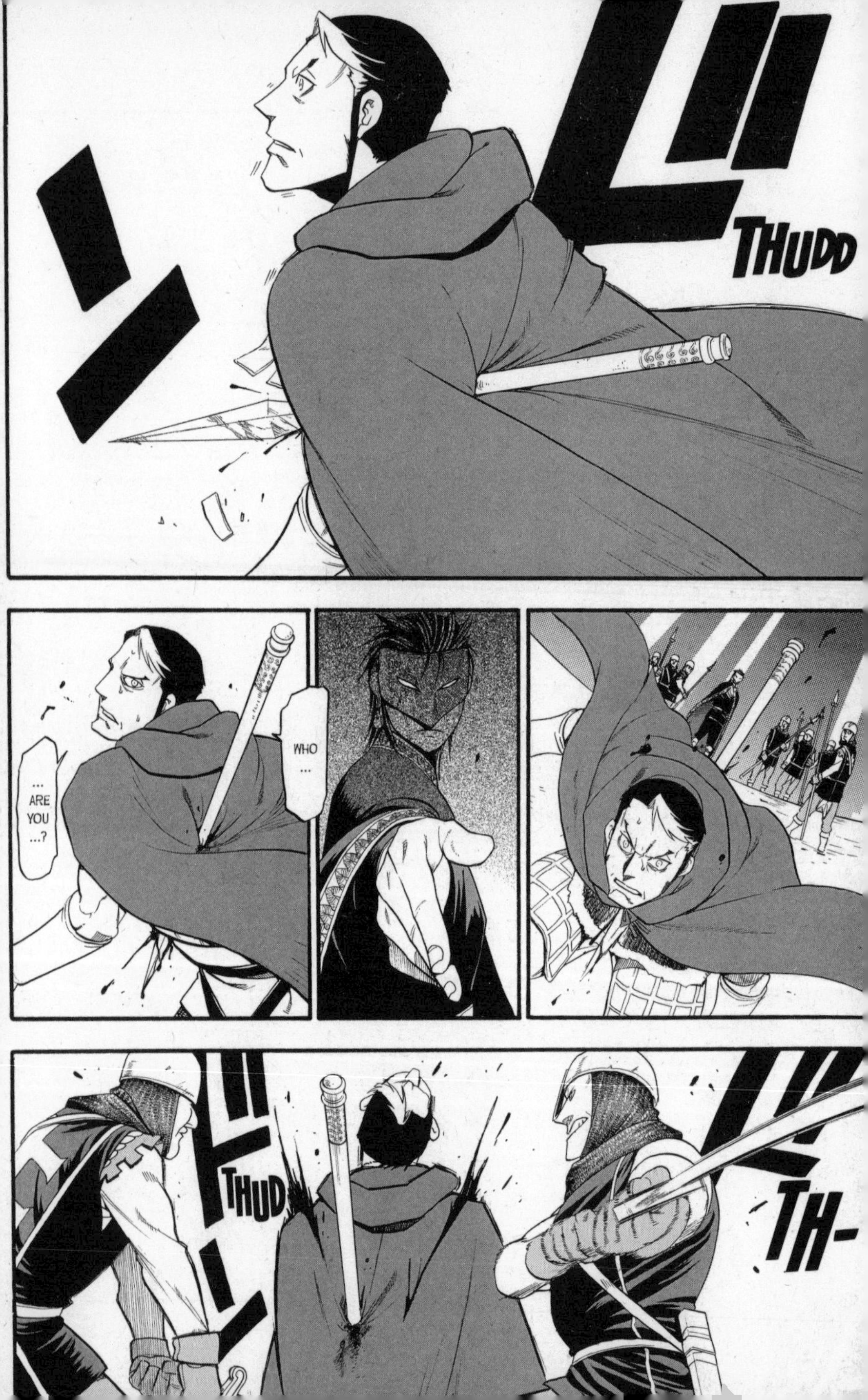
THUDD
WHO ...
... ARE YOU ...?
TH-
THUD

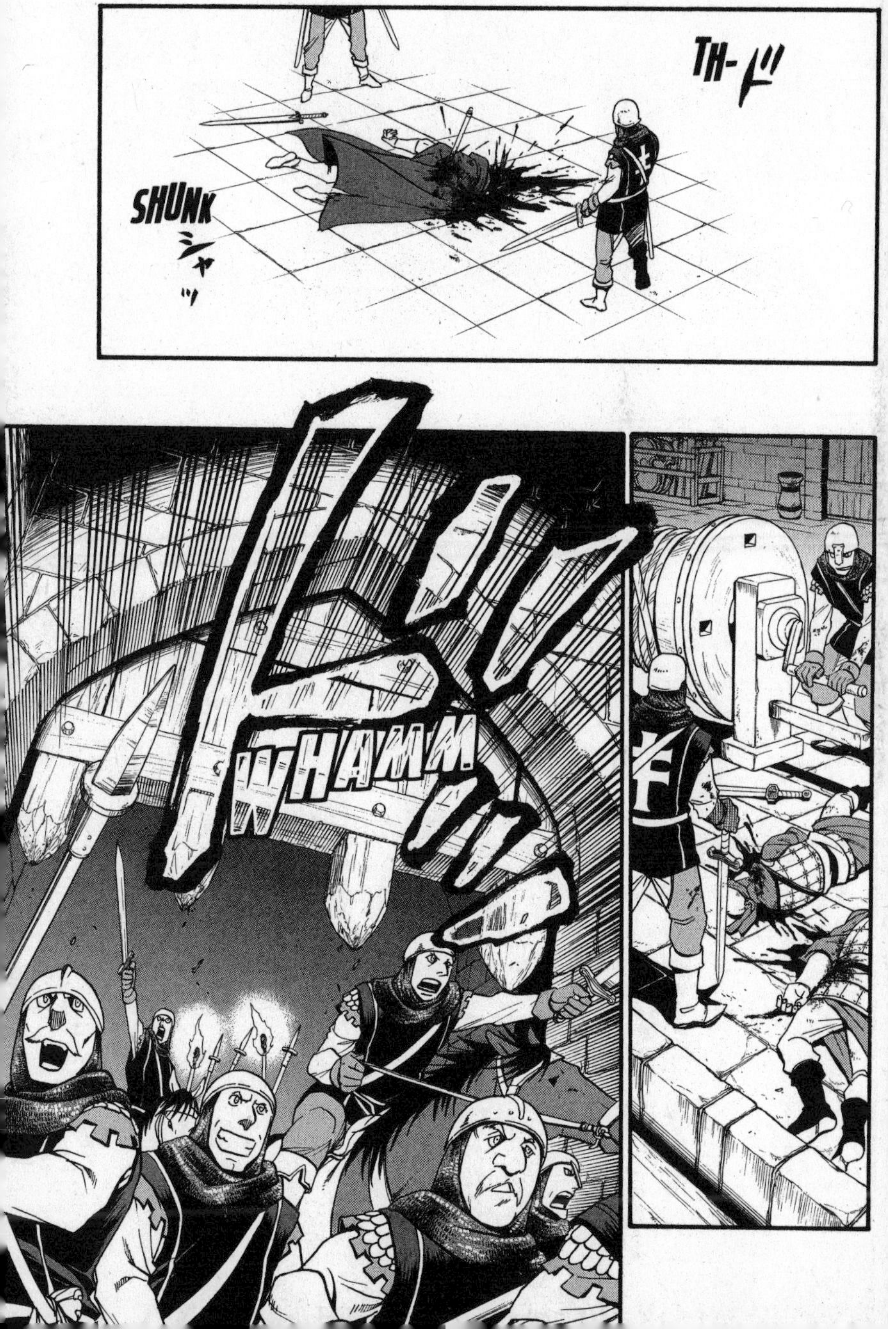
TH-
SHUNK
シャッ
WHAMM

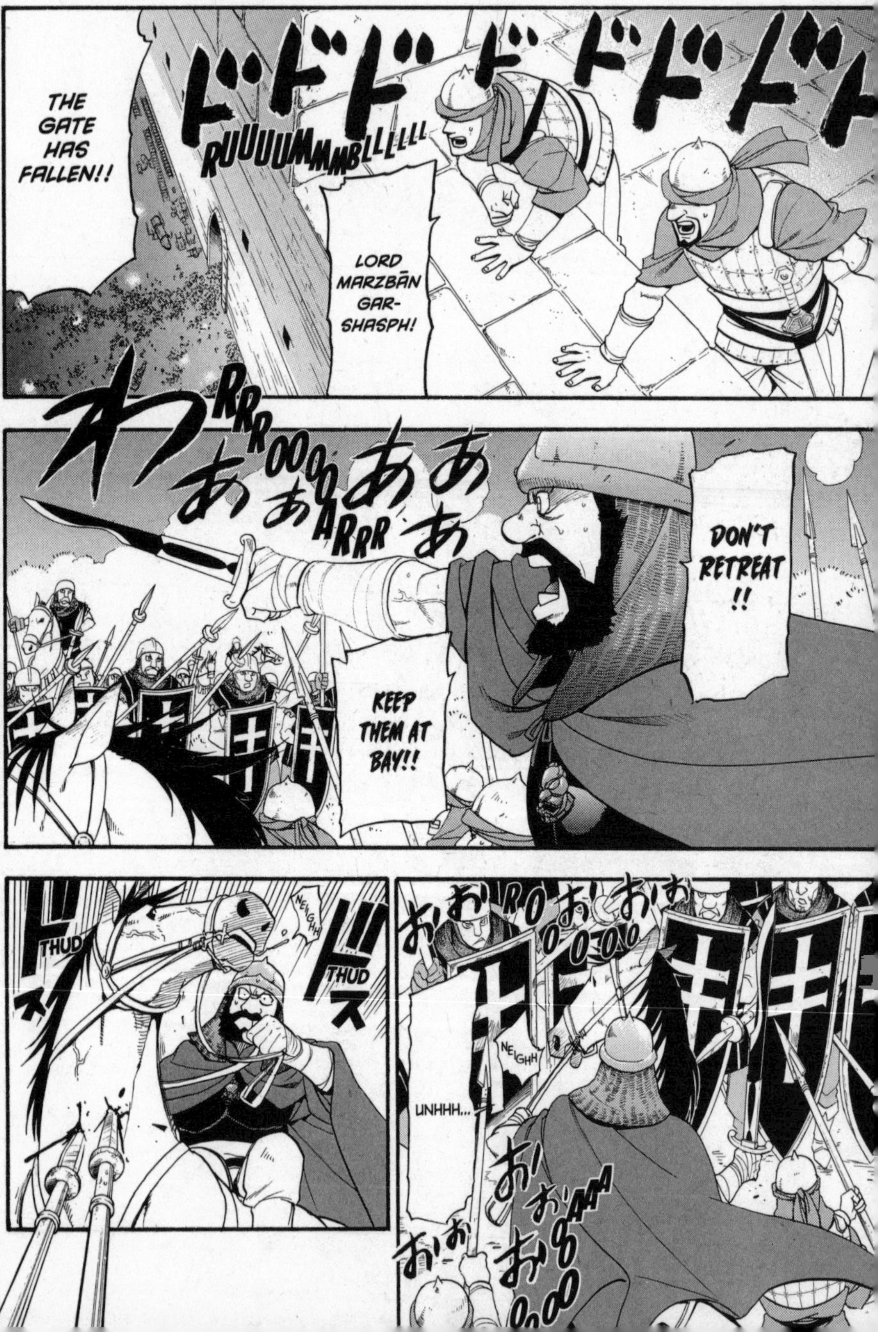
ドドドドドドドド
RUUUUMMMBLLLLLL
LORD MARZBĀN GAR-SHASPH!
THE GATE HAS FALLEN!!
わあああああ
RRROOOOARRR
DON'T RETREAT!!
KEEP THEM AT BAY!!
おおおおおお
ROOOOOO
NEIGHH
UNHHH...
おおおおお
OOOOAAAA
ドス
THUD
NEIGHH
ドス
THUD

STABB

THUD
THUMP
THUMP
THUD
THUMP

WHOAH...

ゴ
ブ
ッ

SPLOSH

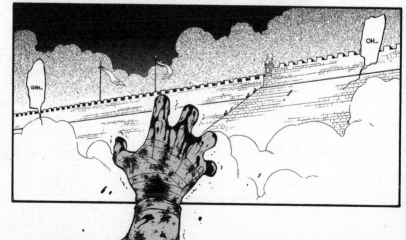

OH...

GAH...

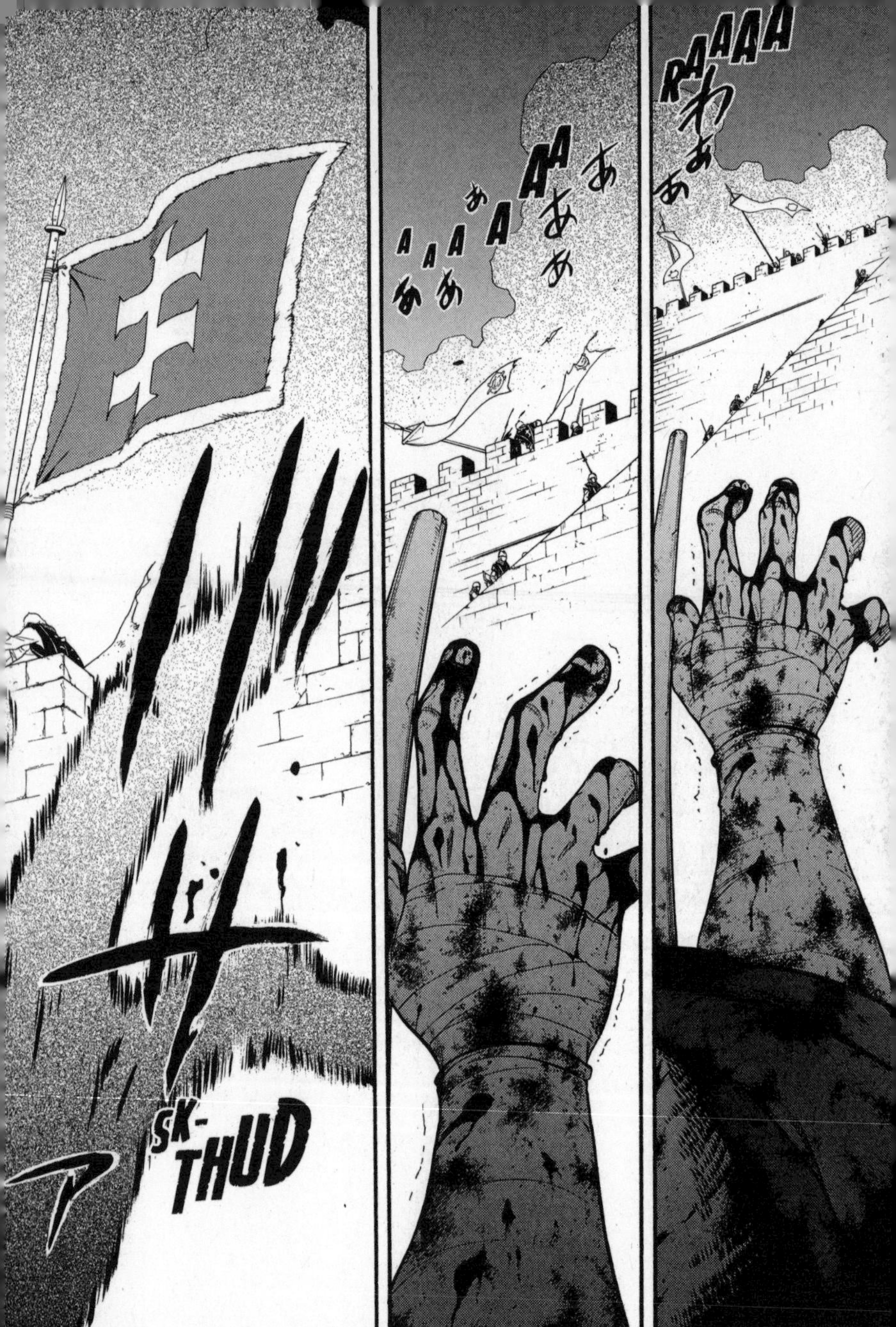
RAAAAA
AAAAAA
SK-THUD

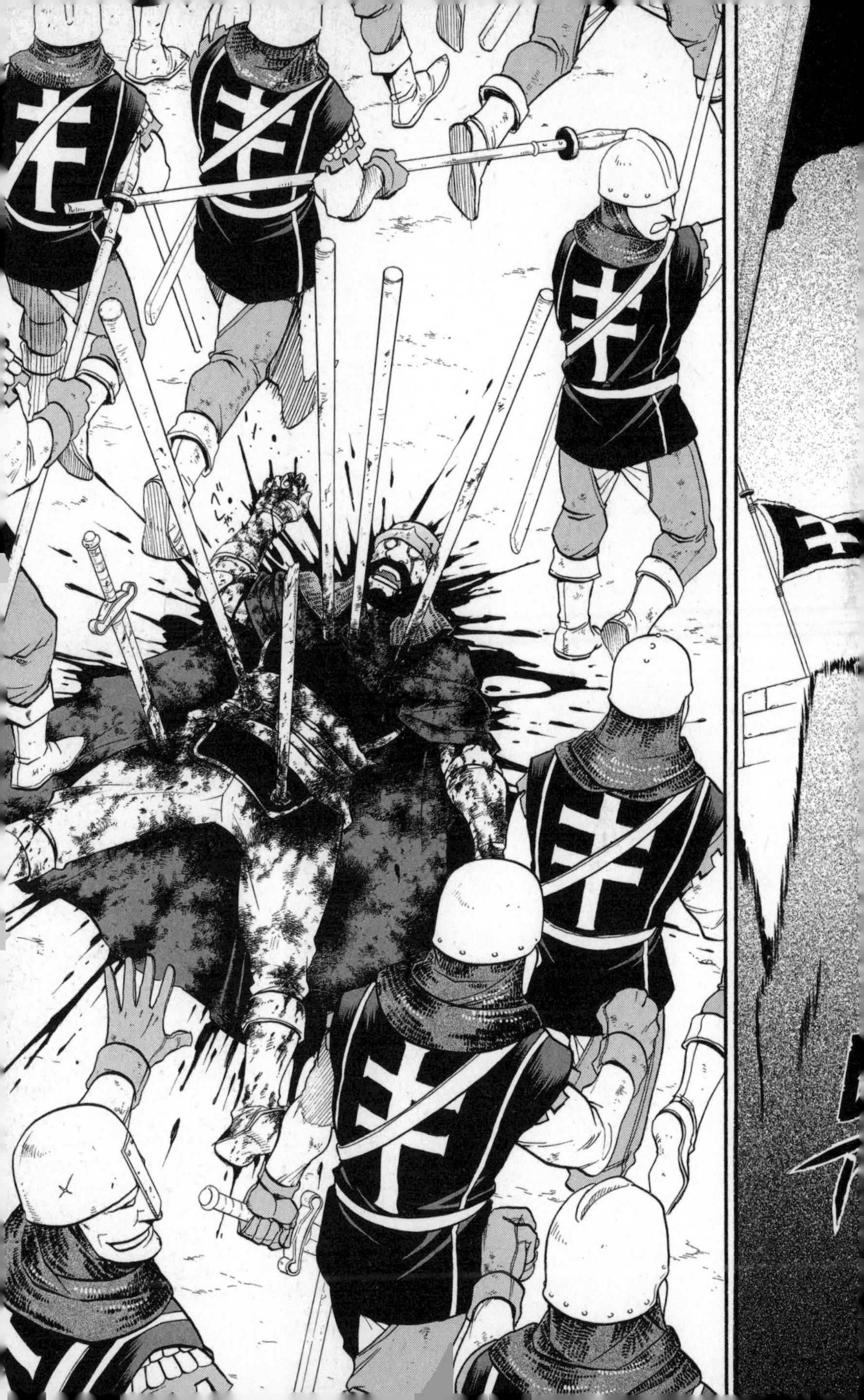
べしゃっ

THE HEROIC LEGEND OF
ARSLAN

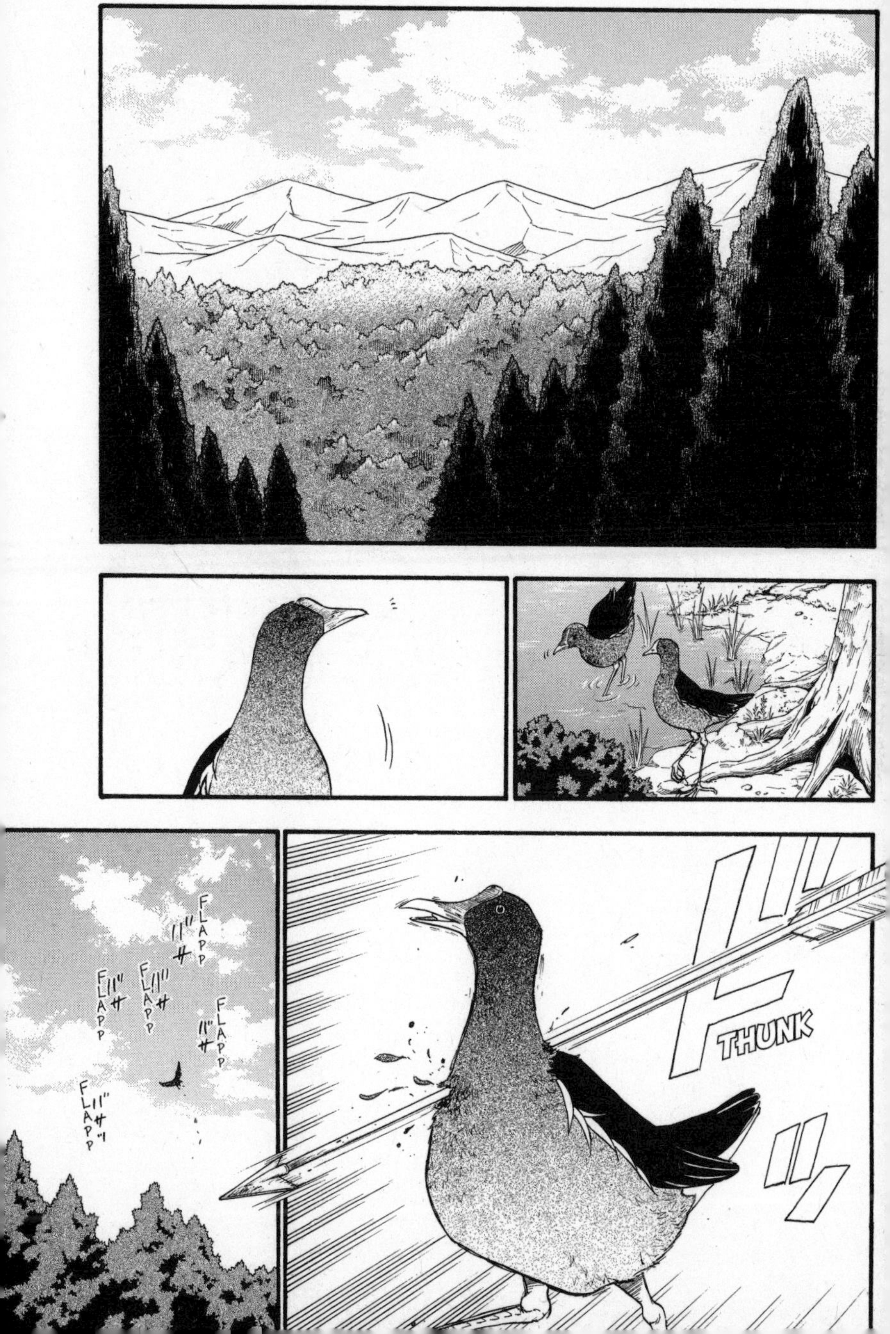

THUNK
FLAPP
FLAPP
FLAPP
FLAPP
FLAPP

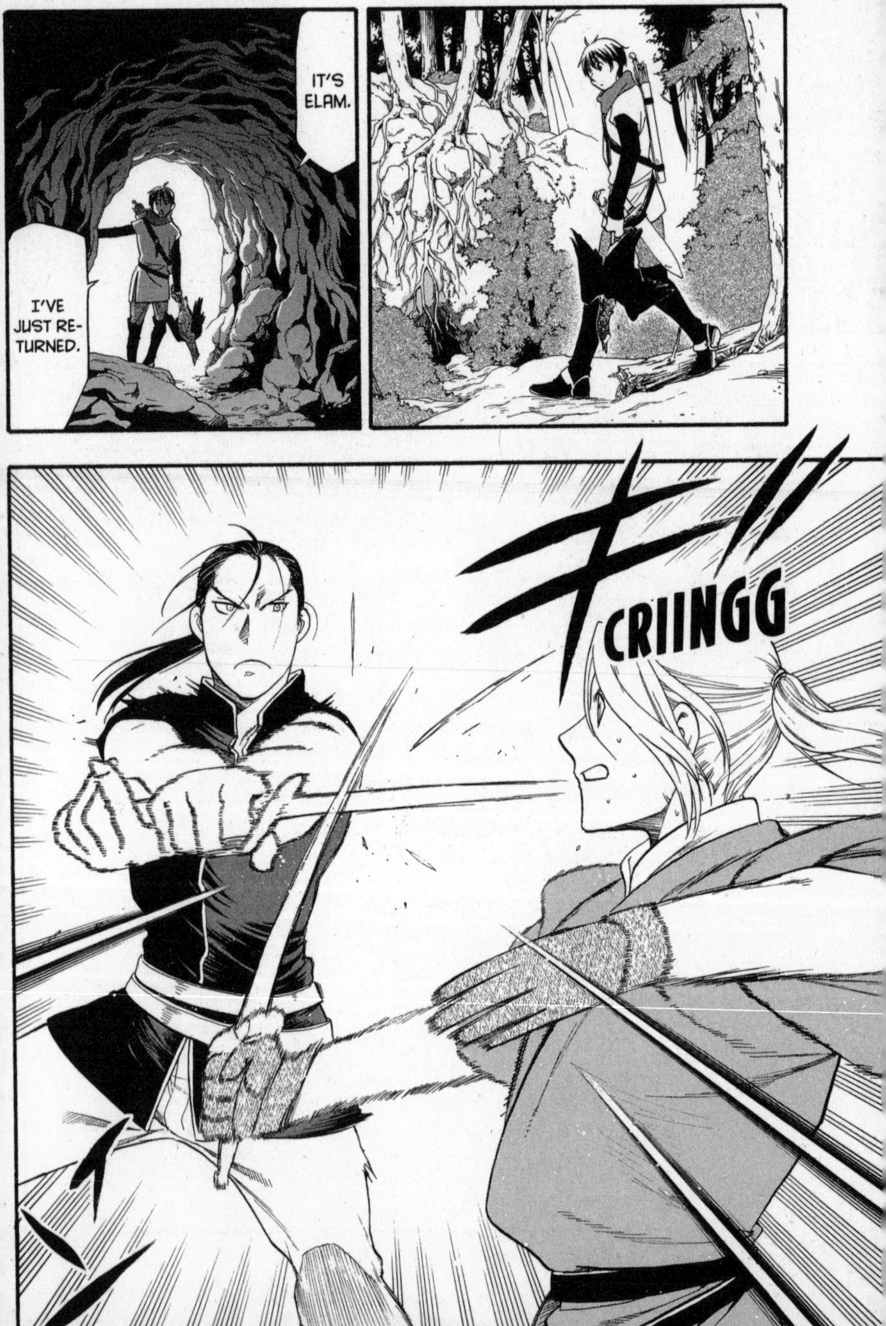
IT'S ELAM.
I'VE JUST RE-TURNED.
CRIINGG

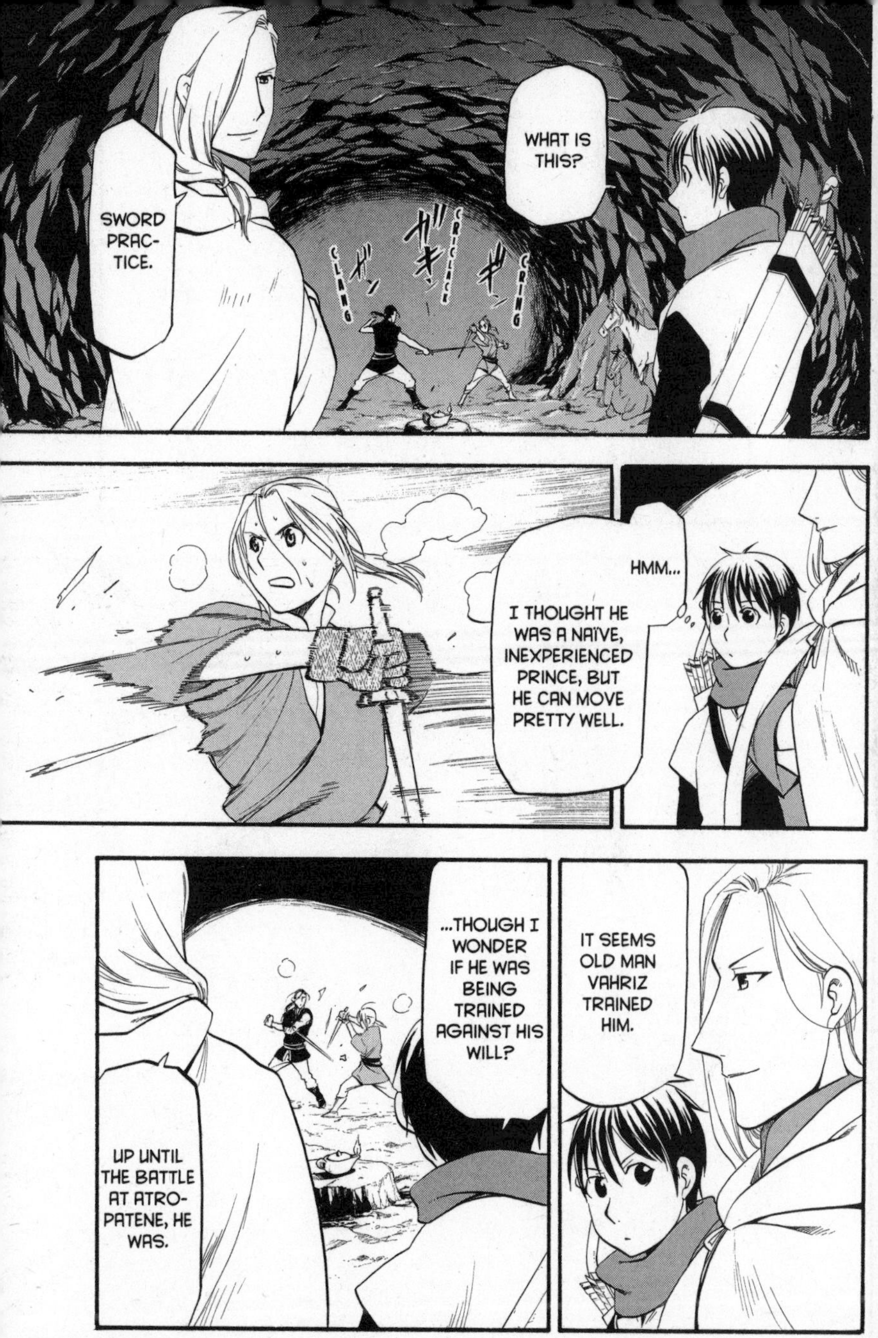
WHAT IS THIS?
SWORD PRAC-TICE.
CRING
CRICLACK
CLANG
HMM...
I THOUGHT HE WAS A NAÏVE, INEXPERIENCED PRINCE, BUT HE CAN MOVE PRETTY WELL.
IT SEEMS OLD MAN VAHRIZ TRAINED HIM.
...THOUGH I WONDER IF HE WAS BEING TRAINED AGAINST HIS WILL?
UP UNTIL THE BATTLE AT ATRO-PATENE, HE WAS.

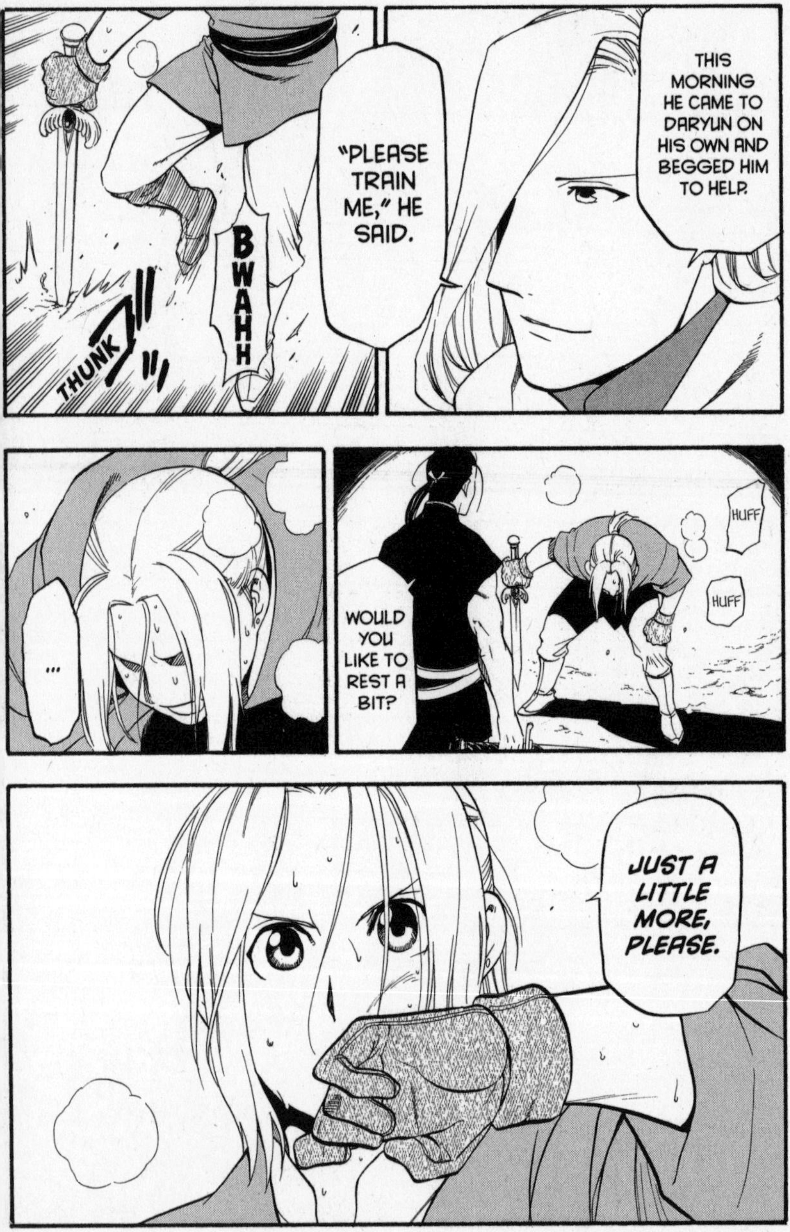
THIS MORNING HE CAME TO DARYUN ON HIS OWN AND BEGGED HIM TO HELP.
"PLEASE TRAIN ME," HE SAID.
BWAHH
THUNK
HUFF
HUFF
WOULD YOU LIKE TO REST A BIT?
...
JUST A LITTLE MORE, PLEASE.

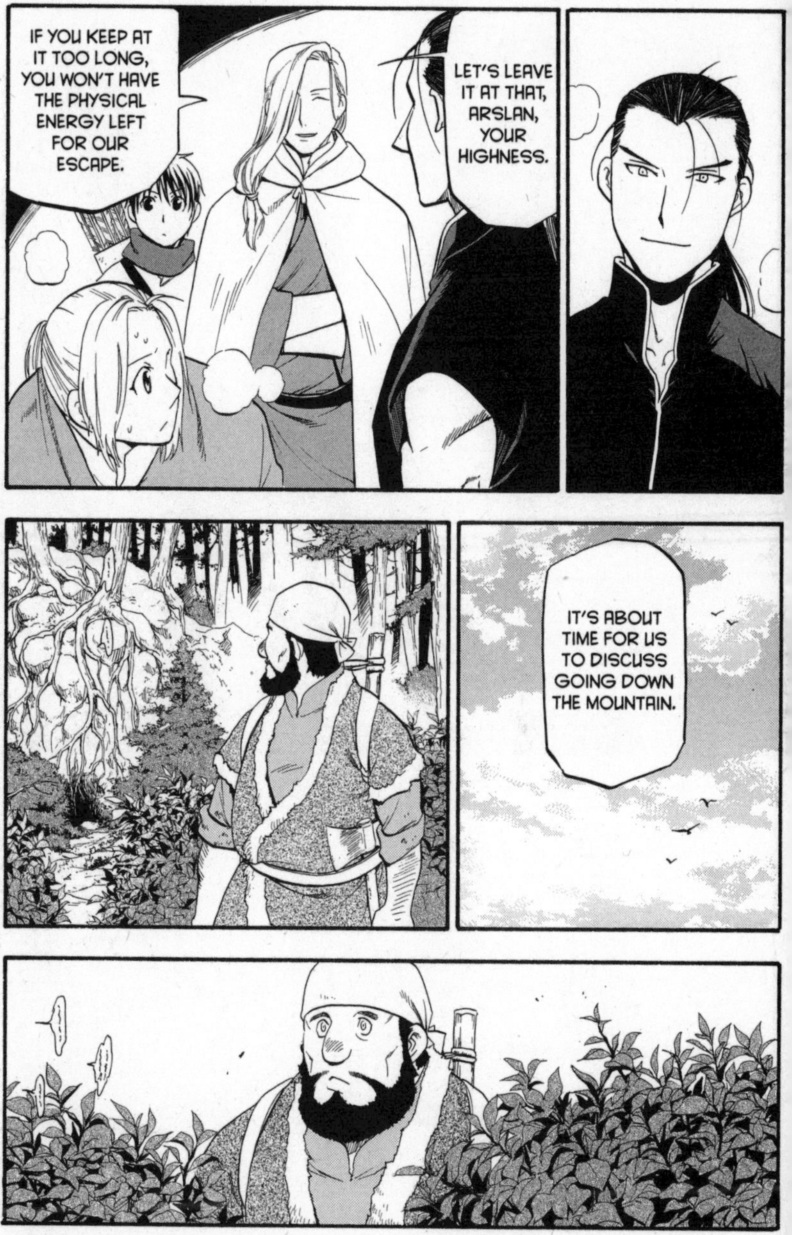
LET'S LEAVE IT AT THAT, ARSLAN, YOUR HIGHNESS.
IF YOU KEEP AT IT TOO LONG, YOU WON'T HAVE THE PHYSICAL ENERGY LEFT FOR OUR ESCAPE.
IT'S ABOUT TIME FOR US TO DISCUSS GOING DOWN THE MOUNTAIN.

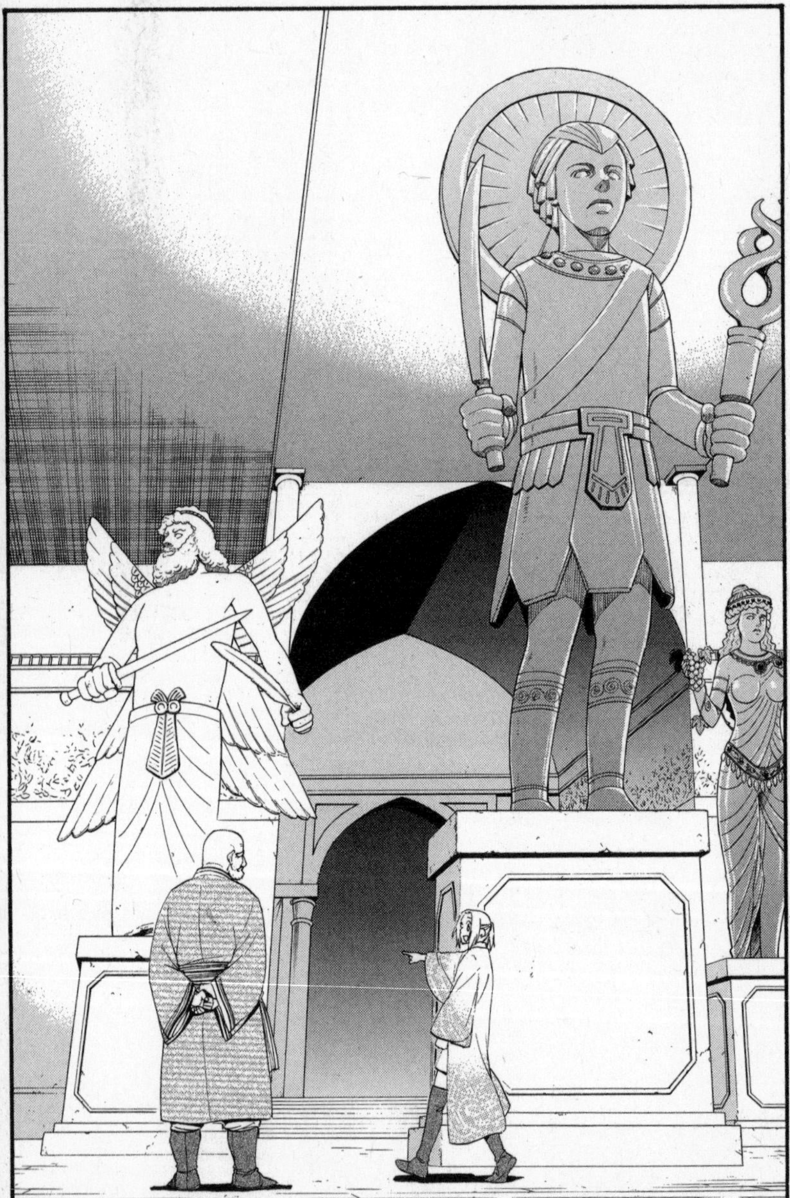

Chapter 9: Bacchanal of Bloodshed

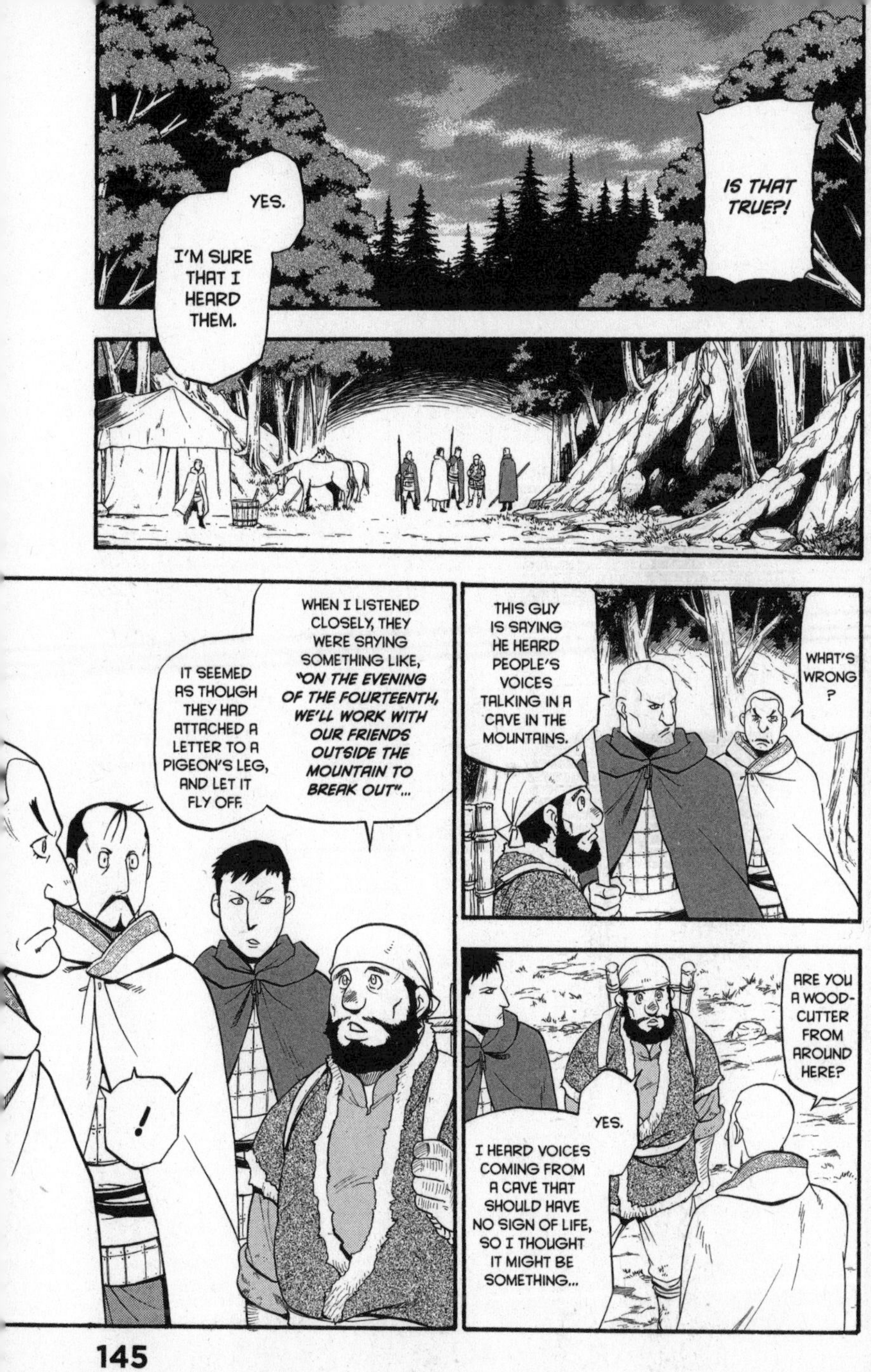
IS THAT TRUE?!
YES.
I'M SURE THAT I HEARD THEM.
WHAT'S WRONG?
THIS GUY IS SAYING HE HEARD PEOPLE'S VOICES TALKING IN A CAVE IN THE MOUNTAINS.
ARE YOU A WOOD-CUTTER FROM AROUND HERE?
YES.
I HEARD VOICES COMING FROM A CAVE THAT SHOULD HAVE NO SIGN OF LIFE, SO I THOUGHT IT MIGHT BE SOMETHING...
WHEN I LISTENED CLOSELY, THEY WERE SAYING SOMETHING LIKE, *"ON THE EVENING OF THE FOURTEENTH, WE'LL WORK WITH OUR FRIENDS OUTSIDE THE MOUNTAIN TO BREAK OUT"*...
IT SEEMED AS THOUGH THEY HAD ATTACHED A LETTER TO A PIGEON'S LEG, AND LET IT FLY OFF.
!

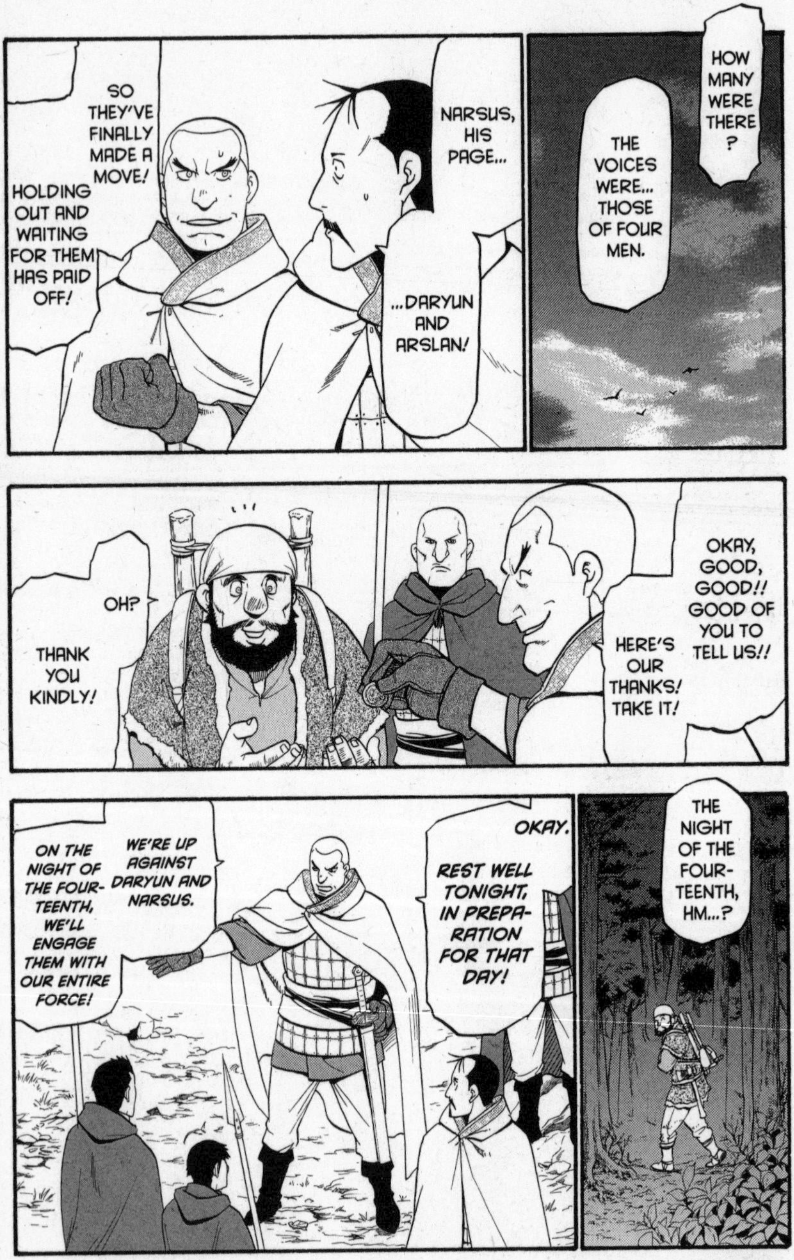

HOW MANY WERE THERE?
THE VOICES WERE... THOSE OF FOUR MEN.
NARSUS, HIS PAGE...
...DARYUN AND ARSLAN!
SO THEY'VE FINALLY MADE A MOVE!
HOLDING OUT AND WAITING FOR THEM HAS PAID OFF!
OKAY, GOOD, GOOD!! GOOD OF YOU TO TELL US!!
HERE'S OUR THANKS! TAKE IT!
OH?
THANK YOU KINDLY!
THE NIGHT OF THE FOUR-TEENTH, HM...?
OKAY.
REST WELL TONIGHT, IN PREPA-RATION FOR THAT DAY!
WE'RE UP AGAINST DARYUN AND NARSUS.
ON THE NIGHT OF THE FOUR-TEENTH, WE'LL ENGAGE THEM WITH OUR ENTIRE FORCE!

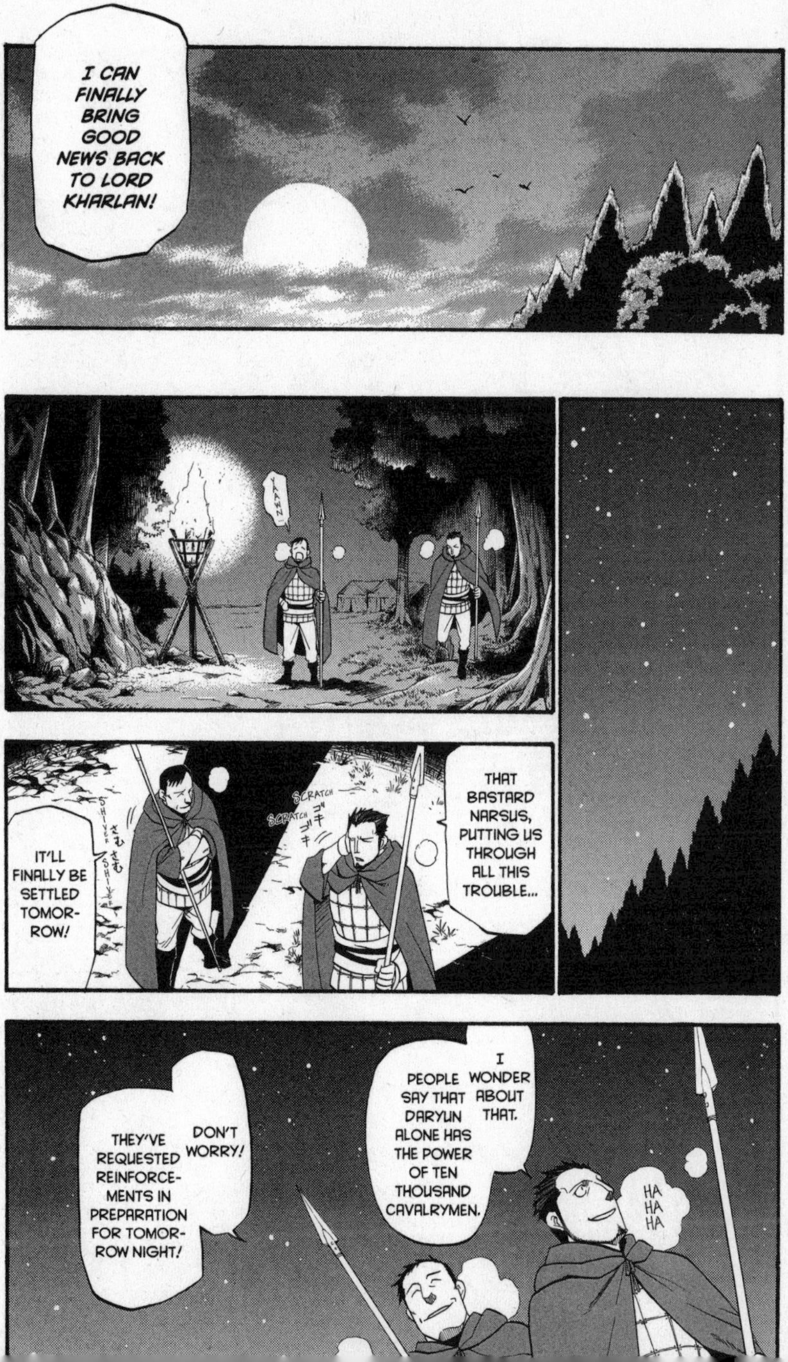
I CAN FINALLY BRING GOOD NEWS BACK TO LORD KHARLAN!
YAWN...
THAT BASTARD NARSUS, PUTTING US THROUGH ALL THIS TROUBLE...
SCRATCH SCRATCH
SHIVER SHIVER
IT'LL FINALLY BE SETTLED TOMORROW!
HA HA HA
I WONDER ABOUT THAT.
PEOPLE SAY THAT DARYUN ALONE HAS THE POWER OF TEN THOUSAND CAVALRYMEN.
DON'T WORRY!
THEY'VE REQUESTED REINFORCEMENTS IN PREPARATION FOR TOMORROW NIGHT!

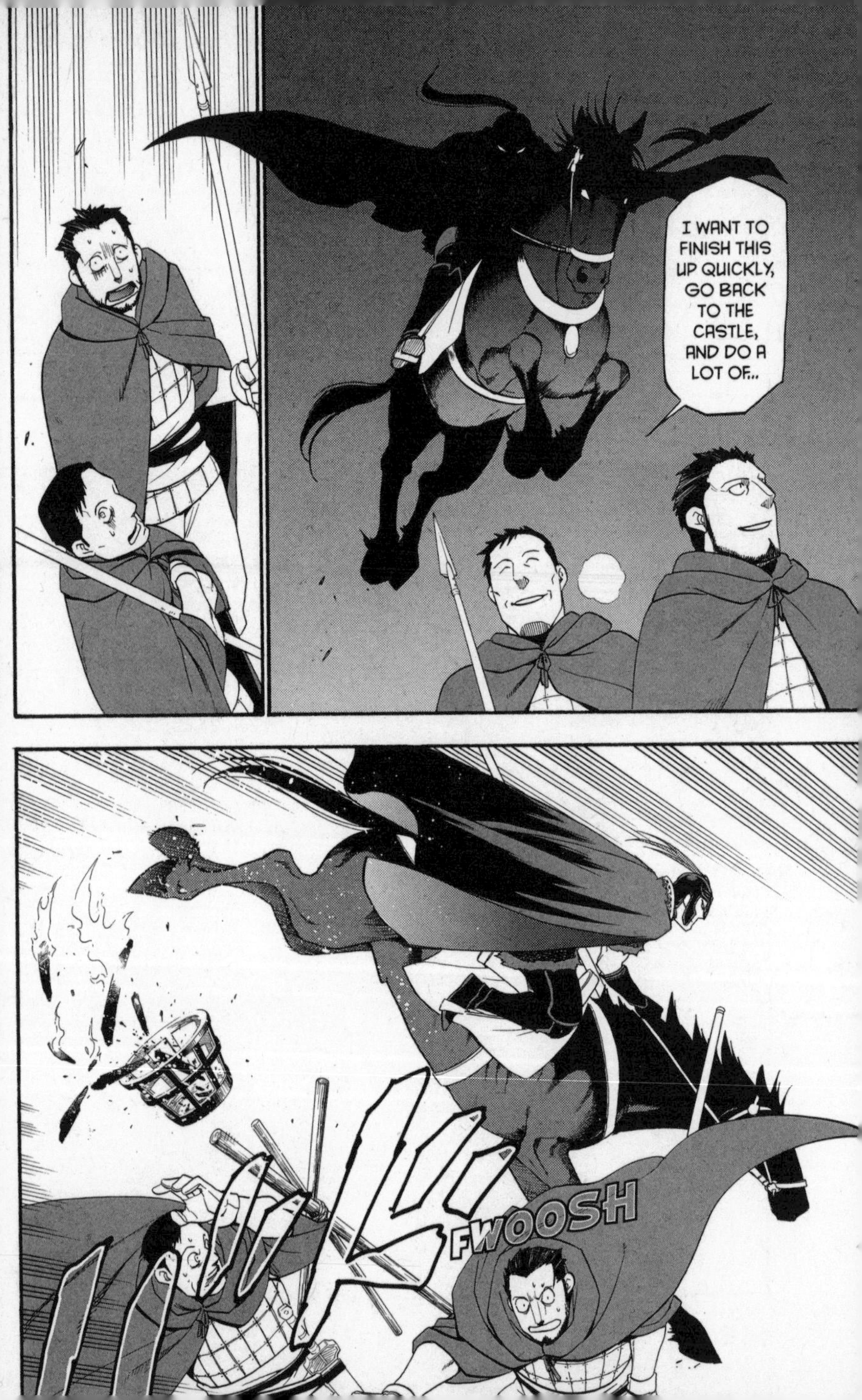
I WANT TO FINISH THIS UP QUICKLY, GO BACK TO THE CASTLE, AND DO A LOT OF...
FWOOSH

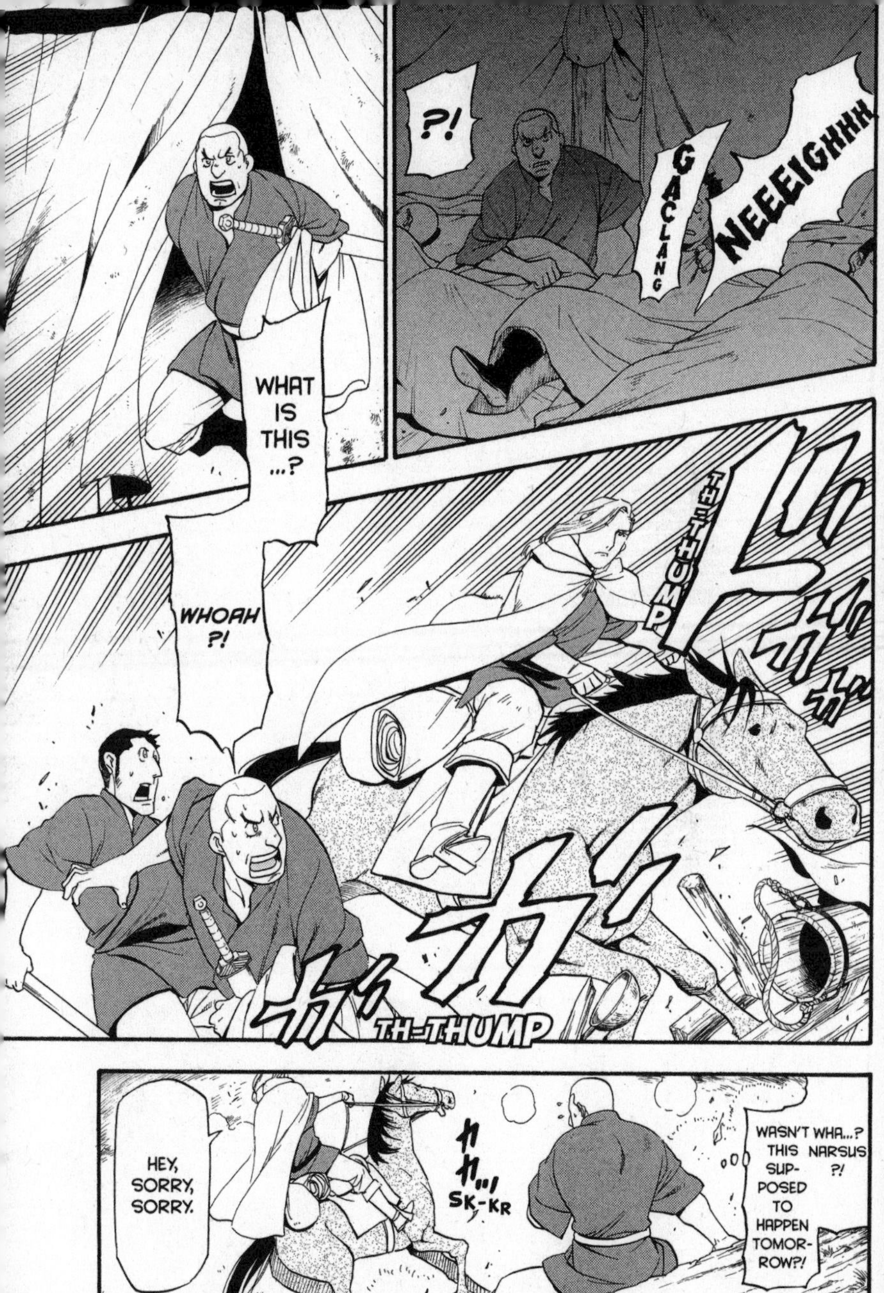
?!
GACLANG
NEEEIGHHH
WHAT IS THIS ...?
WHOAH ?!
TH-THUMP
TH-THUMP
WHA...? NARSUS ?!
WASN'T THIS SUP-POSED TO HAPPEN TOMOR-ROW?!
SK-KR
HEY, SORRY, SORRY.

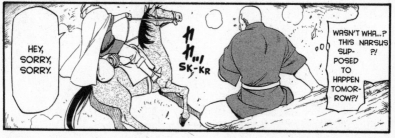

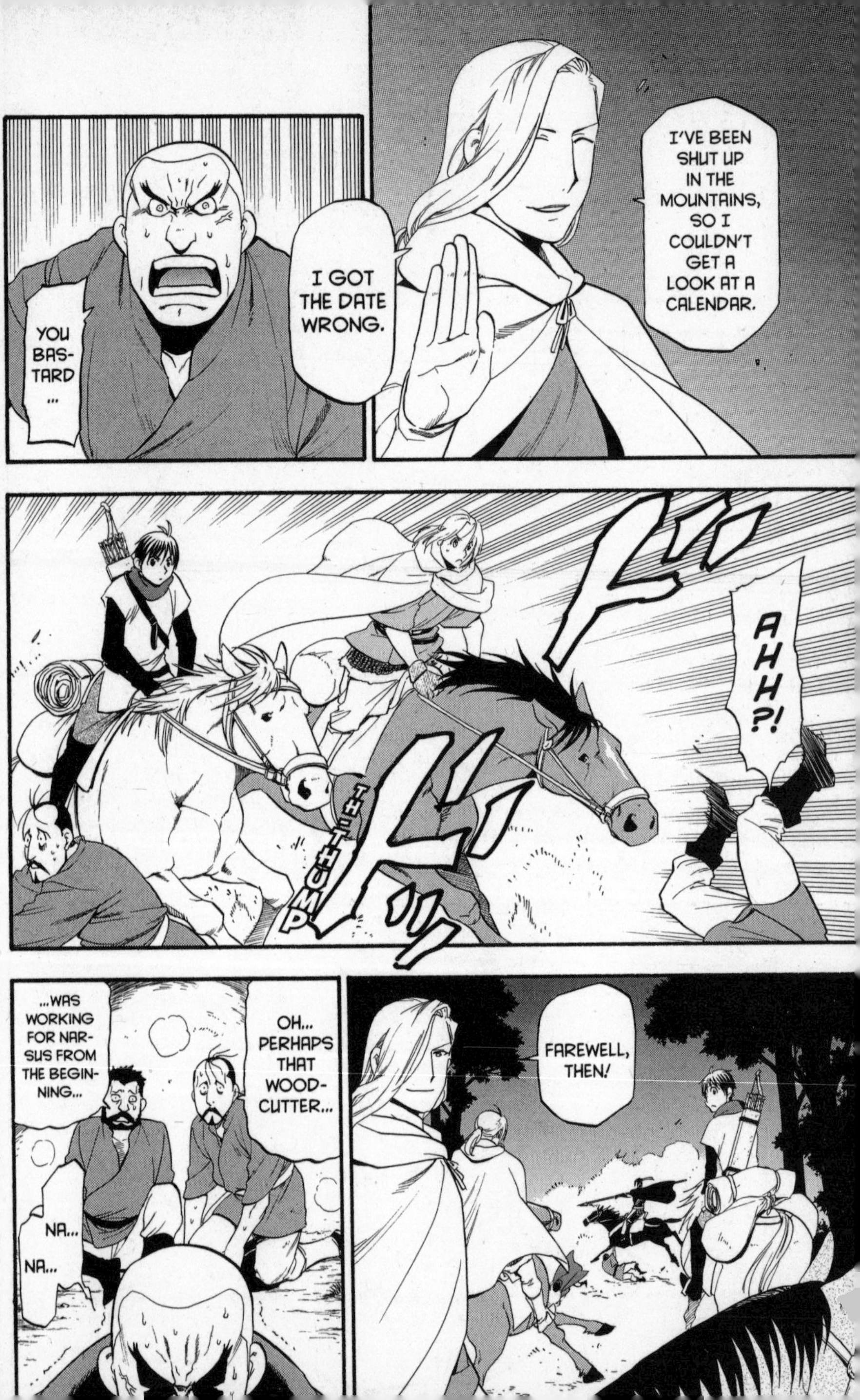
I'VE BEEN SHUT UP IN THE MOUNTAINS, SO I COULDN'T GET A LOOK AT A CALENDAR.
I GOT THE DATE WRONG.
YOU BASTARD...
AHHH?!
TH-THUMP
FAREWELL, THEN!
OH... PERHAPS THAT WOODCUTTER...
...WAS WORKING FOR NARSUS FROM THE BEGINNING...
NA...
NA...

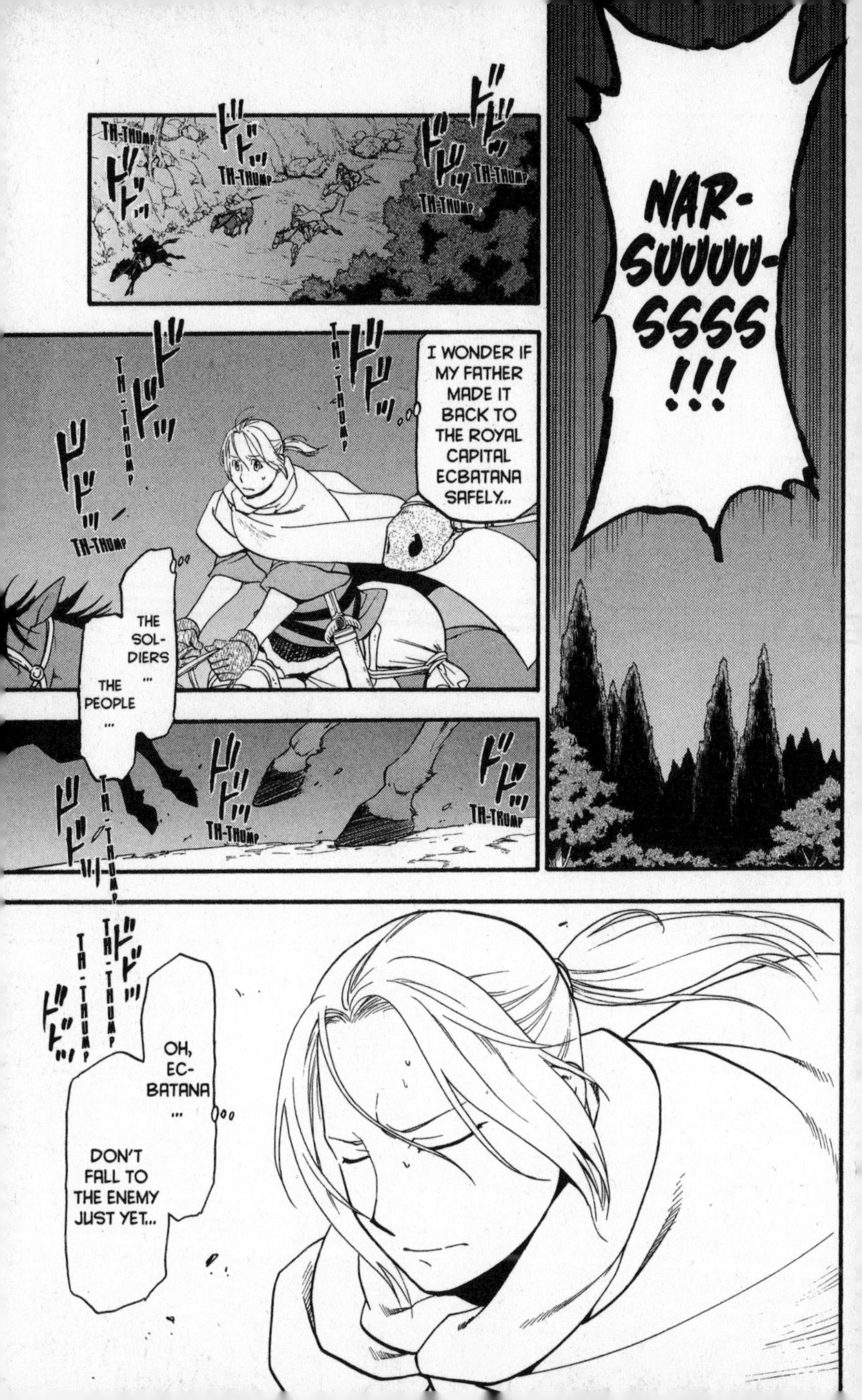
NAR-SUUUU-SSSS!!!
TH-THUMP
TH-THUMP
TH-THUMP
TH-THUMP
TH-THUMP
TH-THUMP
I WONDER IF MY FATHER MADE IT BACK TO THE ROYAL CAPITAL ECBATANA SAFELY...
TH-THUMP
THE SOLDIERS...
THE PEOPLE...
TH-THUMP
TH-THUMP
TH-THUMP
TH-THUMP
TH-THUMP
OH, ECBATANA...
DON'T FALL TO THE ENEMY JUST YET...

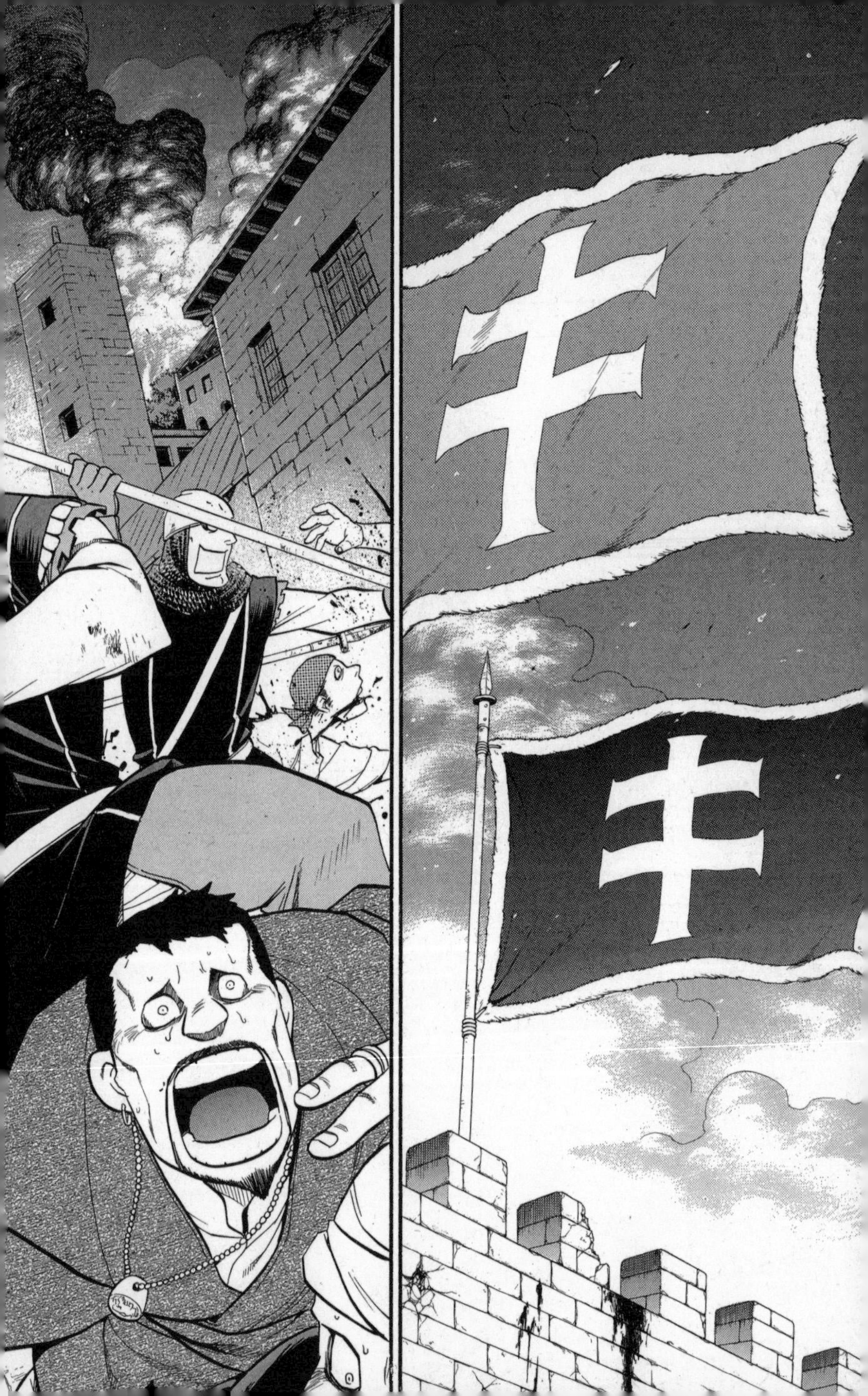

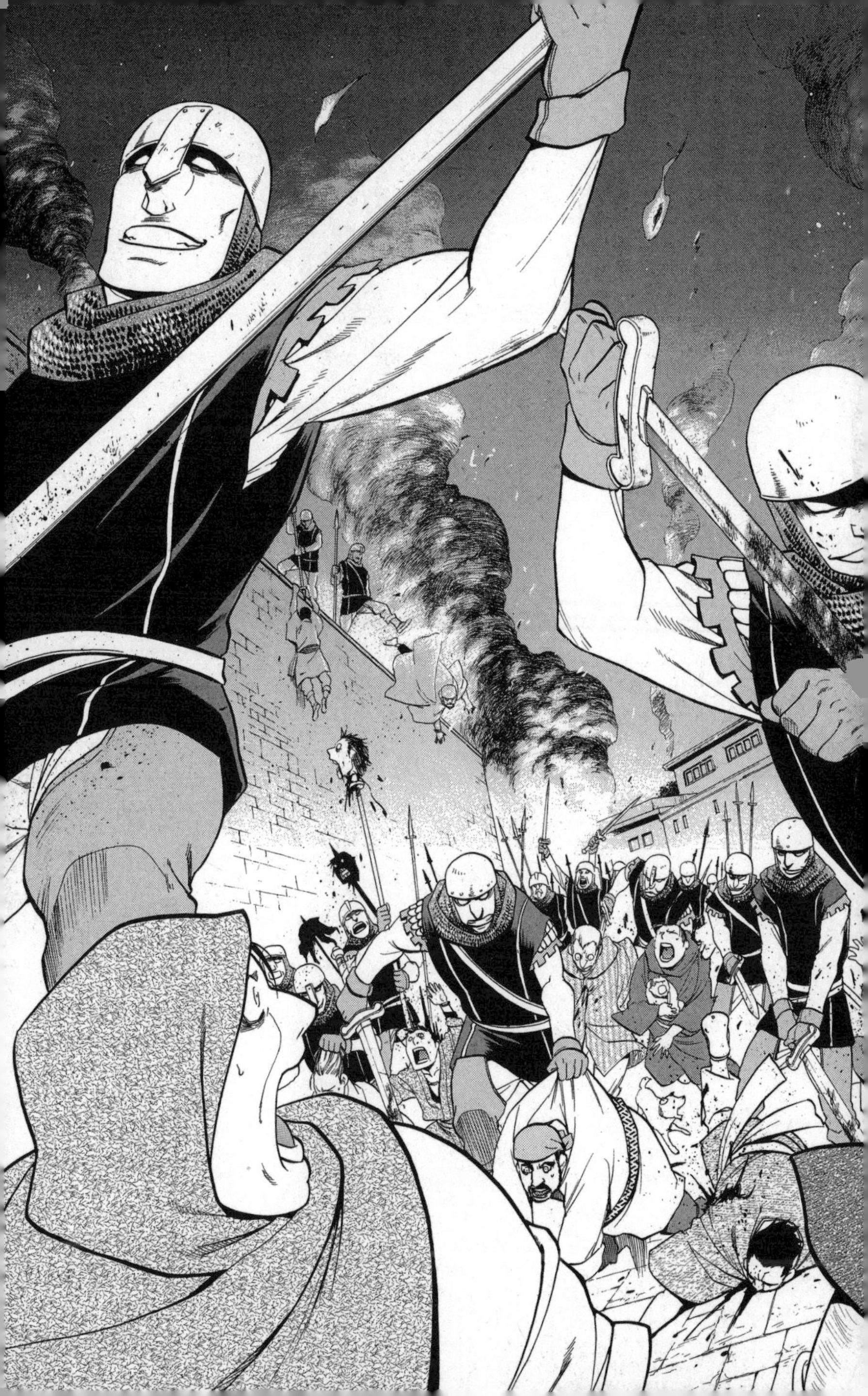

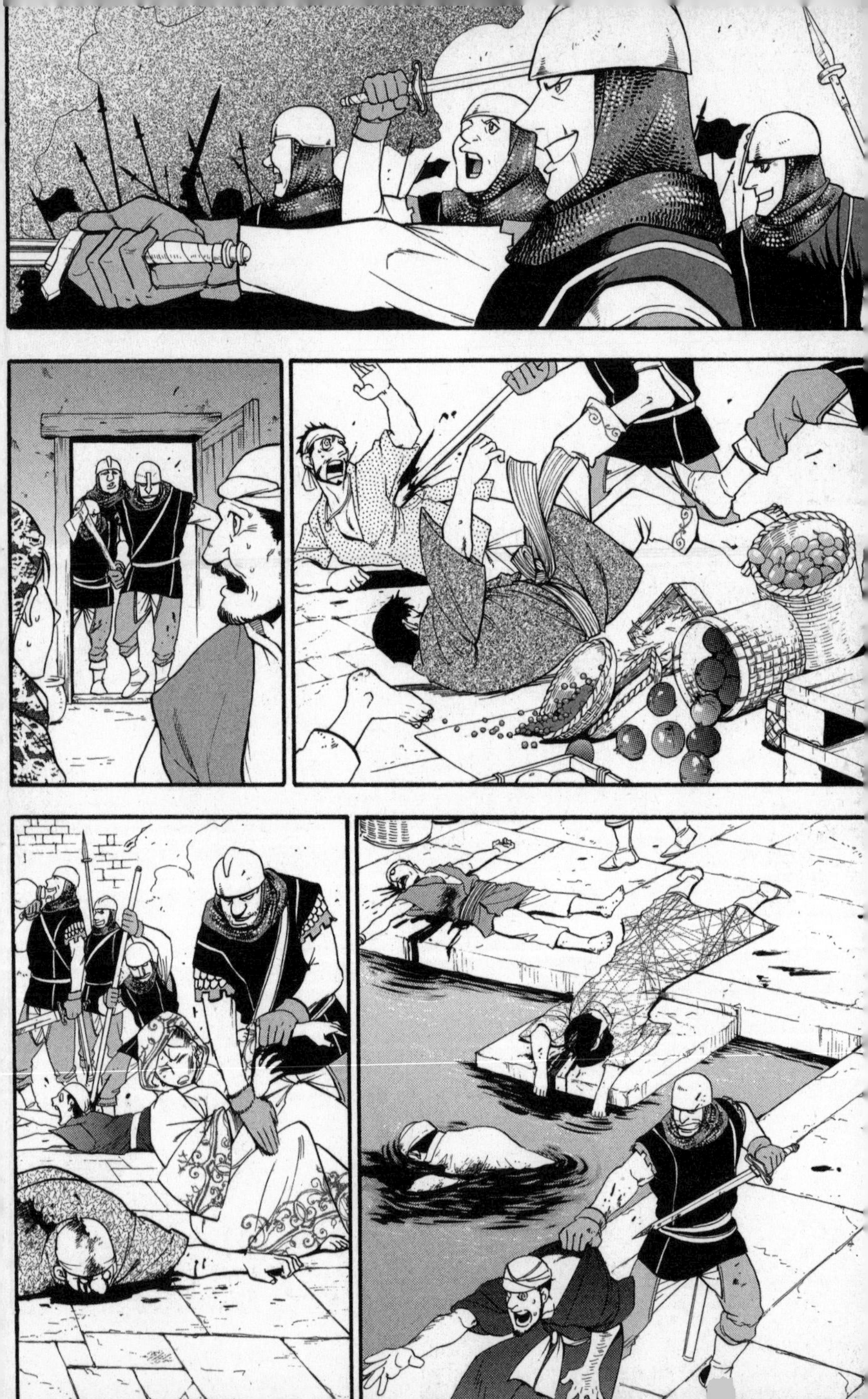

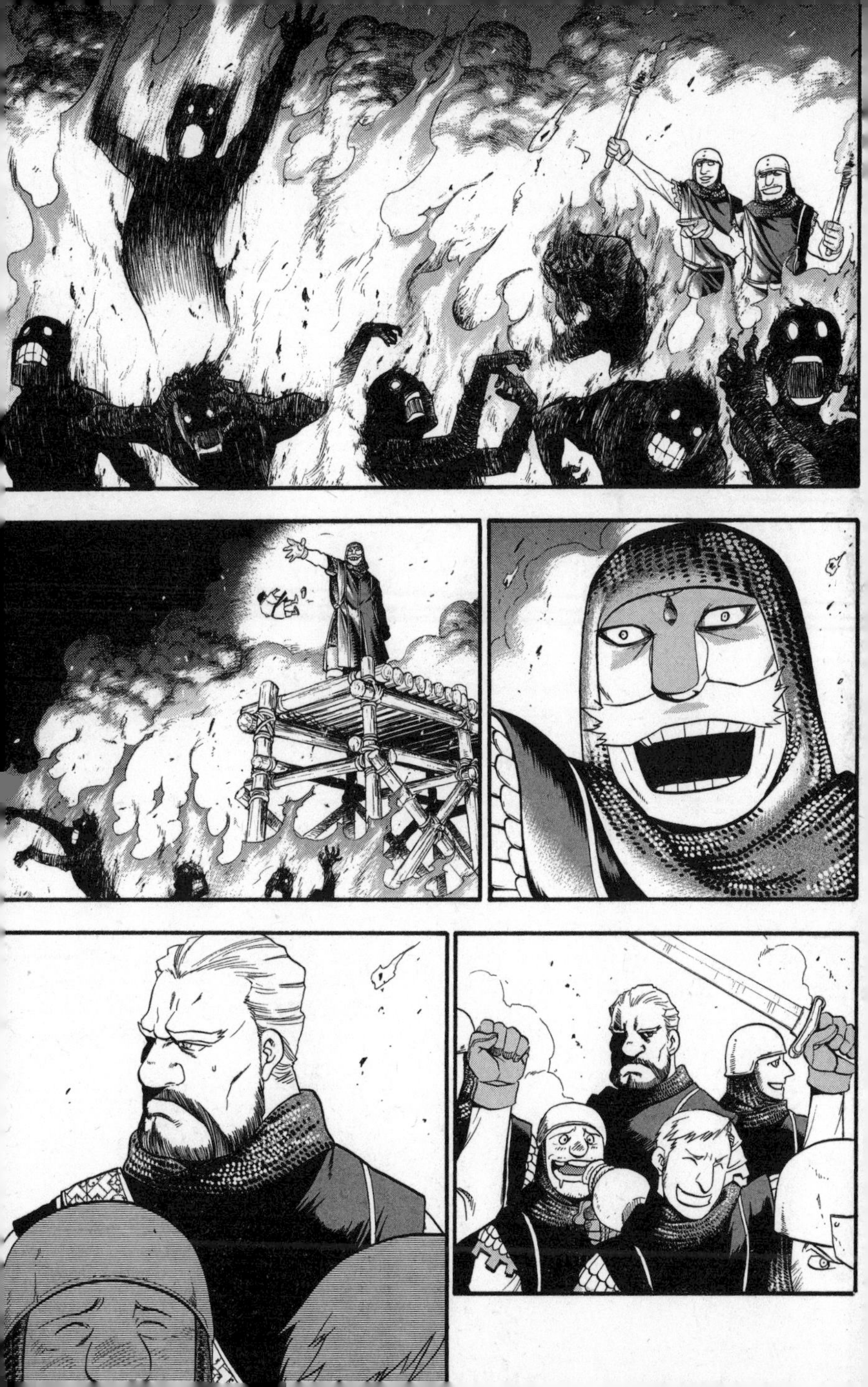

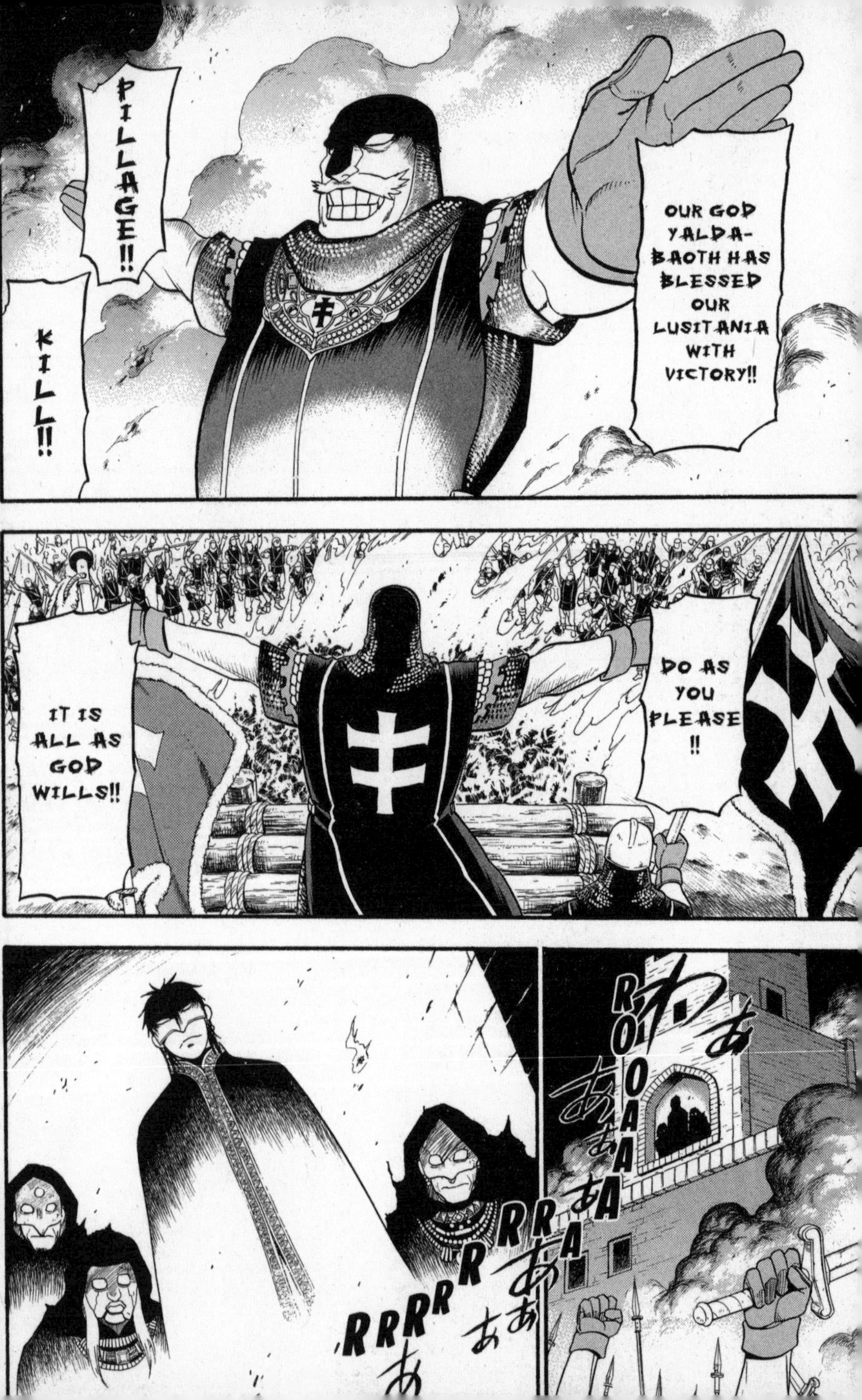
OUR GOD YALDABAOTH HAS BLESSED OUR LUSITANIA WITH VICTORY!!
PILLAGE!!
KILL!!
DO AS YOU PLEASE!!
IT IS ALL AS GOD WILLS!!
ROOAAAARRRRRRR,

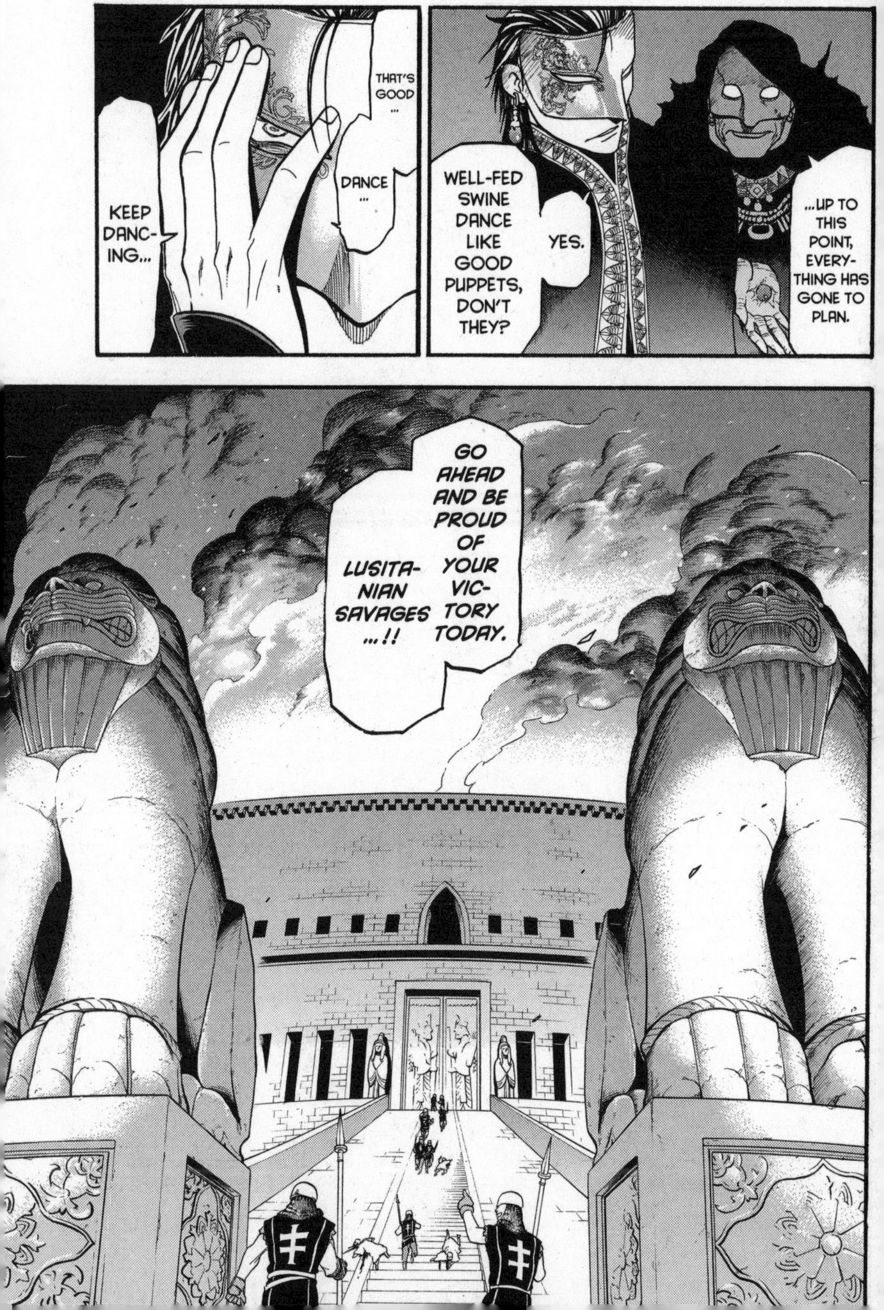
...UP TO THIS POINT, EVERYTHING HAS GONE TO PLAN.
YES.
WELL-FED SWINE DANCE LIKE GOOD PUPPETS, DON'T THEY?
THAT'S GOOD ...
DANCE ...
KEEP DANCING...
GO AHEAD AND BE PROUD OF YOUR VICTORY TODAY.
LUSITANIAN SAVAGES ...!!

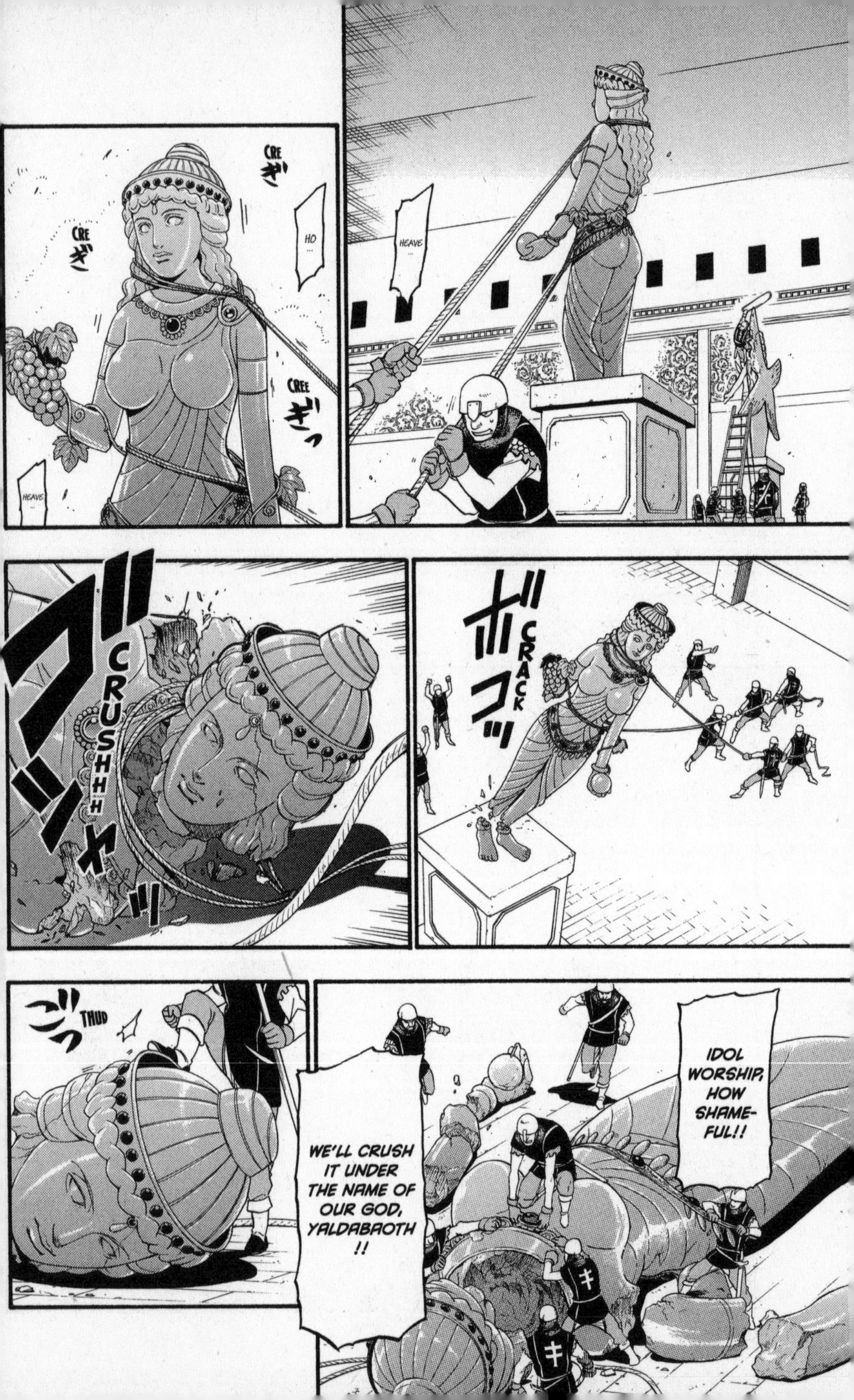
HEAVE …
HO …
CRE ぎ
CRE ぎ
CREE ぎっ
HEAVE …
ボゴッ CRACK
グシャッ CRUSHHH
IDOL WORSHIP, HOW SHAMEFUL!!
WE'LL CRUSH IT UNDER THE NAME OF OUR GOD, YALDABAOTH !!
ごっ THUD

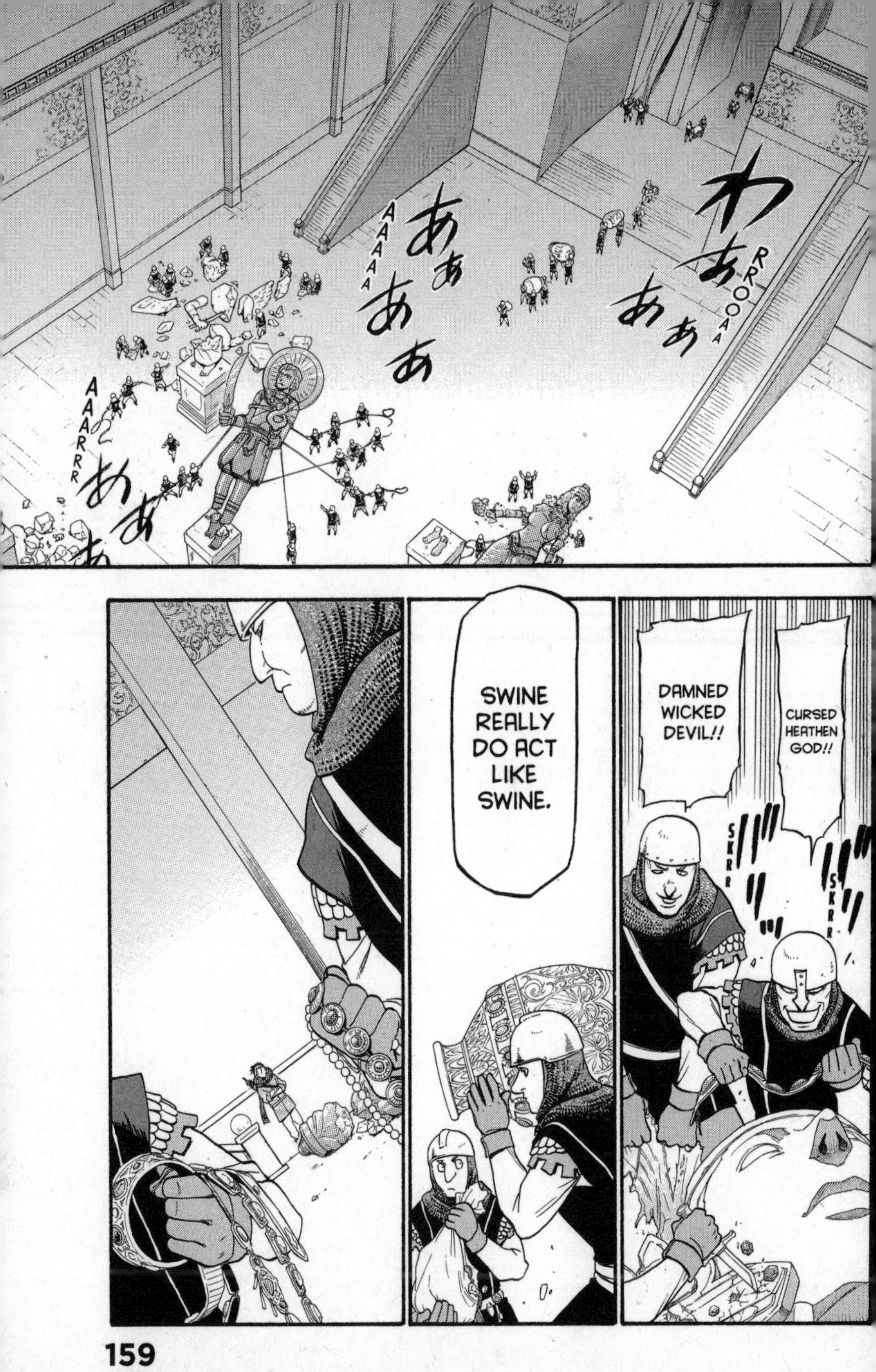
わぁあぁ
RROOAA
あぁああ
AAAAA
AAARRR
ああぁ
CURSED HEATHEN GOD!!
DAMNED WICKED DEVIL!!
SKRR
SKRR
SWINE REALLY DO ACT LIKE SWINE.

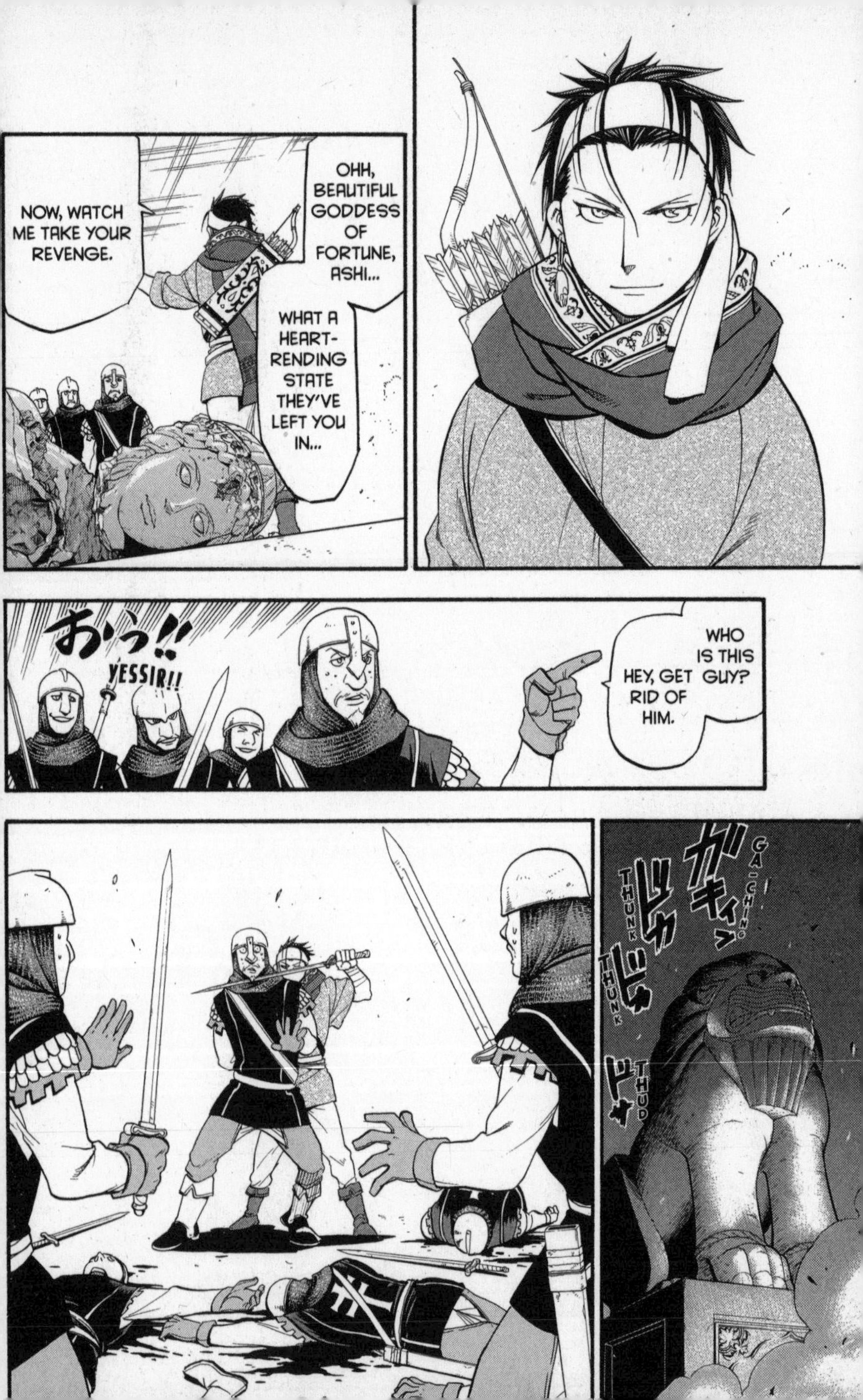
OHH, BEAUTIFUL GODDESS OF FORTUNE, ASHI...
WHAT A HEART-RENDING STATE THEY'VE LEFT YOU IN...
NOW, WATCH ME TAKE YOUR REVENGE.
WHO IS THIS GUY?
HEY, GET RID OF HIM.
おぅ!!
YESSIR!!
ガキィン
GA-CHIN
ドカ
THUNK
ドカ
THUNK
ドッ
THUD

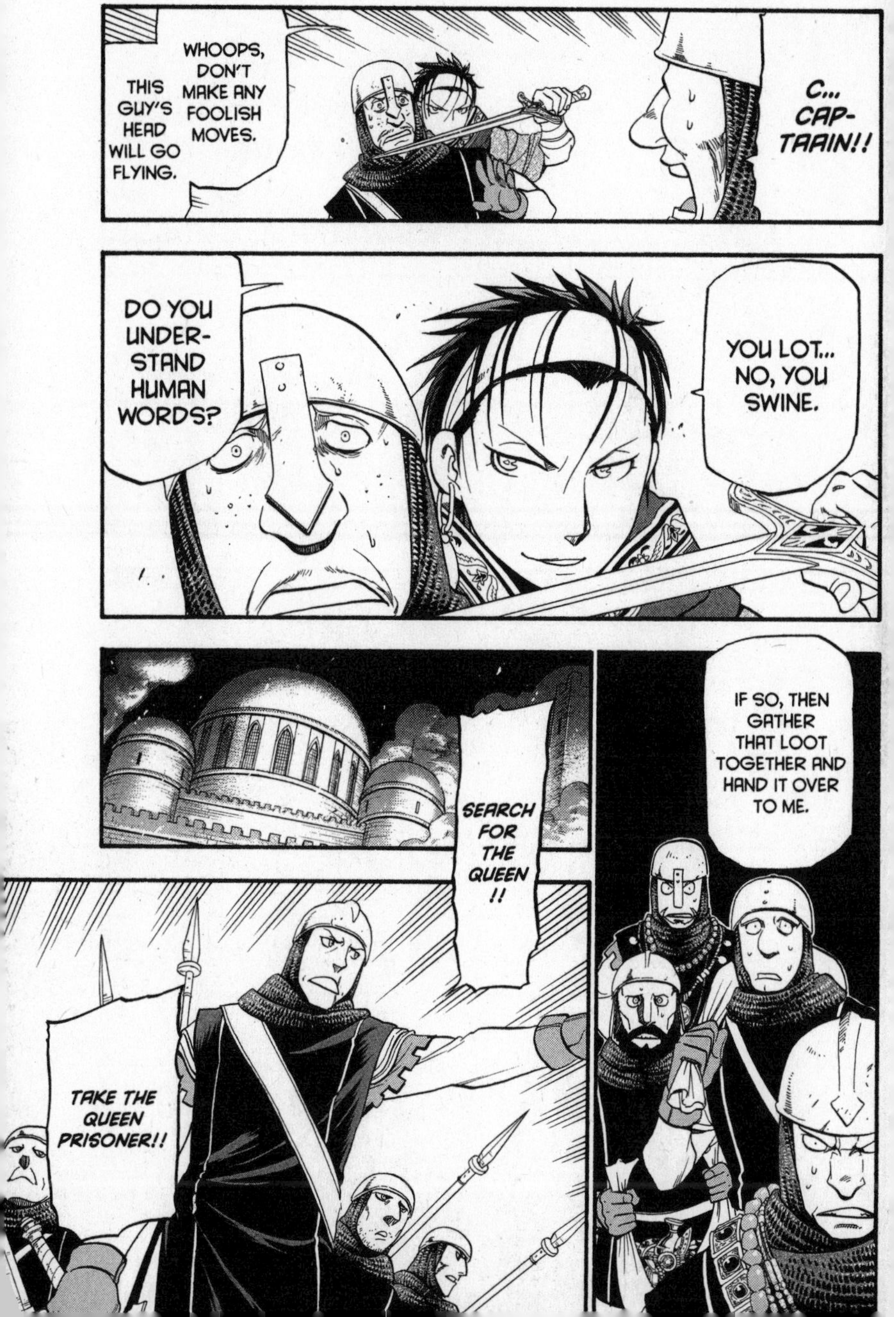
C... CAP-TAAIN!!
WHOOPS, DON'T MAKE ANY FOOLISH MOVES.
THIS GUY'S HEAD WILL GO FLYING.
YOU LOT... NO, YOU SWINE.
DO YOU UNDER-STAND HUMAN WORDS?
IF SO, THEN GATHER THAT LOOT TOGETHER AND HAND IT OVER TO ME.
SEARCH FOR THE QUEEN!!
TAKE THE QUEEN PRISONER!!

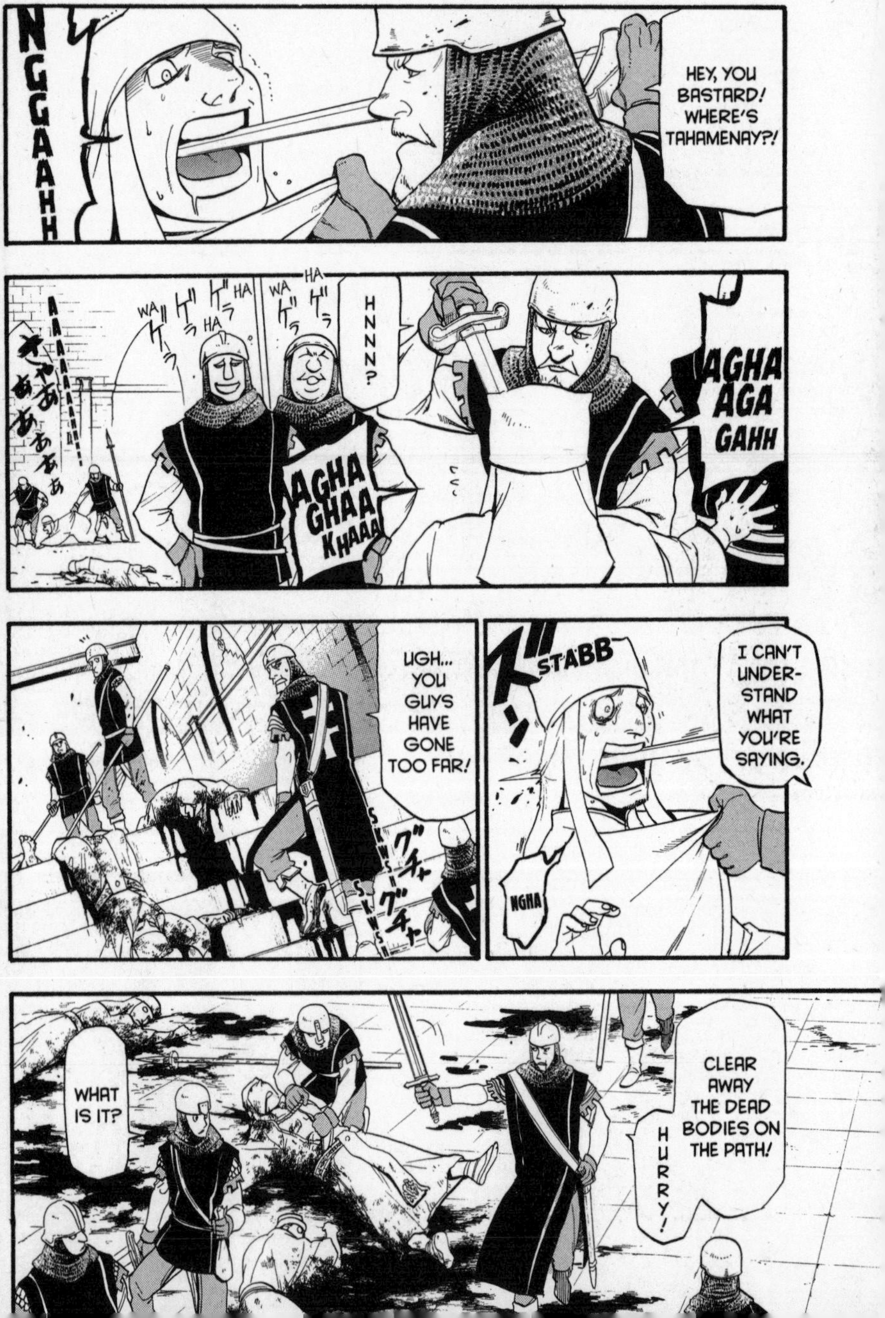
HEY, YOU BASTARD! WHERE'S TAHAMENAY?!
NGGAAHH
AGHA AGA GAHH
HNNN?
WA HA HA
WA HA HA
AGHA GHAA KHAAA
AAAAAAAA!
I CAN'T UNDER-STAND WHAT YOU'RE SAYING.
STABB
NGHA
UGH... YOU GUYS HAVE GONE TOO FAR!
SKWSH
SKWSH
CLEAR AWAY THE DEAD BODIES ON THE PATH!
HURRY!
WHAT IS IT?

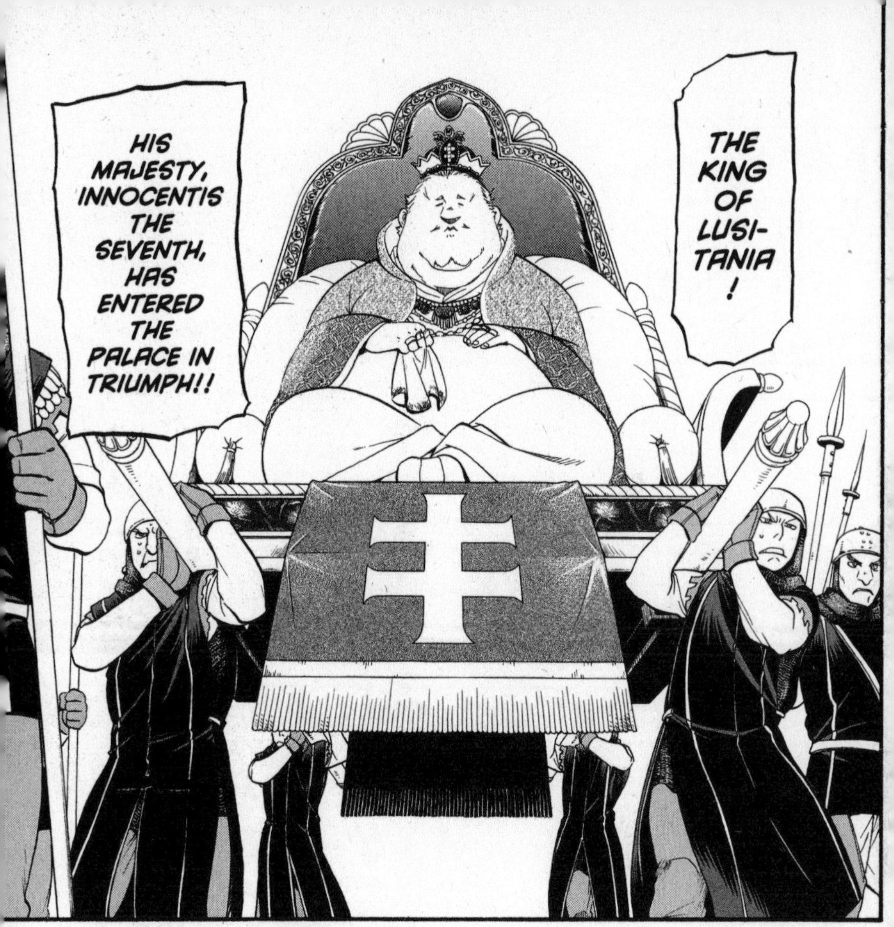
THE KING OF LUSI-TANIA!
HIS MAJESTY, INNOCENTIS THE SEVENTH, HAS ENTERED THE PALACE IN TRIUMPH!!

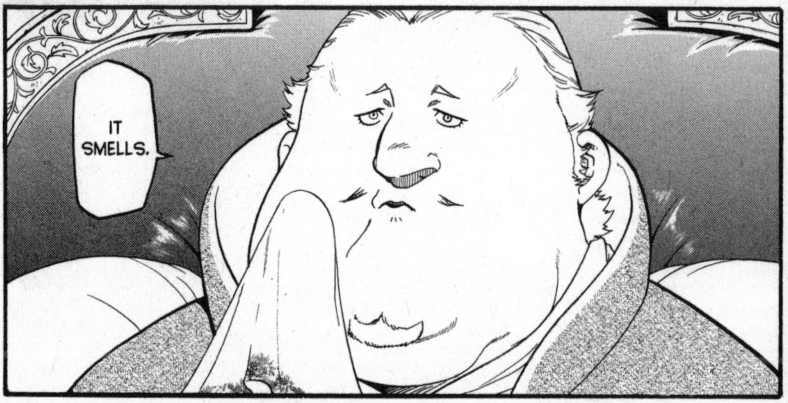
IT SMELLS.

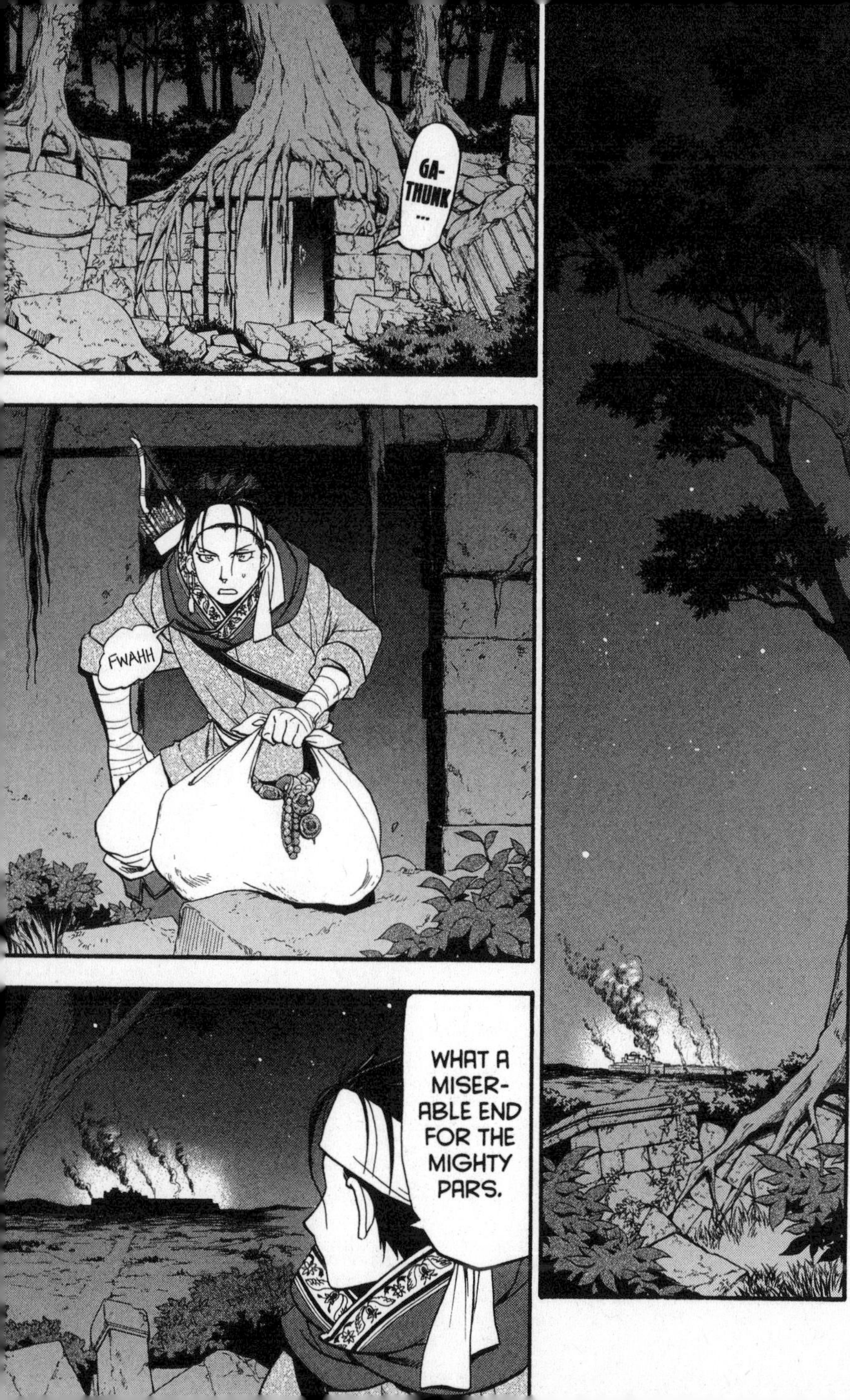
GA-THUNK...
FWAHH
WHAT A MISERABLE END FOR THE MIGHTY PARS.

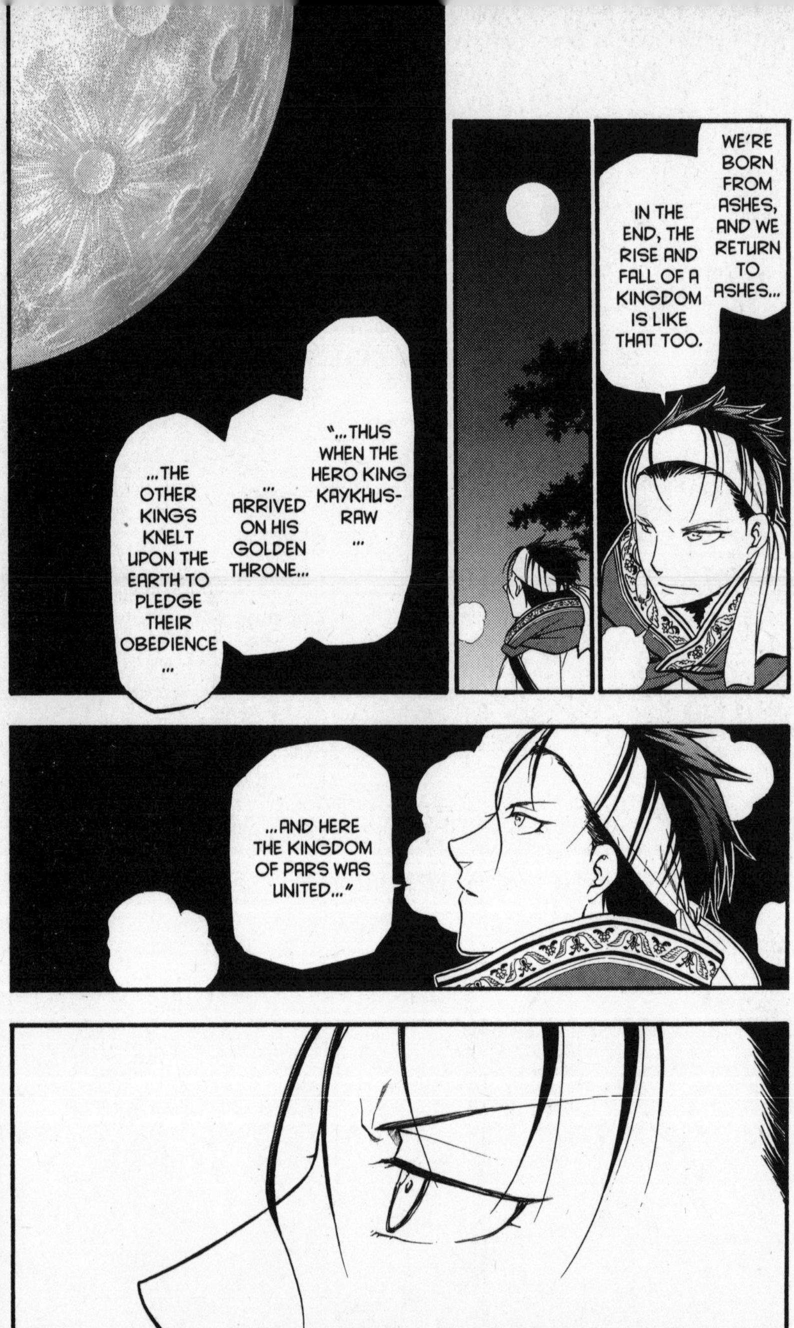
WE'RE BORN FROM ASHES, AND WE RETURN TO ASHES...
IN THE END, THE RISE AND FALL OF A KINGDOM IS LIKE THAT TOO.
"...THUS WHEN THE HERO KING KAYKHUSRAW...
...ARRIVED ON HIS GOLDEN THRONE...
...THE OTHER KINGS KNELT UPON THE EARTH TO PLEDGE THEIR OBEDIENCE...
...AND HERE THE KINGDOM OF PARS WAS UNITED..."

Chapter 10: The Captive Queen

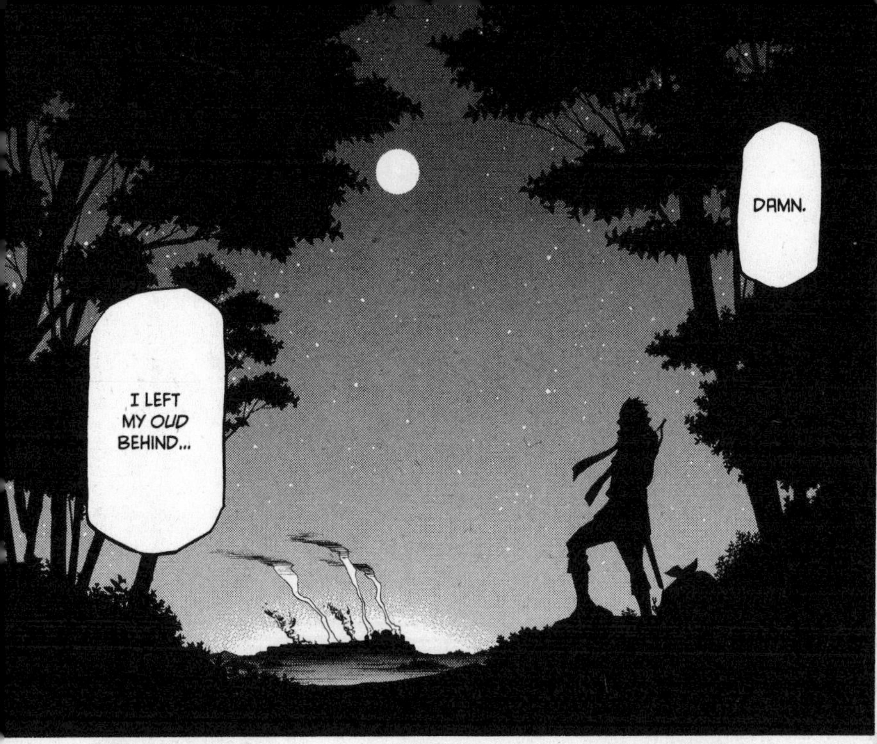
DAMN.
I LEFT MY OUD BEHIND...

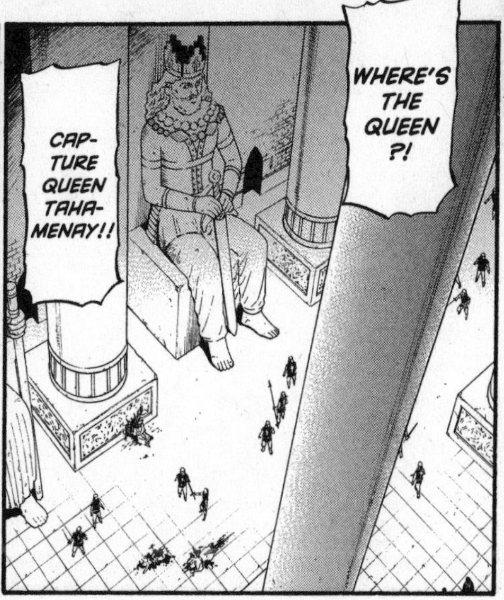
WHERE'S THE QUEEN ?!
CAP-TURE QUEEN TAHA-MENAY!!

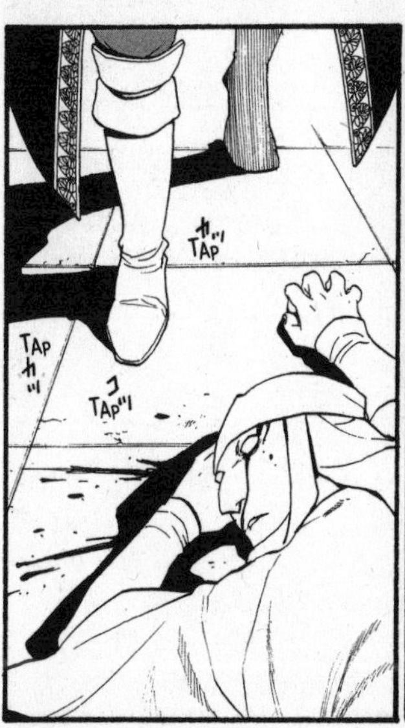
TAP
TAP
TAP

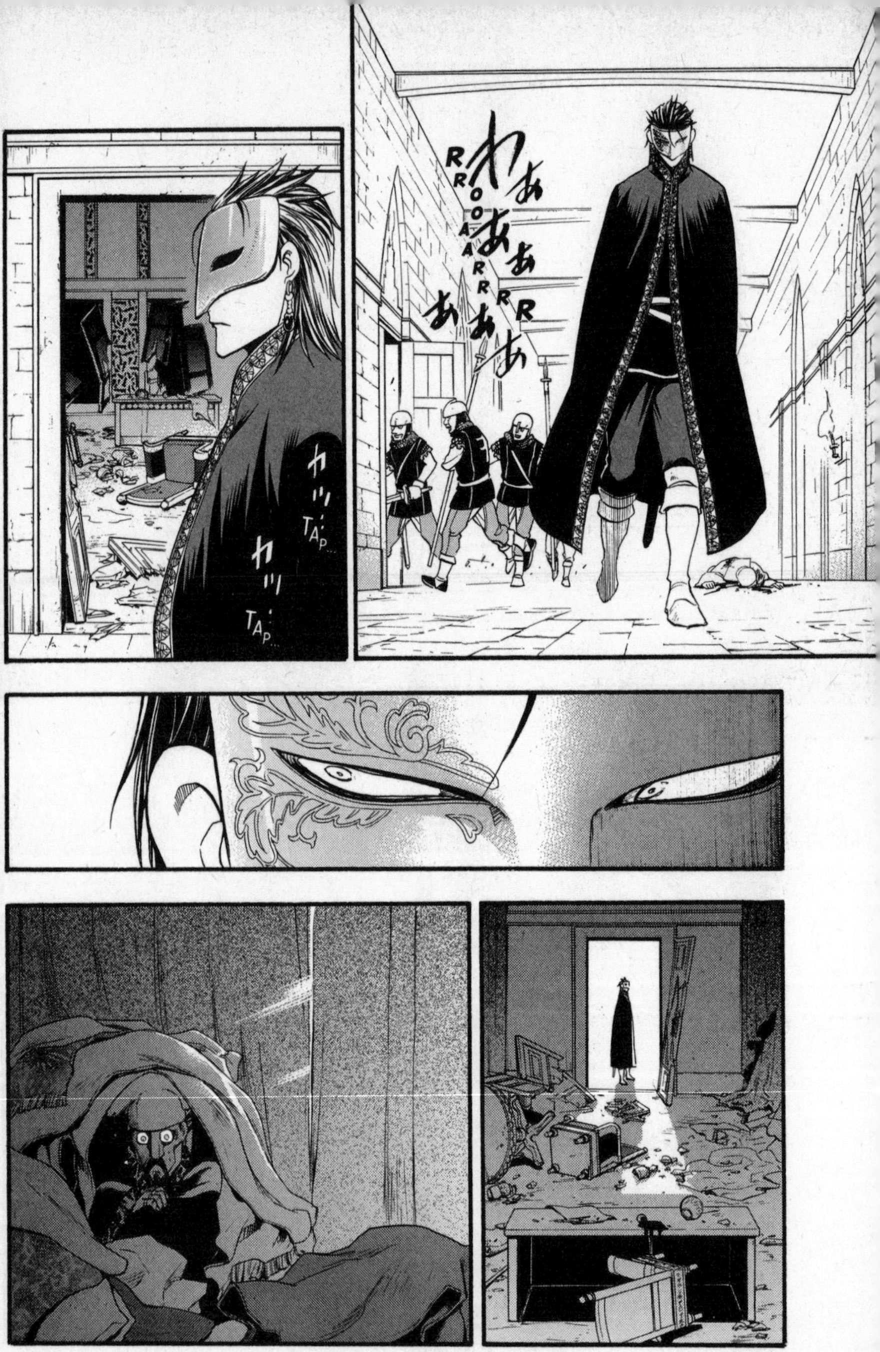
わああああああ
RROOAARRRR
カツ
TAP...
カツ
TAP...

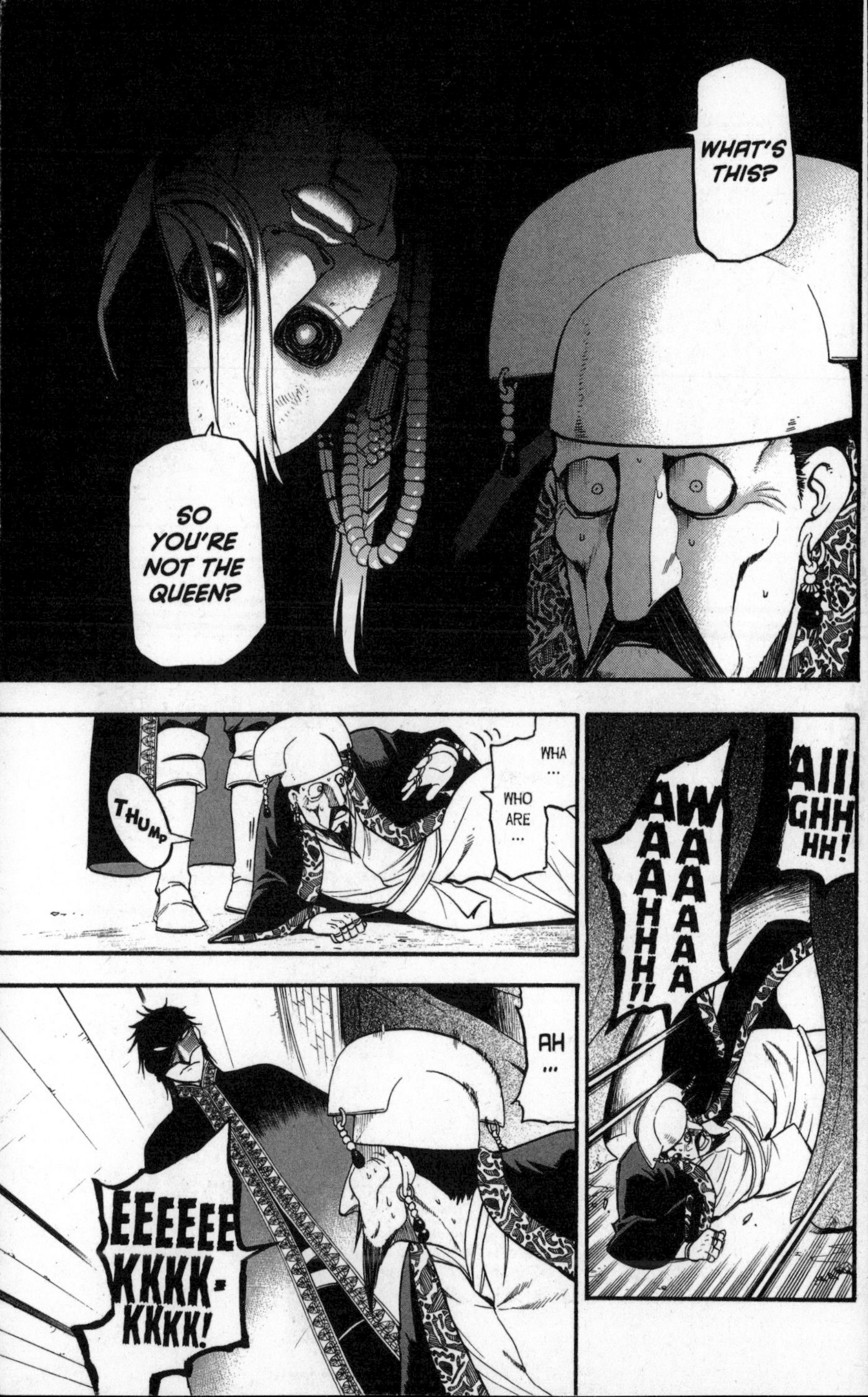
WHAT'S THIS?
SO YOU'RE NOT THE QUEEN?
AIIGHHHH!
WAAAAAA AAAHHHH!!
WHA ... WHO ARE ...
THUMP
AH ...
EEEEEEKKKK-KKKK!

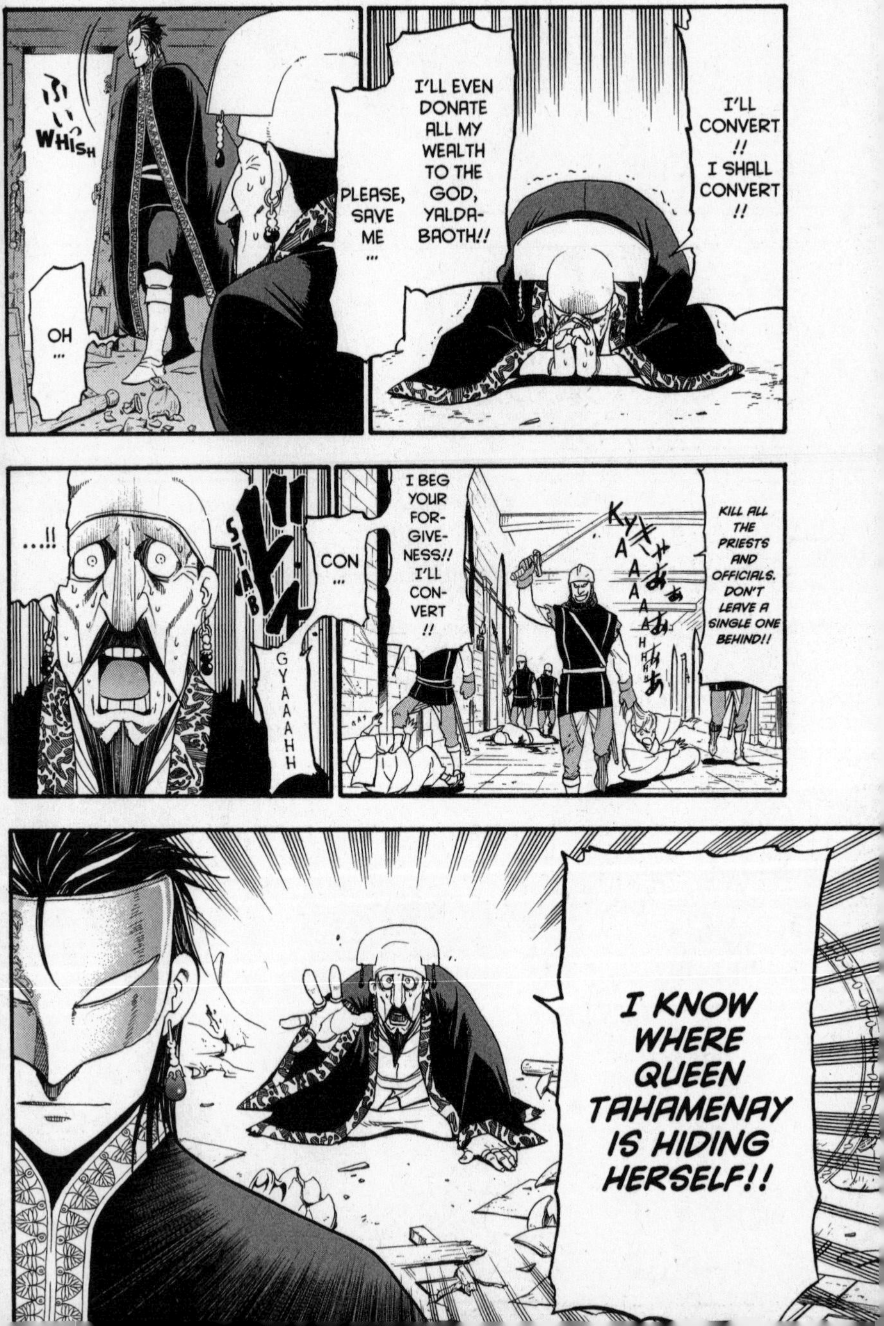

I'LL CONVERT!! I SHALL CONVERT!!
I'LL EVEN DONATE ALL MY WEALTH TO THE GOD, YALDA-BAOTH!!
PLEASE, SAVE ME...
ふいっ WHISH
OH...
KILL ALL THE PRIESTS AND OFFICIALS. DON'T LEAVE A SINGLE ONE BEHIND!!
KYAAAAAHHHH
I BEG YOUR FORGIVENESS!! I'LL CONVERT!!
CON...
STAB
GYAAAAHH
...!!
I KNOW WHERE QUEEN TAHAMENAY IS HIDING HERSELF!!

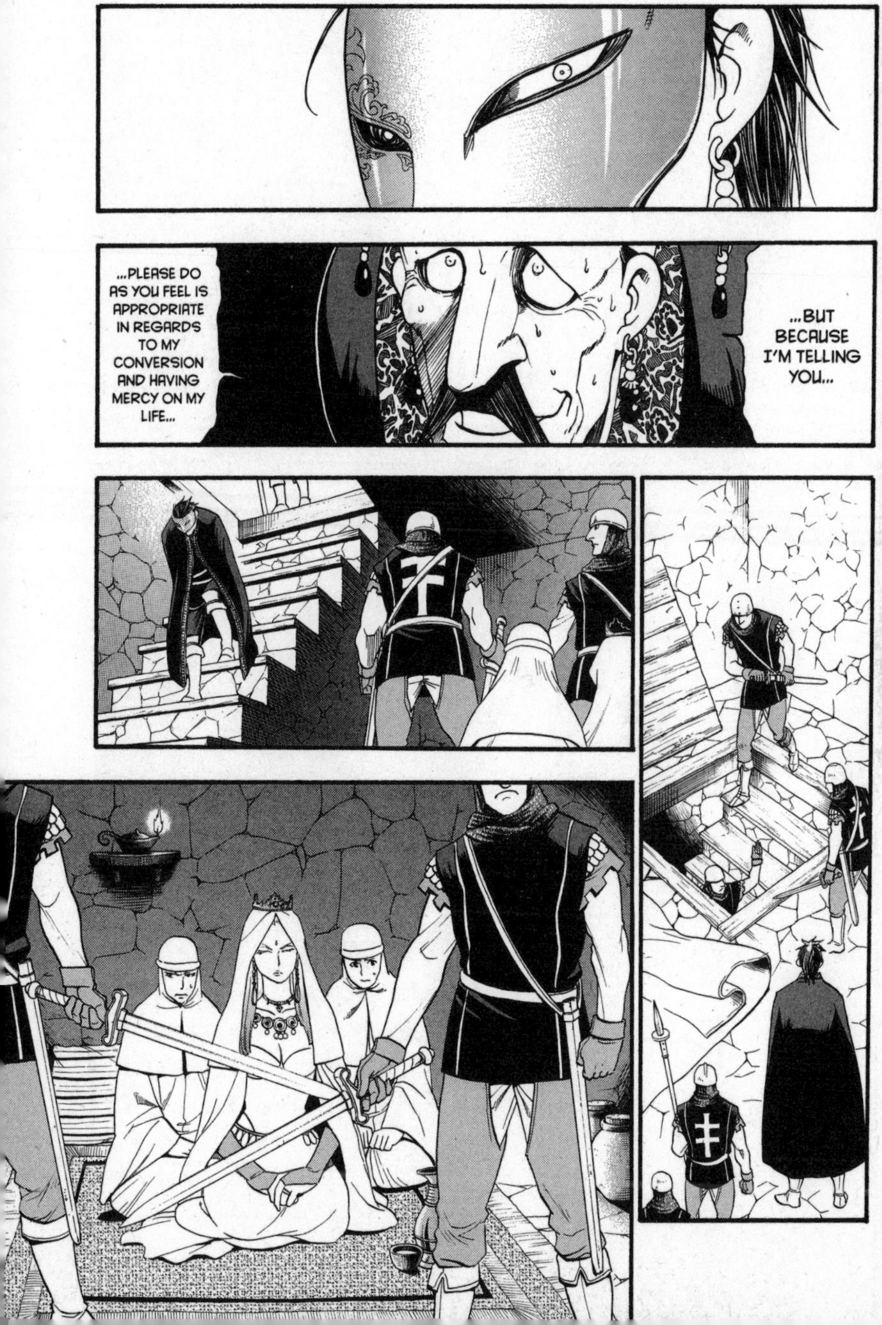
...BUT BECAUSE I'M TELLING YOU...
...PLEASE DO AS YOU FEEL IS APPROPRIATE IN REGARDS TO MY CONVERSION AND HAVING MERCY ON MY LIFE...

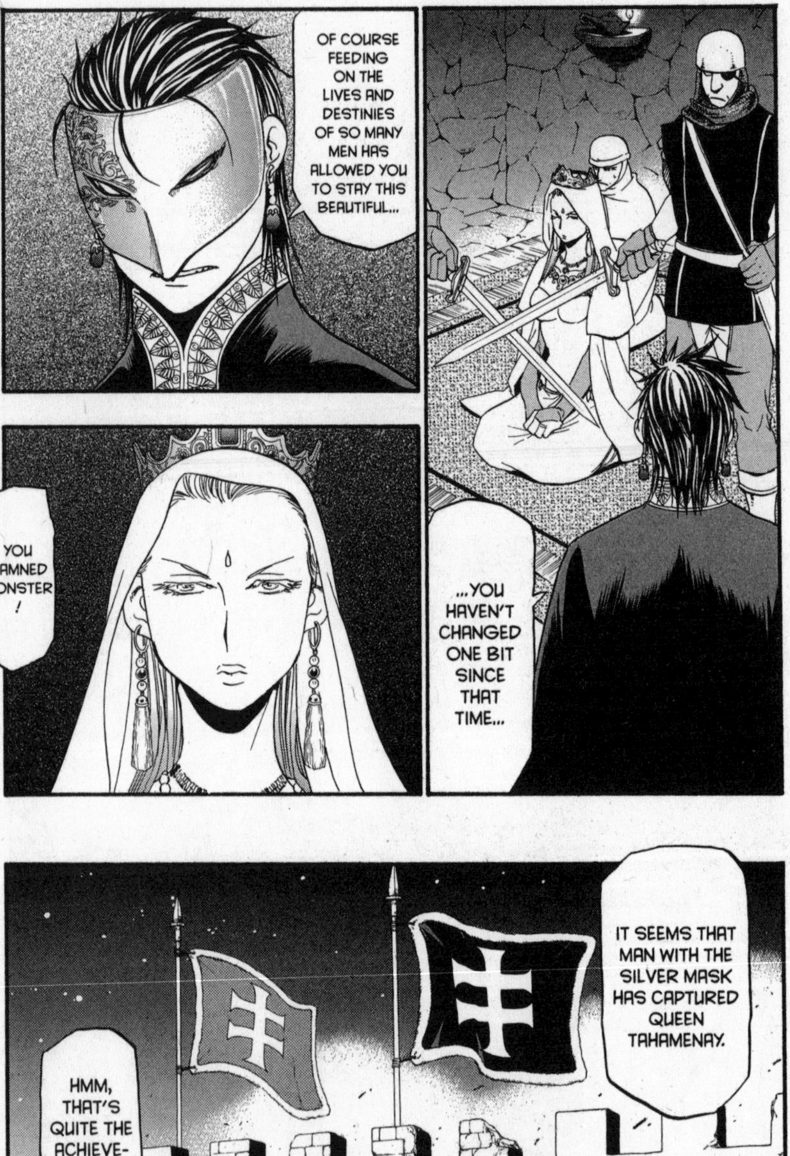
...YOU HAVEN'T CHANGED ONE BIT SINCE THAT TIME...
OF COURSE FEEDING ON THE LIVES AND DESTINIES OF SO MANY MEN HAS ALLOWED YOU TO STAY THIS BEAUTIFUL...
YOU DAMNED MONSTER!
IT SEEMS THAT MAN WITH THE SILVER MASK HAS CAPTURED QUEEN TAHAMENAY.
HMM, THAT'S QUITE THE ACHIEVE-MENT, ISN'T IT?

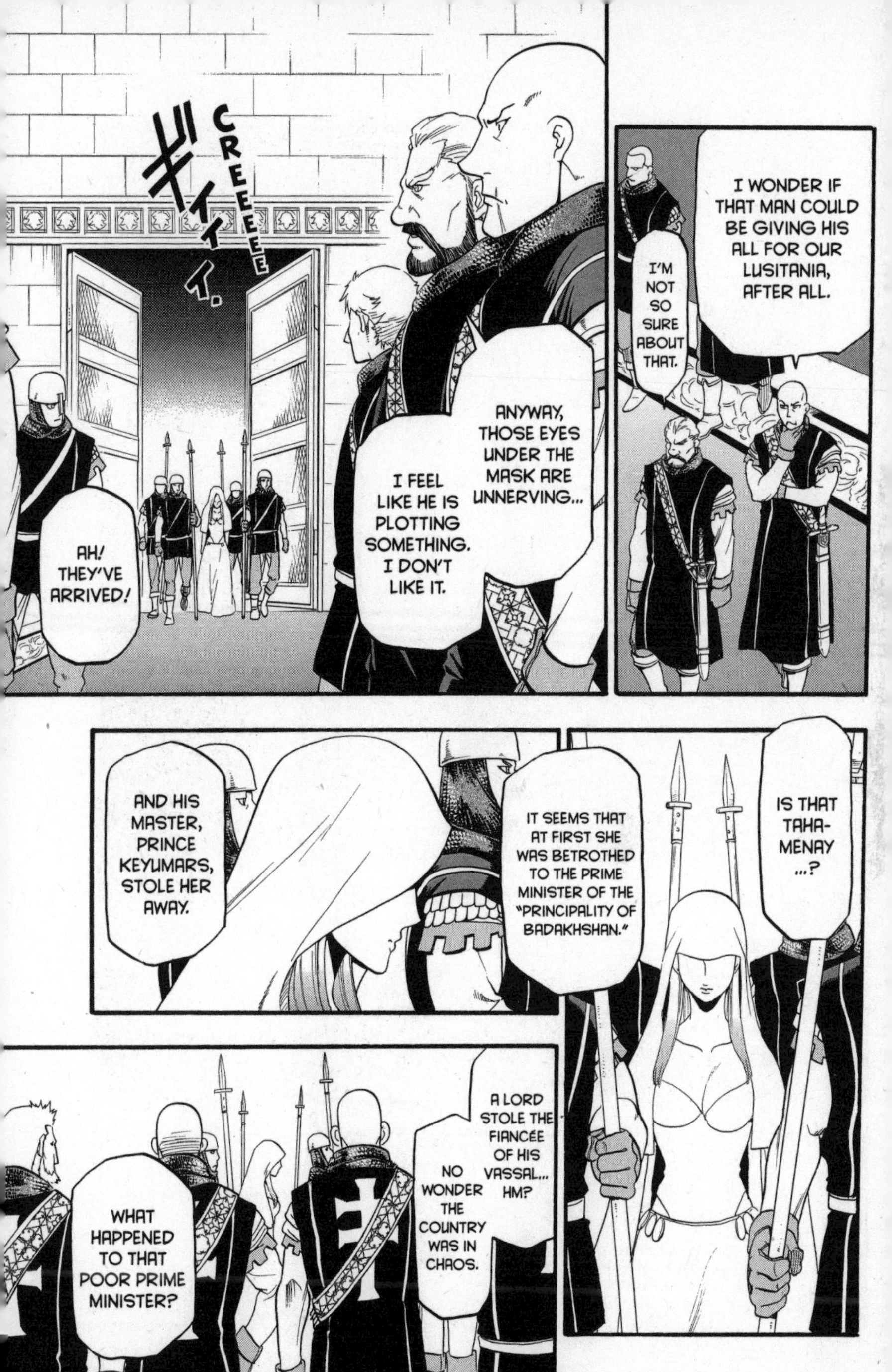
I WONDER IF THAT MAN COULD BE GIVING HIS ALL FOR OUR LUSITANIA, AFTER ALL.
I'M NOT SO SURE ABOUT THAT.
ギイイイ、
CREEEEEE
ANYWAY, THOSE EYES UNDER THE MASK ARE UNNERVING...
I FEEL LIKE HE IS PLOTTING SOMETHING. I DON'T LIKE IT.
AH! THEY'VE ARRIVED!
IS THAT TAHA-MENAY ...?
IT SEEMS THAT AT FIRST SHE WAS BETROTHED TO THE PRIME MINISTER OF THE "PRINCIPALITY OF BADAKHSHAN."
AND HIS MASTER, PRINCE KEYUMARS, STOLE HER AWAY.
A LORD STOLE THE FIANCÉE OF HIS VASSAL... HM?
NO WONDER THE COUNTRY WAS IN CHAOS.
WHAT HAPPENED TO THAT POOR PRIME MINISTER?

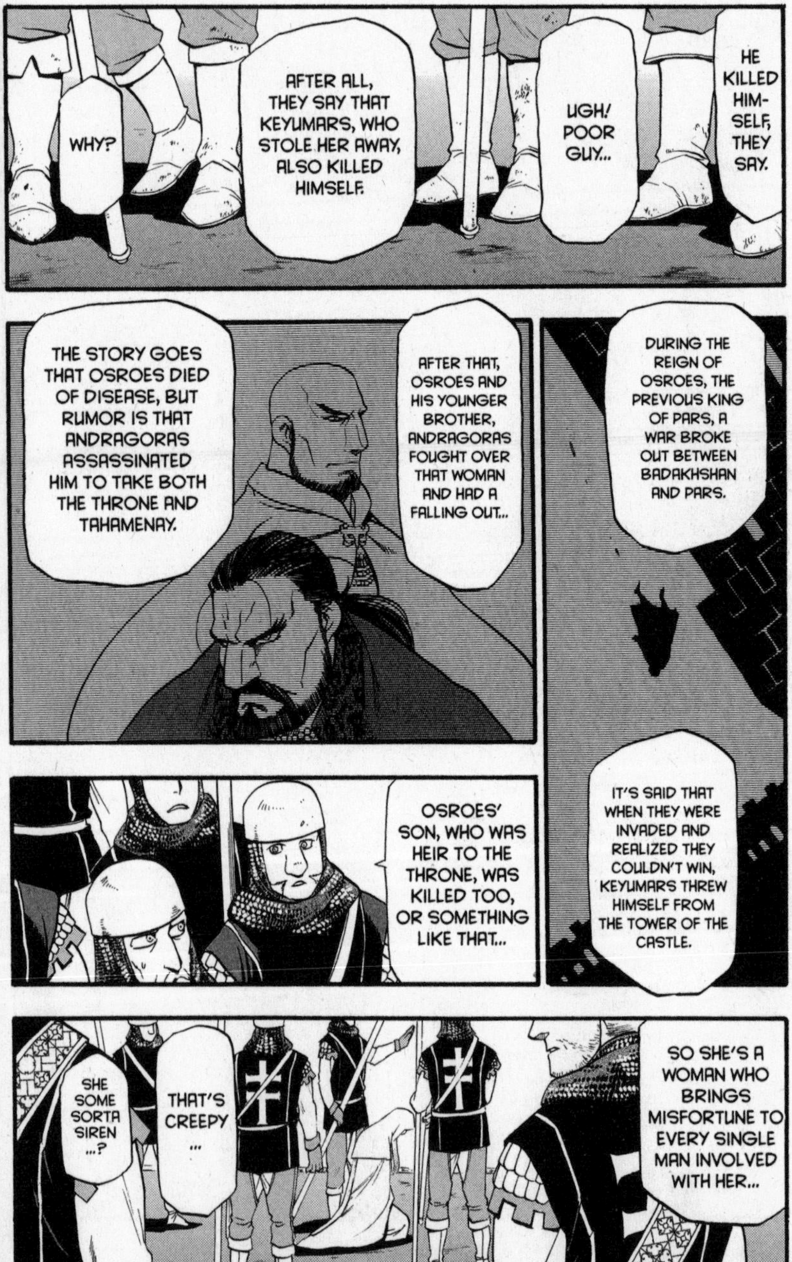
HE KILLED HIMSELF, THEY SAY.
UGH! POOR GUY...
AFTER ALL, THEY SAY THAT KEYUMARS, WHO STOLE HER AWAY, ALSO KILLED HIMSELF.
WHY?
DURING THE REIGN OF OSROES, THE PREVIOUS KING OF PARS, A WAR BROKE OUT BETWEEN BADAKHSHAN AND PARS.
IT'S SAID THAT WHEN THEY WERE INVADED AND REALIZED THEY COULDN'T WIN, KEYUMARS THREW HIMSELF FROM THE TOWER OF THE CASTLE.
AFTER THAT, OSROES AND HIS YOUNGER BROTHER, ANDRAGORAS FOUGHT OVER THAT WOMAN AND HAD A FALLING OUT...
THE STORY GOES THAT OSROES DIED OF DISEASE, BUT RUMOR IS THAT ANDRAGORAS ASSASSINATED HIM TO TAKE BOTH THE THRONE AND TAHAMENAY.
OSROES' SON, WHO WAS HEIR TO THE THRONE, WAS KILLED TOO, OR SOMETHING LIKE THAT...
SO SHE'S A WOMAN WHO BRINGS MISFORTUNE TO EVERY SINGLE MAN INVOLVED WITH HER...
THAT'S CREEPY ...
SHE SOME SORTA SIREN ...?

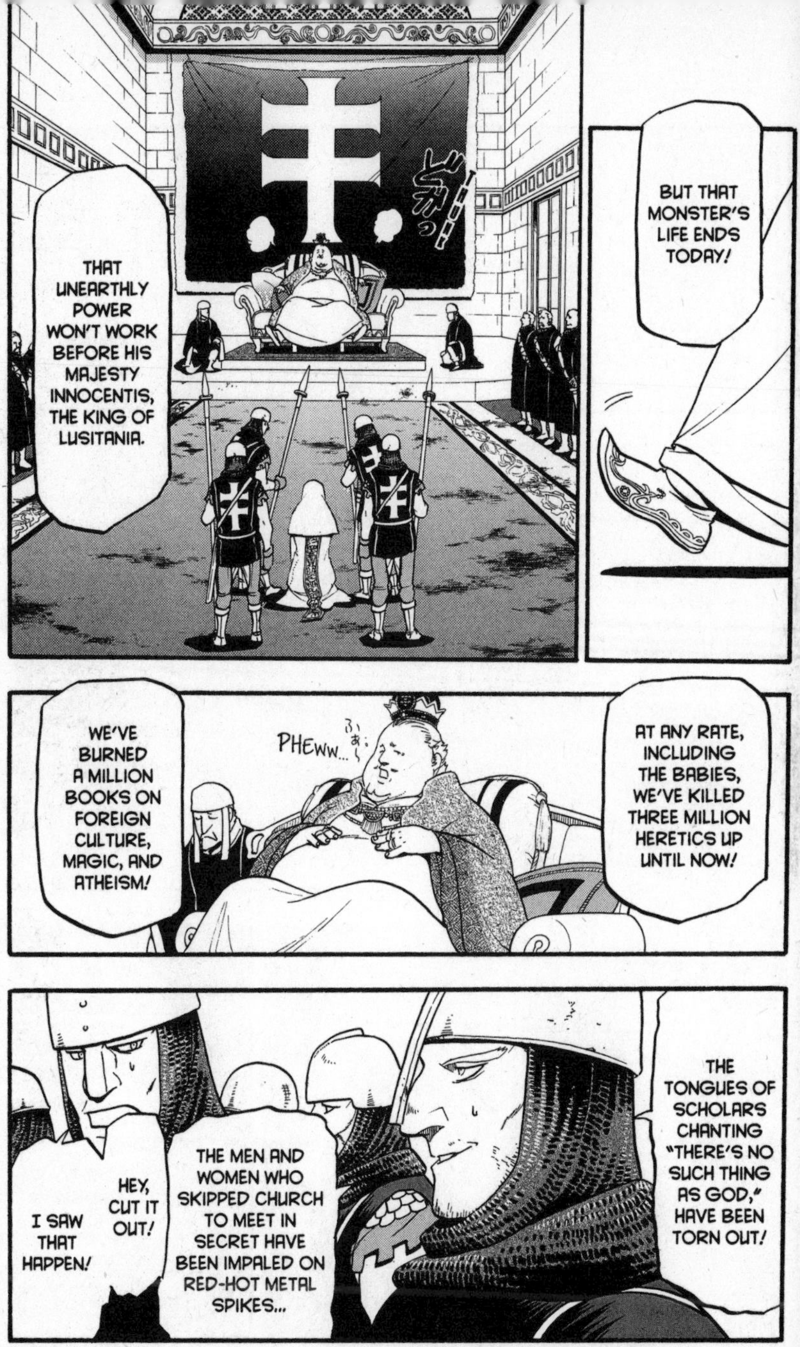
BUT THAT MONSTER'S LIFE ENDS TODAY!
どかっ
THAT UNEARTHLY POWER WON'T WORK BEFORE HIS MAJESTY INNOCENTIS, THE KING OF LUSITANIA.
AT ANY RATE, INCLUDING THE BABIES, WE'VE KILLED THREE MILLION HERETICS UP UNTIL NOW!
ふぉ～
PHEWW...
WE'VE BURNED A MILLION BOOKS ON FOREIGN CULTURE, MAGIC, AND ATHEISM!
THE TONGUES OF SCHOLARS CHANTING "THERE'S NO SUCH THING AS GOD," HAVE BEEN TORN OUT!
THE MEN AND WOMEN WHO SKIPPED CHURCH TO MEET IN SECRET HAVE BEEN IMPALED ON RED-HOT METAL SPIKES...
HEY, CUT IT OUT!
I SAW THAT HAPPEN!

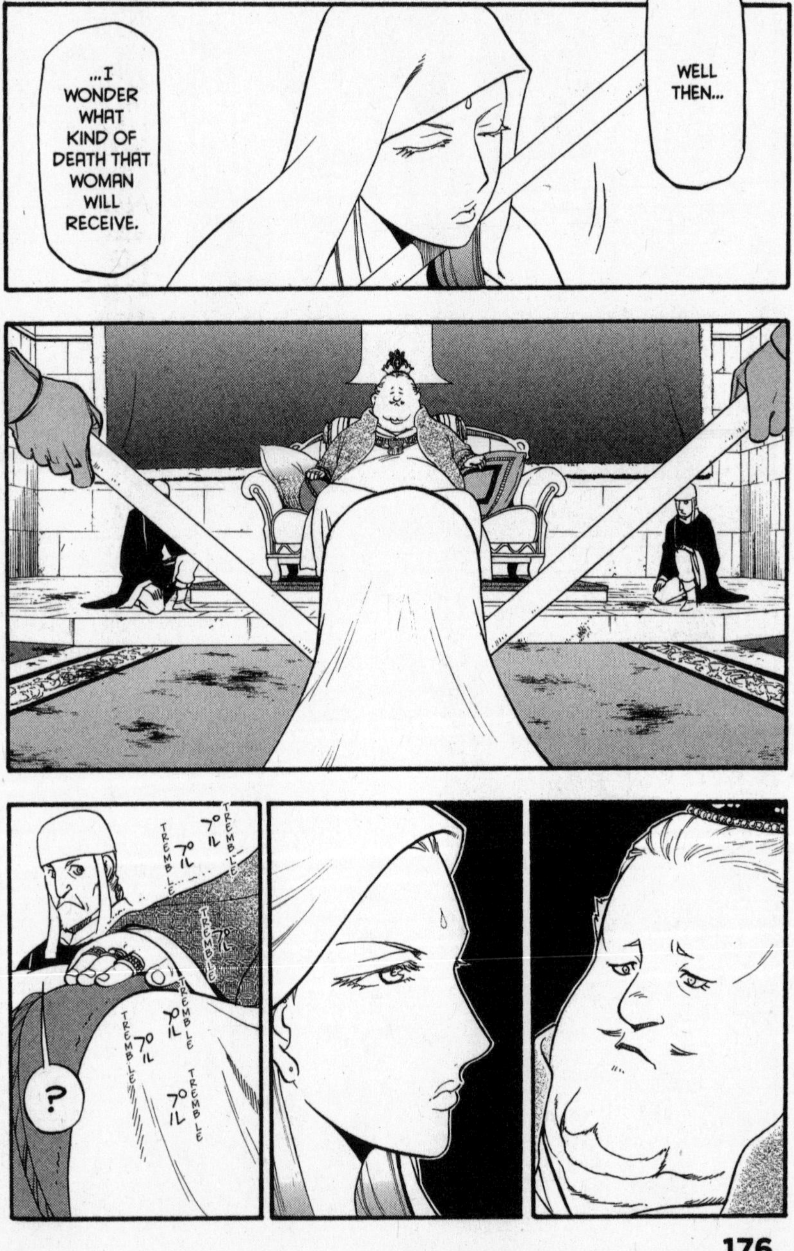
WELL THEN...
...I WONDER WHAT KIND OF DEATH THAT WOMAN WILL RECEIVE.
TREMBLE プル TREMBLE プル
TREMBLE プル
TREMBLE プル
TREMBLE プル
TREMBLE プル
?

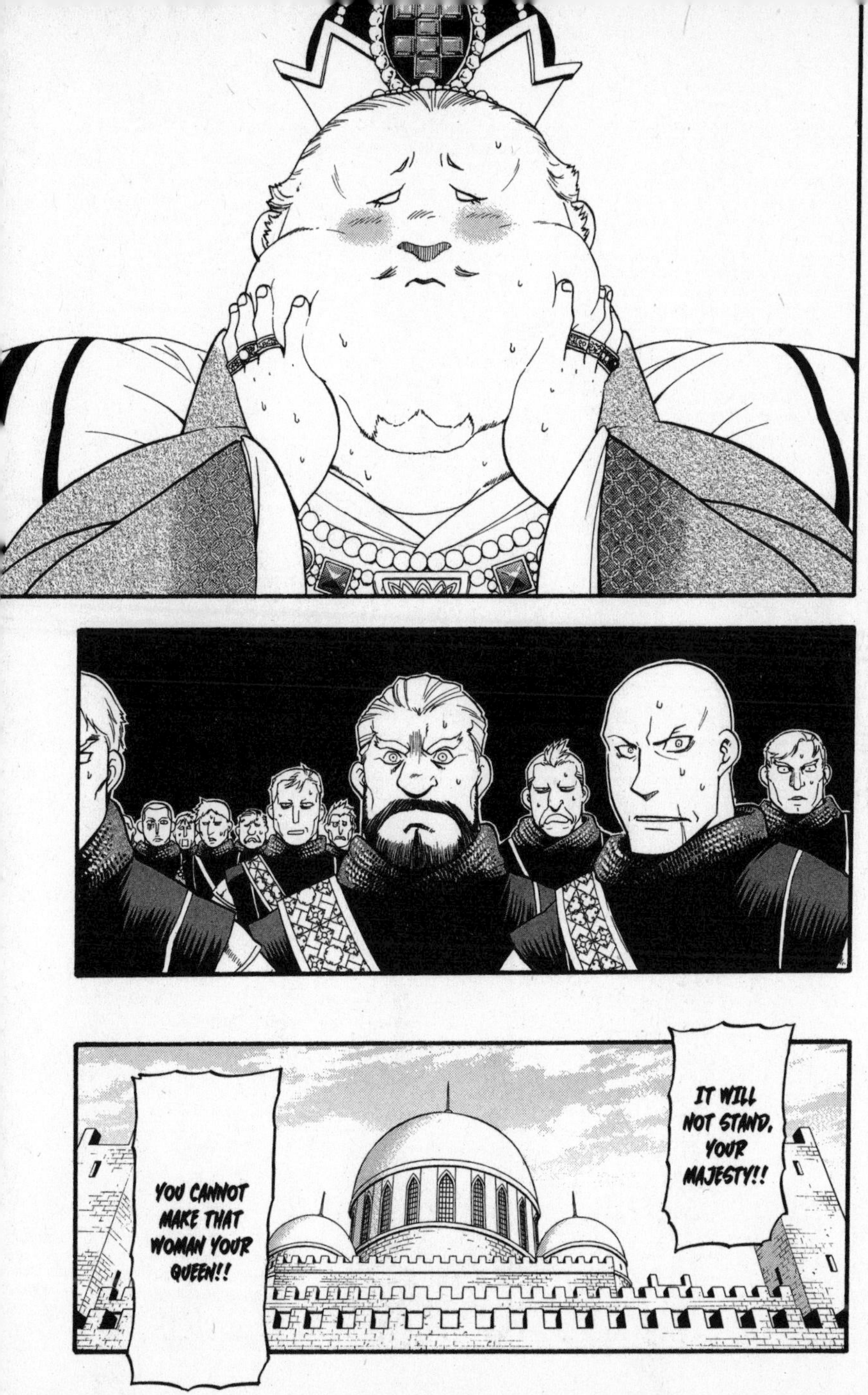

IT WILL NOT STAND, YOUR MAJESTY!!
YOU CANNOT MAKE THAT WOMAN YOUR QUEEN!!

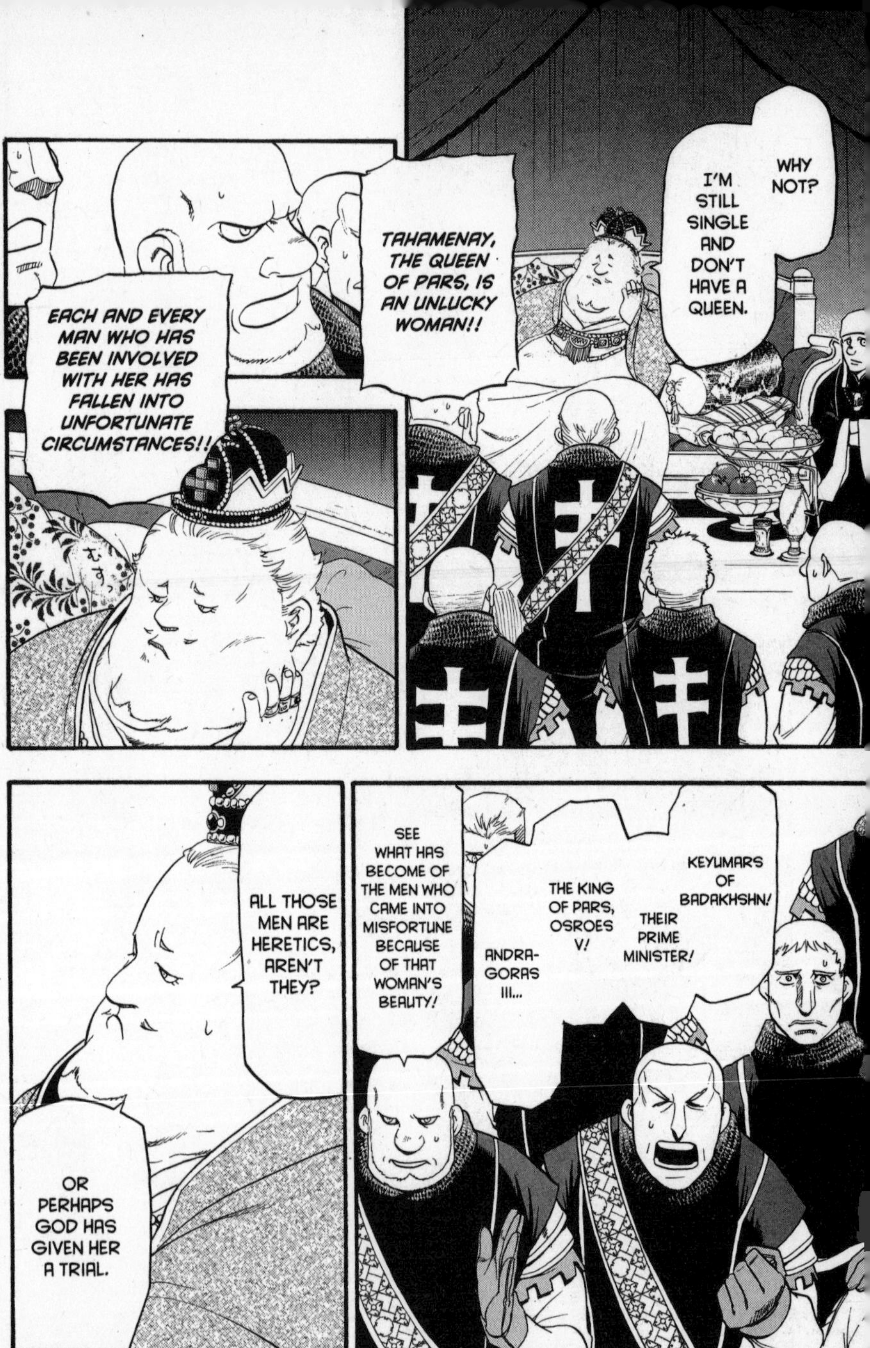
WHY NOT?
I'M STILL SINGLE AND DON'T HAVE A QUEEN.
TAHAMENAY, THE QUEEN OF PARS, IS AN UNLUCKY WOMAN!!
EACH AND EVERY MAN WHO HAS BEEN INVOLVED WITH HER HAS FALLEN INTO UNFORTUNATE CIRCUMSTANCES!!
むすっ
KEYUMARS OF BADAKHSHN!
THEIR PRIME MINISTER!
THE KING OF PARS, OSROES V!
ANDRA-GORAS III...
SEE WHAT HAS BECOME OF THE MEN WHO CAME INTO MISFORTUNE BECAUSE OF THAT WOMAN'S BEAUTY!
ALL THOSE MEN ARE HERETICS, AREN'T THEY?
OR PERHAPS GOD HAS GIVEN HER A TRIAL.

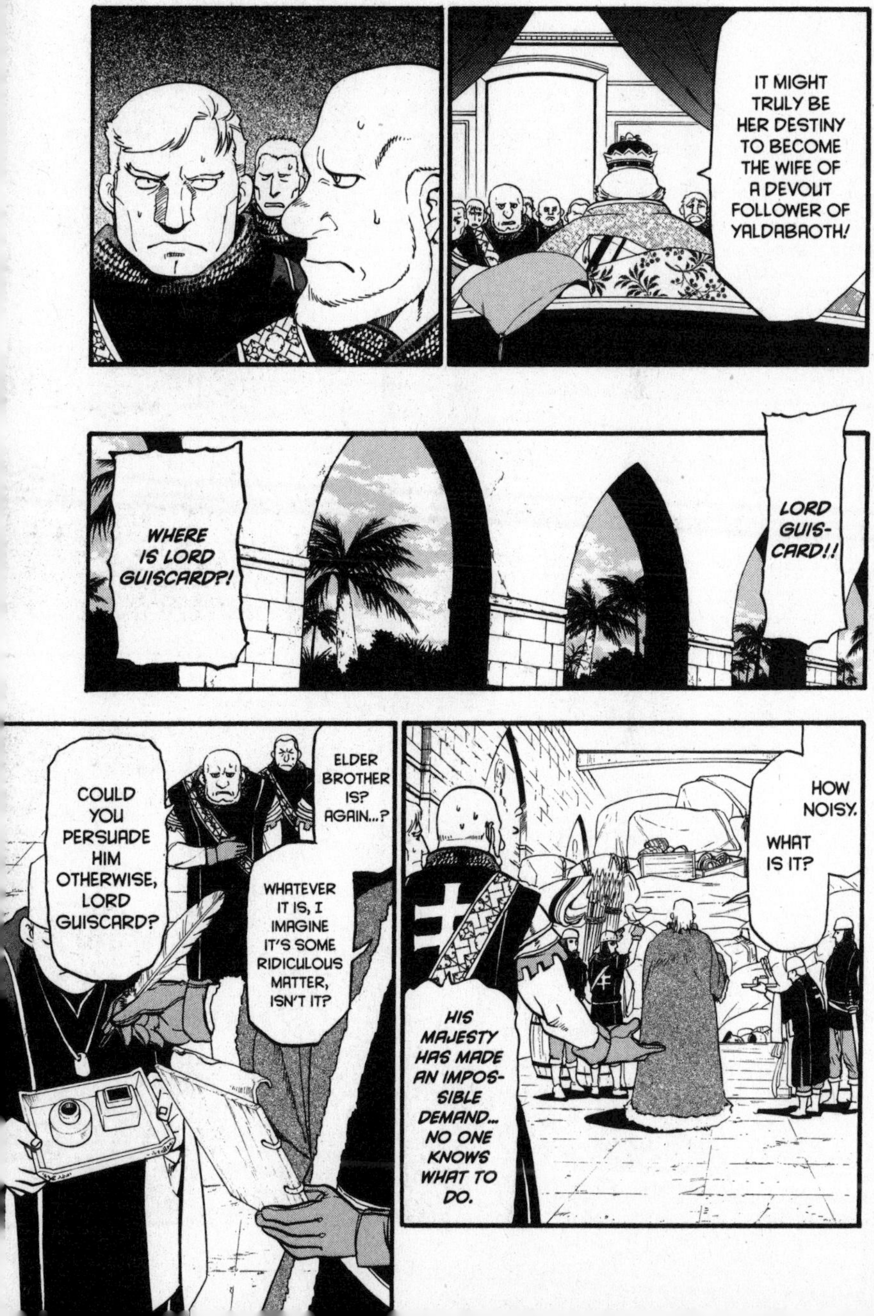
IT MIGHT TRULY BE HER DESTINY TO BECOME THE WIFE OF A DEVOUT FOLLOWER OF YALDABAOTH!
LORD GUIS-CARD!!
WHERE IS LORD GUISCARD?!
HOW NOISY.
WHAT IS IT?
HIS MAJESTY HAS MADE AN IMPOS-SIBLE DEMAND... NO ONE KNOWS WHAT TO DO.
ELDER BROTHER IS? AGAIN...?
WHATEVER IT IS, I IMAGINE IT'S SOME RIDICULOUS MATTER, ISN'T IT?
COULD YOU PERSUADE HIM OTHERWISE, LORD GUISCARD?

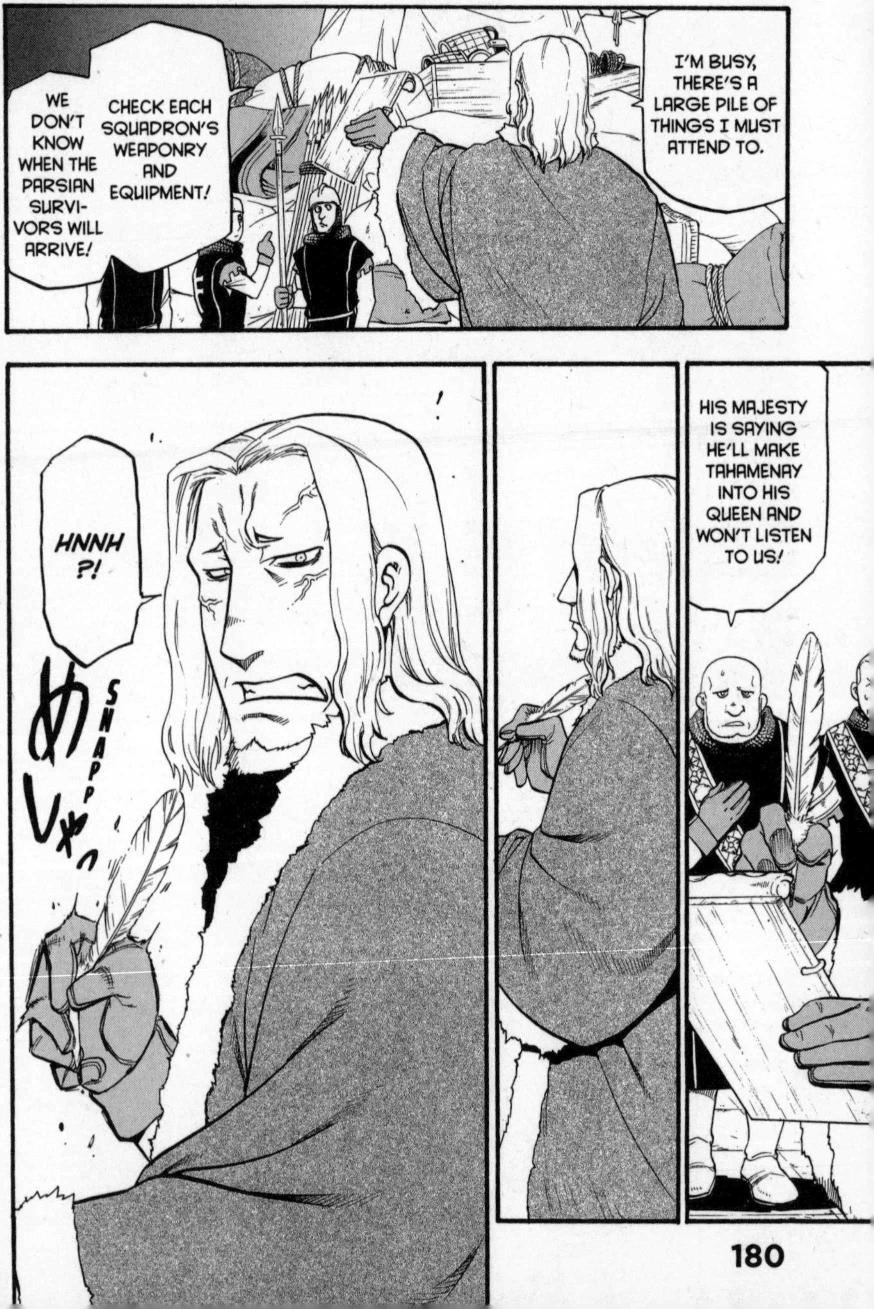
I'M BUSY, THERE'S A LARGE PILE OF THINGS I MUST ATTEND TO.
CHECK EACH SQUADRON'S WEAPONRY AND EQUIPMENT!
WE DON'T KNOW WHEN THE PARSIAN SURVI-VORS WILL ARRIVE!
HIS MAJESTY IS SAYING HE'LL MAKE TAHAMENAY INTO HIS QUEEN AND WON'T LISTEN TO US!
!
HNNH ?!
SNAPP

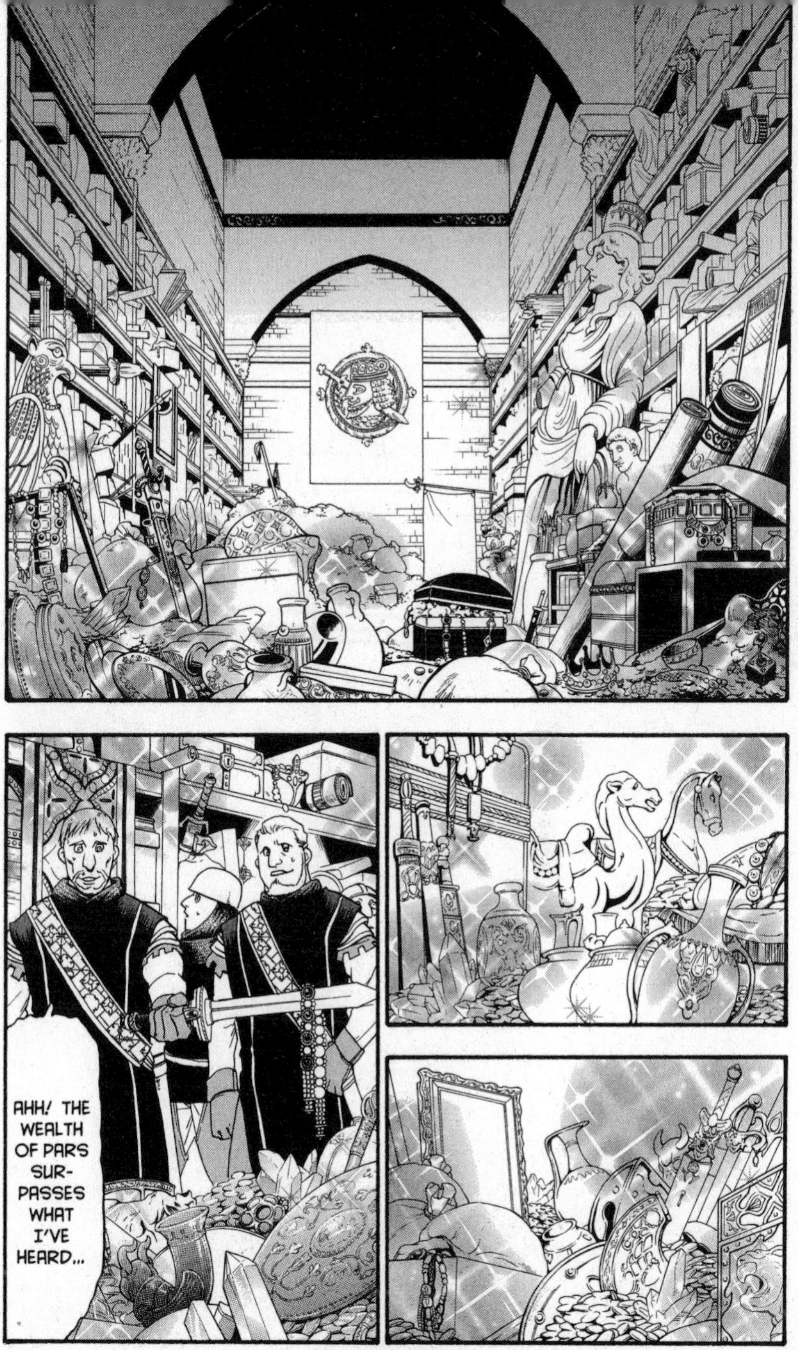
AHH! THE WEALTH OF PARS SUR-PASSES WHAT I'VE HEARD...

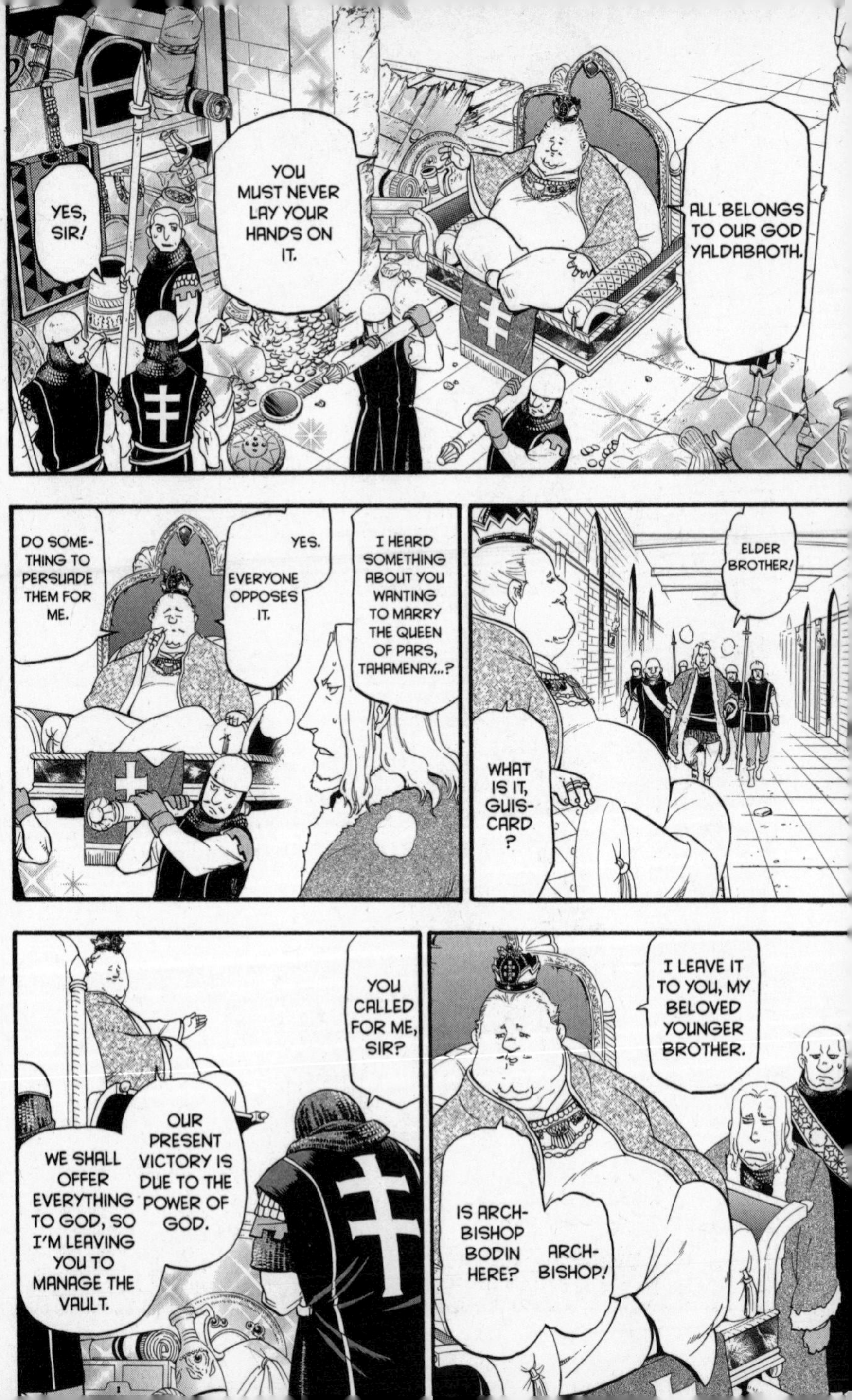
ALL BELONGS TO OUR GOD YALDABAOTH.
YOU MUST NEVER LAY YOUR HANDS ON IT.
YES, SIR!
ELDER BROTHER!
WHAT IS IT, GUIS-CARD?
I HEARD SOMETHING ABOUT YOU WANTING TO MARRY THE QUEEN OF PARS, TAHAMENAY...?
YES.
EVERYONE OPPOSES IT.
DO SOME-THING TO PERSUADE THEM FOR ME.
I LEAVE IT TO YOU, MY BELOVED YOUNGER BROTHER.
ARCH-BISHOP!
IS ARCH-BISHOP BODIN HERE?
YOU CALLED FOR ME, SIR?
OUR PRESENT VICTORY IS DUE TO THE POWER OF GOD.
WE SHALL OFFER EVERYTHING TO GOD, SO I'M LEAVING YOU TO MANAGE THE VAULT.

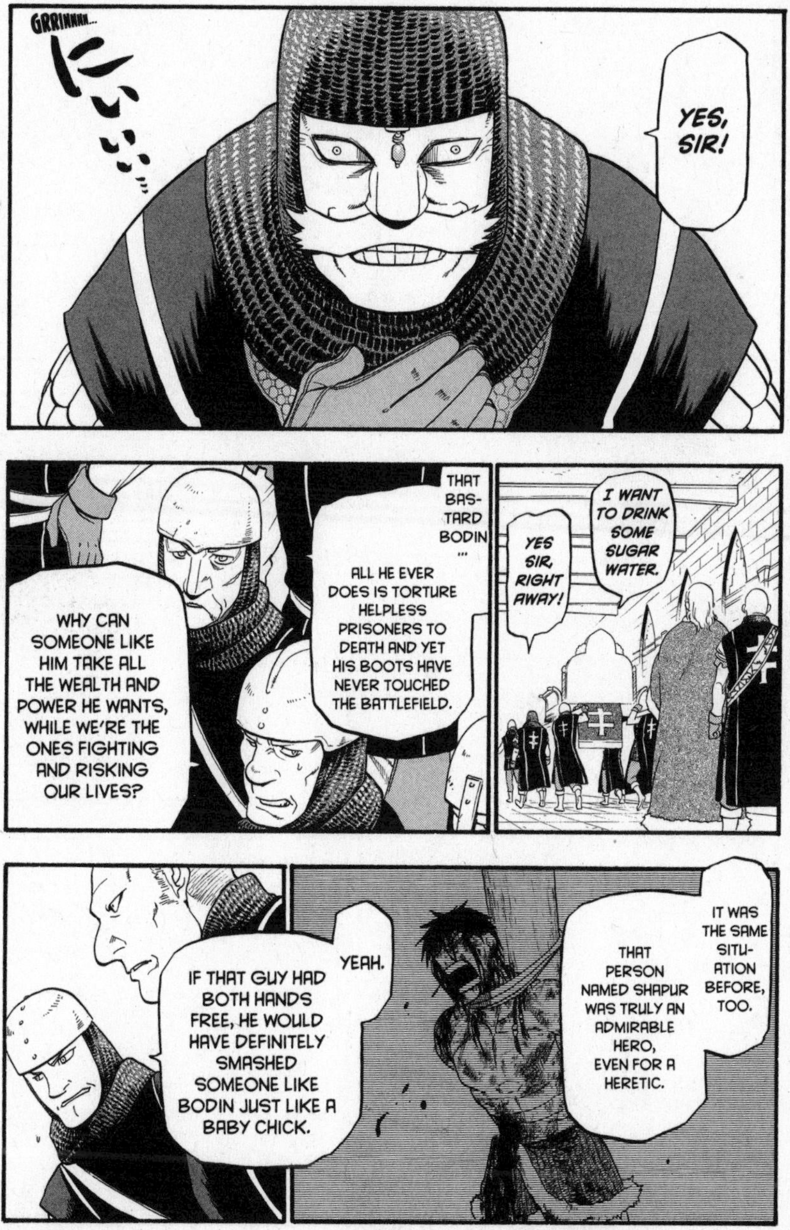
YES, SIR!
GRRINNN...
にぃぃ…
I WANT TO DRINK SOME SUGAR WATER.
YES SIR, RIGHT AWAY!
THAT BASTARD BODIN...
ALL HE EVER DOES IS TORTURE HELPLESS PRISONERS TO DEATH AND YET HIS BOOTS HAVE NEVER TOUCHED THE BATTLEFIELD.
WHY CAN SOMEONE LIKE HIM TAKE ALL THE WEALTH AND POWER HE WANTS, WHILE WE'RE THE ONES FIGHTING AND RISKING OUR LIVES?
IT WAS THE SAME SITUATION BEFORE, TOO.
THAT PERSON NAMED SHAPUR WAS TRULY AN ADMIRABLE HERO, EVEN FOR A HERETIC.
YEAH.
IF THAT GUY HAD BOTH HANDS FREE, HE WOULD HAVE DEFINITELY SMASHED SOMEONE LIKE BODIN JUST LIKE A BABY CHICK.

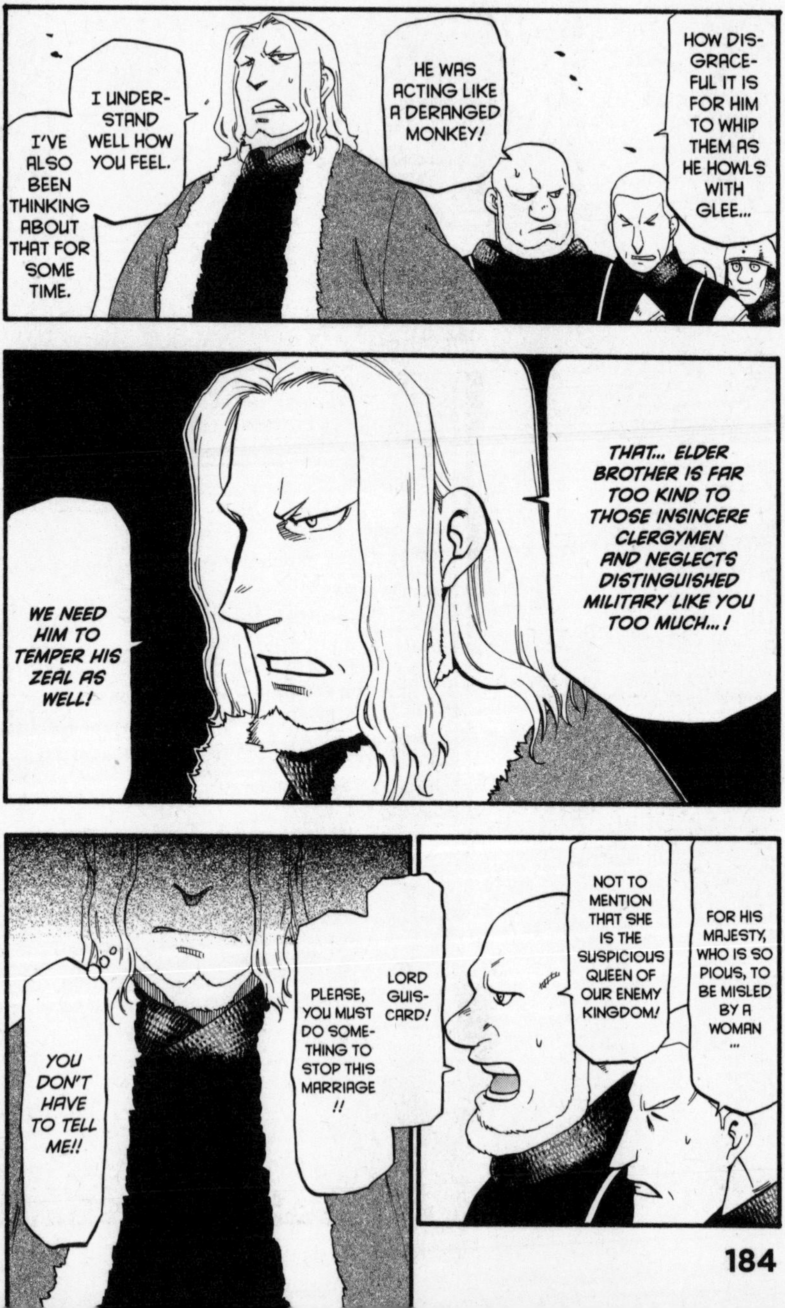
HOW DIS-GRACE-FUL IT IS FOR HIM TO WHIP THEM AS HE HOWLS WITH GLEE...
HE WAS ACTING LIKE A DERANGED MONKEY!
I UNDER-STAND WELL HOW YOU FEEL.
I'VE ALSO BEEN THINKING ABOUT THAT FOR SOME TIME.
THAT... ELDER BROTHER IS FAR TOO KIND TO THOSE INSINCERE CLERGYMEN AND NEGLECTS DISTINGUISHED MILITARY LIKE YOU TOO MUCH...!
WE NEED HIM TO TEMPER HIS ZEAL AS WELL!
FOR HIS MAJESTY, WHO IS SO PIOUS, TO BE MISLED BY A WOMAN ...
NOT TO MENTION THAT SHE IS THE SUSPICIOUS QUEEN OF OUR ENEMY KINGDOM!
LORD GUIS-CARD!
PLEASE, YOU MUST DO SOME-THING TO STOP THIS MARRIAGE !!
YOU DON'T HAVE TO TELL ME!!

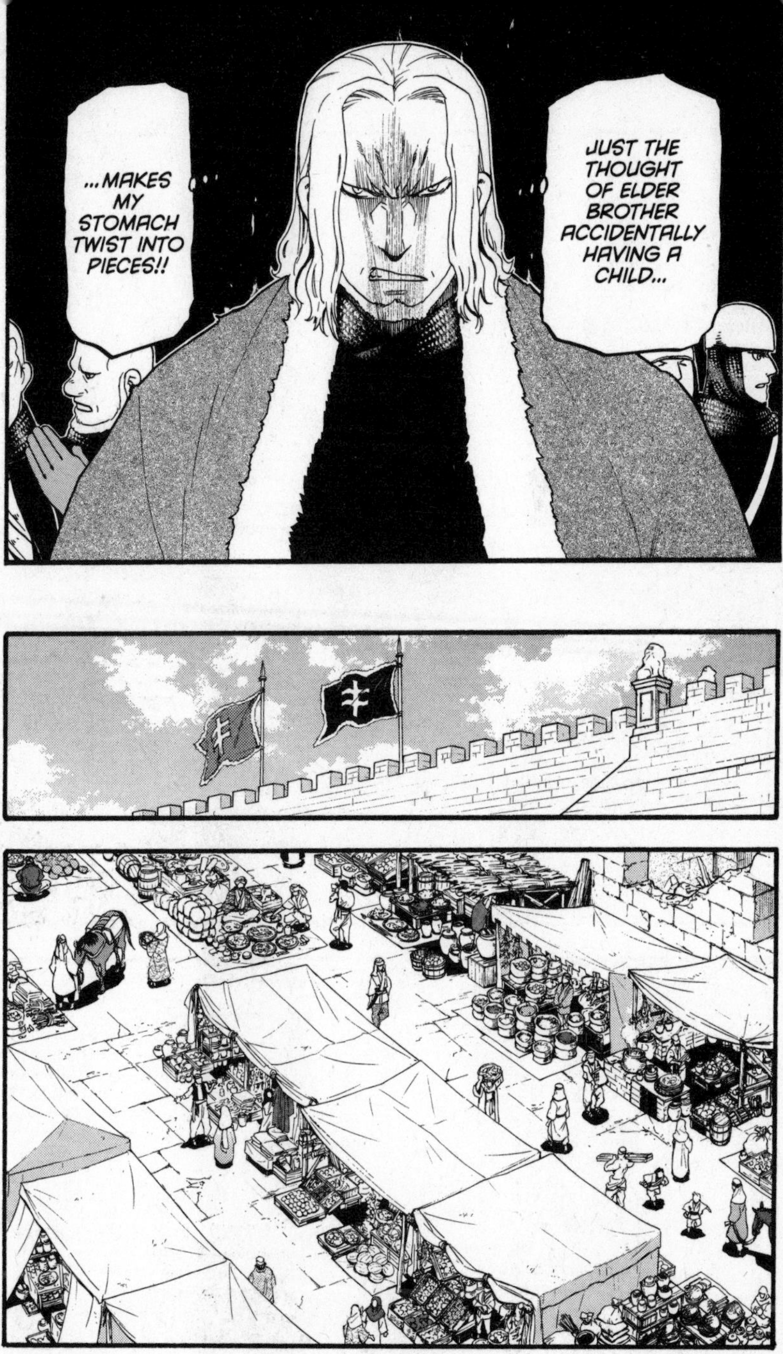
JUST THE THOUGHT OF ELDER BROTHER ACCIDENTALLY HAVING A CHILD...
...MAKES MY STOMACH TWIST INTO PIECES!!

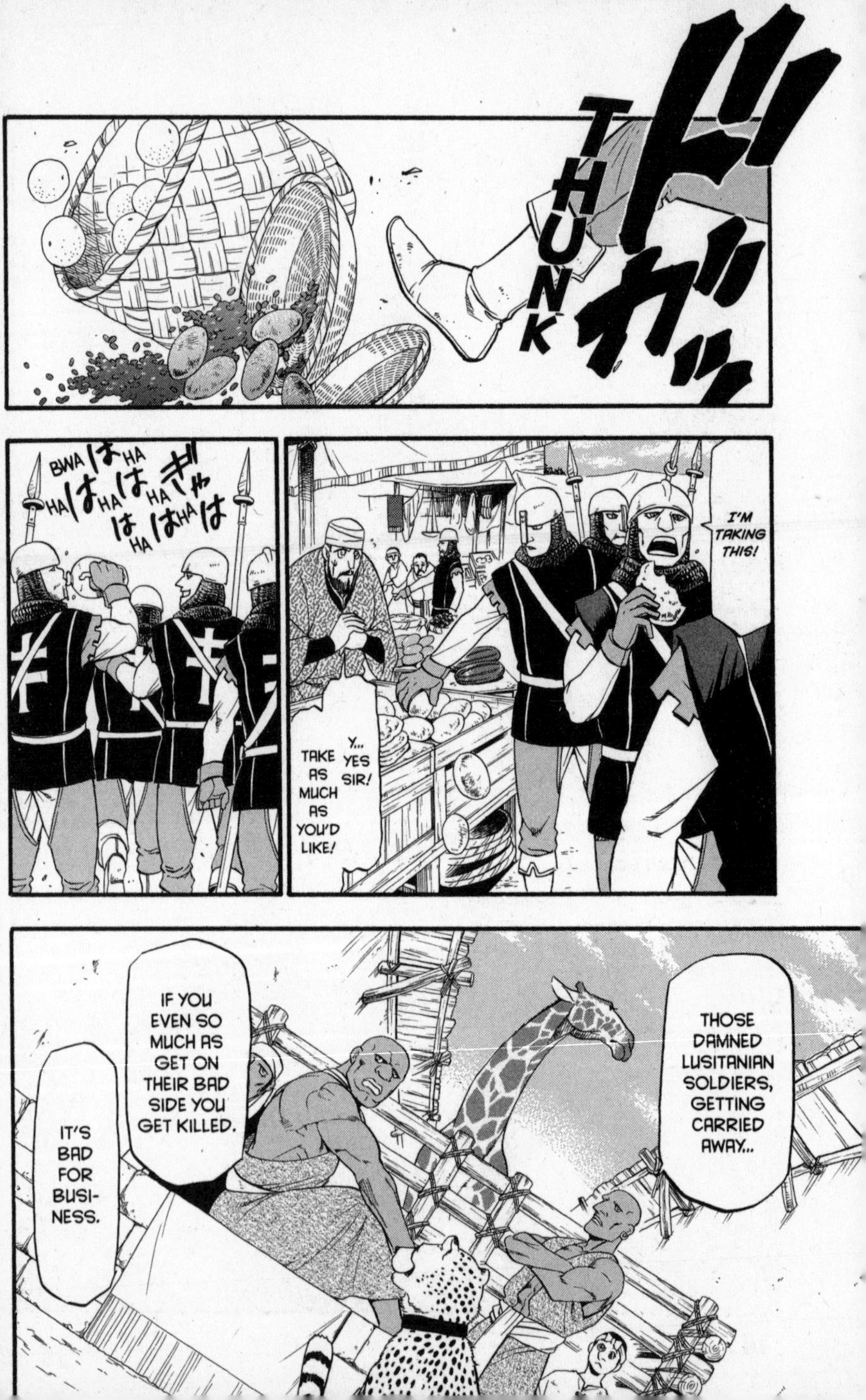
THUNK
I'M TAKING THIS!
Y... YES SIR!
TAKE AS MUCH AS YOU'D LIKE!
BWA HA HA HA HA HA HA
THOSE DAMNED LUSITANIAN SOLDIERS, GETTING CARRIED AWAY...
IF YOU EVEN SO MUCH AS GET ON THEIR BAD SIDE YOU GET KILLED.
IT'S BAD FOR BUSI-NESS.

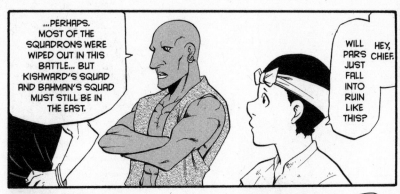

HEY, CHIEF.
WILL PARS JUST FALL INTO RUIN LIKE THIS?
...PERHAPS. MOST OF THE SQUADRONS WERE WIPED OUT IN THIS BATTLE... BUT KISHWARD'S SQUAD AND BAHMAN'S SQUAD MUST STILL BE IN THE EAST.
IF KING ANDRAGORAS COULD UNITE WITH THEM, OR...
THE KING IS ALIVE?!
IF THE KING HAD DIED IN BATTLE, THEN IN ORDER TO DROP THE MORALE OF THE PARSIAN ARMY THE LUSITANIAN ARMY WOULD HAVE BEEN SURE TO SPREAD IT AROUND LOUDLY WHEN THEY SIEGED THE CASTLE.
I SEE! SO THEN THERE'S STILL HOPE!
HUH?
CHIEF! THEY'RE PARSIAN SOLDIERS! PARSIAN SOLDIERS!
THEY'VE COME TO DEFEAT THE LUSITANIANS FOR US!

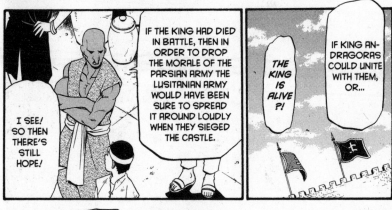

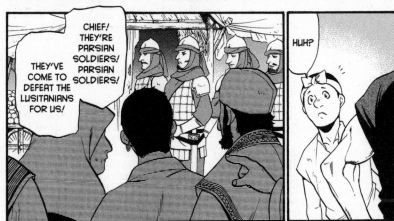

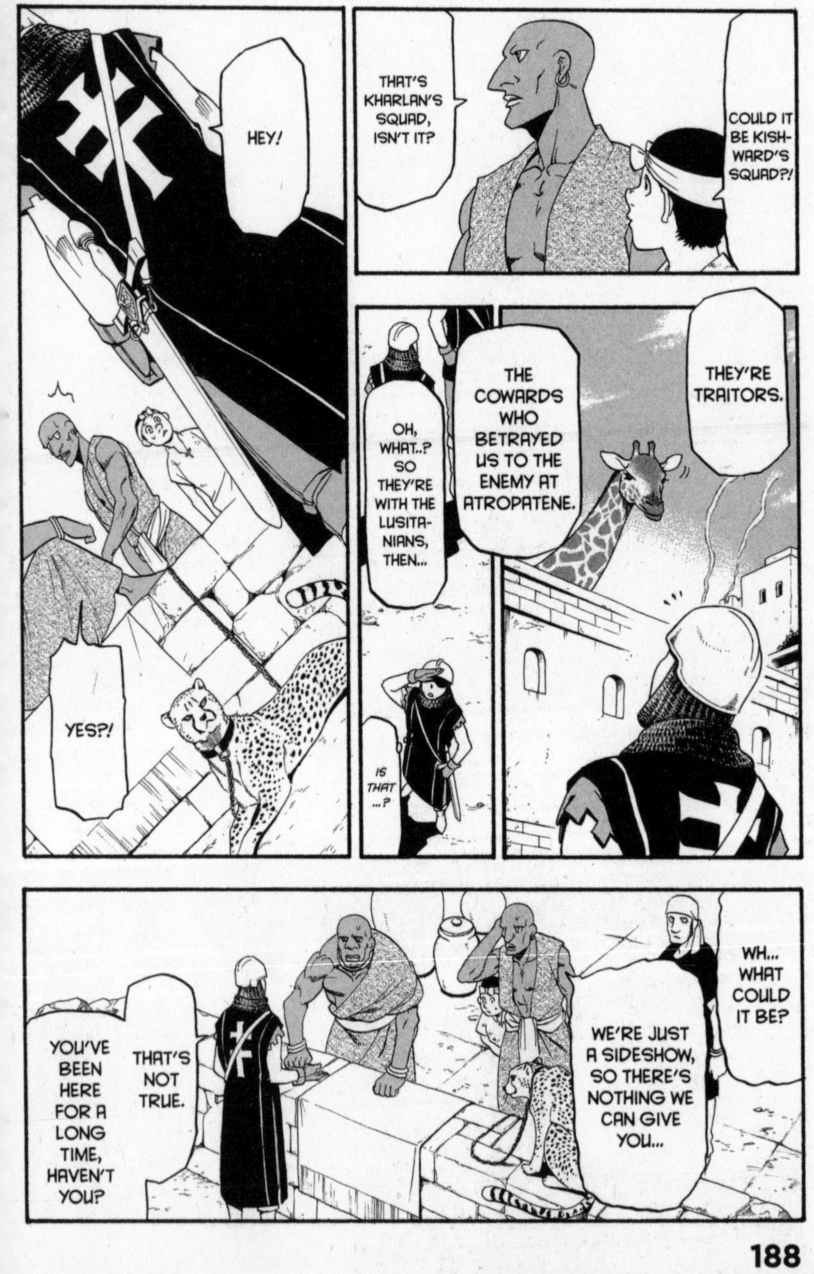
COULD IT BE KISHWARD'S SQUAD?!
THAT'S KHARLAN'S SQUAD, ISN'T IT?
THEY'RE TRAITORS.
THE COWARDS WHO BETRAYED US TO THE ENEMY AT ATROPATENE.
OH, WHAT..? SO THEY'RE WITH THE LUSITANIANS, THEN...
IS THAT ...?
HEY!
YES?!
WH... WHAT COULD IT BE?
WE'RE JUST A SIDESHOW, SO THERE'S NOTHING WE CAN GIVE YOU...
THAT'S NOT TRUE.
YOU'VE BEEN HERE FOR A LONG TIME, HAVEN'T YOU?

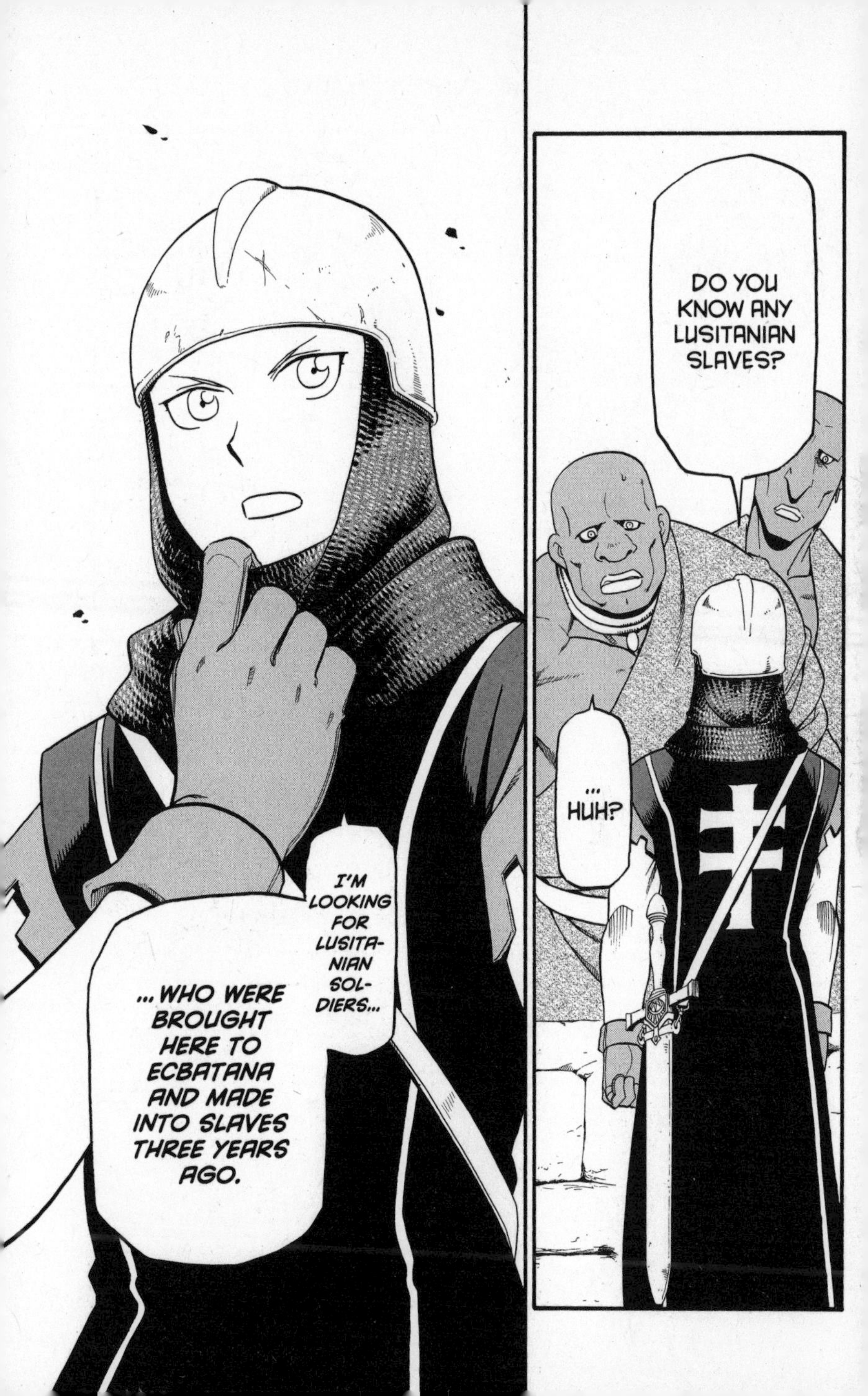
DO YOU KNOW ANY LUSITANIAN SLAVES?
... HUH?
I'M LOOKING FOR LUSITANIAN SOLDIERS...
...WHO WERE BROUGHT HERE TO ECBATANA AND MADE INTO SLAVES THREE YEARS AGO.

- BONUS SKETCHES -

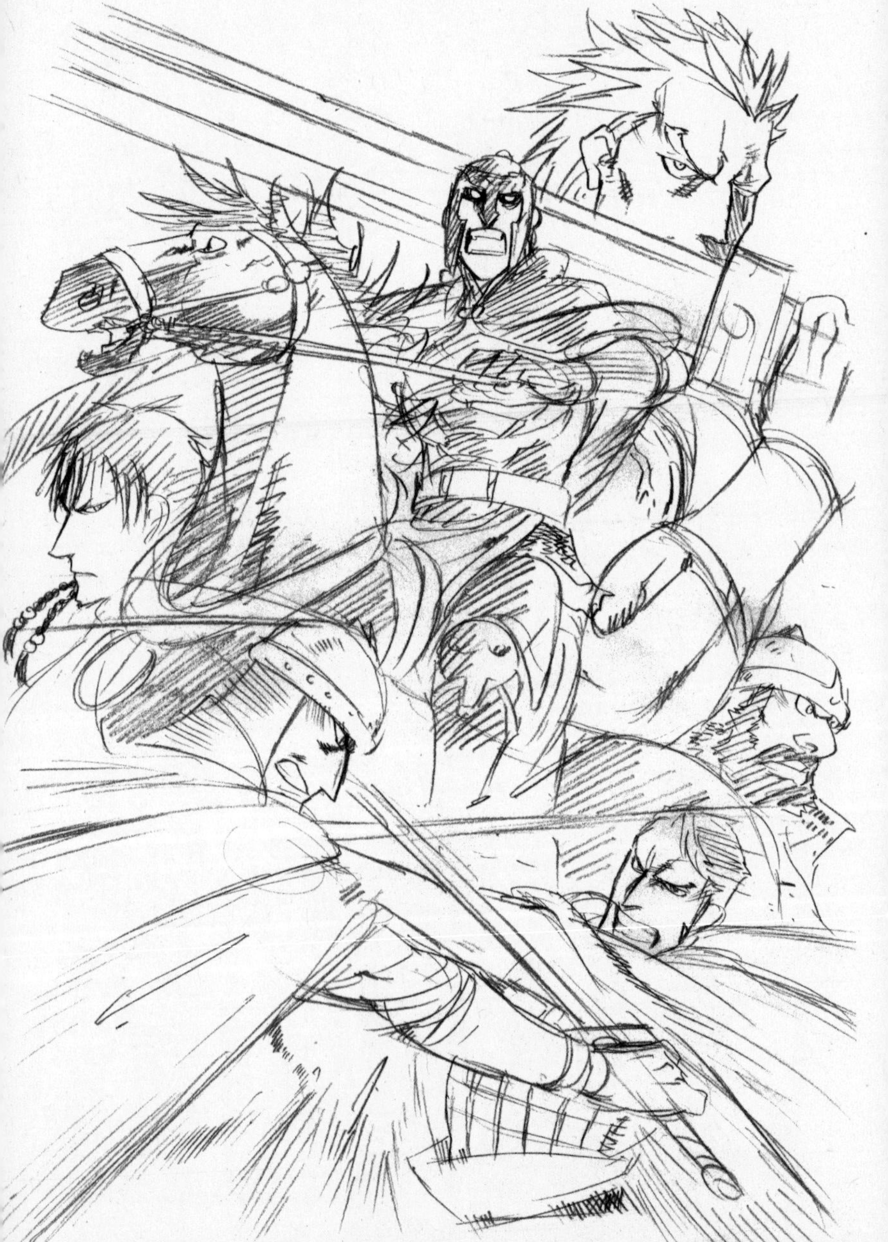

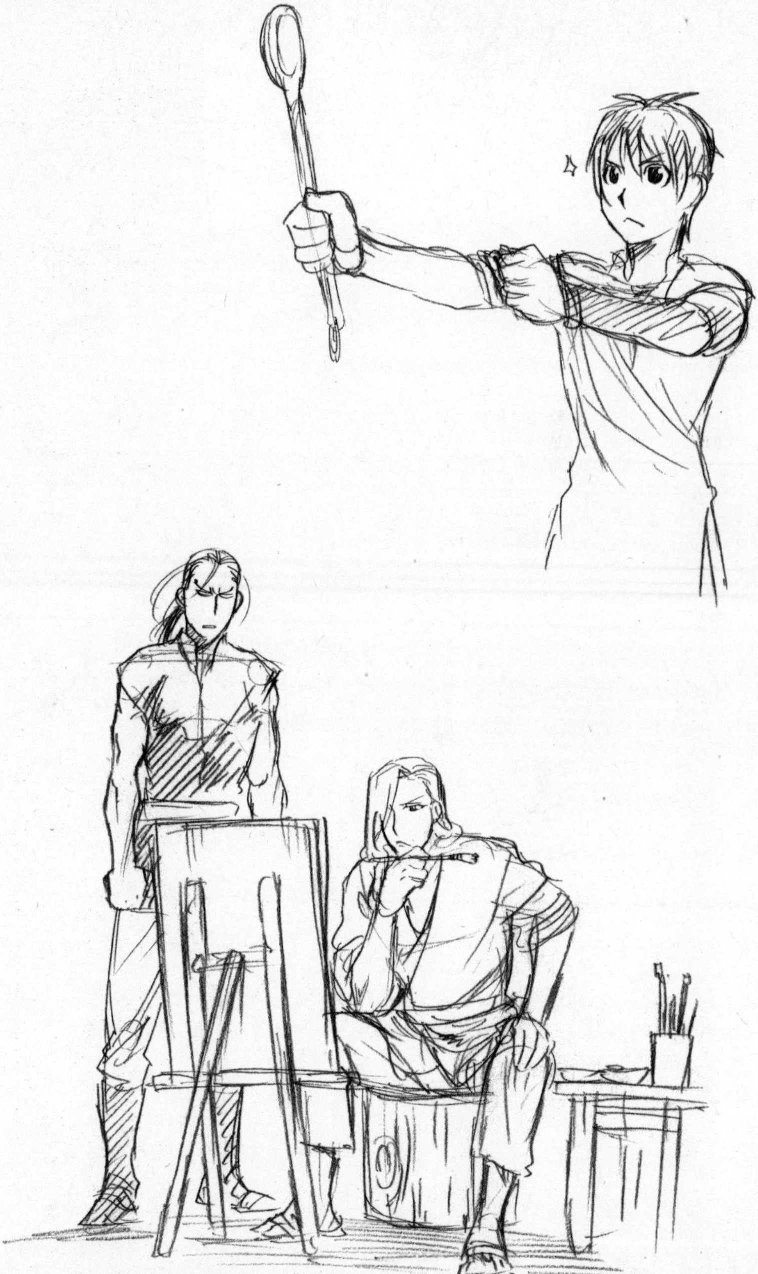

The Heroic Legend of Arslan volume 2 is a work of fiction. Names,
characters, places, and incidents are the products of the author's
imagination or are used fictitiously. Any resemblance to actual events,
locales, or persons, living or dead, is entirely coincidental.

A Kodansha Comics Trade Paperback Original.

The Heroic Legend of Arslan volume 2 copyright © 2014 Hiromu Arakawa
& Yoshiki Tanaka
English translation copyright © 2014 Hiromu Arakawa & Yoshiki Tanaka

All rights reserved.

Published in the United States by Kodansha Comics,
an imprint of Kodansha USA Publishing, LLC, New York.

Publication rights for this English edition arranged through Kodansha Ltd.,
Tokyo.

First published in Japan in 2014 by Kodansha Ltd., Tokyo, as Arslan
Senki volume 2.

ISBN 978-1-61262-973-5

Printed in the United States of America.

www.kodanshacomics.com

9 8 7 6 5 4 3 2 1

Translator: Lindsey Akashi
Lettering: Christy Sawyer & Erika Terriquez
Editing: Ajani Oloye